WALKER EVANS & DAN GRAHAM

Witte de With, center for contemporary art, Rotterdam   29.08.1992 - 11.10.1992

Museum Boymans-van Beuningen, Rotterdam   29.08.1992 - 11.10.1992

Musée Cantini, Marseille   06.11.1992 - 10.01.1993

Westfälisches Landesmuseum für Kunst und Kulturgeschichte, Münster   31.01.1993 - 21.03.1993

Whitney Museum of American Art, New York   17.12.1993 - 17.03.1994

Jean-François Chevrier

Allan Sekula

Benjamin H.D. Buchloh

WALKER
EVANS

&

DAN

GRAHAM

**Westfälisches
Landesmuseum für
Kunst und
Kulturgeschichte**

Musées de Marseille   WHITNEY MUSEUM OF AMERICAN ART

Contents/Sommaire/Inhalt/Inhoud

Walker Evans & Dan Graham

"I have located the original "*Homes for America*" in *Arts Magazine* ... Originally the editor asked for a pictorial essay using my suburban house photos (which had been exhibited in December 1966, in The Contemporary Wing of The Finch Museum of Art, New York, as slides in a show called Projected Art). The final article had removed 4 or 5 of my photos and substituted a 40 year old Walker Evans to celebrate the 40th anniversary of the magazine's founding." (Dan Graham, in a letter written January 14, 1992 to the organizers of the exhibition Walker Evans & Dan Graham).

The Museum Boymans-van Beuningen and Witte de With, center for contemporary art in Rotterdam, the Direction des Musées de Marseille, the Westfälisches Landesmuseum für Kunst und Kulturgeschichte, Münster and the Whitney Museum of American Art in New York are very pleased to present the book *Walker Evans & Dan Graham* which accompanies the exhibition of the same title in our institutions.

The idea for the exhibition came out of the inspiring as well as fruitful discussions that we were able to have over the past two years with the photography and art historian Jean-François Chevrier. Needless to say, the discussions were about the position and the role of photography in the visual arts today. As Jean-François Chevrier remarked in a recent essay, "Whether considered as a matter for specialists or, on the contrary, as one of the forms of 'contemporary art', photography today occupies an ambiguous place between the fine arts and the media." [1] We did not doubt for a moment about inviting Jean-François Chevrier to select, arrange and comment on the works that are included in this exhibition and this book. The choice of Jean-François Chevrier was further accentuated by the research, in which many assisted, that preceded this 'project'.

Such an investigation was imperative because, as Chevrier points out, "Walker Evans is no doubt the best example of a modern artist whose work by virtue not only of its internal complexity but also of the rich echoes it has found in contemporary art, utterly transcends the tradition of straight photography. Evans, as MoMA's John Szarkowski has shown in his exhibitions and catalogues, certainly exerted an influence on Frank, Winogrand and Friedlander. Yet all too often this genealogy, which Europeans are probably less aware of (or blinded by) than Americans are, conceals the historical importance of other trends - for example the work of post-Pop artists like Dan Graham and the new interest in realism and the contemporary environment guiding artists like Thomas Struth." [2]

It may then also come as no surprise that when Dan Graham proposed his 'photojournalism' in the format of a magazine article to the American *Arts Magazine*, one of the magazine's staff members replaced the architectural photographs of Graham with the photograph "*Wooden Houses, Boston*" (1930) from *American Photographs* by Walker Evans, published by The Museum of Modern Art in New York in 1938. [3] We know that Graham himself considered the photography of Walker Evans important for the development of his own work, "... I can see that I like Walker Evans very much and what is highly interesting about his work is that it was published in magazines and had a big influence on Pop Art. It allowed certain things to work, like the idea of representation of the representation, which was crucial to Pop and Conceptual Art. Besides that, I think that Evans and also Ruscha roused an interest in vernacular architecture, by making it available in a printed form, in the way Godard used vernacular architecture or Robert Venturi and Rem Koolhaas." [4]

With this exhibition and this book we want to clarify the relationship between the oeuvres of the American artists Walker Evans (1903-1975) and Dan Graham (1942) and to compare two different visions - each a product of its time - on the American urban environment, as well as to shed light into the history of photography and the visual arts. This is more than necessary now that the links between photography and the visual arts are increasingly, and often superficially, being brought closer together.

We are pleased to present as well in this book, next to the opinion of Jean-François Chevrier, the critical views of the art historian Benjamin H.D. Buchloh and the photographer and critic Allan Sekula. We are pleased to present to you the essay, "Moments of History in the Work of Dan Graham", by Benjamin H.D. Buchloh, previously included as an afterword, in the by now practically unfindable publication, *Dan Graham Articles*, published in 1977 by the Stedelijk Van Abbemuseum in Eindhoven. [5] This essay still prevails as one of the most rich and, at the same time, precise discussions on the oeuvre of Dan Graham. The same may be said for the detailed and often provocative essays that Allan Sekula has published over the past ten years on specific themes from the 'independent art' of photography. But, as Sekula asks, "independence from what?" [6]

Art institutions should ask themselves precisely such questions when they wish to engage in the complex discipline of photography: whether with regard to the formation of collections, exhibition policies, and even with regard to the establishment of new institutions that are specifically oriented towards the field of photography. From the architectural photographs of Thomas Struth and James Welling in the Modern Art collection of the Museum Boymans-van Beuningen, to exhibitions such as De Afstand and Ken Lum in Witte de With, to the role of the future 'Foto-instituut' in Rotterdam. From such recent exhibitions as Edward Hopper, Moholy Nagy and Le Pont Transbordeur et la Vision Moderniste in Les Musées de Marseille, to the initiative, taken by the Westfälisches Landesmuseum für Kunst und Kulturgeschichte in Münster of dedicating a special museum for the works of contemporary artists who employ photographic means. The Whitney Museum of American Art in New York is concerned with understanding and appreciating photography's unique role in the construction of twentieth-century art, and is specifically interested in the ways in which photography has become integrated into contemporary art and has precipitated the endgame of Modernism.

The exhibition Walker Evans & Dan Graham is at home in Rotterdam, Marseille, Münster and New York. Our cities are frequently confronted by new cultural developments; especially those architectural developments that speak about the reconstruction and the new layouts of old city centers, and, lest we forget, the rapid expansions which occur on the edges of our cities. To this end one can also make an appeal to the history and development of the architecture that exists in front of the cameras of Walker Evans and Dan Graham.

As mentioned above, we began the preparations for the exhibition and book *Walker Evans & Dan Graham*, of which the results are now visible, very early on. We want to extend our thanks to all those who were directly or indirectly helpful to us: in the first place to Dan Graham, who with every new question has advised and assisted us; and to his assistant, Regina Möller; Marian Goodman and the staff of the Marian Goodman Gallery, especially Elaine Budin and Priamo Lozada; and furthermore to Galerie Art & Project; Vito Acconci; Art Gallery of Ontario; Judith Barry and Ken Saylor; Gustinet Bartomeo Mari; Jane Ryan Beck and Craig Winkelman; Galerie Jürgen Becker; Benjamin H.D. Buchloh; The Carnegie Museum of Art and Mark Francis, Lisa Corrine Isenberg; DIA Center for the Arts and Karen Kelly; Rosalind Cutforth; Herman Daled; Lili Dujourie; Galerie Durand-Dessert; Yves Gevaert; Claude Gintz; André Goeminne; Kim Gordon; Ydessa Hendeles Art Foundation; Friedrich Wolfram Heubach; John Hilliard; Galerie Pierre Hubert; Galerie Johnen & Schöttle; John Knight; Kasper König; Lisson Gallery and Sharon Essor; Produzentengalerie Hamburg; Rotterdamse Kunststichting and Anne-Mie Devolder; Thomas Lawson; Galerie Meert Rihoux; Ernst Mitzka; Galerie Roger Pailhas; Birgit Pelzer; Galleria Pieroni; René Pulfer; Gerhard Richter; Harry Ruhé; Galleria Lia Rumma; Bob Rogers; Galerie Rüdiger Schöttle; Shimada Gallery; Hans Sonneveld; Stedelijk Van Abbemuseum and Jaap Guldemond; Galerie Micheline Szwajcer; Johan Van Heddegem; Galerie Vega; Jeff Wall; Lawrence and Alice Weiner.

For their investigative work on Walker Evans, we thank especially Sandra Alvarez de Toledo; as well as The Art Institute of Chicago and David Travis, J. Russel Harris; The Estate of Walker Evans and John Hill; The Metropolitan Museum of Art and Maria Morris-Hambourg, Margaret Kannan; The Minneapolis Institute of Arts and Carol T. Hartwell, Peggy Tolbert; The Museum of Modern Art and Peter Galassi, Susan Kismaric, Nicole Friedler; Sylviane De Decker Heftler. And of course we want to thank all of the lenders who entrusted us with their works for such a long period. Our special thanks goes to the staff of Witte de With which was responsible for the organization of both the exhibition and the book. On behalf of them, we want to thank Craigie Horsfield for his encouragement. Finally, we want especially to thank Jean-François Chevrier, without whose persistence and enthusiasm this exhibition and book would never have been realized.

Chris Dercon
Witte de With, center for contemporary art, Rotterdam
Wim Crouwel
Museum Boymans-van Beuningen, Rotterdam
Bernard Blistène
Directeur des Musées de Marseille
Klaus Bußmann
Westfälisches Landesmuseum für Kunst und Kulturgeschichte, Münster
David A. Ross
Whitney Museum of American Art, New York

1 Chevrier, Jean-François, "Entre les beaux-arts et les médias", *Galeries Magazine*, no. 37, juin/julliet 1990.
2 ibid.
3 Graham, Dan, "Homes for America, Early 20th-Century Possessable House to the Quasi-Discrete Cell of '66", *Arts Magazine*, vol. 41, no. 3, December 1966 - January 1967. In the spring of 1971 Dan Graham reconstructed and published his original maquette in the lithography workshop of the Nova Scotia College for Art and Design, Halifax, Nova Scotia.
4 Dercon, Chris, "Dan Graham, I enjoy that closeness where I take two things that are very close and just slightly overlap them", *Forum International*, vol. II, no. 9, September-October 1991.
5 We thought it best to present the German version of Benjamin H.D. Buchloh's essay, "Augenblicke der Geschichte in der Arbeit von Dan Graham", as it appeared in *Braco Dimitrijevic, Dan Graham, On Kawara, Roman Opalka*, Galerie René Block Berlin/DAAD. This version is somewhat different from the English version which was published in the catalogue *Dan Graham Articles*, Stedelijk Van Abbemuseum, Eindhoven, 1977.
6 Sekula, Allan, "Some American Notes" in Issues and Commentary I, *Art in America*, no. 2, February 1990.

Walker Evans & Dan Graham

"'*Homes for America*' a été publié à l'époque dans *Arts Magazine* ... A l'origine le rédacteur en chef voulait un article illustré par mes photos d'architecture de banlieue (qui avaient été exposées en décembre 1966, dans l'aile contemporaine du Finch Museum of Art, à New York, sous la forme de projections - l'exposition s'appelait Projected Art). Quand l'article est paru, mes 4 ou 5 photos avaient disparu et avaient été remplacées par une image de Walker Evans d'il y a quarante ans, pour fêter le quarantième anniversaire de la création du magazine..." (Dan Graham, dans une lettre du 14 janvier 1992 adressée aux organisateurs de cette exposition).

Le Musée Boymans-van Beuningen et Witte de With, centre pour l'art contemporain de Rotterdam, la Direction des Musées de Marseille, le Westfälisches Landesmuseum für Kunst und Kulturgeschichte de Münster et le Whitney Museum of American Art de New York sont heureux de présenter le catalogue de l'exposition *Walker Evans & Dan Graham*, qui se tiendra successivement dans ces cinq institutions.

L'idée de l'exposition est née de nombreuses et fructueuses conversations échangées depuis deux ans avec l'historien de l'art Jean-François Chevrier. Il était bien entendu question, au cours de ces conversations, de la place et du rôle qu'occupe aujourd'hui la photographie dans les arts visuels. Comme Jean-François Chevrier le faisait remarquer dans un article récent, "Considérée comme une affaire de spécialistes ou, au contraire, comme une des formes de l'art dit 'contemporain', la photographie se situe surtout aujourd'hui entre les beaux-arts et les médias." [1] Nous avons proposé à Jean-François Chevrier de faire la sélection des oeuvres, de décider de la structure de l'exposition et d'en écrire le texte du catalogue. Le travail de recherche - mené à plusieurs - pour conduire ce projet à sa réalisation, ne fit que confirmer ses options.

Ce projet prenait tout son sens, puisque, comme l'écrit Chevrier, "Walker Evans est sans doute le meilleur exemple d'un artiste moderne dont l'oeuvre dépasse largement la tradition de la photographie documentaire, pure ou directe [straight], et cela aussi bien par la complexité interne de son propos que par les échos qu'elle a reçus dans l'art contemporain. Cette oeuvre s'est actualisée - on le sait depuis les expositions et les commentaires de John Szarkowski, au MoMA - chez Frank, Winogrand, Friedlander. En admettant même qu'on le sache moins bien en Europe qu'aux Etats-Unis, dans tous les cas, cette généalogie ne doit pas masquer d'autres possibilités d'approches, à travers une nouvelle exigence de réalisme qui traverse l'art actuel et détermine certains recours à l'enregistrement photographique, ne serait-ce que pour rendre compte de l'environnement contemporain. (Thomas Struth, notamment)." [2]

Il semble déjà moins surprenant, dès lors, qu'un des membres de la rédaction de la revue américaine *Arts Magazine* ait pris l'initiative de remplacer une des photographies d'architecture de Dan Graham, inclues dans sa proposition de 'photojournalisme', comme il qualifie lui-même ce travail, par cette photographie de Walker Evans, "Wooden Houses, Boston" (1930), publiée dans le catalogue de l'exposition American Photographs, au Museum of Modern Art de New York en 1938. [3] On sait l'importance que Graham lui-même attachait à l'oeuvre d'Evans pour l'évolution de ses propres recherches: "J'aime beaucoup l'oeuvre de Walker Evans; je trouve particulièrement intéressant qu'il ait travaillé pour des magazines, et qu'il ait eu de l'influence sur le Pop Art. Grâce à lui certaines idées ont fait leur chemin, cette idée de la représentation de la représentation par exemple; c'était important pour le Pop Art et l'art conceptuel. Je pense aussi, qu'au même titre qu'Ed Ruscha, Walker Evans a su éveiller un intérêt pour l'architecture vernaculaire, en la mettant à la portée de tout le monde par des publications dans des imprimés. Godard, Robert Venturi ou Rem Koolhaas aussi se sont intéressé à l'architecture vernaculaire." [4]

Cette exposition et ce livre voudraient éclairer les liens entre les oeuvres de ces deux artistes américains, Walker Evans (1903-1975) et Dan Graham (1942), mettre en regard leurs visions respectives - chacune en son temps - de l'environement urbain américain; elle voudrait également apporter quelques éclaircissements sur l'histoire de la photographie et des art visuels, à une époque où on les confronte sans cesse, et souvent à tort.

Nous avons l'honneur de publier dans ce livre, à côté du texte de Jean-François Chevrier, les points de vue de l'historien d'art Benjamin H.D. Buchloh et du photographe et critique Allan Sekula. Nous sommes heureux que soit réédité à cette occasion le texte de Benjamin H.D. Buchloh, "Moments d'histoire dans l'oeuvre de Dan Graham", publié par le Stedelijk Van Abbemuseum d'Eindhoven en 1977, comme postface au recueil désormais introuvable des *Dan Graham Articles*. [5] Ce texte demeure aujourd'hui, de l'avis général, le commentaire le plus riche et le plus précis de l'oeuvre de Dan Graham. Il en est de même des textes détaillés et souvent polémiques de Sekula, publiés ces dix dernières années sur le sujet précis de la photographie comme 'art indépendant'. Mais, "indépendant par rapport à quoi?", demande Sekula. [6]

De telles interrogations pourraient être celles des institutions artistiques qui abordent un domaine aussi complexe que la photographie. Qu'il s'agisse, pour elles, de constituer une collection, d'engager une politique d'expositions ou même de considérer la création de nouvelles institutions exclusivement consacrées à la photographie. Que l'on pense aux acquisitions des photographies de Thomas Struth ou de James Welling pour la collection d'Art Moderne du Musée Boymans-van Beuningen, aux expositions comme De Afstand ou Ken Lum, organisées par Witte de With, ou au rôle que s'apprête à jouerle futur 'Foto-instituut' de Rotterdam. Aux expositions récentes présentées par les Musées de Marseille - Edward Hopper, Moholy-Nagy, ou Le Pont Transbordeur et la Vision Moderniste-, et à l'initiative prise par le Westfälisches Landesmuseum für Kunst und Kulturgeschichte à Münster de consacrer un musée aux œuvres d'artistes contemporains utilisant la photographie. Comprendre et apprécier le rôle unique de la photographie dans l'art de XXème siècle est une des préoccupations majeures du Whitney Museum of American Art à New York qui est particulièrement intéressé par les manières selon lesquelles la photographie s'est intégrée à l'art contemporain et a précipité la fin du modernisme.

Rotterdam, Marseille, Münster et New York sont quatre villes de prédilection pour une telle exposition. Elles sont toutes les trois confrontées en permanence au phénomène de l'évolution culturelle, aux questions architecturales posées par la reconstruction et le réaménagement des vieux quartiers au centre des villes, et à celles du développement tentaculaire des périphéries. Il n'est pas absurde, pour aborder ces questions, de faire appel à l'histoire, à l'histoire de l'architecture, et à la vision qu'en ont eue Walker Evans et Dan Graham.

La réalisation de cette exposition et de ce livre fut un travail de longue haleine. Nous tenons à remercier tous ceux qui, de manière directe ou indirecte, y ont contribué: avant tout Dan Graham, qui a bien voulu répondre à chacune de nos questions, ainsi que son assistante, Regina Möller; Marian Goodman et toute l'équipe de sa galerie, et en particulier Elaine Budin et Priamo Lozada; Galerie Art & Project; Vito Acconci; Art Gallery of Ontario; Judith Barry et Ken Saylor; Gustinet Bartomeo Mari; Jane Ryan Beck et Craig Winkelman; Galerie Jürgen Becker; Benjamin H.D. Buchloh; The Carnegie Museum of Art et Mark Francis, Lisa Corrine Isenberg; DIA Center for the Arts et Karen Kelly; Rosalind Cutforth; Herman Daled; Lili Dujourie; Galerie Durand-Dessert; Yves Gevaert; Claude Gintz; André Goeminne; Kim Gordon; Ydessa Hendeles Art Foundation; Friedrich Wolfram Heubach; John Hilliard; Galerie Pierre Hubert; Galerie Johnen & Schöttle; John Knight; Kasper König; Lisson Gallery et Sharon Esser; Produzentengalerie Hamburg; Rotterdamse Kunststichting et Anne-Mie Devolder; Thomas Lawson; Galerie Meert Rihoux; Ernst Mitzka; Galerie Roger Pailhas; Birgit Pelzer; Galleria Pieroni; René Pulfer; Gerhard Richter; Galleria Lia Rumma; Bob Rogers; Galerie Rüdiger Schöttle; Harry Ruhé; Shimada Gallery; Hans Sonneveld; Stedelijk Van Abbemuseum et Jaap Guldenmond; Galerie Micheline Szwajcer; Johan Van Heddegem; Galerie Vega; Jeff Wall; Lawrence et Alice Weiner.

Pour leur travail de recherche sur Walker Evans nous tenons à remercier spécialement Sandra Alvarez de Toledo; ainsi que l'Art Institute of Chicago, David Travis et J.Russel Harris; le Fonds Walker Evans et John Hill; le Metropolitan Museum ofArt, Maria Morris-Hambourg et Margaret Kannan; le Minneapolis Institute of Arts, Carol T. Hartwell et Peggy

Tolbert; le Museum of Modern Art de New York, Peter Galassi, Susan Kismaric et Nicole Friedler; Sylviane De Decker Heftler.

Et évidemment tous les prêteurs qui ont accepté de nous confier leurs oeuvres et de s'en dessaisir pendant une aussi longue période. Nous remercions particulièrement l'équipe de Witte de With, qui s'est chargé de l'organisation de l'exposition et de la réalisation du livre. De leur part, nous remercions Craigie Horsfield, dont les encouragements n'ont jamais faibli. Enfin, et plus particulièrement, nous remercions Jean-François Chevrier sans l'enthousiasme et la persévérance duquel ni l'exposition ni le livre n'auraient vu le jour.

Chris Dercon
Witte de With, centre d'art contemporain, Rotterdam.
Wim Crouwel
Musée Boymans-van Beuningen, Rotterdam.
Bernard Blistène
Directeur des Musées de Marseille.
Klaus Bußman
Westfälisches Landesmuseum für Kunst und Kulturgeschichte, Münster.
David A. Ross
Whitney Museum of American Art, New York

1 Jean-François Chevrier, "Entre les beaux-arts et les médias", *Galeries Magazine*, no.37, juin/juillet 1990.
2 ibid.
3 Dan Graham, "Homes for America, Early 2Oth Century Possessable House to the Quasi-Discrete Cell of '66", in *Arts Magazine*, vol.41, no.3, décembre 1966-janvier 1967. Au cours du printemps 1971, Dan Graham en a reconstruit et publié la maquette originale dans l'atelier de lithographie de Nova Scotia College for Art and Design, Halifax, Nova Scotia.
4 Chris Dercon, "Dan Graham, "*I enjoy that closeness where I take two things that are very close and just slightly overlap them*", in *Forum International*, vol. II, no. 9, septembre-octobre 1991.
5 Nous avons préféré publier ici la version allemande du texte de Benjamin H.D. Buchloh, "Augenblicke der Geschichte in der Arbeit von Dan Graham", paru dans *Braco Dimitrijevic, Dan Graham, On Kawara, Roman Opalka*, Galerie René Block, Berlin, DAAD. Cette version diffère légèrement de la version anglaise publiée dans le catalogue *Dan Graham, Articles*, publié par le Stedelijk Van Abbemuseum, Eindhoven, 1977.
6 Allan Sekula, "Some American Notes", in Issues and Commentary 1, *Art in America*, no.2, février 1990.

Walker Evans & Dan Graham

"Ich habe die originalen "*Homes for America*" in *Arts Magazine* gefunden... Ursprünglich hatte der Herausgeber um einen Bild-Essay mit meinen Fotos der Vororthäuser gebeten (die im Dezember 1966 im Zeitgenössischen Flügel des Finch Museum of Art, New York, in einer Ausstellung mit dem Titel Projected Art als Dias gezeigt worden waren). In der schließlich gedruckten Fassung waren 4 oder 5 von meinen Fotos durch ein 40 Jahre altes von Walker Evans ersetzt worden, um das 40jährige Bestehen der Zeitschrift zu feiern." (Dan Graham in einem Brief vom 14. Januar 1992 an die Organisatoren der Ausstellung Walker Evans & Dan Graham.)

Das Museum Boymans-van Beuningen und Witte de With, Zentrum für zeitgenössische Kunst in Rotterdam, die Direktion der Musées de Marseille, das Westfälische Landesmuseum für Kunst und Kulturgeschichte in Münster und das Whitney Museum of American Art in New York freuen sich, das Buch *Walker Evans & Dan Graham* zu präsentieren, das die gleichnamige Ausstellung in unseren Häusern begleitet.

Die Idee zu dieser Ausstellung entstand aus den inspirierenden wie fruchtbaren Diskussionen, die wir während der letzten zwei Jahre mit dem Kunsthistoriker und Fotografie-Spezialisten Jean-François Chevrier führten. Es versteht sich von selbst, daß diese Diskussionen sich um die Position und Rolle der Fotografie in der bildenden Kunst von heute drehten. Wie Jean-François Chevrier in einem jüngst erschienen Essay bemerkte, "ob man sie nun als Angelegenheit der Spezialisten oder, im Kontrast dazu, als eine der Formen 'zeitgenössischer Kunst' betrachtet, die Fotografie besetzt heute einen mehrdeutigen Platz zwischen der bildenden Kunst und den Medien." [1] Für uns bestand zu keinem Moment auch nur der geringste Zweifel, Jean-François Chevrier einzuladen, und die Auswahl, Anordnung und Kommentierung der in dieser Ausstellung und in diesem Buch gezeigten Arbeiten zu übernehmen. Die Entscheidung für Jean-François Chevrier wurde durch die von vielen geleisteten Forschungsarbeiten, die diesem 'Projekt' vorausgingen, noch unterstrichen.

Derartige Untersuchungen waren geboten, da, Chevrier zufolge, "Walker Evans zweifellos das beste Beispiel eines modernen Künstlers ist, dessen Werk nicht nur wegen seiner inneren Komplexität, sondern auch aufgrund des starken Widerhalls, den es in der zeitgenössischen Kunst gefunden hat, die Tradition der konventionellen Fotografie völlig überschreitet. Wie John Szarkowski vom MoMA in seinen Ausstellungen und Katalogen gezeigt hat, waren Frank, Winogrand und Friedlander zweifellos von Evans beeinflußt. Allerdings verdeckt diese Genealogie, derer sich die Europäer weniger bewußt sind als die Amerikaner (oder von der sie geblendet sind), nur allzu oft die historische Bedeutung anderer Strömungen - zum Beispiel die Arbeit von Post-Pop-Künstlern wie Dan Graham und das neue Interesse am Realismus oder das heutige Umfeld, von dem Künstler wie Thomas Struth sich führen lassen." [2]

So ist es denn auch nicht verwunderlich, daß, als Dan Graham dem amerikanischen *Arts Magazine* seinen 'Fotojournalismus' in Form eines Zeitschriftenartikels vorschlug, ein Mitarbeiter der Redaktion Grahams Architekturfotos durch das Foto "*Wooden Houses, Boston*" (1930) aus dem 1938 vom Museum of Modern Art in New York herausgegebenen *American Photographs* von Walker Evans ersetzte. [3] Wir wissen, daß Graham selbst die fotografische Arbeit Walker Evans' als wichtig für die Entwicklung seiner eigenen Arbeit betrachtete, "... ich merke, daß ich Walker Evans sehr mag, und das überaus Interessante an seinen Arbeiten ist die Tatsache, daß sie in Zeitschriften veröffentlicht wurden und einen großen Einfluß auf die Pop Art hatten. Seine Arbeit ließ bestimmte Dinge funktionieren, wie zum Beispiel die Darstellung der Darstellung, die für die Pop Art und die Konzept-Kunst entscheidend war. Daneben weckten Evans und auch Ruscha meiner Meinung nach ein Interesse an einheimischer Architektur, indem sie sie in gedruckter Form zur Verfügung stellten, in der Art, wie Godard oder Robert Venturi und Rem Koolhaas einheimische Architektur nutzten." [4]

Mit dieser Ausstellung und diesem Buch möchten wir die Beziehungen zwischen den Werken der amerikanischen Künstler Walker Evans (1903-1975) und Dan Graham (1942) klären und die beiden unterschiedlichen Sichtweisen - jede ein Produkt ihrer Zeit - der amerikanischen Vorortumgebung miteinander vergleichen, aber auch die Geschichte der Fotografie und der bildenden Kunst erhellen. Das ist heute, da die Verbindungen zwischen Fotografie und bildender Kunst - oft auf oberflächliche Weise - immer enger werden, mehr als notwendig.

Wir freuen uns, in diesem Buch neben den Ansichten Jean-François Chevriers auch die kritische Sicht des Kunsthistorikers Benjamin H.D. Buchloh, sowie die des Fotografen und Kritikers Allan Sekula vorstellen zu können. Wir freuen uns, Ihnen den Essay "Moments of History in the Work of Dan Graham" von Benjamin H. D. Buchloh präsentieren zu können, der in der heute praktisch nicht mehr auffindbaren, 1977 vom Stedelijk Van Abbemuseum herausgegebenen Publikation *Dan Graham Articles* als Nachwort veröffentlicht worden war. [5] Dieser Essay stellt nach wie vor eine der fruchtbarsten und gleichzeitig präzisesten Abhandlungen des Werks von Dan Graham dar. Dasselbe gilt für die detaillierten und oft provokativen Essays, die Allan Sekula während der letzten zehn Jahre zu spezifischen Themen der 'unabhängigen Kunst' der Fotografie veröffentlicht hat. Nur, so fragt Sekula, "Unabhängigkeit wovon?" [6]

Kunstinstitute sollten sich gerade diese Frage stellen, wenn sie sich im Bereich der komplexen Disziplin der Fotografie engagieren wollen - ob nun im Hinblick auf den Aufbau von Sammlungen oder auf die Ausstellungspolitik, ja selbst im Hinblick auf die Einrichtung neuer Institute, die speziell auf das Feld der Fotografie ausgerichtet sind: von den Architekturfotografien von Thomas Struth und James Welling in der Modernen Sammlung des Museums Boymans-van Beuningen über Ausstellungen wie De Afstand und Ken Lum im Witte de With bis hin zur Rolle des zukünftigen 'Foto-Instituut' in Rotterdam; von den jüngst gezeigten Ausstellungen wie Edward Hopper, Moholy-Nagy und Le Pont Transbordeur et la Vision Moderniste in den Musées de Marseille bis hin zu der auch vom Westfälischen Landesmuseum für Kunst und Kulturgeschichte in Münster ergriffenen Initiative, den Arbeiten zeitgenössischer Künstler, die fotografische Mittel einsetzen, ein eigenes Museum zu widmen. Das Whitney Museum for American Art in New York fördert das Verständnis und die Wertschätzung der besonderen Rolle, welche die Photographie in der Entwicklung der Kunst des zwanzigsten Jahrhunderts spielt. Das Museum ist insbesondere daran interessiert, die Art und Weise, wie Photographie in Gegenwartskunst integriert wurde, zu verstehen und damit das Endspiel des Modernismus beschleunigte.

Die Ausstellung Walker Evans & Dan Graham ist in Rotterdam, Marseille, Münster und New York zuhause. Unsere Städte werden häufig mit neuen kulturellen Entwicklungen konfrontiert; das sind zu einem nicht unerheblichen Teil architektonische Entwicklungen der Rekonstruktion und Neugestaltung alter Stadtzentren und, nicht zu vergessen, die rapide Expansion, die an den Rändern unserer Städte stattfindet. Um das zu zeigen, kann man durchaus die Geschichte und Entwicklung der Architektur anrufen, die vor den Kameras von Walker Evans und Dan Graham stattgefunden hat und stattfindet.

Wie bereits erwähnt haben wir mit den Vorbereitungen für die Ausstellung und das Buch Walker Evans & Dan Graham, deren Ergebnisse nun vorliegen, bereits sehr früh begonnen. Wir möchten all denen, die uns direkt oder indirekt dabei geholfen haben, herzlich danken: an erster Stelle Dan Graham, der uns bei jedem neu auftauchenden Problem beraten und geholfen hat, sowie seiner Assistentin Regina Möller; Marian Goodman und den Mitarbeitern der Marian Goodman Gallery, vor allem Elaine Budin und Priamo Lozoda; desweiteren Galerie Art & Project; Vito Acconci; Art Gallery of Ontario; Judith Barry und Ken Saylor; Gustinet Bartomeo Mari; Jane Ryan Beck und Craig Winkelman; Galerie Jürgen Becker; Benjamin H.D. Buchloh; The Carnegie Museum of Art und Mark Francis, Lisa Corrine Isenberg; DIA Center for the Arts und Karen Kelly; Rosalind Cutforth; Herman Daled; Lili Dujourie; Galerie Durand-Dessert; Yves Gevaert; Claude Gintz; André Goeminne; Kim Gordon; Ydessa Hendeles Art Foundation; Friedrich Wolfram Heubach; John Hilliard; Galerie Pierre Hubert; Galerie Johnen & Schöttle; John Knight; Kasper König; Lisson Gallery und Sharon Essor; Produzentengalerie Hamburg; Rotterdamse Kunststichting und Anne-Mie Devolder; Thomas Lawson; Galerie Meert Rihoux; Ernst Mitzka; Galerie Roger Pailhas; Birgit Pelzer; Galleria Pieroni; René Pulfer; Gerhard Richter; Harry Ruhé; Galleria Lia Rumma; Bob Rogers; Galerie Rüdiger Schöttle;

Shimada Gallery; Hans Sonneveld; Stedelijk Van Abbemuseum und Jaap Guldemond; Galerie Micheline Szwajcer; Johan Van Heddegem; Galerie Vega; Jeff Wall; Lawrence und Alice Weiner.

Für ihre Nachforschungen über Walker Evans danken wir Sandra Alvarez de Toledo; The Art Institute of Chicago sowie David Travis und J. Russel Harris; The Estate of Walker Evans und John Hill, The Metropolitan Museum of Art sowie Maria Morris-Hambourg und Margaret Kannan, The Minneapolis Institute of Arts sowie Carol T. Hartwell und Peggy Tolberg, The Museum of Modern Art sowie Peter Galassi, Susan Kismaric und Nicole Friedler; Sylviane De Decker Heftler.

Und natürlich danken wir allen Leihgebern, die uns ihr Vertrauen schenkten und sich für einen so langen Zeitraum von ihren Werken trennen. Unser ganz besonderer Dank gilt den Mitarbeitern von Witte de With, die für die Organisation der Ausstellung wie auch für die Publikation des Buches die Verantwortung übernahmen. In ihrem Namen möchten wir Craigie Horsfield für seine beständige Ermutigung danken. Und schließlich danken wir ganz speziell Jean-François Chevrier, ohne dessen Beharrlichkeit und Enthusiasmus diese Ausstellung und dieses Buch nicht zustande gekommen wären.

Chris Dercon
Witte de With, Zentrum für zeitgenössische Kunst, Rotterdam
Wim Crouwel
Museum Boymans-van Beuningen, Rotterdam
Bernard Blistène
Directeur des Musées de Marseille
Klaus Bußmann
Westfälisches Landesmuseum für Kunst und Kulturgeschichte, Münster
David A. Ross
Whitney Museum of American Art, New York

1 Chevrier, Jean-François, "Entre les beaux-arts et les médias", Galeries Magazine, no. 37, juin/juillet 1990.
2 Ebenda.
3 Graham, Dan, "Homes for America, Early 20th Century Possessable House to the Quasi-Discrete Cell of `66", Arts Magazine, vol. 41, no. 3, December 1966-January 1967. Im Frühjahr 1971 rekonstruierte und publizierte Dan Graham den Original-Entwurf in der Lithografie-Werkstatt des Nova Scotia College for Art and Design, Halifax, Nova Scotia.
4 Dercon,Chris, "Dan Graham, I enjoy that closeness where I take two things that are very close and just slightly overlap them", Forum International, vol. II, no. 9, September/October 1991.
5. Wir haben uns im deutschen Textteil für die Fassung von Benjamin H. D. Buchlohs Essay, "Augenblicke der Geschichte in der Arbeit von Dan Graham" entschieden, wie sie in Braco Dimitrijevic, Dan Graham, On Kawara, Roman Opalka, Galerie René Block Berlin/DAAD erschienen ist. Diese Fassung unterscheidet sich zum Teil von der englischen Fassung, die im Katalog Dan Graham Articles, Stedelijk Van Abbemuseum, Eindhoven 1977 erschien.
6. Sekula, Allan, "Some American Notes", in Issues and Commentary I, Art in America, no. 2, February 1990.

Walker Evans & Dan Graham

"Ik heb de originele "*Homes for America*" gevonden in *Arts Magazine* ... Aanvankelijk vroeg de redacteur om een essay waarbij mijn foto's van huizen in buitenwijken geplaatst zouden worden (die als dia's getoond waren in december 1966, in The Contemporary Wing van het Finch Museum of Art, New York, in een tentoonstelling met de titel Projected Art). In het uiteindelijke artikel waren 4 of 5 van mijn foto's verwijderd en vervangen door een 40 jaar oude foto van Walker Evans om het 40-jarig jubileum van het blad te vieren." (Dan Graham in een brief aan de organisatoren van de tentoonstelling Walker Evans & Dan Graham, 14 januari 1992).

Het Museum Boymans-van Beuningen, Witte de With, centrum voor hedendaagse kunst, beide in Rotterdam, de Direction des Musées de Marseille, het Westfälisches Landesmuseum für Kunst und Kulturgeschichte, Münster en het Whitney Museum of American Art in New York zijn zeer verheugd u het boek *Walker Evans & Dan Graham* voor te stellen dat de gelijknamige tentoonstelling in onze instituten begeleidt.

Het idee voor de tentoonstelling is voortgesproten uit even inspirerende als vruchtbare gesprekken die wij de afgelopen twee jaar mochten voeren met de Franse kunst- en fotografiehistoricus Jean-François Chevrier. Die gesprekken gingen, hoe kan het anders, over de plaats en de rol van de fotografie in de beeldende kunst. Zoals Jean-François Chevrier opmerkte in een recent essay: "Of ze nu beschouwd wordt als een zaak voor specialisten of, in tegendeel, als een van de uitingsvormen van 'hedendaagse kunst', vandaag neemt de fotografie een dubbelzinnige plaats in tussen de kunst en de media." [1] Wij hebben dan ook geen moment getwijfeld om Jean-François Chevrier uit te nodigen om de werken die in de tentoonstelling en het boek *Walker Evans & Dan Graham* zijn opgenomen, uit te kiezen, te ordenen en te becommentariëren. De keuze van Jean-François Chevrier is verder aangescherpt door het onderzoek, waaraan velen hebben meegewerkt, dat aan dit project vooraf ging.

Een dergelijk onderzoek was noodzakelijk want, aldus Chevrier: "Walker Evans is zonder twijfel het beste voorbeeld van een moderne kunstenaar wiens werk, niet alleen door het complexe karakter dat het van zichzelf heeft, maar ook door de grote weerklank die het vond in de hedendaagse kunst, de traditie van de pure fotografie overtreft. Evans, zoals John Szarkowski van het MoMA aantoonde in zijn tentoonstellingen en catalogi, oefende zeker invloed uit op Frank, Winogrand en Friedlander. Toch verbergt zulk een genealogie, waarvan Europeanen zich waarschijnlijk minder bewust zijn (of waardoor ze verblind zijn) dan Amerikanen, het historische belang van andere stromingen, bijvoorbeeld het werk van post-Pop kunstenaars als Dan Graham en de hernieuwde belangstelling voor realisme en de dagelijkse omgeving van hedendaagse kunstenaars als Thomas Struth." [2]

Het mag dan ook geen verrassing zijn dat toen Dan Graham zijn 'photojournalism' in de vorm van een magazine-artikel voorstelde aan het Amerikaanse *Arts Magazine*, één van de medewerkers van het blad de architectuurfoto's van Graham verving door de foto "*Wooden Houses, Boston*" (1930) uit *American Photographs* van Walker Evans, gepubliceerd door het Museum of Modern Art in New York in 1938. [3] We weten dat Graham zelf de fotografie van Walker Evans belangrijk achtte voor de ontwikkeling van zijn eigen fotografie: "... ik weet dat ik erg veel van zijn werk houd. Wat zeer interessant is aan zijn werk is dat het in tijdschriften gepubliceerd werd en een enorme invloed had op de Pop Art. Daardoor konden bepaalde dingen werken, zoals het idee van de afbeelding van de afbeelding, een idee dat cruciaal was voor de Pop Art en de conceptuele kunst. Daarenboven denk ik dat Evans en ook Ruscha belangstelling hebben gewekt voor de locale architectuur door die te presenteren in een gedrukte vorm, zoals Godard of Robert Venturi en Rem Koolhaas de lokale architectuur gebruikten." [4]

Met deze tentoonstelling en dit boek willen wij niet alleen de relatie tussen de oeuvres van de Amerikaanse kunstenaars Walker Evans (1903-1975) en Dan Graham (1942) verhelderen en twee verschillende, door de tijd ingegeven, visies op de ontwikkeling van de Amerikaanse stedelijke omgeving vergelijken, maar ook willen wij een licht werpen op de geschiedenis van de fotografie en de beeldende kunst. Zulks is meer dan nodig, nu al dan niet willekeurig, de banden tussen fotografie en beeldende kunst steeds nauwer worden aangehaald.

Wij zijn dan ook zeer vereerd dat wij in dit boek naast het standpunt van Jean-François Chevrier, u ook de kritische inzichten van kunsthistoricus Benjamin H.D. Buchloh en fotograaf en criticus Allan Sekula kunnen voorstellen. Wij hebben gemeend u het essay "Moments of history in the work of Dan Graham", van Benjamin H.D. Buchloh voor te leggen, eerder als nawoord gepubliceerd in de inmiddels haast onvindbare publicatie *Dan Graham Articles*, uitgegeven in 1977 door het Stedelijk Van Abbemuseum in Eindhoven.[5] Dit essay geldt nog steeds als een van de meest rijke en tegelijkertijd precieze verhandelingen over het oeuvre van Dan Graham. Hetzelfde geldt voor de gedetailleerde en vaak provocerende essays die Allan Sekula de laatste tien jaar heeft gepubliceerd over specifieke thema's van de 'onafhankelijke kunst' van de fotografie. Maar, vraagt Sekula, "onafhankelijk van wat?" [6]

Het zijn juist zulke vragen waarmee kunstinstituten zich bezig dienen te houden wanneer zij zich wensen in te laten met de complexe discipline van de fotografie: hetzij met betrekking tot collectievorming, tentoonstellingsbeleid, ja zelfs met betrekking tot de oprichting van nieuwe instituten die zich richten op het terrein van de fotografie. Van de architectuurfoto's van Thomas Struth en James Welling in de collectie Moderne Kunst van het Museum Boymans-van Beuningen, over tentoonstellingen als De Afstand en Ken Lum in Witte de With, tot de rol van het toekomstige 'Foto-instituut' in Rotterdam. Van de tentoonstellingen van Edward Hopper, Moholy Nagy en Le Pont Transbordeur et la Vision Moderniste die in het recente verleden hebben plaatsgevonden in Les Musées de Marseille tot het initiatief, mede geïniteerd door het Westfälisches Landesmuseum für Kunst und Kulturgeschichte in Münster, om een speciaal museum te wijden aan werken van hedendaagse beeldende kunstenaars die fotografische middelen hanteren. En het Whitney Museum of American Art in New York, dat een grote waarde hecht aan en begrip wil kweken voor de bijzondere rol van de fotografie in de ontwikkeling van de kunst van deze eeuw, is zeer geïnteresseerd in de wijze waarop de fotografie verweven is met de hedendaagse kunst en het eindspel van het modernisme heeft versneld.

De tentoonstelling Walker Evans & Dan Graham is perfect op zijn plaats in Rotterdam, Marseille, Münster en New York. Want onze steden hebben met elkaar gemeen dat ze telkens geconfronteerd worden met nieuwe culturele ontwikkelingen, niet in het minst architectonische ontwikkelingen die de wederopbouw en de nieuwe inrichting van oude stadskernen betreffen, en niet te vergeten de razendsnelle uitbreidingen die zich afspelen aan de randen van onze steden. Ook hiervoor kan men een beroep te doen op de geschiedenis en de ontwikkeling van de architectuur die zich voltrekt voor de camera's van Walker Evans en Dan Graham.

Zoals hierboven gemeld hebben wij de voorbereidingen voor de tentoonstelling en het boek *Walker Evans & Dan Graham*, waarvan nu de resultaten zichtbaar zijn, reeds in een vroeg stadium gestart. Onze dank gaat uit naar al diegenen die ons hierbij direct of indirect behulpzaam waren: in de eerste plaats naar Dan Graham die ons met raad en daad, bij iedere nieuwe vraag, heeft bijgestaan; zijn medewerker, Regina Möller; Marian Goodman en de staf van de Marian Goodman Gallery, vooral Elaine Budin en Priamo Lozada, en verder Vito Acconci; Galerie Art & Project; Art Gallery of Ontario; Judith Barry en Ken Saylor; Gustinet Bartomeo Mari; Jane Ryan Beck en Craig Winkelman; Galerie Jürgen Becker; Benjamin H.D. Buchloh; The Carnegie Museum of Art en Mark Francis, Lisa Corrine Isenberg; DIA Center for the Arts en Karen Kelly; Rosalind Cutforth; Herman Daled; Lili Dujourie; Galerie Durand-Dessert; Yves Gevaert; Claude Gintz; André Goeminne; Kim Gordon; Ydessa Hendeles Art Foundation; Friedrich Wolfram Heubach; John Hilliard; Galerie Pierre Hubert; Galerie Johnen & Schöttle; John Knight; Kasper König; Lisson Gallery en Sharon Essor; Produzentengalerie Hamburg; Rotterdamse Kunststichting en Anne-Mie Devolder; Thomas Lawson; Galerie Meert Rihoux; Ernst Mitzka; Galerie Roger Pailhas; Birgit Pelzer; Galleria Pieroni; René Pulfer; Gerhard Richter; Harry Ruhé; Galleria Lia Rumma; Bob Rogers; Galerie Rüdiger Schöttle; Shimada Gallery; Hans Sonneveld; Stedelijk Van Abbemuseum en Jaap Guldemond; Galerie Micheline Szwajcer; Johan Van Heddegem; Galerie Vega; Jeff Wall; Lawrence en Alice Weiner.

Sandra Alvarez de Toledo danken wij voor het opzoekingswerk omtrent Walker Evans, evenals The Art Institute of Chicago en David Travis, J. Russel Harris; The Estate of Walker Evans en John Hill; The Metropolitan Museum of Art en Maria Morris-Hambourg, Margaret Kannan; The Minneapolis Institute of Arts en Carol T. Hartwell, Peggy Tolbert; The Museum of Modern Art en Peter Galassi, Susan Kismaric, Nicole Friedler; Sylviane De Decker Heftler.

Uiteraard danken wij alle bruikleengevers die in ons hun vertrouwen hebben gesteld en hun werken aan ons hebben afgestaan voor zulk een lange periode. Onze speciale dank gaat uit naar de staf van Witte de With die verantwoordelijk was voor de organisatie van de tentoonstelling en het boek. In naam van hen zijn wij Craigie Horsfield erkentelijk voor zijn aanmoedigingen. Tenslotte willen wij hier vooral Jean-François Chevrier bedanken zonder wiens vasthoudendheid en enthousiasme deze tentoonstelling en dit boek nooit gerealiseerd hadden kunnen worden.

Chris Dercon
Witte de With, center for contemporary art, Rotterdam
Wim Crouwel
Museum Boymans-van Beuningen, Rotterdam
Bernard Blistène
Directeur des Musées de Marseille
Klaus Bußmann
Westfälisches Landesmuseum für Kunst und Kulturgeschichte, Münster
David A. Ross
Whitney Museum of American Art, New York

1 Chevrier, Jean-François, "Entre les beaux-arts et les médias", *Galeries Magazine*, no. 37, juin/juillet1990.
2 ibid.
3 Graham, Dan, "Homes for America, Early 20th-Century Possessable House to the Quasi-Discrete Cell of '66", *Arts Magazine*, vol. 41, no. 3, December 1966 - January 67. In het voorjaar van 1971 reconstrueerde en publiceerde Dan Graham zijn oorspronkelijke maquette in de lithografie werkplaats van het Nova Scotia College for Art and Design, Halifax, Nova Scotia.
4 Dercon, Chris, "Dan Graham, I enjoy that closeness where I take two things that are very close and just slightly overlap them", *Forum International*, vol. II, no. 9, September-October 1991.
5 Wij hebben gemeend in het Duitse tekstdeel van dit boek u de versie van Benjamin H.D. Buchlohs essay, "Augenblicke der Geschichte in der Arbeit von Dan Graham", te moeten presenteren, zoals die verschenen is in *Braco Dimitrijevic, Dan Graham, On Kawara, Roman Opalka*, Galerie René Block Berlin/DAAD. Deze versie wijkt enigszins af van de Engelse versie zoals die is verschenen in de catalogus *Dan Graham Articles*, Stedelijk Van Abbemuseum, Eindhoven.
6 Sekula, Allan, "Some American Notes" in Issues and Commentary I, *Art in America*, no. 2, February 1990.

Dual Reading

Jean-François Chevrier

"Dan, you've been called a poet and a critic and a photographer. Are you an artist now?" asked Lucy Lippard during a roundtable radio broadcast in 1970. Dan Graham replied: "I don't define myself, but whatever I do, I think, is defined by the medium. I did printed matter about three or four years ago. Things in print, things for magazines, things that use photography. I've done things in all the areas that other people have worked in and I think they define themselves."[1] This declaration should be enough to immediately settle any vain debate about the photographic nature of a part of Dan Graham's work. If the artist is defined by his activities, which are themselves defined by the tools employed, it becomes pointless to ask whether Dan Graham is 'really' a photographer or not. He is a photographer when he uses photography, and what he does in this domain has a certain autonomy, relative to be sure, but sufficient to justify independent examination.

In 1970, however, the question of artistic definitions had been exacerbated by the recent multiplication of activities cutting across established genres and categories. The radio conversation, led by Lucy Lippard and also including Carl Andre, Douglas Huebler, and Jan Dibbets, is quite telling on this point. The four artists were brought together because they were "four visual artists who have used words in one way or the other." Like Carl Andre, Dan Graham sets himself apart from so-called 'conceptual' art: "I don't think I am doing conceptual art." But he also refuses to situate himself in the divide between objects and words. He is not an artist who prefers words to objects. He pushes aside the 'word-object dichotomy', to foreground the notion of information. As he makes very clear, "I was never interested in words or syntax in poetry, but more in information. I wanted the things I did to occupy a particular place and to be read in a particular present time. The context is very important. I wanted my pieces to be about place as in-formation which is present."

With Homes for America (*Arts Magazine*, December 1966 - January 1967), photography found its role in this strategic context, as visual information to be combined with written information, in a space - the page, or the double-page spread of a magazine - that constitutes the locus of a reading experience. Insofar as it is a montage material, photography becomes a tool of in-formation, of the putting into form of experience. Such was the procedure adopted, which can always be called 'conceptual' if one so desires. In reality, Dan Graham situates himself above all as a post-pop artist, working directly on and with the mass media, rather than appropriating media iconography and effects as the pop artists did.[2]

A further concern was to assimilate art criticism to artistic activity, concretely, materially, so as to resorb the gap of the

separated, a posteriori judgment. This gap had to be placed (displaced) within the very structure of the work. When he published Homes for America, Dan Graham did not even need to indicate "This is not a work of art", as Marcel Broodthaers did a few years thereafter on the labels of the collection "*Der Adler von Oligozän bis heute*", exhibited in Düsseldorf (as part of "*Musée d'Art Moderne. Département des Aigles, Section des Figures*", Städtische Kunsthalle, Düsseldorf, May-June 1972). Homes for America is a magazine article. The commentary is not a secondary reflection on a separate (and past) artwork. It is no longer a reflection of art's autonomy. The commentary is coextensive to the work (which neither negates nor denies itself). The work and the commentary are copresent in a single space of perception, which is that of information. The latter is no longer information on; it is in-formation of. The commentary itself is artistic form.

In the late sixties, Dan Graham simultaneously set himself a number of critical goals. He wished to return Pop Art to its place of origin (the media), to synchronize the watches of artistic activity and its critical reception, and thus to identify the art object with its social production, where formalist doctrine tended on the contrary to isolate it in a strict autonomy (carefully distanced from the media sphere). Finally, he recognized that Minimalism (with its 'primary structures') is never anything more than a hyperformalism, and he sought to restore the links between the form-type of the minimal object and the architectural models - like the serialized cube of suburban housing tracts - that this object transforms in an ideal or negative mode (Donald Judd and Tony Smith respectively). This, of course, was the relation that a mystifying aesthetic discourse denied.

When Homes for America appeared in December 1966, Robert Smithson had already undertaken a contextualization of Minimalism in his early critical texts, and particularly in his less than orthodox interpretation of the architectural models of a mannerist Donald Judd.[3] Dan Graham's strategy was of the same order and perhaps more radical, for at that time he had no desire (or possibility) to create plastic objects and as yet had only produced verbal structures and photographic images. A few months earlier he had taken part in an exhibition called Projected Art, where he had in effect projected transparencies of suburban dwellings; these are the images that should have illustrated Homes for America.[4] Following a logic of fiction - which was hastily confounded with 'conceptual' procedures, as a way of reducing its specificity - the article delivered to *Arts Magazine* became the work "*Homes for America*", by an art critic and photographer, or a photographer/ architecture critic, or better yet, a minimal artist, critic, and photographer who chose not to produce plastic objects, as there are architects who have chosen not to build.[5]

In "Entropy and the New Monuments", published some six months prior to Homes for America, Smithson recognized the negative qualities of the suburban environment (dullness, vapidity) in the structures of Judd, Morris, LeWitt, and Flavin. He also compared them with the visual models furnished by the interminable "printed matter" of the Gutenberg Galaxy described by McLuhan.[6] A neo-romantic, Smithson puts the monument (and its function of remembrance) to the test of time. He speaks of Flavin's "instant monuments" and details the paradox of the "new monuments" in terms that irresistably evoke photographic recording: "They are not built for the ages, but rather against the ages. They are involved in a systematic reduction of time down to fractions of seconds, rather than representing the long spaces of centuries. Both past and future are placed into an objective present." In an essay published the following year, "The Monuments of Passaic" (*Artforum*, December 1967), Smithson illustrated a narrative parodying memories of a "grand tour" in Italy with photographs taken in the course of an excursion to his native city.[7] Here he plays on the ambiguity between the historical monument (vestige of a memorable cultural past) and the monument's larger value as a work of memory, whose model is constituted by documentary photography, but which the latter reduces to an intangible optical appearance.[8]

Like Smithson and before him, Dan Graham used photography to work toward a redefinition of the monument. In the same period, Douglas Huebler renounced the creation of objects and undertook conceptual actions using photography, after concluding from his participation in the exhibition Primary Structures (Jewish Museum, New York, 1966) that a cube can be just as 'real' as any utilitarian object - a table, a chair - but that it cannot be erected outdoors on a monumental scale without being exposed to a crushing comparison with nature.[9] This difficulty never presented itself to Dan Graham, as he never felt any attraction to the untrammeled spaces of a natural world without urbanism. Smithson contrasts the monument of the past, the incarnation of a historic ideal, with the exhaustion of this ideal in the no man's land of galleries and para-urban spaces. But this exhaustion is grandiose; it rivals geologic phenomena, laying the groundwork of a new archaism, a return to the origin. For Dan Graham, on the other hand, the monument has always already undergone the reduction (miniaturization and dematerialization) of the photographic image, which therefore constitutes an effective model. Thus he never worked against the monument in general, nor even more particularly against the urban monument.[10] His first glass pavilions appeared at the end of the seventies, after the performances, video works, and mirror installations; they were a necessary and logical extension of the critical investigation of specific urban structures which had begun with photography.

Here we must return to the early photographs, taken in 1965-66, outside New York, in New Jersey: for they already establish the parameters of the dialectic of socio-psychological perception, founded on social divisions, which will be developed later on. Shown in a gallery, the transparencies introduce (project) an exterior within the exclusive space of the immaculate 'white cube'. This exterior is made up of a specific piece of information, characterized by a double remove: to the periphery of New York (New Jersey) and to the recent past of the post-war period, from which dates the construction program of the tract houses, during the early childhood of Dan Graham (born in 1942). This way of being nearby, yet elsewhere - in both space and time - is the mark of the photographic (documentary) present, which for this reason represents the model of the later works. It suffices to consider the structures employed in the performances and videos of the 1970s, where the present hic et nunc of the action (or the reception) is constantly altered by the proximity of a mirror reflection or the immediate past of a recording. In "*Yesterday/Today*" (1975) for example, an audio recording brings a recent past (yesterday) and a video intrusion from nearby (the activities occurring in the room next door) into the present space of the viewer.[11] Five years later (1979-80), "*Video View of Suburbia in an Urban Atrium*" again introduces the proximate distance of the suburbs into a privileged urban space.[12]

Another video installation, "*Edge of the City*" (1981), very precisely designates the relation of the suburbs to the urban center. By this time, though, Dan Graham's field of investigation has considerably enlarged. If the suburban margin was his first historical subject, he now begins to examine another moment of the modernist utopia. The recent past has been displaced: it is now the sixties, the period of the first atriums at the feet of the glass towers raised by the multinational corporations. While Post-Modernism is busy negating the history of Modernism in the name of all its nostalgic 'revivals', Dan Graham conceives and constructs his "*Pavilions*", using the most banalized, most devalued typological models of the International Style. He himself speaks of "clichés of modern architecture".[13]

As attested in two particularly elaborate texts, both published in *Artforum* ("Art in Relation to Architecture/ Architecture in Relation to Art", February 1979, and "Not Post-Modernism...", December 1981), Dan Graham's thought in the period around 1980 is essentially articulated on the basis of historical givens, though without abandoning the psycho-sociological models that had oriented his previous experiments. He shifts from the information system to the architectural object, while retaining the axial question of the perception of alterity and the modes of its experience (or construction). He returns - with all the gains of his performance and video work - to the historical contextualization of Minimalism that he had undertaken in "*Homes for America*". The minimalist cube, opened up, multiplied, given over to the baroque, is now linked to the modernist utopia of a center-city reconciled with nature; the corporate atrium is the exemplary (caricatural) manifestation of this utopia, at a time when public space is being privatized.

Conceived as a (critical) monument to utopia, the architecture of the "*Pavilions*" resumes the fictional transparency and the play of mirrors which characterize the glass towers. This critical sculpture-architecture is above all founded on a historical analogy mobilizing far more distant references: the pavilion is to the primitive hut imagined in the eighteenth century - the paradigm of modernist architecture's originary primitivism - what the atrium is to the picturesque garden (the model of the urban park).[14] By putting the city/suburb division back into the historical movement of the Enlightenment's culture-nature dialectic, Dan Graham broadens the narrow context of Minimalism. He can now work with all the mediating terms that will allow him to concretely articulate the two essential determinants of the minimalist model: architectural modernism (in the form that spread throughout America with the triumph of the International Style) and the pop environment of the suburbs. As "*Alteration of a Suburban House*" already prefigured in 1978, the constructed object of art (the pavilion) reflects - both literally and in the sense of a critical 'reflection' - the contemporary environment and its historical models. The urban utopia of the corporate buildings, with their baroque outgrowths (the atriums), is the resumé, or the miniaturized reflection, of the pop environment of the suburbs, which has achieved an up-to-date blend of city and nature symbolized by exuberant commercial signs, abundance, and the community of consumption.

The environment of pop sign-systems having become the present context of the modernist utopia since the sixties, it was quite logically through an interpretation of Pop Art and its cultural ambivalence, in Lichtenstein's work and above all in that of the architect Robert Venturi, that Dan Graham elaborated the principle of his own constructions. A passage of "Not Post-Modernism..." is particularly illuminating: "Venturi, like the more academic of the pop artists, never accepted popular culture simply on its own terms, but correlated it to formalist and architectural-historical readings that placed popular readings in a dialectical perspective. A Venturi, Rauch and Scott Brown building may be read from both a 'high' architecture framework, as well as one assimilable to popular, ephemeral readings. Both readings are correct. Owing to its seeming ephemerality in terms of the popular code, such work cannot be immediately assimilated into academic architecture: conversely, the work cannot be immediately assimilated and coopted by mass culture because of its anchoring in 'high' architecture. The fact that it cannot be immediately assimilated allows the work to question both positions, but from within (not in contradiction to) popular culture and architectural values, both formal and historical." [15]

Describing Lichtenstein's ambivalence toward popular culture in the same terms, Dan Graham speaks of a "dual reading" - and it is precisely this "dualism," also called for by Robert Venturi in his 1966 volume *Complexity and Contradiction in Architecture*, that allows him to construct an appropriate (because ambiguous) image of the permanence of the modernist utopia in its debased, alienating, and oppressive uses.[16] It is not then a question of 'deconstructing' the

modernist model, nor one of treating the signs of popular culture with irony, nor even of parodying the mediatized masterpieces of the past. Here, critical acumen consists in an exaltation of the historical contradictions present in a utopian model that has been transformed into a structure of alienation. This is effected less by discriminating between things or ideas (as in the etymological sense of the word 'criticism') than by constructively dramatizing ambiguity as the coexistence of contradictory points of view and the montage of dissimilar historical moments.

The insightful beauty of the photographs produced since 1965 is bound up with this "dual reading," whose principle emerged from an analysis of Pop Art. These pictures are at once rigorous images of architecture, formalized to the point of abstraction, and also magazine illustrations without any pretension to 'art', assimilable to the ephemeral creations of the mass media. Their current presentation, in the form of prints displayed like autonomous works, has a tendency to blur their initial attachment to the pop culture of the media. However, this development corresponds to the aesthetic claim that appeared with the "*Pavilions*", which are defined nonetheless (and this is worth stressing) as "clichés of modern architecture", thus maintaining their relation to the media culture of brand-name images. These photographs may also be compared with the treatment of similar subjects in contemporary 'creative' photography - consider, for example, the documentary chatter of Bill Owens in "*Suburbia*" (1973) - to confirm that they have indeed retained their double pertinence to the modernist tradition (as transmitted by 'academic' minimalism) and to pop culture.

In 1965, the choice of transparencies and the corresponding standardization of color qualities signaled a refusal of all the refinements composing the 'beautiful image', colorist saturation effects as well as the nuances of black and white values. At this time, Dan Graham was more drawn to Dan Flavin's industrial neons than to the chromatic play of 'straight photography' in its differing versions (Helen Levitt, Eliot Porter, etc.), all of which finally participate in craft as opposed to industry. Attached, at the same time, to the austere rigour of Modernism, Graham also turned away from the kitsch exuberance of Hollywood-style magazine illustrations (that exuberance would come later, in the atrium images). Historians of photography made no mistake: they did not include him in their panoramas and obviously considered his project to be irredeemably conceptual, in other words involving a use of photography that remains irreducible to the canonic forms and yet does not, for all that, present the typical aspect of 'conceptual photography' à la Sol LeWitt.

Dan Graham upheld the principle of the dual reading before he even formulated it. It was enough for him to use photography as it had emerged historically, between the fine arts and the media. Its ambiguous situation had lasted throughout the entire period of modern art's development and gradual acceptance, from 1850 up to the 1960s, when Warhol, then Richter produced their first photographic 'tableaux'. But the ambiguity was still not resolved. Warhol subsequently seemed to opt for the side of the media, while Richter little by little came to privilege abstraction (maintaining nonetheless the counterpoint of the photographic model). American photorealism, for its part, prolonged its stubborn attempt to exalt (or attain) the impersonal exactness of the photographic image, in an overly perfect pictorial mechanics. By using the photograph as he did, for what it is, between the object of exhibition (even in the form of projected transparencies) and the media tool, Dan Graham revealed the historical situation of Pop Art, between Modernism (assimilated to 'high art') and popular culture. This is precisely where he rejoined the example of Walker Evans, at the sources of pop.

Judging from the testimony one can gather today, the artists of the conceptual circle had recognized this lineage by the end of the 1960s.[17] But in the early sixties many pop artists or artists close to pop had already mentioned the precedent of Walker Evans, and particularly his billboard images. Jim Dine speaks of them in an interview with Gene Swenson in 1963.[18] In 1967, Allan Kaprow evoked Evans with respect to the European décollage artists (Hains, Villeglé, Rotella), in a text that insists on the nostalgic resonances of pop, with all its references to the thirties and forties, the childhood years of its exponents.[19] Four years earlier, Warhol had produced his famous homage to Rauschenberg, "*Let Us Now Praise Famous Men*", where he used family photos of Rauschenberg (taken in the thirties), and to which he gave the title of the cult book by James Agee and Walker Evans.[20] This book, moreover, had been reprinted in 1960. As for *American Photographs*, the book-length catalogue of the Evans exhibition at The Museum of Modern Art, New York in 1938 - containing the images mentioned by Dine and Kaprow - it was reprinted in 1962.

If we add that *Many Are Called* (the subway portraits) and *Message from the Interior* both appeared in 1966, and also that Garry Winogrand and Lee Friedlander were in a certain way officially recognized as the inheritors of Walker Evans in 1966-67, we reach the conclusion that the sixties, which opened with Pop Art, were also the years when a certain image of America took hold in art via photography, an image founded on the wealth of vernacular culture documented since the thirties, and of which Evans could be taken as the eponymous figure.[21] This is what the editors of *Arts Magazine* signified when they replaced Dan Graham's row houses with a lineup of wooden houses photographed by Evans in Boston in 1930, already familiar as the cover image of the 1962 edition of *American Photographs* (see reproduction, page 109).

In 1965-66, Dan Graham did not know the work of Walker Evans; he discovered it later, after the publication of "*Homes for America*", when his friend Mel Bochner showed him *American Photographs*. His interest for the functional urban

and suburban architecture of the post-war period - where the reversal of the modernist utopia into a structure of alienation is so massively manifest - came to him from the direct observation of New York and its suburbs, and beyond this immediate experience, from two artistic models much closer to him in time than Walker Evans: Minimalism of course, but also certain European filmmakers (Antonioni, Godard) who developed their work out of post-war Italian Neo-Realism, in which the themes of the modern city and the suburbs as sites of psychological disturbances and existential wandering were omnipresent.[22] One could even quite easily assimilate the structure of "*Homes for America*" to the document-fiction dialectic that Godard brings systematically into play.[23]

These references to cinema were in fact widely shared in the avant-garde circles of New York in the late sixties. Complementing "*Made in USA*", Godard's "*Deux ou trois choses que je sais d'elle*".appeared in 1966 as the fulfillment of a cinematic synthesis linking the timeliness of Pop Art and the 'nouveau roman' to a documentary dramatization inspired by Neo-Realism.[24] Throughout this period Walker Evans held completely aloof from vanguard circles, and we cannot be certain that he followed the evolution of post-war European film. It is nonetheless true that his friend James Agee was an attentive observer of these developments from 1941 to 1948, writing articles on Rossellini, Vittorio de Sica, and Georges Rouquier ("*Farrebique*") for the left American journal *The Nation*, somewhat as André Bazin did more systematically in France. In any case, the essential remains: a convergence effectively took place in the sixties between the history of a 'realist' cinema leading to Godard and Antonioni, and the photographic project of Walker Evans - which reached its culmination at this time, when the publication of the subway portraits from the late thirties came to complete *American Photographs*.

In a context strongly marked by the anti-liberal stance of the radical Marxist left and the anti-humanism of structuralist thought (rejoined by the 'literalism' of Robbe-Grillet), Evans was above all esteemed for his images of architecture and of urban signs. Dan Graham, like everyone else, saw the Pop Art principle of the reproduction of reproduction in *American Photographs*, but he also and more particularly saw what he himself had observed in the suburbs immediately bordering on New York (in New Jersey). This was the image of Main Street, as both historical reality and the paradigm of suburban urbanism: standardized houses lined up along the railroad tracks, in short, the architecture of commerce and communication in its mechanized form, common to the totality of the industrial world, and in its vernacular aspect quite specific to America.

The portion of Evan's work that could be imputed to the humanist ideology of Rooseveltian social-democracy was shunted aside. Like any portrait bearing the slightest trace of empathy, the images of *Let Us Now Praise Famous Men* appeared too close to the "mythology" (Barthes) developed by Edward Steichen in The Family of Man at The Museum of Modern Art, New York in 1955. In the eyes of Dan Graham (and his friends), all 'normal' photography was caught in the mystifications of liberal humanism. He stresses, however, that this rejection was also a repression, and that what he refused in the sixties has recently resurfaced, in the "*Children's Pavilion*" project undertaken with Jeff Wall.[25]

In reality Evans was no less reserved, or ambivalent, toward all the rhetorical appeals for communion in the image. He did not take part in The Family of Man. His perspective on social reality was too distant, he was both too moralistic (or puritan) and too much the dandy to fit in with the sentimental exaggeration and spectacular effects of an imagery of universal community. As early as 1931, in an essay published by Lincoln Kirstein in *Hound and Horn*, he had violently criticized Steichen's commercial aesthetism.[26] A few years later, while working for the Farm Security Administration (FSA) (from 1935 to 1938), he resisted his employers' propaganda program and even more forcefully opposed the dramatic excess and emotional pandering of Margaret Bourke-White and Erskine Caldwell in their 1937 bestseller, *You Have Seen Their Faces*.[27] His revulsion was moral and aesthetic. The style of Margaret Bourke-White, the star photographer of *Life* (whose first cover she did in 1936), represented the exact equivalent in the media of the 'monumental order' characterizing official architecture in the thirties, in its conception as the symbol of an authoritarian power incarnating the organic unity of a people. Evans, with his self-proclaimed 'bohemian' origins and taste for Baudelaire and Flaubert, could only draw back from his own sympathies for the downtrodden, refusing any belief in art's capacity to "improve society".[28] Throughout his life he was confronted by the dilemma of the bohemian artist: he had to stay outside of left-leaning programs while also avoiding establishment frameworks.[29] He could neither belong to the people nor appoint himself their enlightened spokesman (or self-interested panegyrist, after the example of Bourke-White).

The artistic position which results from this dilemma is necessarily ambiguous. Evans formulated it several times, in terms that resemble Dan Graham's remarks on Pop Art. In a 1971 interview occasioned by a retrospective of his oeuvre at The Museum of Modern Art, New York, he summed up his double refusal of (photographic) art and commerce, whose conflation he had seen in Steichen's work forty years before: "I was doing non-artistic and non-commercial work. I felt - and it's true - I was on the right track."[30] He was an outsider - one of those who open up a new field of inquiry and who, when they are recognized, run the risk of being co-opted by the establishment, a risk he had to face as early as 1938 (he responded by going 'underground', to photograph the passengers in the subway - producing images that remained practically unknown until the sixties.) In 1971, to dissociate himself once again from the functional (and commercial) criteria of the informational image, he advanced the idea of the

'documentary style', a magic compromise-formula between high art and the information trade. But he remains most true to himself with the model of affirming a negation, as when he declares: "Theorists claim almost everything for the camera except the 'negation' that it can be made not to think and not to translate its operator's emotion."[31]

He had already written in the 1931 essay "The Reappearance of Photography": "America is really the natural home of photography if photography is thought without operators." But the previously quoted assertion - introducing images that Evans situates in the years around 1940 - is the more radical. It is the negative response to the ideological programs of the thirties, indeed to all the debased utopias of the Machine Age, to which the text of '31 still seems to subscribe.[32] Presenting the subway portraits, Evans describes an ideal project (which he never carried out), a project in total conformity to the impersonality and absence of aesthetic choice that characterize the Duchampian ready-made: "I would like to be able to state flatly that sixty-two people came unconsciously into range before an impersonal fixed recording machine during a certain time period, and that all these individuals who came into the film frame were photographed, and photographed without any human selection for the moment of lens exposure."[33] In this, one can clearly recognize the radicalism of late sixties' conceptual procedures. But if we consider the images themselves, it must be acknowledged that their dramatic resonance is quite foreign to the postulated principle of indifference. In his attempts to push the (blind) confidence of early Modernism to the extreme, to the absurd, Evans revealed the dark side of Modernism as the age of the machine.

The Berlin filmmakers of the twenties had gone down this road before him: Fritz Lang above all, with "*Metropolis*" (1924) but also with "*M.*" (1931). When Evans indicates that the figures in the subway pictures are "the ladies and gentlemen of the jury", one may assume that he wanted to apply the police photographer's method of typological inventory to the common man, raised to the status of juror.[34] In "*M.*", Lang had already transformed an underground crowd of criminals into a somber tribunal. By citing Daumier as a reference, Evans suggests that all these plays of reversal between the 'common' and the criminal in the figure of the man of the crowd are foreshadowed at the moment when an artist first comes to suspect modern justice. The underground subway is Murnau's "street film" - as Kracauer described it - transformed into the tribunal of the unconscious, the most common of all, where the crime is judged by the criminal. It may be added, in support of this interpretation, that the example Evans found in the street photography of Paul Strand was distilled, for him, in the single portrait of the blind newspaper vendor, "*Blind Woman*" (1915).

This dark side of Modernism, theater of the figures (or masks) of the unconscious, had been isolated by the Berlin filmmakers during the crisis of the twenties, in the streets of the 'big city' ["Großstadt"]. It is logical that photographers, at the edges of the cinema, in New York - the modern city par excellence - should have given the first indications of it, and that Walker Evans, on the far side of another crisis, should have produced the synthesis of the two historical moments, relating them to the archaic modernity of the Baudelairean city, marked by the stigmata of sin. In a passage from *My Heart Laid Bare*, Baudelaire had stated his 'theory of true civilization': "It is not in gas, nor in steam, nor in spiritist tables, it is in the diminution of the traces of original sin." [35] By grouping the subway portraits under the title *Many Are Called* (but few are chosen...), Evans returns to the allegorical - and melancholic - vein that runs through *The Flowers of Evil* (which was, for a time, to be entitled *Limbo*). Finally, one must recall that Baudelaire associated all caricature with "the satanic laugh", and that he particularly admired Daumier.[36]

None of this is foreign to the American art of the sixties. Smithson's black humor is a variant of "the satanic laugh", as the outlet of a melancholy for which the suburbs furnish abundant allegorical motifs. Because he was not romantic enough to play 'the devil's advocate', Dan Graham stuck to a stricter realism, the simple acknowledgment of the negative utopia realized in the suburban environment. And yet his study, since the late 1960s, of the typological models of Modernism - their formation and recent transformations - brought him very exactly to the site of Baudelairean remembrance: limbo, the twilight region of waiting, which absorbs all the historical scrap-ends ferried along by the constituted utopias. In this intermediary zone, the immobile, indifferent time of melancholy lays bare the utopian content (the 'non-place') of the clichés of universal happiness. Thus the Baudelairean model, in the form that it took for Evans, reappears behind the Warholean figure of the dandy.

Long before Warhol, the Duchampian principle of indifference came into play in Walker Evans' work as the negative and objectively dramatic exaltation - via photography - of the egalitarian dream of American society. For this indifference is also, even primarily, that of the dandy who struggles in vain to break the bohemian mold and who, like Baudelaire, admires Daumier. Placed in this genealogy, the subway portraits were able to bring a historical interpretation to the crisis of Modernism in the thirties, one that converges with the observations that Walter Benjamin drew from his study of the Baudelairean city. The crowd, manipulated by the mechanisms of totalitarian propaganda, is the element of 'number' in which the bohemian artist both achieves the dissolution of his subjectivity and finds the stimulating force of his activity. Art must answer the machine with the machine, not in the manner of the media-inflected epic (celebrating a pseudo-organic community) but in a lyric mode attuned to the diversity of the common.

Here lies the great discovery of Evans in the thirties, which Dan Graham has inherited: the vernacular of American culture in all its diversity, irreducible to Modernist typologies. There is

no American people, but a spectacle of America. Far more rich and complex than the rare masterpieces inspired by a modernism of European origin, it cannot for all that be assimilated to the cliché of an Edenic 'New World', protected from industrial civilization. Of all the 'masters' of modern American photography, Walker Evans is no doubt the only one to have entirely broken free of an idea of Nature, the only one to have rigorously taken the side of signs and of history (to use the distinction established by Roland Barthes at the time of *Mythologies*): the only one who did not seek to found a mastery of photography on the ability to make nature talk, or to reveal its secret messages (through the magic of technics). His oeuvre began in earnest with the crisis of '29, and developed primarily in that crisis. For him, the spectacle of America is essentially urban, marked by the signs of the city (or of commerce) and their violent but ephemeral hold on the environment. The recording need not isolate the permanent form of a symbol (Weston's "thing itself") but must rather fix an image-sign, a document-monument.

For all the photographers of the twenties, influenced by Strand and gathered under the banner of anti-pictorialist 'straight photography', nature was simultaneously (or successively) the model of the ideal machine - thus assimilable to the work of art - and the salutary answer to the deleterious effects of an ideal of mechanicity. Whatever the option taken, these photographers required a 'quality' that would relate the image to the art object, or to what Fernand Léger called "le bel objet": the industrial object, perfectly delineated, perfectly functional, with a design obeying that of nature. Although he appreciated the cut of technical objects, even (or above all) the most ordinary ones - as attested by his article "Beauties of the Common Tool", published in *Fortune* in 1955 - Evans essentially saw them as examples of a technical culture having more to do with an anthropological (or historical) repertory of ideal figures than with the eternal laws of nature. In any case, regardless of the subject under study, his model was not the natural or industrial object but the image, aligned by filiation and function with the printed or posted signs used for communication.

Here, the difference from his immediate predecessors is decisive. Ralph Steiner, for example, who passed on his technique to Evans, had in the twenties already glimpsed the richness of the documentary material later assembled in *American Photographs*. This is apparent in his illustrations for a 1930 article in *Fortune*, at the very beginning of the Depression. The aim of these views anticipates that of Evans: "a record - not of the new America, its skyscrapers, its airplanes, its dynamos - but of the America which remains unregenerate, its backporches and backyards, its ugliness and its waste." [37] The same text also has the merit of stating the 'mythological' reasoning proper to the nationalist imagination of *Fortune*'s editors, which would later make it possible for Evans to work for the magazine: "Essentially, the English scene is sad and the American scene is happy. It is smelly, but it is also exuberant and vigorous to strew the countryside with things worn out and left over. Every garbage dump, every row of ramshackle houses lining the railroad track, is evidence of our boundless wealth. This is space we do not need, we have so much." But these parallels merely underscore everything that set Evans apart. Steiner was no doubt a particularly early case of adaptation to a demand for cultural identity, a demand that the ideology of technological progress could not fully satisfy (because it left too many things by the wayside). But Steiner was too attached to the value that traditional (pre-industrial) 'high art' placed on the accomplished work. Strand, whom he discovered in 1926-27, exemplified this value: "Strand stunned me by showing me his Mexican prints. I was pole-axed; I had never seen prints so rich - with such real texture - and so glorious in tonal values." [38] Evans, on the contrary, ceaselessly pushed aside these criteria of 'historic' quality and polished execution, going so far as to declare in 1971, while exhibiting once again at The Museum of Modern Art, New York: "I'm no longer comfortable in a museum. I don't want to go to them, don't want to be 'taught' anything, don't want to see 'accomplished' art. I'm interested in what's called vernacular." [39]

However if we wish to take the most precise measure of Evans' artistic lucidity, we must not ignore the ambiguity of his position. In 1971, the vernacular - "what's called vernacular" - is a specialty recognized by the very establishment that Evans claims to oppose. *Fortune* had cleared the path for this recognition forty years before, followed by The Museum of Modern Art, New York. At the end of his life, Walker Evans is himself a 'historic' artist, a master, with a teaching position at Yale; he almost seems to be repeating his own lectures. In 1969, writing for a collective volume entitled *Quality: Its Image in the Arts* - a title that goes without commentary - he sketches a portrait of the typical street photographer, piling on the figures of the bourgeois hero exempt from morality and polite society (the voyeur, the spy, the irresponsible child), just as they are to be found in the image popularized by novelists ever since the nineteenth century (he actually quotes Nabokov). Even if Steiglitz succeeded in bringing the photographer into the museum, Evans maintains that his place is in the street: "For his eye, the raw feast: much-used shops, bedrooms, and yards, far from the halls of full-dress architecture, landscaped splendor, or the more obviously scenic nature." [40] This term-by-term opposition of the repertories of 'high' and 'low' is clearly a bit too eloquent; it shares in the institutional rhetoric it seeks to contradict (and only denies). It would be easy to conclude that Evans finally did not escape what he called the "paradigmatic position" occupied by Steiglitz, in whom he recognized "a brand of humorless post-Victorian bohemianism".

But this ambiguity is also the effect of lucidity. In Atget, Evans had found a more convincing example than Steiglitz (or Strand). But he could not accept the mold of the artist-collector building up a clandestine oeuvre even as he furnishes

documents to the institutions and the academic artists. He therefore had to 'establish' his project, that is, both to give it an institutional support - outside the media - and a specific form. [41] This is why he seized the chance offered by his exhibition at The Museum of Modern Art, New York in 1938, the chance to publish *American Photographs*: a book, between the magazine and the museum wall, where the images are simply reproduced, not framed like precious works, left without captions but isolated in a coherent way, each one printed on a single page without a facing image. Thus he avoided the two solutions, contrary but equally mystifying, of Steiglitz and Margaret Bourke-White. He also avoided any didacticism, whether of simple propaganda or of a more 'critical' turn, such as that which characterized photomontage - but which produced such fewer successes (excepting rare figures like Heartfield) than the alignment of art on the communication techniques of advertising.

Montage, in Evans' case, remains a cinematographic (and therefore syntactic) model, a model of editing. Through the intermediary of Jay Leyda in particular, Evans had become familiar with the films of Eisenstein and Vertov. Montage became a way of organizing images whose autonomy, as necessary as it may be, can never be definitive, never final. Always this refusal of 'accomplished art'! Indeed, he ceaselessly altered the framing of his photos, fragmenting them, extracting details that he would then combine with other images. This mobility is rich with a double resonance: it corresponds to practices (the cinema and the press) which are exterior to the fine arts, and it proceeds from a specific conception of the image-sign, as a moment in an open work.

In 1931, in the previously quoted text from *Hound and Horn* which examines the recent developments (the 'renaissance') of photography in Germany, Evans mentions, of course, the volume published by Albert Renger-Patzsch, *Die Welt ist schön* (The World is Beautiful); but his approbation is partial, for he finds it still too tied up with the traditional debate between photography and painting. The construction of Renger-Patzsch's book is, in effect, very static, overly divided; it also reflects the organic conception of relations between nature and industry, tradition and modernity. On the other hand, Evans quickly recognizes himself in Franz Roh's text for the book *foto-auge*, from which he quotes long excerpts; he is particularly struck by the appeal to the amateur's freedom - negligence, imperfection, incompletion - which culminates in photography's assimilation to the "underestimated history of non-professional productivity". The most positive note, however, comes at the end of the article and concerns the portraits of August Sander: "*Antlitz der Zeit* is more than a book of 'type studies'; [it is] a case of the camera looking in the right direction among people. This is one of the futures of photography foretold by Atget. It is a photographic editing of society, a clinical process..."

In these few lines, written at a turning point in his career,

Evans announces his own program: "a photographic editing of society", which subsequently he will never cease to reaffirm, stretching it to its extreme in the subway portraits. All the elements of this project came into play early on, around the idea of type, or typology. His first architectural studies date from 1928, already displaying greater affinities for European notions of 'new vision' than for the examples of Stieglitz and Strand.[42] He also tried his hand, with success, at street photography, basing his approach on a model of social typology loosened up by the uncertainties of snapshot recording. Much later he would recall: "I had a few prescient flashes and they led me on. I found I wanted to get a type in the street, a 'snapshot' of a fellow on the waterfront, or a stenographer at lunch. That was a good vein. I still mine that vein." He tells, additionally, of the compulsion that rules the artist-collector.[43] But as the remark on Sander indicates and as his publications confirm, this model of snapshot typology, however stimulating it may have been, was not enough. He needed a more solid structure, permitting an ordering of social (and historical) diversity that would not reduce it to a picturesque typology, and would not sacrifice intuition to the overly restrictive procedures of the 'study'. Atget had fixed the figure-types of the Parisian street, by enlarging the model of workmen's genre scenes [petits métiers] drawn from the picturesque tradition; but Atget's project was far more ambitious, integrating urban architecture and interiors. What distinguishes Evans, in *American Photographs* and *Many Are Called*, from the good street photographers who were so numerous around 1940, is summed up quite well in the superiority that Baudelaire accords to Daumier over the caricaturist Henri Monnier (the inventor of "Monsieur Prudhomme"): "Many of his *Scènes populaires* are undeniably pleasurable; otherwise we would have to deny the cruel and surprising charm of the daguerreotype. But Monnier has no idea how to create, to idealize, to arrange." [44]

On one side are the inhabitants of the city (large or small); on the other, its architecture (vernacular). These are the two borders of the attempt at social editing, as they appear in *American Photographs*. From one side to the other flows a constant circulation of signs (modern or historic): because architecture itself, in the typological diversity characteristic of American eclecticism, is a system, or at least an assemblage of signs. To edit (to cut, to splice) is to transform types into a collection of ordered images: human and architectural types, running from the archetype to the stereotype, with all the possible hybrids in between. The collection expands compulsively, mirroring the proliferation of urban signs; but its fashioning (its organization in sequences) is reasoned, if not constructive. The cumulative wealth of assemblage which characterizes the urban and suburban environment must be ordered and exalted by the rigour of sequential montage.

Thus there is a very close relationship between the work of editing carried out in *American Photographs* and the image of American architecture, as it is formed in the second half of

the book. The 'pop' architect Robert Venturi - in whom Dan Graham has been so interested since the late seventies - will say: "Main Street is almost all right." Walker Evans already shows what this success consists of: the rhythmic combination of straight line and irregular figures (symbolic or decorative), summed up in the double image of urban signs, which answer a functional need for communication but also proceed from less direct (or 'gratuitous') interests. This combination is omnipresent in the book. The order may be very strict, dictated now by the austere regularity of the frame houses or the neo-classical alignments, now by the uniformity of a standardized shot (frontality and shallowness of field, for example) - but this order is always contradicted by the discordance, indeed the incongruity of the details, and by the accelerations of the montage.

Much has been made of Evans' 'classicism' (simplicity, economy of means, refusal of the romantic picturesque, anti-expressionism). It is possible that the model of Main Street, associated to the Georgian-type row houses, holds a faraway echo of the syntax of classical architecture, where the five distinct 'orders' - according to the typology fixed during the Renaissance - are symbolized by emblematic ornamental figures: Doric, Ionic, etc. But the complexity of eclectic assemblage is quite different from the simplicity (or rigour) of the paradigmatic orders. Evans had witnessed the birth of the International Style (with The Museum of Modern Art, New York exhibition and the book by Philip Johnson, in 1932); but he could not adhere to it, no more than he could subscribe to the ideal of technological progress underlying the universalism of Mies van der Rohe. Without being regionalist, his language is that of a mid-range or mitigated urbanism with all its vernacular specificities, situated between the metropolitan and rural worlds, where the rare examples of 'high' architecture share in the diversity of slapped-together constructions and borrowed styles: between the more or less primitivist archetype (such as Laugier's famous hut, mentioned above with respect to Dan Graham) and the historicist, industrial stereotype. A situation corresponding exactly to that of photography, between the fine arts and the media.

By seeking his models in nineteenth-century literature (Flaubert, Baudelaire), Evans was able to turn away from the various rallying cries of a utopian or amnesia-ridden Modernism, which transformed Enlightenment cosmopolitanism into a nationalism founded on the triumphant universality of a free-enterprise model (as Dan Graham's generation would recognize in the post-war period). Indeed, his first coherent documentary project, carried out for Lincoln Kirstein in 1930-31, bore on Victorian architecture (Boston, Saratoga Springs, etc.). But he is not a photographer of America's heartland, ennobling the vacuum of Main Street or the poverty of ruined farmers. The second section of American photographs opens and closes on images of broken ornaments - 'relics' - crumpled like cardboard or cut paper. These ornaments are fake vestiges of Antiquity, reducing the historical archetype to the stereotype of melancholic desolation. One can hardly imagine images more apt to convey Baudelairean allegory, described in the same period by Walter Benjamin as the exemplary irony that the artist-collector turns back upon himself. Exemplary, because it makes melancholy into the condition of possibility for an exaltation of modern signs, disengaged from any nostalgic longing for a communal bond (and, of course, from all futurist reverie).

Conjured in the form of cast-off debris - through (falsely historicist) quotes - these signs are already tightly at grips with desolation; thus they can stand forth from it as from their own fundament. Here the image of human beings emerges in its turn, not so much against an architectural background as among the ruins (the work-site) of urban signs, including architecture: the image emerges, animated and organized by the photographer's double activity (collecting-editing). The humanism of Walker Evans, like that of Baudelaire, can burst out in a moment of compassion, and all the more easily since Evans is less given to the "satanic laugh". But this humanism stems mainly from another 'pathos', one which fixes on the signs and traces of destruction, referring the collector back to his own passion.

Here is the key to the gradual shift of the final twenty years. In the best works, it is no longer a question of the spectacle of the street, but of interiors where the image of the occupants - themselves absent - coalesces in the assemblage of a few object-signs, like a very clear, if only relatively decipherable message (to recall the word from the 1966 volume, *Message from the Interior*). Evans had been interested in these interior arrangements ever since 1930, and especially during the period of the FSA, when he entered farmers' homes. Around 1930, and also in parallel with his activity for the FSA, he had occasionally photographed his own place of lodging and of work (especially his darkroom). But "*The Child's Room*" (1951), "*The Parlor Chairs*" (1958), and "*The Home Organ*" (1968) should be related to the inquiries on Victorian architecture and to the paradigm of historical ruins, as *Message from the Interior* clearly establishes by associating the first two of these three images to views of abandoned or dilapidated architecture, broken ornaments, and extremely run-down dwelling places. This side of Evans' work is not merely the indication of an old man's tired retreat, but the effect of the compulsion - measured, held back - which pushes the collector to search through others' lives for the signs of his own melancholy. The interior, with its 'decorative' arrangements, is not so much a place of refuge as the figure of a story and a history c a l l e d b a c k at the very border of the erasure imposed by forgetting and by the fatality of the banal (of normalized sameness).

The artist, Dan Graham no less than Walker Evans, cannot reduce this fatality to a process of social alienation, whose indifferently objective or strictly 'critical' witness he becomes - unless he is willing to pay the price of total submission to

melancholy. The 'satanic laugh' is the romantic hero's solution. But those who cannot or will not be the devil's advocate are necessarily exposed to the ambiguous pathos of the individualized (decorative, formalized) signs of the common - above all if they forbid themselves recourse to a universal abstracted from its historical determinants. Dan Graham's dual reading of Pop Art culminates in this pathos, which his photographic images simultaneously concentrate and hold at a distance. If Walker Evans was able to invent the image of America inherited by Pop Art, it was because he had given himself the ability to transform his melancholy passion into a lyrism attached - at a distance - to the lot of the common.

1 On the request of Jeanne Siegel, director of art broadcasts for the New York radio station WBAI, Lucy Lippard invited four visual artists - Douglas Huebler, Dan Graham, Carl Andre, and Jan Dibbets - to speak together on March 8, 1970. The text of this meeting was published in: Lippard, Lucy, *Six Years: The Dematerialization of the Art Object*, New York, Praeger, 1973, pp.155-159.
2 Dan Graham has expressed this idea several times, each time stressing that his works for magazines were both a radicalization of Pop Art and a transformation of Minimalism (through schematization and critical highlighting of the context of presentation). See in particular "My Works for Pages", in *Dan Graham*, cat. Art Gallery of Western Australia, Perth 1985, pp. 8-11: "If 'Minimal' art took its meaning from the notion that the gallery is an objective support, by comparison Pop Art took its meaning from the surrounding media-world of images. Pop wished to undermine the notions of quality in fine art by using mass-cultural content. Since it fed its pictures through the magazines back into popular culture, Pop Art also made an ironic comment about popular culture to itself. What Pop pointed out was that the information media, such as magazines, could be used dialectically with the art system. That is, a work could function in terms of both the art language and the popular language of the media at the same time, commenting on and placing in perspective the assumptions of each. I designed works for magazine pages which would be both self-defined and would relate through the context, to the surrounding information on the other printed pages.... The most 'absolute' of these works is "*Schema*" (March 1966). Each published example of this piece appears as an isolated page in different magazines.... Conventionally, art magazines reproduce second-hand art which exists first, as phenomenological presence, in galleries. Turning this upside down, "*Schema*" only exists by its presence in the functional structure of the magazine and can only be exhibited in a gallery second-hand.... I wanted to make a Pop Art which was more literally disposable (an idea which was alluded to in Warhol's idea of replacing 'quality' by 'quantity,' the logic of a consumer society). I wanted to make an art-form which could not be reproduced or exhibited in a gallery/museum, and I wanted to make a further reduction of the 'minimal' object to a not necessarily aesthetic two-dimensional form (which was not painting or drawing): printed matter which is mass produced and mass disposable information."
In an interview with Eugenie Tsai, published in *Robert Smithson: Drawings*, cat., Münster-Sorø-München, 1988-90, pp. 8-23),
Dan Graham insists on the idea of the disposable, both in his early magazine pieces and in the work of those artists (especially Flavin and LeWitt) whom he had exhibited in the ephemeral John Daniel's Gallery (October 1964 - June 1965): "When I showed Sol LeWitt, his instruction to me after the show was to use the wood for firewood; he would never say that again but he really had no interest in value... Nobody really had a sense that this stuff had any value; people didn't think that way back then. A key idea of the sixties, in clothes, fashion, as well as rock music, was of the disposable. So I was just doing something that was disposable, but didn't take an interest in having to produce. I never thought that anyone would put it in a museum: I was completely against that." op. cit., p. 8.
3 Smithson's first published essay, in 1965, on Judd, already contained this idea. See "Donald Judd", *7 Sculptors*, cat. Institute of Contemporary Art, Philadelphia, 1965, pp. 21-23, reprinted in Holt, Nancy, *The Writings of Robert Smithson*, New York, New York University Press,1979, pp. 13-16. Smithson interprets Judd's structures as a speculation on matter, on "the very form of matter", and remarks: "Just as the mannerist artists of the Sixteenth Century permuted the facts of the Classic Renaissance, so has Judd permuted the facts of Modern Reality. By such means, Judd discovered a new kind of 'architecture,' yet his contrary methods make his 'architecture' look like it is built of 'anti-matter.' Perhaps 'primary matter' and 'anti-matter' are the same thing."
Dan Graham recalls that Judd didn't at all appreciate this interpretation ("Judd didn't like the essay, he hated it.") Smithson had "invented Judd (in that essay) like Borges invents a fictional character." The divergence between these two artists reflects the split in the vanguard American art of the sixties, between the minimalists and conceptualists attached to puritan morality and close to the New Left, on the one hand, and the pop artists, closer to rock'n'roll and the culture of 'fun', on the other. Smithson, according to Dan Graham, "was much more out of Pop Art, and he liked to be the devil's advocate. If you think about it, that's the mannerist part, because the mannerists took that position relative to Renaissance values. Minimal people couldn't understand; they could never be mannerist. That's where his disagreement with Judd comes in. He was putting Judd in a mold that may or may not be historically true, but Judd never saw it that way. And Judd would be very moralistic, even though his position, I would say, is right-wing, he's still idealistic and moralistic in the way he takes it." (Interview with Eugenie Tsai, op. cit., note 2 , p. 14.)
4 Things worked out differently, as we know: the editors of *Arts Magazine* replaced

Dan Graham's images with a photograph by Walker Evans, "*Wooden Houses, Boston*" (1930), reproduced in the book *American Photographs*, cat. The Museum of Modern Art, New York, 1938; reprint 1962. Projected Art was presented in November 1966 at the Finch College Museum of Art, New York, by Elayne Varian. It would appear that Dan Graham was the only artist in this exhibition to project transparencies. This initiative would have to be resituated in the long history of the transparency, both in its use as a pedagogical tool (especially in the study and teaching of architecture, since Fredrick Henry Evans at the turn of the century) and as a way of enlarging a photograph to be employed as a pictorial model (Lichtenstein, Richter, the photorealists). At the time of Projected Art, no one in the art world considered the color transparency as an end in itself. This was not the case at the beginning of the century - after the invention of 'autochrome' plates by the Lumière brothers - in the circles of the American photographic Secession (Stieglitz, Steichen) and of international pictorialism. One might also recall that photographers of the Farm Security Administration (FSA) in the thirties used the new Kodak technique that appeared in 1935 to produce several hundred color transparencies, some comparable to those of Dan Graham (these early slides were completely neglected, however, until their recent rediscovery by Sally Stein in the archives of the Library of Congress in Washington). At the end of the sixties, Dan Graham was not concerned - any more than he is now - with the history of photography, but the other references given above were familiar to him. He also associated the luminous projection of transparencies with Flavin's neons and was interested, as his later works have proved, in the idea of the (glassy) 'transparency' and its relation to the projected image.

5 The article in *Arts Magazine*, Homes for America, must be distinguished from the work "*Homes for America*" which was created later, in 1970-71, as a reconstitution of the original layout of the article, by the printing workshop of the Nova Scotia College of Art and Design in Halifax, Nova Scotia. The reconstitution is accompanied by numerous variants, among them the double panel of the Daled collection, reproduced here on page 132; it includes views of figures taken in 1967, after the publication of the article. This distinction between the article and the work allows us to take stock of the anti-art position implied by the choice of the disposable in the magazine pieces. But that choice was untenable, because it was irreconciliable with the complex demands of a critical fiction in text and images. Dan Graham originally wanted to publish in a magazine like *Esquire*, but had to settle for an art journal which itself did not faithfully carry out his project. In fact, because of its complexity this project was irreducible to instant consumption from the very beginning, and thus was destined for deferred realization in an 'artistic' form. The principle of the 'disposable' (in which every consumer article shares) could only be a model for an article of critical fiction - and a fictive, untenable ideal for the artist Dan Graham. To that must be added the force of necessity. After 1970, at the time when he was creating "*Homes for America*", Dan Graham - like all the artists of a conceptual bent presented by John Gibson in New York - realized that photography, without being fully attached to the fine arts, was still a possible source of income.

6 "Judd has a labyrinthine collection of 'printed matter,' some of which he 'looks' at rather than reads. By this means he might take a math equation, and by sight, translate it into a metal progression of structured intervals. In this context, it is best to think of 'printed matter' the way Borges thinks of it, as 'The Universe (which others call the library)', in other words as an unending 'library of Babel.'" Holt, op. cit., note 3 , p. 15.

7 The original title of the text was "A Tour of the Monuments of Passaic, New Jersey". The text is reprinted in Holt, op.cit. note 3, pp. 52-57. Smithson presents his photographs of monuments as film stills. The first monument, a bridge over the Passaic river, sets the tone: "Noon-day sunshine cinema-ized the site, turning the bridge and the river into an over-exposed picture. Photographing it with my Instamatic 400 was like photographing a photograph. The sun became a monstrous light-bulb that projected a detached series of 'stills' through my Instamatic into my eye. When I walked on the bridge, it was as though I was walking on an enormous photograph that was made of wood and steel, and underneath the river existed as an enormous movie film that showed nothing but a continuous blank."

8 The distinction between the two senses of the word 'monument' is clearly established by Françoise Chaoy in "A propos du culte et des monuments", the preface to the French translation of Aloïs Riegl's 1903 text *Der moderne Denkmalkultus* (*Le culte moderne des monuments*, Paris, Editions du Seuil, 1984, p.11). "The notion of the historical monument is not a cultural invariant... For if the monument - that is to say (etymologically) the artefact that calls out to make us remember - can be said to participate in a universal 'art of memory' found in almost every culture, the invention of the historical monument is bound up with that of the concepts of art and history. It belongs to post-Gothic Europe, which elaborated the concept in the successive stages of a long process, whose first stratum can be seen in the Quattrocento".

9 See Huebler's interview with Irmeline Lebeer at the moment of his exhibition at the Kunstverein Münster(December 1972 - January 1973), *Chroniques de l'art vivant,* no. 38, April 1973; pp. 21-23: "My main concern (at the time of "*Primary Structures*") was to create sculptures so large that they couldn't fit inside a museum. That's why I installed them outside. Now, the primary structures are interesting in that they become real: a cube is as real as a table or a chair. When I put these absolutely real forms outside, I had to admit that they didn't entertain the same harmonious relationship with nature as a statue, a nude, and so on, but functioned instead as real objects in competition with all the other real objects in the world outside. I realized that unless they were integrated in an architectonic frame - a special structure designed to receive them - my sculptures didn't stand up to a confrontation with the trees and the sky; nature was more powerful. Of course I could produce bigger forms, monumental sculptures, but the truth was that the world didn't need me to add still more objects to those that already exist. This experience incited me to a fundamental change of orientation."

10 In the course of an interview with Daniela Salvioni, *Flash Art*, no. 152, May-June 1990: pp.142-144, Dan Graham remarked: "I'm not necessarily against monumentality. Conceptual art had been interested in the disposable, non-museum collectible work that refused a permanent historical appropriation. From an architectural point of view, instead, monumentality designates place, history. The meaning of things that last for a longer historical period of time is more open-ended. It is not a meaning that I or an art audience put out. I'm not saying it is a better meaning, it is just more open-ended.
A time duration that is long enough so that the work's meaning might be modified, maybe misinterpreted." This interest in the monument, opposed in its perdurability to the ephemeral productions destined for consumption, recalls the antivitalist interpretation of traditional artistic culture in Hannah Arendt's writing (where life is consumption).
For Arendt, the utilitarian object and, a fortiori, the art object are fundamentally distinct from the object of consumption. Dan Graham did not take this approach in the late 1960s. However, one cannot speak of a turnabout. This development corresponds to a reevaluation of the modernist heritage, inspired by Walter Benjamin's method of historical (not historicist) interpretation, here applied to the recent past. Modernism no doubt led to the International Style of triumphant post-war capitalism, but through its very contradictions it produces the in-between space of a critical acuity, when it is compared to its utopian models from the period of the Enlightenment. Dan Graham pointed out the enduring ambivalence of these models as early as 1967, when he remarked the conjunction of hippie pacifism and the pastoral (as well as communal) utopia that, in the history of Modernism, accompanies and doubles the ideal of technological progress. See "Eisenhower and the Hippies", published in the winter 1968-69 issue of the journal *0 to 9*, and reprinted in *Dan Graham Articles,* cat. Stedelijk Van Abbemuseum, Eindhoven, 1977, pp. 23-26. Twenty years later, in the course of an interview with Birgit Pelzer (*Dan Graham*, cat ARC, Musée de la ville de Paris, Paris, 1987, pp. 33-38), Dan Graham summed up his current position: "Walter Benjamin proposed to recover historical memory. Because today's ideology has wiped out the past, it has to be reconstructed as though it were springing up anew. Modernism was against monuments. Me, I'm completely for them: monuments mark time.... Monuments are linked to the city's memory and personally, I think that what interests me the most for the moment is to recover the recent past, the historical memory of the recent past. Concerning the sixties, a period that most living people actually went through, it's as though collective memory were struck with amnesia. The media have to continually erase the recent past in order to fabricate their present utopia." This utopia of the present moment is precisely what Dan Graham has always sought to pervert, first by feigning conformism (the model of the disposable) then by playing with all sorts of chronological perturbations in his performances, mirror installations, and videos (especially through delays in recording). "The present", he said to Birgit Pelzer, "does not exist. The impossibility of reaching this absolute present is the failure of the modernist ideal, according to which you can achieve tabula rasa."

11 "*Yesterday/Today*" is described in Benjamin Buchloh's anthology of Dan Graham's video works and texts on video from 1970 to 1978, *Video-Architecture-Television,* Halifax/New York, The Press of the Nova Scotia College of Art and Design, New York University Press, 1979, p. 42. One year before, in 1974, Dan Graham had already created several time-delay video installations in divided spaces ("*Time Delay Rooms*"), which simultaneously produce a systematic subversion of the essential characteristics of video ("a present-time medium") and an alteration of the public's copresence (as well as each viewer's immediate presence to him/herself). But "*Yesterday/Today*" introduced a new parameter into this trap-like structure: the specificity of the architectural space and of the (recorded) daily activity that takes place there. It then became a question of articulating the disjunctions of lived space produced by the alterations of the "video present" with the givens of the contemporary environment, by choosing particularly significant architectural structures as sites for intervention (installation). As Anne Rorimer has underscored in "Dan Graham: An Introduction", *Dan Graham Pavillons*, cat. Kunstverein München, München, 1988, p. 24, "*Picture Window Piece*" from 1974, before "*Yesterday/Today*", represents the first step in this direction. It is at this same watershed moment, in 1974-75, that we find the second important ensemble of photographs (after those of 1965-67), serving as orientations or departure-points for later video installations and pavilions.

12 "*Video View of Suburbia in an Urban Atrium*" is described by Anne Rorimer. op. cit. note 11, p. 26. This piece provides a perfect illustration of the continuity of Dan Graham's architectural interests since "*Homes for America*". Additionally, it must be noted that several photographs of suburban homes (for one or two families) date from 1978. Though very comparable to the images of 1965-66, they are distinguished by the closer attention given to detached houses, with their particular morphology, or even physionomic aspect. "*Alteration of a Suburban House*" also dates from 1978. The text of this (impossible) project refers explicitly to the glass house built by Mies van der Rohe and Philip Johnson at the close of the forties. Thus all the facets of Modernism are concentrated, for Dan Graham, in figure of the suburban house.

13 Dan Graham used the phrase in an interview with Brian Hatton in 1991 (brochure published for the exhibition at the Galerie Roger Pailhas, Marseille, in June-July 1991), to characterize the form of his pavilions: "The forms are usually clichés of modern architecture. Like ten years ago there was a return by Pelli and many people to a Boullée-Ledoux kind of pantheon, from grottoes and children's playgrounds to the World's Fair and the United Nations. La Géode, the 360 degree cinema at La Villette, was part of that. So I'm thinking of all those typological forms. Also, although I don't do what Venturi does, i.e., literally inflect towards things in the environment, I've always been interested in the inflection in another sense. The materials and forms are inflecting towards the most recent phase of the modern city as well as the historical clichés it might be based on." These clichés of modern architecture had already been evoked by Dan Graham in his 1979 text "Art in Relation to Architecture/ Architecture in Relation to Art", *Artforum*, February 1979: pp. 22-29, in a comment on Mies van der Rohe's glass buildings and their function as brand-name images for the multinational corporations and American capitalism: "Mies' classicist glass towers and apartment buildings became the new standard of American technology, especially as this style was easily exported to other areas of the world by American big business. Mies' classicism was based on apparent trueness to materials (materials being seen for what they were, instead of disguised by the use of ornamentation) wedded to an idealized, 'universal,' and highly abstract, notion of space. These modernist structures soon became popular packages for international (multinational) corporate branch offices in the 'Free World'."

14 Among the many historical reference-points for his pavilions, Dan Graham has often mentioned the "primitive hut", described in a 1753 essay by Marc-Antoine Laugier as the archetype of all architecture. This speculative model, characteristic of Enlightenment primitivism, corresponds to Rousseauist exaltation of the goodness of natural man as opposed to the corrupting force of urban civilization. Dan Graham discovered it in the late seventies, in the works of authors engaged in the postmodern debate on the urban utopia (Manfredo Tafuri, Léon Krier). See especially: "Not Post-Modernism: History as Against Historicism, European Vernacular in Relation to American Commercial Vernacular, and the City as Opposed to the Individual Building", Artforum, December 1981; pp. 50-59.
The antecedents and critical fortunes of Laugier's model had been reconstituted a few years earlier by Rykwert, Joseph, On Adam's House in Paradise, New York/Chicago, 1972, as the central figure of reasoned architectural primitivism, from which Modernism largely springs, even in the work of Gropius (compare, for instance, the Blockhaus Somerfeld built in 1921 in the suburbs of Berlin, influenced by Frank Lloyd Wright's prairie houses).

15 "Not Post-Modernism..." op. cit., note 14 p. 57.

16 Dan Graham speaks of a "dual reading" with respect to Lichtenstein in "Art in Relation to Architecture/Architecture in Relation to Art", op. cit., note 13. In support of his thesis he quotes statements that Lichtenstein made to Gene Swenson in 1963 on Pop Art and its relationships to mass culture. Lichtenstein: "It is an involvement with what I think to be the most brazen and threatening characteristics of our culture, things we hate, but which are also powerful in their impingement on us. I think art since Cézanne has become extremely romantic and unrealistic, feeding on art; it is utopian. It has less and less to do with the world, it looks inward - neo-Zen and all that. This is not so much a criticism as an obvious observation. Outside is the world; it's there. Pop Art looks out in the world; it appears to accept its environment, which is not good or bad, but different - another state of mind." And: "The heroes depicted in comic books are fascist types, but I don't take them seriously in these paintings - maybe there is a point in not taking them seriously, a political point. I use them for purely formal reasons, and that's not what those heroes were intended for... Pop Art has very immediate and of-the-moment meanings which will vanish - that kind of thing is ephemeral - and Pop takes advantage of this 'meaning,' which is not supposed to last, to divert you from its formal content. I think the formal statement in my work will become clearer in time." Dan Graham sums up: "A work by Lichtenstein can be both 'art for art's sake' and something assimilable to popular cultural meanings.
Both readings are correct." There is, in short, a veritable ambivalence in Pop Art with respect to the media, an ambivalence irreducible to the strategies of critical distantiation which would relate Pop Art to certain Brechtian positions of the New Left. This ambivalence nonetheless has a critical bearing - since distantiation still does intervene as a simple effect of the artistic approach - if it is resituated and developed in a historical context larger than the limited sphere of the fine arts; that is to say more specifically, if it is placed in relation to the most clearly political questions of architecture. In any case, Dan Graham is not looking for the (art historical) truth of Pop Art; he interprets it in order to obtain a model. -The Lichtenstein-Swenson interview figured in the series "What is Pop Art?", published in two parts in *ARTnews* (November 1963, February 1964), reprinted in Mashun, Carol Anne, *Pop Art: The Critical Dialogue*, Ann Arbor, UMI Research Press,1989, pp. 111-115.

17 Alice Weiner: "Seeing Dan's photographs from that period was like seeing a Walker Evans photograph but without people" (conversation with Chris Dercon, 14 April 1992). Dan Graham recalls that the relationship between his images and those of Walker Evans was pointed out to him by Mel Bochner, who had actually met Evans (unpublished interview with the author, 27 July 1991).

18 It was in the series of interviews mentioned above, "What is Pop Art?", that Jim Dine referred to Walker Evans, after evoking the beauty of billboards (which he recognized long before he began using them as a model). "It's not a unique idea - Walker Evans photographed them in 1929. It's just that the landscape around you starts closing in and you've got to stand up to it."op. cit., note 16, p. 115. Jim Dine's last remark is the exact definition of the 'picturalization' of the landscape effected by a photographer when he isolates a portion of it in his viewfinder.

19 Allan Kaprow remarks: "For all its directness, apparent objectivity and detachment from personal emotions, most Pop Art evokes a romance of the era of about twenty to thirty years ago, the time of the artist's childhood. It's very much like the mood we find in the novels of Jack Kerouac. Villeglé's, Hain's and Rotella's tattered posters, seeing America from afar, whose proclamations and has-been goddesses are beaten by weather and age, recall Walker Evans' photos of years ago; Lichtenstein's cartoons and products have an iconography and style of the forties..." "Pop Art: Past, Present, and Future", *The Malahat Review,* July 1967, reprinted in Carol Anne Mashun's anthology, op. cit., note 16, pp. 61-74.

20 On this point, see Rosenthal, Nan, "Let Us Now Praise Famous Men: Warhol As Art Director", *The Work of Andy Warhol,* DIA Art Foundation Discussions in Contemporary Culture no.3, Gary Garrels (ed.), Seattle, Washington, Bay Press, 1989, pp. 47-50.

21 Establishing itself through numerous mediations, Evans' exemplarity emerges as the fulfillment of an American model of 'documentary photography' inherited from the nineteenth century. In the postface to *American Photographs,* Lincoln Kirstein reaches back to Mathew Brady, the portraitist of Abraham Lincoln, as the point of origin for Walker Evans; Kirstein situates Brady alongside his European counterparts (Nadar, Cameron, Hill). He also notes: "Walker Evans is giving us the contemporary civilization of eastern America and its dependencies as Atget gave us Paris before the war and as Brady gave us the War between the States." In the journal he ran during the early thirties, *Hound and Horn,* Kirstein published an article by Charles Flato presenting Brady's images of the Civil War as landmark indications of "enormous possibilities of simplicity and directness." A recent commentator of this 1933 article noted: "Without mentioning Steiglitz or pictorialism, Flato implicitly sets Brady against the heritage of *Camerawork.*" See Trachtenberg, Allan, *Reading American Photographs: Images as History, Mathew Brady to Walker Evans,* New York, Hill & Wang, 1989, pp. 231-235. When he speaks of Brady as being "really a delineator of manners, of the ephemeral and the universal that it indicates", Flato quite clearly rejoins Baudelaire's famous observations on "the double composition of the beautiful" ("an eternal, invariable element" and "a relative, circumstantial element"), developed in the opening pages of *The Painter of Modern Life,* dedicated to Constantin Guys (a painter-chronicler, notably of the Crimean War). Already we have the principle of the dual reading! Thirty years after the texts of Kirstein and his associates, when John Szarkowski presented the exhibition New Documents at The Museum of Modern Art, New York in 1967 (regrouping Diane Arbus, Lee Friedlander, and Garry Winogrand), the American-style documentary model had become the unifying principle of 'Modernism' in photography. *American Photographs* was reissued the same year as Szarkowski took up his position at The Museum of Modern Art, New York. Robert Frank's book, *The Americans,* had been published three years earlier, after Evans introduced a first selection of Frank's images in *US Camera Annual* from 1958. Under the common rallying cry of the 'document', a solid genealogical sequence now designates a ridge-line from which individual authors emerge, far above the mass of anonymous images in which the essence of the medium has been formed and deposited.
In 1966, in the brief postface to *Message from the Interior,* Szarkowski notes with a deep sense of rhetorical balance: "Evans' style seems as inevitable and anonymous as that of the early daguerreotypists, yet the character of his imagery - frontal, concisely plain, remotely passionate - is unchallengeably his own."

22 Dan Graham has recently mentioned on several occasions the importance of post-war cinema for the formation of his interest in architecture. See especially the interview with Chris Dercon of May 1991, published in *Forum International,* vol. II, no. 9, (september-oktober 1991): pp. 73-80. The reference to Neo-Realism (Rossellini, Antonioni) came up in the course of an unpublished interview with the author in Los Angeles (27 July 1991).

23 Godard has always insisted on the necessity of basing fiction in documentary givens. "*Deux ou trois choses que je sais d'elle*" (1966)- the film that Dan Graham mentions the most frequently - was inspired by a report that appeared in a magazine about prostitution in large suburban apartment complexes. But the document-fiction relationship also opens out on the relationship between reality and imaginary figures. Speaking of "*Vivre sa vie*"(1962) in an interview published in *Cahiers du cinéma,* no. 138, (decembre 1962), he said: "I began with the imaginary and I discovered the real; but behind the real is the imaginary again." This is what leads Godard to speak of "theater-truth," or "theatrical realism." Finally, he has always defined his films as "attemps" [essais]. Their documentary aspect therefore concerns their own progression first of all. Referring to "*Deux ou trois choses que je sais d'elle*", he notes: "I watch myself filming, and you hear me thinking.
In short, it's not a film, it's an attempt at a film and it presents itself as such. It's not a story, it's meant to be a document." Jean-Luc Godard, *2 ou 3 choses que je sais d'elle,* Paris, Seuil/Avant Scène,1971, p. 12.

24 In a collective volume published in London in 1967 (Studio Vista) Stij Björkman says of "*Deux ou trois choses que je sais d'elle*": "The film reflects a kind of new realism with the 'nouveau roman': economy and precision of detail; a vision giving an extraordinary depth of perspective through the sudden switches between close-up and long-shot."
This remark could also be applied to the montage of "*Homes for America*". Following the self-reflexive documentary logic described above, the apartment complex where the film's heroine lives refers, as Godard himself indicates, to the idea of being (or living) together, but also to the ensemble constituted by the film. "It's a question of describing an 'ensemble." Architecture is the metaphor of the film-description.
The object described is the subject of the film. "One should put it all in a film." And this all should be organized as a complex ensemble, inhabited by people, an interior-exterior, a subject-object. "I can't ignore the fact that everything exists both from the interior and from the exterior. This, for example, can be made palpable by filming a building from the exterior, then from the interior, as if you were entering inside a cube, inside an object.
It's the same with a person, his face is usually seen from the exterior." op. cit., note 23, p. 15.

25 Dan Graham discusses this question in the interview with Brian Hatton in 1991. op. cit., note 13 .

26 "The Reappearance of Photography", *Hound and Horn,* vol. 5, no.1, October-December 1931; reprint, Trachtenberg, Alan, *Classic Essays on Photography,* New Haven, Conn., Leete's Island Books, 1980, pp. 185-188.

27 This book seems to have constituted a veritable counter-example for Agee and Evans, who saw the enterprise of their predecessors as "a double outrage: propaganda for one thing, and profit-making out of both propaganda and the plight of the tenant farmers." Quoted in Stott, William, *Documentary Expression and Thirties America,* Chicago, The University of Chicago Press, 1973, reprint 1986, p. 222.

28 William Stott ,op. cit., note 27, p. 320, quotes this remark, made to him by Evans when they met near the end of the photographer's life: "I do have a weakness for the disadvantaged, for poor people, but I'm suspicious of it. I have to be, because that should not be the motive for artistic or aesthetic action. If it is, your work is either sentimental or motivated toward 'improving society.' I don't believe an artist should do that with his work."

29 Evans says exactly: "The problem is one of staying out of Left politics and still avoiding Establishment patterns" (quoted by W. Stott, ibid.).

30 Interview with Paul Cummings, 13 August 1971, "Archives of American Art", quoted by Alan Trachtenberg, op. cit., note 21 , p. 237.

31 This assertion opens an undated note drafted by Evans for the introduction to an edition of the subway portraits (1938-1941). The statement, therefore, came after the portraits themselves. It was finally published in *Walker Evans at Work,* New York,Harper and Row 1982, p.160, a volume assembled in1982 under the direction of the Evans estate. After this opening remark, the text develops a description of the project: "This collection is at least an impure chance-average lottery selection of its subjects - human beings in a certain established time and place." Evans insists nonetheless on the conceptual value of the project, whose realization is an approximation and not a fulfillment. "The locale was picked for practical reasons only, for rigidity of technical working conditions. Actually the ultimate purity of this method of photography - the record method - has not been achieved here, but it is present as an unfulfilled aim..." The final remark establishes a typical place, the city, a situation - people seated in the subway - and a date, 1940: "This is a fair run of the people in the city who actually do sit in this place, the subway bench; and the time is 1940, more or less."

32 The Machine Age was the exhibition organized in 1927 by Jane Heap's vanguard journal, *The Little Review*. But the expression designates a social reality extending far beyond artistic horizons. The organizers of the 1927 exhibition were quite clear about this, as they showed "actual machines, parts, apparatuses, photographs and drawings of machines, plants, constructions, etc., in juxtaposition with architecture, paintings, drawings, sculpture, constructions, and inventions by the most vital of the modern artists" (text reprinted with French translation in *Léger et l'esprit moderne: Une alternative d'avant-garde à l'art non-objectif (1918-1931)*, cat. Musée d'art moderne de la ville de Paris, Paris, 1982, p. 216). In a text from the original catalogue, "The Americanization of Art", the Russian immigrant, precisionist painter Louis Lozowick (very well-versed in European Cubo-Futurism and Constructivism) remarks: "The history of America is a history of stubborn and ceaseless effort to harness the forces of nature..., of gigantic engineering feats and colossal mechanical construction" (quoted by Richard Guy Wilson, in *The Machine Age in America*, cat. The Brooklyn Museum, New York, 1986, p. 30). In the early twenties, the first photographers of the machine (Paul Strand and Ralph Steiner in particular) stuck to a more measured and individualized vision of the machine, even if Strand did call it "The New God" in his famous 1922 essay. Lozowick's exaltation of the grandiose and the colossal would only find its photographic illustration in the last years of the decade, particularly in Margaret Bourke-White's attraction for massive images. In his very early photographs of industrial monuments - among them the celebrated "*Armco Steel, Ohio*" of 1922 - Edward Weston had used the architectural model above all as a way to break with pictorialism (just as Strand had used the machine); but his fascination was short lived. He only retained from this period a certain sense of descriptive emphasis, which he applied to motifs from pre-industrial culture, charging them with erotico-cosmic resonances. At the close of the twenties Evans contributed for a time to the aesthetic justification of American-style technological Modernism, but his engagement was even briefer than Weston's, and he did not adopt the same solution to escape it. He contributed, for instance, to a book by the poet Hart Crane entitled *The Bridge*, celebrating the symbolic beauty of the Brooklyn bridge in 1930. But he was also interested in another urban spectacle: Broadway signs (jumbled or broken), the crowd on the streets (or on the beach at Coney Island). Even his images of skyscrapers and of architectural alignments have the qualities of an improvisational study, distinguishing them from the more accomplished, clearly drawn views produced by Strand's disciples, and relating them to the experimental thrust of the Bauhaus-style 'new vision' in Europe. In 1971, however, Evans renounced his initial period of activity (1928-31) in its entirety, declaring it to be too "romantic" - which we may interpret as meaning too closely linked to the romanticism of the machine that characterized the twenties and helped usher in the triumph of industrialism in the thirties. See *Walker Evans at Work* (op. cit., note 31, p. 42). Finally, it must be stressed that beyond the pseudo-cubist architecture of the building complexes, the aspects of urban reality that attracted Evans' closest attention were not at all indifferent to the concerns of the ideologues of industrialization and the modern city. Lewis Mumford, for example, had declared in 1931 that the subway and the "cheap popular lunchrooms" were the "two main sources of the modern style at the present" (quoted by R. G. Wilson, op. cit., note 32, p. 30).

33 As pointed out above (note 31), the date of this text is uncertain. However, the authors of *Walker Evans at Work* have published another note drafted for the same purpose and dated 1962. It is tempting to use this chronological benchmark to confirm the comparison with Duchamp. It was in effect during a roundtable discussion organized by The Museum of Modern Art, New York at the time of the exhibition The Art of Assemblage in 1961 - and no earlier - that Duchamp declared: "A point that I want very much to establish is that the choice of these 'readymades' was never dictated by an aesthetic delectation. This choice was based on a reaction of visual indifference with at the same time a total absence of good or bad taste." This declaration is largely explained by its context: Duchamp wanted to set himself apart (as he did in effect several times) from the aesthetic appropriation of the found object, the industrial waste product, etc., as practiced by the 'assemblage' artists (neo-dadas or nouveaux réalistes). He recalled that an artistic decision is not a simple act of "appropriation of the real" celebrating the beauty of "industrial folklore" (two phrases used by Pierre Restany, the theorist of Nouveau Réalisme). Given his own interests and his links to The Museum of Modern Art, New York, it is improbable to think that Walker Evans remained unaware of the exhibition organized by William Seitz and never himself grappled with the problematic developed by Duchamp (even if he did not actually hear Duchamp speak). For a historical discussion of the principle of Duchampian indifference and particularly of his remarks in the 1961 talk "Apropos of 'Readymades'", see Camfield,William I, *Marcel Duchamp: Fountain*, Houston, The Menil Collection-Houston Fine Art Press, 1989, pp. 42-47.

34 Evans' full remarks are as follows: "The portraits on these pages were caught by a hidden camera, in the hands of a penitent spy and an apologetic voyeur. But the rude and impudent invasion involved has been carefully softened, and partially mitigated by a planned passage of time. These pictures were made twenty years ago, and deliberately preserved from publication. As it happens, you don't see among them the face of a judge or a senator or a bank president. What you do see is at once sobering, startling, and obvious: these are the ladies and gentlemen of the jury." *Walker Evans at Work*, op. cit., note 31. All this takes on the air of a moral fable: acknowledging his guilt ("a penitent spy") and having already punished himself by not publishing his images for twenty years, the artist recognizes - somewhat ironically, as befits a dandy - the existence of a popular jury, and therefore, of a common moral law. He had additionally given himself Daumier (and Dickens) as a model, that is to say an aesthetic authority, but also a moral and political one: "The crashing non-euphoria of New York subway life may some day be recorded by a modern Dickens or Daumier. The setting is a sociological gold mine awaiting a major artist." The reference to Daumier returns in 1971 in an interview with Leslie Katz , *Art in America*, March-April, 1971, reprint in Goldberg, Vicki, *Photography in Print: Writings from 1816 to the Present*, New York, Simon and Schuster,1981, pp. 358-369.: "Daumier's "Third Class Carriage" is a kind of snapshot of actual people sitting in a railway carriage in France in the mid-nineteenth century. Although he didn't use a camera, he sketched people on the spot, like a reporter..."

35 Baudelaire, "Mon coeur mis à nu", *Oeuvres complètes*, vol. I, Paris, Gallimard, Pléiade, 1975 p. 697.

36 Baudelaire analyzes the tenor of the 'satanic laugh' in "De l'essence du rire", a theoretical essay summing up his observations on caricature. The "satanic laugh" manifests the contradictory nature of man, divided between "the idea of his own superiority" and his obvious "misery": "Laughter emerges from the perpetual collision or clash [choc] of these two infinities." In short, the Pascal's tragic vision of "fallen man", conjoined to romantic heroism. However, Baudelaire finds the purest example outside France (Hoffmann). Molière himself is not "fierce" enough; and in the end, not a single sketch-book caricaturist is mentioned. And yet in another text, "Quelques caricaturistes français", it is precisely Molière who is compared with Daumier: "His caricature is of redoubtable amplitude, but without rancor or gall. Throughout his oeuvre there is a fundament of honesty and good-naturedness." *Oeuvres complètes*, op. cit. vol. II, pp. 532-534; 556-557. It is difficult to speak of 'good-naturedness' with respect to Evans, but it is certainly alongside Daumier that Baudelaire's typology would place him, and there indeed he places himself, leaving the heritage of the satanic laugh to surrealist 'black humor' with from time to time - as *Many Are Called* perhaps attests - a few regrets.

37 Quoted by Lesley K. Baier, in *Walker Evans at Fortune, 1945-1965*, cat. Wellesly College Museum, Wellesley, Mass., 1977-78, pp. 10-11. A double-page spread of photographs by Steiner originally published in *Fortune* (May 1930) is reproduced in *Photography Rediscovered: American Photographs, 1900-1930*, cat. Whitney Museum of American Art, New York, 1979, pp. 104-105.

38 Steiner,Ralph *A Point of View*, Middletown,Wesleyan University Press, 1978, p. 104-105.

39 Interview with Leslie Katz, op. cit., note 34, p. 367. In the course of the same interview Evans stresses: "Both Ansel Adams and Paul Strand are really great technicians. They sometimes show they're too great. They do the perfect thing with the camera, and you say ohh and ahh, how perfect. Then you don't get their content clearly enough, however."

40 Evans, Walker, "Photography", *Quality: Its Image in the Arts*, Louis Kronenberger, Marshall Lee (eds.),New York, Atheneum, 1969; reprinted in Liebling, Jerôme (ed.), *Photography: Current Perspectives*, Rochester, Light Impressions, 1978, pp. 16-18.

41 It is quite necessary to take the verb 'establish' in this double sense. In the 1971 interview with Paul Cummings, op. cit., note 30, p. 238, Walker Evans does exactly that, when he declares, "That took some time to establish" - speaking of his method, his 'style', and then going on to discuss its institutional recognition.

42 Here we can complete certain observations introduced above (note 32). The image reproduced in this book at the opening of the group of plates devoted to Walker Evans is particularly significant. It is quite easy to recognize, in the anti-descriptive stance taken here - the black zone, without detail, in the center of the network of metallic structures - the contribution of the expressionism underlying the constructivist experiments going on in Europe. This is what distinguishes Evans' approach, in 1929, from the descriptive rigour of photographers like Weston ("*Armco Steel, Ohio*", 1922) or Charles Scheeler in his views of the Ford Plant ("*Criss Crossed Conveyors*", 1927). Later, in 1947, Evans will take a shot of the Ford Plant (*First and Last*, New York, Harper and Row, 1978, p. 173) that is very similar to that of Scheeler, for at this point he has renounced the 'romanticism' of his first architectural studies and adapted himself, with a certain opportunism, to straight photography's doctrine of design. He continued to distinguish himself nonetheless from the falsely expressionistic tendency of industrial heroism, as celebrated by authors such as Margaret Bourke-White.

43 Interview with Leslie Katz ,op. cit., note 34, p. 362. "A collector", remarks Evans, "becomes excessively conscious of a certain kind of object, falls in love with it, then pursues it. I notice that in my work for a certain time I'm interested in nothing but a certain kind of face or type of person. You start selecting people with the camera. It's compulsive and you can hardly stop. I think all artists are collectors of images."

44 Baudelaire, op. cit., note 36 , pp. 556-557.

Double lecture

Jean-François Chevrier

A la question de Lucy Lippard au début d'une rencontre radiophonique en 1970 - "Dan, on t'a considéré comme un poète, un critique et un photographe. Es-tu un artiste maintenant?" - Dan Graham répondit: "Je ne me définis pas, mais, quoi que je fasse, c'est toujours le médium, je crois, qui le définit. Il y a trois ou quatre ans, j'ai fait des choses imprimées, pour les magazines, des choses qui passent par la photographie. J'ai fait des choses dans tous les domaines où d'autres ont travaillé et je crois qu'elles se définissent d'elles-mêmes.[1] "Cette déclaration devrait suffire pour écarter d'entrée de jeu tout débat inutile sur la nature photographique d'une partie de l'oeuvre de Dan Graham. Dès lors que l'artiste est défini par ses activités, elles-mêmes définies par les outils utilisés, il devient inutile de se demander si Dan Graham est ou non un 'vrai' photographe. Il est photographe quand il utilise la photographie, et ce qu'il fait dans ce domaine possède une autonomie relative mais suffisante pour justifier un examen spécifique.

En 1970, toutefois, la question des définitions artistiques était exarcerbée par la multiplication récente d'activités transversales aux catégories et genres institués. La rencontre, animée par Lucy Lippard, avec Carl Andre, Douglas Huebler et Jan Dibbets, est sur ce point très parlante. Les quatre artistes ont été réunis parce que ce sont "quatre artistes visuels qui ont, d'une manière ou d'une autre, utilisé les mots." Comme Carl Andre, Dan Graham se démarque de l'art dit 'conceptuel': "Je ne pense pas faire de l'art conceptuel." Mais il refuse également de se situer dans un partage entre les mots et les objets. Il n'est pas un artiste qui préfère les mots aux objets. Il repousse la 'dichotomie mot-objet', pour mettre en avant la notion d'information. Il précise: "Je ne me suis jamais intéressé à la question des mots ou de la syntaxe dans la poésie, mais bien plus à l'information. Je voulais que les choses occupent un lieu donné et soient lues dans un présent donné. Le contexte est très important. Je voulais que mes pièces traitent du lieu comme présent de l'in-formation."

Depuis H o m e s f o r A m e r i c a (*Arts Magazine*, décembre 1966 - janvier 1967), la photographie a trouvé sa place dans ce contexte stratégique, comme information visuelle combinée à l'information écrite, dans un espace - la page, ou la double page de magazine - qui constitue le lieu d'une expérience de lecture. La photographie est un outil d'in-formation, de mise en forme de l'expérience, dans la mesure où elle est un matériau de montage. Voici pour la procédure adoptée, que l'on peut toujours, si on le souhaite absolument, appeler 'conceptuelle'. En réalité, Dan Graham se situe surtout comme un artiste post-pop, travaillant directement sur et avec les médias, au lieu de s'en approprier l'iconographie et les effets, comme l'avaient fait les artistes pop.[2]

Il s'agissait aussi d'assimiler la critique d'art à l'activité artistique, concrètement, matériellement, afin d'absorber l'écart du jugement séparé (*a posteriori*). Cet écart devait être placé, déplacé, dans la structure même de l'oeuvre. En publiant H o m e s f o r A m e r i c a, Dan Graham n'avait même pas besoin de préciser. "Ceci n'est pas une oeuvre d'art", comme le fit quelque temps plus tard Marcel Broodthaers sur les étiquettes de la collection, "*Der Adler vom Oligozän bis heute*", qu'il présenta à Düsseldorf ("*Musée d'Art Moderne. Département des Aigles, Section des Figures*", Städtische Kunsthalle, Düsseldorf, mai-juillet 1972). H o m e s f o r A m e r i c a est un article de magazine. Le commentaire n'est plus une réflexion seconde sur une oeuvre séparée (et passée). Il n'est plus un reflet de l'autonomie de l'art. Le commentaire est co-extensif à l'oeuvre (qui ne se nie ni ne se dénie). L'oeuvre et le commentaire sont coprésents dans un même espace de perception qui est celui de l'information. Celle-ci n'est plus information sur; elle est information de. Elle est la forme artistique même.

A la fin des années soixante, Dan Graham s'est fixé simultanément plusieurs enjeux critiques. Il veut rapporter le Pop Art à son lieu d'origine (les médias), remettre l'activité artistique à l'heure de sa réception critique et identifier ainsi l'objet d'art à sa production sociale, quand toute la doctrine formaliste tend au contraire à l'isoler dans une stricte autonomie (soigneusement distincte de la sphère médiatique). Enfin, il a reconnu que le minimalisme (les 'structures primaires') n'est jamais qu'un hyperformalisme, et il veut rapporter la forme type de l'objet minimal aux modèles architecturaux - tel le cube sérialisé des pavillons de banlieue - dont cet objet est la transformation idéale (Donald Judd) ou négative (Tony Smith), alors même que tout le discours mystifiant qui l'entoure dénie cette relation.

Quand H o m e s f o r A m e r i c a paraît fin 1966, Robert Smithson a déjà entrepris cette contextualisation du minimalisme dans ses premiers textes critiques et, particulièrement, dans son interprétation peu orthodoxe des modèles 'architecturaux' d'un Judd maniériste.[3]. La stratégie de Dan Graham est du même ordre et peut-être plus radicale, car il n'a alors aucune tentation (ni possibilité) de fabriquer des objets plastiques et n'a produit à ce jour que des structures verbales et des images photographiques. Il avait en effet participé quelques mois plus tôt à une exposition intitulée *Projected Art* en projetant, effectivement, des vues diapositives d'habitations suburbaines, et ce sont ces images qui auraient dû illustrer H o m e s f o r A m e r i c a.[4] Selon une logique de fiction - que l'on s'empressa de rattacher à l'art 'conceptuel' pour en réduire la spécificité - l'article donné à *Arts Magazine* devint l'oeuvre "*Homes for America*" d'un critique d'art photographe, ou d'un photographe critique d'architecture, ou, mieux encore, d'un artiste minimal, critique et photographe, qui a choisi de ne pas fabriquer d'objet plastique, comme il existe des architectes qui ont choisi de ne pas construire.[5]

Dans "Entropy and the New Monuments" publié quelque six mois avant H o m e s   f o r   A m e r i c a , Smithson avait reconnu aux structures de Judd, Morris, LeWitt et Flavin les qualités négatives (platitude et monotonie [*vapidity, dullness*]), de l'environnement suburbain. Il les assimilait également aux modèles visuels fournis par l'innombrable "matière imprimée" (*printed matter*) de la Galaxie Gutenberg décrite par McLuhan.[6] Néoromantique, Smithson met le monument (et sa fonction de remémoration) à l'épreuve du temps. Il parle des "*instant monuments*" de Flavin et décrit le paradoxe des "nouveaux monuments" en des termes qui suggèrent irrésistiblement l'enregistrement photographique: "Ils ne sont pas construits pour traverser le âges mais plutôt pour s'y opposer. Ils participent d'une réduction systématique du temps aux fractions de secondes, au lieu de représenter la longue étendue des siècles. Le passé et le futur sont situés l'un et l'autre dans un même présent objectif." Dans un essai publié l'année suivante, "The Monuments of Passaïc" (*Artforum*, décembre 1967), Smithson illustra de photographies, qu'il avait prises au cours d'une excursion dans sa ville natale, un récit parodiant les souvenirs d'un Grand Tour en Italie.[7] Il joue ici de l'ambiguïté entre le monument historique (vestige d'un passé culturel mémorable) et la valeur plus large du monument comme oeuvre de mémoire, dont la photographie documentaire constitue le modèle mais qu'elle réduit à une apparence optique sans consistance.[8]

Comme Smithson et avant lui, Dan Graham a travaillé avec la photographie à une redéfinition du monument. A la même époque, Douglas Huebler renonce à fabriquer des objets et entreprend des actions conceptuelles utilisant la photographie, après avoir conclu de sa participation à l'exposition *Primary Structures* (Jewish Museum, 1966) qu'un cube peut être aussi 'réel' que n'importe quel objet utilitaire - une table, une chaise-, mais qu'il ne peut être élevé en plein air à une échelle monumentale sans être exposé à une comparaison écrasante avec la nature.[9] Cette difficulté ne s'est jamais présentée à Dan Graham, comme il n'a jamais ressenti d'attraction pour les espaces vierges d'une nature sans urbanisme. Smithson oppose au monument du passé, incarnation d'un idéal historique, l'épuisement de cet idéal dans le *no man's land* des galeries et des espaces para-urbains. Mais cet épuisement est grandiose, il est à la mesure des phénomènes géologiques et jette les bases d'un nouvel archaïsme. Pour Dan Graham, le monument a toujours déjà subi la réduction (miniaturisation et dématérialisation) de l'image photographique, qui constitue dès lors un modèle effectif. Il n'a donc jamais travaillé contre le monument, en général, ni même, plus particulièrement, contre le monument urbain.[10] Ses premiers pavillons de verre apparurent à la fin des années soixante-dix, après les performances, les travaux vidéos et les dispositifs de miroirs, comme une extension nécessaire et logique de l'investigation critique de structures urbaines spécifiques engagée avec la photographie.

Il faut revenir ici aux premières photographies, prises en 1965-66 hors de New York, dans le New Jersey. Car elles produisent déjà les paramètres d'une dialectique de la perception socio-psychologique, fondée sur des divisions sociales, telle qu'elle a été dévoloppée ultérieurement. Projetées dans une galerie, les diapositives introduisent (projettent) un extérieur dans l'espace réservé du 'cube blanc' immaculé. Cet extérieur est constitué d'une information spécifique, caractérisée par un double déplacement: à la périphérie de New York (le New Jersey) et dans le passé proche de l'après-guerre, dont date le programme de construction des *tract houses*, et qui correspond à la petite enfance de Graham (né en 1942). L'ailleurs proche - dans l'espace et dans le temps - est la marque du présent photographique (documentaire) qui représenta, de ce fait, le modèle des travaux suivants. Il suffit en effet de penser aux dispositifs des performances et des vidéos des années soixante-dix, où le présent, *hic et nunc*, de l'action (ou de la réception) est constamment altéré par l'à-côté du reflet en miroir et par le passé immédiat de l'enregistrement. Dans "*Yesterday/Today*", par exemple, en 1975, c'est un enregistrement sonore qui accompagne d'un passé proche (hier) l'intrusion vidéo de l'à-côté (ce qui se passe dans la pièce à côté) dans l'espace actuel du spectateur.[11] Cinq ans plus tard, en 1979-80, "*Video View of Suburbia in an Urban Atrium*" introduit de nouveau l'ailleurs proche de la banlieue dans un espace urbain privilégié.[12]

Une autre installation vidéo, "*Edge of the City*", en 1981, désigne exactement la relation de la banlieue à la ville. Mais, à cette époque, le champ d'investigation de Dan Graham est considérablement élargi. Si la marge suburbaine avait été son premier sujet historique, il examine désormais un autre moment de l'utopie moderniste. Le proche passé s'est déplacé: ce sont maintenant les années soixante, l'époque des premiers atriums au bas des immeubles de verre des entreprises multinationales. Tandis que le postmodernisme est en train de nier, au nom de tous les *revivals* nostalgiques, l'histoire du modernisme, Dan Graham conçoit et construit des pavillons ("*Pavilions*"), en utilisant les modèles typologiques du 'style international' les plus banalisés, les plus dévalués. Il parle lui-même de "*clichés of modern architecture*."[13]

Comme en témoignent deux textes particulièrement développés, publiés dans *Artforum* ("Art in Relation to Architecture/Architecture in Relation to Art", février 1979, et "Not Post-Modernism...", en décembre 1981), la pensée de Dan Graham, autour de 1980, s'articule essentiellement sur des données historiques, sans pour autant abandonner les modèles psycho-sociologiques qui avaient orienté ses expérimentations antérieures. Du dispositif d'information, il passe à l'objet d'architecture, en conservant la question axiale de la perception et des modes d'expérience (ou de construction) de l'altérité. Il reprend - avec tous les acquis de la performance et de la vidéo - la contextualisation historique du minimalisme qu'il avait entreprise dans "*Homes for America*". Le cube minimaliste ouvert et démultiplié, baroquisé, est maintenant rapporté à l'utopie moderniste de la cité réconciliée avec la nature, dont les atriums d'entreprises (*corporate atriums*) sont la manifestation exemplaire (caricaturale) au temps d'une privatisation de l'espace public.

Conçue comme un monument (critique) de l'utopie, la sculpture-architecture des "*Pavilions*" résume les fictions de transparence (et les jeux de miroir) de l'architecture de verre. Mais elle est fondée aussi et surtout sur une analogie historique qui mobilise des références plus lointaines: le pavillon est à la hutte primitive imaginée au XVIIIe siècle - paradigme du primitivisme originel de l'architecture moderniste - ce que l'atrium est à la tradition du jardin pittoresque, modèle des parcs urbains.[14] En replaçant le partage ville-banlieue dans l'histoire de la dialectique ville-nature des Lumières, Dan Graham élargit le contexte étroit du minimalisme. Il dispose désormais de toutes les médiations qui lui permettent d'articuler concrètement les deux déterminations essentielles du modèle minimaliste: le modernisme architectural, tel qu'il s'est diffusé en Amérique avec le triomphe du 'style international', et l'environnement pop des banlieues. Comme "*Alteration of a Suburban House*" l'a préfiguré en 1978, l'objet d'art construit (le pavillon) reflète, littéralement et sur le plan de la 'réflexion' critique, l'environnement contemporain et ses modèles historiques. L'utopie urbaine des immeubles, avec leur excroissances baroquisantes (les atriums), est bien le résumé, ou la réflexion miniature, de cet environnement pop des banlieues où s'est accompli un mixte *up to date* de la ville et de la nature, symbolisé par l'exubérance des signes du commerce, de l'abondance et de la communauté de consommation.

En toute logique, l'environnement des signes pop étant clairement depuis les années soixante le contexte effectif de l'utopie moderniste, c'est en interprétant le Pop Art et son ambivalence culturelle, chez Lichtenstein et surtout chez l'architecte Robert Venturi, que Dan Graham a élaboré le principe de ses propres constructions. Un passage de "Not Post-Modernism..." est sur ce point particulièrement éloquent: "Venturi, comme les artistes pop les plus tradionnels (*academic*) n'a jamais accepté la culture populaire en elle-même mais l'a traitée dans une perspective dialectique, en relation avec le formalisme et l'histoire de l'architecture. Un bâtiment de Venturi, Rauch et Scott-Brown peut être rattaché au 'grand' art, comme assimilé aux productions éphémères de la culture populaire. Les deux lectures sont correctes. Par ce qui obéit dans ses apparences au code populaire de l'éphémère, ce bâtiment ne peut pas être rangé immédiatement dans l'architecture académique. Inversement, ce qui l'inscrit dans la 'grande' architecture empêche son intégration dans la culture de masse. Cette résistance à l'assimilation, d'un côté comme de l'autre, permet à l'oeuvre de mettre en question de l'intérieur - et non par opposition -

les deux systèmes de valeurs, formelles et historiques, de la culture populaire et de l'architecture."[15]

Décrivant dans les mêmes termes l'ambivalence de Lichtenstein à l'égard de la culture populaire, Dan Graham parle de "double lecture" (*dual reading*), et c'est précisément ce "dualisme" - tel que le revendiquait Robert Venturi dans son livre de 1966, *Complexity and Contradiction in Architecture* - qui lui permet de construire une image juste, parce qu'ambigüe, de la permanence de l'utopie moderniste dans ses usages dégradés, aliénants et oppressifs.[16] Il ne s'agit pas dès lors de 'déconstruire' le modèle moderniste ni de traiter avec ironie les signes de la culture populaire, ni même de parodier les chefs-d'oeuvre médiatisés du passé. La justesse critique consiste dans l'exaltation des contradictions historiques d'un modèle utopique transformé en structure d'aliénation. Elle ne procède pas tant d'un acte de discrimination (selon le sens étymologique de la critique) que d'une dramatisation constructive de l'ambiguïté comme coexistence de points de vue contradictoires et montage de moments historiques hétérogènes.

De cette "double lecture", dont le principe s'est dégagé du Pop Art, participent la justesse et la beauté des photographies produites depuis 1965. Ce sont à la fois des images d'architecture rigoureuses, formalisées jusqu'à l'abstraction, et des illustrations de magazine sans prétention à l''art', assimilables à la production éphémère des médias. Leur présentation actuelle, sous forme d'épreuves exposées comme des oeuvres autonomes, tend à gommer leur appartenance initiale à la culture pop des médias, mais cette évolution correspond à la revendication esthétique apparue dans les "*Pavilions*", qui se définissent néammoins - il faut le rappeler - comme des "clichés de l'architecture moderne" et maintiennent ainsi leur relation à la culture médiatisée des images de marque. On peut aussi comparer ces photographies avec le traitement de sujets similaires dans la photographie 'créative' contemporaine - considérer, par exemple, le bavardage documentaire de Bill Owens dans "*Suburbia*", paru en 1973 - pour vérifier qu'elles ont bien conservé la marque de leur double appartenance à la tradition moderniste (transmise par le minimalisme 'académique') et à la culture pop.

Opter en 1965 pour la couleur sans qualités des diapositives supposait un refus des raffinements de la belle image, des effets coloristes de saturation aussi bien que des nuances de valeurs du noir et blanc. Dan Graham pensait alors aux néons industriels de Flavin plus qu'aux jeux chromatiques de la *straight photography*, dans ses différentes versions (Helen Levitt, Eliot Porter, etc.), qui participent toutes en fin de compte de l'artisanat opposé à l'industrie. Attaché, en même temps, à la rigueur austère du modernisme, il se détournait également de l'exubérance kitsch des illustrations de magazines à grand tirage, façon Hollywood (cette exubérance étant arrivée chez lui plus tard, avec les images d'atriums). Les historiens de la photographie ne s'y sont d'ailleurs pas trompé ils ne l'ont pas inclus dans leurs panoramas et considèrent manifestement que son propos relève d'un conceptualisme irrécupérable, c'est-à-dire d'un usage de la photographie irréductible aux canons historiques et qui n'a pas, pour autant, l'aspect type de la 'photographie conceptuelle' à la Sol LeWitt.

Dan Graham s'est conformé au principe de la double lecture avant de l'avoir énoncé. Il lui suffit d'utiliser rigoureusement la photographie comme elle s'est définie, entre les beaux-arts et les médias. Situation ambiguë, maintenue pendant toute la période où s'est développé et imposé l'art moderne, depuis 1850 jusqu'au début des années 1960, quand Warhol, puis Richter produisirent leurs premiers tableaux photographiques. L'ambiguïté n'était pas alors résolue pour autant. Warhol sembla ensuite choisir le camp des médias et Richter privilégia peu à peu l'abstraction (en conservant toutefois le contrepoint du modèle photographique). Le photoréalisme américain, quant à lui, s'obstinait à exalter (ou accomplir), dans une trop parfaite mécanique picturale, l'exactitude impersonnelle de l'image photographique. En utilisant la photographie comme il le fit, pour ce qu'elle est, entre l'objet d'exposition (même sous forme de diapositives projetées) et l'outil médiatique, Dan Graham révéla la situation historique du Pop Art, entre le modernisme (assimilé au 'grand' art) et la culture populaire. C'est ici précisément qu'il retrouva l'exemple de Walker Evans, en amont du Pop Art.

D'après les témoignages que l'on peut recueillir aujourd'hui, les artistes du cercle conceptuel avaient, à la fin des années soixante, reconnu cette parenté.[17] Mais, depuis le début de la décennie, plusieurs artistes pop ou proches du Pop Art avaient déjà mentionné le précédent de Walker Evans, et particulièrement ses images de panneaux publicitaires (billboards). Jim Dine en parle dans un entretien avec Gene Swenson en 1963.[18] En 1967, Allan Kaprow l'évoque à propos des décollagistes européens (Hains, Villeglé, Rotella) dans un texte qui insiste sur les résonances nostalgiques du Pop Art, avec ses références aux années trente-quarante, les années d'enfance des artistes pop.[19] Quatre ans plus tôt, Warhol avait produit son fameux hommage à Rauschenberg, "Let Us Now Praise Famous Men", où il utilisait des photos de famille de Rauschenberg (prises dan les années trente), et auquel il donna le titre du livre-culte de James Agee et Walker Evans.[20] Ce livre avait d'ailleurs connu une réédition en 1960. Quant à American Photographs, le livre-catalogue de l'exposition Evans au Museum of Modern Art, New York, en 1938, où se trouvent les images mentionnées par Dine et Kaprow, il était reparu en 1962.

Si l'on ajoute que c'est en 1966 que parurent Many Are Called (les portraits du métro) et Message from the Interior, et en 1966-67, également, que Garry Winogrand et Lee Friedlander furent en quelque sorte investis officiellement de l'héritage d'Evans, on peut conclure que les années soixante, les années ouvertes par le Pop Art, furent aussi celles où s'imposa dans l'art, via la photographie, une certaine image de l'Amérique, fondée sur la richesse de la culture vernaculaire documentée depuis les années trente, dont Evans pouvait être tenu pour la figure éponyme.[21] C'est ce que les éditeurs d'Arts Magazine ont signifié quand ils ont remplacé les row houses de Dan Graham par un alignement de maisons en bois de Boston photographié par Evans en 1930: l'image reproduite en couverture de l'édition de 1962 d'American Photographs p.109.

En 1965-66, Dan Graham ne connaissait pas Walker Evans, qu'il découvrit un peu plus tard, quand son ami Mel Bocher, après la parution de "Homes for America", lui montra American Photographs. Son intérêt pour l'architecture fonctionnelle urbaine et suburbaine de l'après-guerre - où se manifeste massivement le renversement de l'utopie moderniste en une structure d'aliénation - lui est venu d'une observation directe de New York et de sa banlieue, et, en dehors de cette expérience immédiate, de deux modèles artistiques plus proches - dans le temps - que Walker Evans: le minimalisme bien sûr, mais aussi un cinéma d'auteurs européens (Antonioni, Godard) dérivé du néoréalisme italien de l'après-guerre, dans lequel les thèmes de la ville moderne et de la banlieue, comme lieux d'égarement psychologique et d'errance, étaient omniprésents.[22] On pourrait même aisément rattacher la structure de "Homes for America" à la dialectique document-fiction mise en oeuvre systématiquement par Godard.[23]

Ces références au cinéma étaient en fait largement partagées dans le milieu d'avant-garde new yorkais de la fin des années soixante. "Deux ou trois choses que je sais d'elle" de Godard, complétant "Made in USA," apparut en 1966 comme l'accomplissement d'un cinéma associant l'actualité du Pop Art et du nouveau roman à une dramatisation documentaire inspiré du néoréalisme.[24] A cette époque, Walker Evans se tenait tout à fait en dehors des milieux d'avant-garde, et l'on ne peut pas affirmer qu'il avait pris connaissance de l'évolution du cinéma européen depuis l'après-guerre. On peut toutefois rappeler que son ami James Agee fut de 1941 à 1948 un observateur attentif de ce cinéma, écrivant pour le journal de la gauche américaine, The Nation, des articles sur Rossellini, Vittorio de Sica, ou Georges Rouquier ("Farrebique"), comme le faisait en France, plus systématiquement, André Bazin. Mais l'essentiel reste la convergence qui s'opéra effectivement dans les années soixante entre une histoire du cinéma 'réaliste', qui conduit à Godard et Antonioni, et le projet photographique d'Evans, qui trouva alors son aboutissement, quand la publication des portraits du métro de la fin des années trente vint compléter American Photographs.

Dans un contexte marqué fortement à la fois par un anti-libéralisme de la gauche radicale marxisante et par un anti-humanisme de la pensée structuraliste - à laquelle se rattachait le littéralisme de Robbe-Grillet -, Evans était surtout considéré pour ses images d'architecture et de signes urbains.

Dan Graham, comme tout le monde, retrouva dans *American Photographs* le principe de la reproduction de reproduction du Pop Art, mais aussi, plus particulièrement, ce qu'il avait lui-même observé dans l'immédiate banlieue de New York (le New Jersey): l'image de *Main Street* - réalité historique et paradigme de l'urbanisme suburbain -, les maisons standardisées alignées le long d'une voie ferrée; en somme, l'architecture du commerce et de la communication, dans sa forme mécanisée, commune à l'ensemble du monde industrialisé, et sous un aspect vernaculaire, propre à l'Amérique.

La part de l'oeuvre d'Evans assimilable à l'idéologie humaniste de la social-démocratie rooseveltienne était écartée. Les images de *Let Us Now Praise Famous Men*, comme tout portrait chargé de la moindre trace d'empathie, apparaissaient surtout trop proches de la "mythologie" (Barthes) développée par Edward Steichen dans *The Family of Man* au Museum of Modern Art, New York, en 1955. Aux yeux de Dan Graham (et de ses amis), toute photographie 'normale' ressortissait des mystifications de l'humanisme libéral. Il précise toutefois que ce rejet était aussi un refoulement et que ce qu'il repoussait dans les années soixante a resurgi récemment dans le projet "*Children's Pavilion*" entrepris avec Jeff Wall.[25]

En réalité, Evans n'était pas moins réservé, ou ambivalent, à l'égard des appels rhétoriques à la communion par l'image. Il n'avait pas participé à *Family of Man*. Son regard sur la réalité sociale était trop distant, trop moral (ou puritain) et trop dandy pour s'accorder à l'emphase sentimentale et aux effets spectaculaires d'une imagerie de la communauté universelle. Dès 1931, dans un essai publié par Lincoln Kirstein dans *Hound and Horn*, il avait violemment critiqué l'esthétisme publicitaire de Steichen.[26] Quelques années plus tard, quand il travaillait pour la Farm Security Administration (FSA) (entre 1935 and 1938), il s'opposa au programme de propagande de ses commanditaires et, plus encore, à l'outrance dramatique et au racolage des bons sentiments pratiqués par Margaret Bourke-White et Erskine Caldwell dans leur bestseller de 1937, *You Have Seen Their Faces*.[27] Sa répulsion était morale et esthétique. Le style de Margaret Bourke-White, photographe phare de *Life* (dont elle avait réalisé la couverture du premier numéro en 1936), représentait l'équivalent exact, dans les médias, de 'l'ordre monumental' qui caractérise l'architecture officielle des années trente, conçue comme le symbole d'une puissance autoritaire incarnant l'unité organique d'un peuple. Venu, comme il le dit lui-même, de la Bohème, lecteur de Baudelaire et de Flaubert, Evans devait se garantir de sa sympathie pour les défavorisés et refuser de croire que l'art puisse "améliorer la société".[28] Il resta toute sa vie confronté au dilemme de l'artiste bohème: il devait se tenir en dehors des programmes de gauche, tout en évitant les cadres de l'*establishment*.[29] Il ne pouvait ni appartenir au peuple ni s'en faire le porte-parole éclairé (ou intéressé, à la manière de Bourke-White).

La position artistique qui résulte de ce dilemme est nécessairement ambigue. Evans l'a formulée à plusieurs reprises en des termes similaires aux propos de Dan Graham sur le Pop Art. Au cours d'un entretien en 1971, au moment où le Museum of Modern Art de New York lui consacre une rétrospective, il résume le double refus de l'art (photographique) et du commerce, dont il avait, quarante ans plus tôt, observé la conjugaison chez Steichen: "Je faisais un travail non-artistique et non-commercial. Je sentais - à juste titre - que j'étais sur la bonne voie." [30] Il était un *outsider*. Mais de ceux qui ouvrent un nouveau champ de recherches et qui, lorsqu'ils sont reconnus, risquent d'être assimilés à l'*establishment*, comme cela lui était arrivé dès 1938 (à quoi il avait répondu en allant photographier les passagers du métro, *underground*, produisant alors des images qui allaient rester quasiment inédites jusqu'aux années soixante). En 1971, également, pour se démarquer une nouvelle fois du critère fonctionnel (et commercial) de l'image d'information, il avança l'idée de 'style documentaire', formule magique de compromis entre le grand art et le métier d'information. Mais c'est encore sur le modèle de l'affirmation de la négation qu'il est le plus conforme à lui-même, quand il déclare: "Les théoriciens attribuent à l'appareil photographique à peu près tous les pouvoirs, sauf le fait négatif *(negation)*, qu'il puisse servir ni à penser ni à traduire les émotions de son opérateur ."[31]

Il avait déjà écrit en 1931 dans "The Reapparance of Photography": "L'Amérique est vraiment la demeure naturelle de la photographie si on la définit sans penser à l'opérateur." La formule citée précédemment - qui introduit des images situées par Evans en 1940 - est plus radicale. C'est la réponse négative aux programmes idéologiques de la décennie passée, comme à toutes les utopies, dégradées, du *Machine Age*, auxquelles le texte de 1931 pouvait sembler souscrire.[32] Présentant les portraits du métro, Evans énonce un projet idéal (qu'il n'a pas accompli), parfaitement conforme à l'impersonnalité et à l'absence de choix esthétique, qui définissaient le *ready made* duchampien: "Je voudrais pouvoir dire tranquillement que soixante-deux personnes sont venues inconsciemment se placer l'une après l'autre, pendant une période déterminée, devant un appareil d'enregistrement impersonnel et fixe, et que *tous*, quand ils sont passés dans le cadre du viseur, ont été photographiés, et photographiés sans qu'aucune décision humaine n'ait déterminé le moment de la prise de vue."[33] On peut bien sûr reconnaître ici le radicalisme des procédures conceptuelles de la fin des années soixante. Mais, si l'on considère les images elles-mêmes, il faut bien constater que leur résonance dramatique est étrangère à l'indifférence revendiquée. En cherchant à pousser à l'extrême, jusqu'à l'absurde, la confiance (aveugle) du premier modernisme dans les pouvoirs de la machine, Evans a révélé le versant sombre *(the dark side)* du modernisme comme âge de la machine.

Les cinéastes berlinois des années vingt l'avaient précédé dans cette voie: Fritz Lang, notamment, avec "*Metropolis*" (1924) mais aussi "*M. Le Maudit*" (1931). Quand Evans indique que les personnages du métro sont 'les dames et les messieurs du jury', on peut penser qu'il a voulu appliquer à l'homme du commun, promu à l'exercice de la justice, la méthode d'inventaire typologique de la photographie policière.[34] Lang, dans "*M. Le Maudit*," avait déjà transformé en un sombre tribunal une foule *underground* de criminels. En se donnant Daumier comme référence, Evans rapporte aux premiers soupçons d'un artiste sur la justice moderne tous ces jeux de renversement entre le 'commun' et le criminel dans la figure de l'homme des foules. Le métro souterrain est 'le cinéma des rues' de Murnau ("*street films*" dit Kracauer) transformé en ce tribunal de l'inconscient, le plus commun; où le crime est jugé par le criminel. On peut ajouter, à l'appui de cette interprétation, que l'exemple trouvé par Evans dans la photographie de rue de Paul Strand, se concentrait pour lui dans le portrait de la marchande de journaux aveugle, "*Blind Woman*", de 1916.

Ce versant sombre du modernisme, théâtre des figures (ou masques) de l'inconscient, le cinéma berlinois l'avait isolé, en temps de crise, dans les rues de la 'grande ville' *(Großstadt)*. Il est logique que ce soit à New York -la ville moderne par excellence- que des photographes, à l'orée du cinéma, en aient donné les premières indications et que Walker Evans, au terme d'une autre crise, ait produit la synthèse des deux moments historiques, en les rapportant à la modernité archaïque de la ville baudelairienne, marquée par les stigmates du péché. Dans un fragment de *Mon coeur mis à nu*, Baudelaire avait énoncé sa "théorie de la vraie civilisation": "Elle n'est pas dans le gaz, ni dans la vapeur, ni dans les tables tournantes, elle est dans la diminution des traces du péché originel."[35] En rassemblant les portraits du métro sous le titre *Many Are Called* (beaucoup d'appelés... mais peu d'élus), Evans reprend la veine allégorique et mélancholique du poète des *Fleurs du Mal* (qui durent pendant quelque temps s'appeler *Les Limbes*). Il faut enfin se rappeler que Baudelaire rattachait la caricature dans son ensemble au "rire satanique" et qu'il admirait particulièrement Daumier.[36]

Tout ceci n'est pas étranger à l'art américain des années soixante. L'humour noir de Smithson participe du 'rire satanique', comme exutoire d'une mélancolie dont la banlieue fournit des motifs allégoriques. Parce qu'il n'était pas assez romantique pour se faire ainsi 'l'avocat du diable', Dan Graham s'en est tenu à plus de réalisme, c'est-à-dire au constat de l'utopie négative accomplie dans l'environnement suburbain. En étudiant, depuis la fin des années soixante-dix, les modèles typologiques du modernisme -leur formation et leurs transformations récentes-, il a, toutefois, retrouvé exactement la situation de la remémoration baudelairienne: les limbes, région crépusculaire de l'attente, absorbant tous les déchets historiques transportés par les utopies constituées. Dans cette région intermédiaire, le temps immobile, égal, de la mélancolie révèle négativement le contenu utopique (le non-lieu) des poncifs de bonheur pour tous. Le modèle baudelairien, tel qu'il

avait pu jouer pour Evans, reparaît ainsi derrière le dandysme warholien.
Bien avant Warhol, le principe d'indifférence duchampien a joué en effet chez Walker Evans comme l'exaltation négative, et objectivement dramatique, via la photographie, du rêve d'égalitarisme de la société américaine. Car cette indifférence est aussi et d'abord celle du dandy qui cherche, en vain, à échapper à la bohème et, comme Baudelaire, admire Daumier. En ce plaçant dans cette généalogie, les portraits du métro apportèrent une interprétation historique de la crise du modernisme dans les années trente, qui converge avec les observations tirées par Walter Benjamin de son étude de la ville baudelairienne. La foule, manipulée par les machines de propagande totalitaire, est l'élément du nombre dans lequel l'artiste bohème (ou le 'peintre de la vie moderne') accomplit la dissolution de sa subjectivité et trouve les impulsions de son activité. L'art doit répondre à la machine par la machine, non pas sur le mode de l'épopée médiatisée (qui célèbre une pseudo organicité communautaire) mais sur un mode lyrique accordé à la diversité du commun.

C'est là que réside la grande invention d'Evans dans les années trente, dont hérite Dan Graham: le vernaculaire de la culture américaine, dans sa diversité irréductible aux typologies modernistes. Il n'y a pas de peuple américain mais un spectacle de l'Amérique. Plus riche et plus complexe que les rares chefs-d'oeuvre inspirés d'un modernisme d'origine européenne, il ne répond pas pour autant au poncif d'un Nouveau monde édénique, protégé de la civilisation industrielle. De tous les 'maîtres' de la photographie moderne américaine, Walker Evans est sans doute le seul qui se doit entièrement dépris de l'idée de Nature, qui ait pris rigoureusement le parti des signes et de l'histoire -pour reprendre la distinction établie par Barthes au moment des *Mythologies*- ; le seul qui n'ait pas cherché à fonder une maîtrise de la photographie dans l'habileté à faire parler la nature ou à en révéler les messages secrets (par la magie de la technique). A peu de choses près, son oeuvre a commencé avec la crise de 1929, à New York, et a cessé avec elle. Pour lui, le spectacle de l'Amérique est essentiellement urbain, marqué par les signes de la ville (ou du commerce) et leur emprise violente mais éphémère sur l'environnement. L'enregistrement ne doit pas isoler la forme permanente d'un symbole ("*the thing itself* " de Weston) mais fixer une image-signe, un document-monument.

Pour tous les photographes des années vingt influencés par Strand et ralliés à la *straight photography* (antipictorialiste), la nature fut à la fois, ou successivement, le modèle de la machine idéale -assimilable de ce fait à une oeuvre d'art- et la réponse salutaire aux effets négatifs du machinisme. Il leur fallait, d'un côté comme de l'autre, obtenir une 'qualité' qui apparente l'image à l'objet d'art ou à ce que Fernand Léger appelait "le bel objet": l'objet industriel, parfaitement dessiné, fonctionnel, dont le *design* obéit au dessin de la nature. Bien qu'il fût sensible à l'épure des objets techniques, même et surtout les plus ordinaires -comme l'atteste sa publication dans *Fortune* en 1955, "Beauties of the Common Tool" , Evans y voyait essentiellement les exemples d'une culture technique participant plus d'un imaginaire anthropologique (et historique) que des lois constantes de la nature. Dans tous les cas, quel que fût le sujet d'étude, son modèle n'était pas l'objet (naturel ou industriel) mais l'image, alliée, par parenté et par fonction, aux signes imprimés, affichés, utilisés pour la communication.

La différence avec ses prédécesseurs immédiats est ici décisive. Ralph Steiner, par exemple, qui lui transmit sa technique, avait entrevu dans les années vingt la richesse du matériau documentaire rassemblé ultérieurement dans *American Photographs*. En témoignent ses illustrations d'un article de *Fortune* en 1930, au début de la crise, dont le propos était déjà précisément celui d'Evans: "un constat: non pas l'Amerique récente, avec ses gratte-ciels, ses avions et ses générateurs, mais une Amérique avant restauration *(unregenerate)*, avec ses vérandas et ses arrière-cours, sa laideur et son gâchis."[37] Le même texte a, par ailleurs, le mérite d'énoncer clairement les raisons 'mythologiques', dans l'imaginaire nationaliste des éditeurs de *Fortune*, qui allaient permettre à Evans de travailler pour ce magazine: "Fondamentalement, l'Angleterre est triste, et l'Amérique est gaie. Elle sent mauvais, mais elle a assez d'exubérance et d'énergie pour couvrir le pays de vieilles choses usées, laissées à l'abandon. Chaque décharge, chaque alignement de maisons délabrées le long de la voie ferrée est le signe même de notre infinie richesse. C'est de l'espace dont nous n'avons pas besoin. Nous en avons tant." Mais ces convergences rendent d'autant plus sensible ce qui différencie Evans. Steiner s'était sans doute adapté particulièrement tôt à une demande d'identité culturelle que l'idéologie du progrès technologique ne pouvait entièrement satisfaire (parce qu'elle laissait trop de choses à l'écart). Mais il s'était trop attaché aux valeurs d'accomplissement du 'grand art' traditionnel (pré-industriel) exemplifiées par Strand, dont il avait eu la révélation en 1926-27: "Strand m'a montré ses photos mexicaines. J'étais stupéfait, sidéré: jamais je n'avais vu des tirages aussi riches -avec une texture aussi sensible-, aussi somptueux par leurs valeurs tonales."[38] Evans, au contraire, n'a cessé de repousser ce critère de qualité 'historique' et de fini dans l'exécution, jusqu'à déclarer en 1971, alors qu'il expose une fois de plus au Museum of Modern Art de New York: "Maintenant je suis mal à l'aise dans un musée. Je ne veux pas y aller, je ne veux pas qu'on m''apprenne' quoi que ce soit, je ne veux pas voir d'art 'accompli'. Je m'intéresse à ce qu'on appelle le vernaculaire."[39]

Il ne faut cependant pas ignorer ce qu'il y eut d'ambigü dans la positon d'Evans, si l'on veut mesurer précisément sa lucidité aristique. En 1971, le vernaculaire -"ce qu'on appelle le vernaculaire"- est une spécialité reconnue par l'*establishment*, auquel il prétend s'être opposé. *Fortune* avait, quarante ans plus tôt, ouvert la voie, suivi par le Museum of Modern Art de New York. Dans les dernières années de sa vie, Evans est lui-

même un artiste 'historique', un maître, qui enseigne à Yale: il donne l'impression de répéter sa propre leçon. En 1969, dans un ouvrage collectif intitulé *Quality: Its Image in the Arts* - titre qui se passe de commentaire-, il dresse un portrait type du photographe de rue, en multipliant les figures du héros bourgeois excepté de la morale et de la bonne société -le voyeur, l'espion, l'enfant irresponsable-, tel qu'il a été popularisé par la littérature romanesque depuis le XIXe siècle (Nabokov est d'ailleurs cité). Bien que Stieglitz ait réussi à faire entrer la photographie au musée, la place du photographe est 'dans la rue': "Son festin visuel est fait d'un matériau brut: boutiques, chambres à coucher, cours usagées, loin des espaces de l'architecture solennelle, avec ses entours magnifiques, ou d'une nature encore plus évidemment pittoresque."[40] Cette opposition des deux répertoires *high and low* est évidemment trop éloquente et participe de la rhétorique institutionelle qu'elle veut contredire (et ne fait que dénier). On pourrait en conclure facilement qu' Evans n'a finalement pas échappé à la "position paradigmatique"- selon ses propres termes- de Stieglitz, chez qui il reconnaissait "l'absence d'humour caractéristique de la bohème post-victorienne."

Mais cette ambiguïté est aussi l'effet de la lucidité. Evans avait trouvé chez Atget un exemple plus convaincant que Stieglitz (et Strand). Mais il ne pouvait pas être l'artiste collectioneur qui constitue une oeuvre clandestine en fournissant des documents aux institutions et aux artistes académiques. Dans l'Amérique des années vingt-trente, la stratégie documentaire d'Atget correspondait trop bien au programme d'un magazine comme *Fortune*. Il devait donc 'établir' son propos, c'est-à-dire lui donner à la fois un support institutionnel, hors des médias, et une forme spécifique.[41] C'est ce qu'il fit quand il profita d'une exposition au Museum of Modern Art de New York, en 1938, pour publier *American Photographs*: un livre, entre le magazine et la cimaise, où les images sont simplement reproduites -et non encadrées comme des oeuvres précieuses-, mais sans légendes, régulièrement isolées, chacune publiée seule sur une page sans vis-à-vis. Il évitait de cette manière les deux solutions, contraires mais également mystifiantes, de Stieglitz et de Margaret Bourke-White. Il évitait aussi le didactisme, qu'il fût de simple propagande ou plus 'critique', qui caractérisait le photomontage mais produisit moins de réussites (en dehors d'exceptions comme Heartfield) qu'un alignement de l'art sur les techniques de communication publicitaire.

Si l'on parle de montage, celui-ci reste pour Evans un modèle cinématographique, donc syntaxique, d'*editing*. Par l'intermédiaire de Jay Leyda, notamment, il connaissait les films d'Eisenstein, de Vertov. Le montage est une manière d'organiser des images dont l'autonomie, aussi nécessaire soit-elle, ne doit jamais être définitive, aboutie. Toujours son refus de l'art 'accompli'! Il ne cesse d'ailleurs de modifier le cadrage de ses photos, de les fragmenter, d'en tirer des détails qu'il combine avec d'autres. Il y a là une mobilité à double résonance: elle correspond à des pratiques -le cinéma et la presse- extérieures aux beaux-arts, et procède d'une conception spécifique de l'image-signe, comme moment d'une oeuvre ouverte.

En 1931, dans le texte déjà cité de *Hound and Horn*, qui examine les récents développements (la "renaissance") de la photographie en Allemagne, Evans mentionne, bien sûr, le livre d'Albert Renger-Patzsch, *Die Welt ist schön* (Le monde est beau), mais il ne l'apprécie qu'à moitié, car il le trouve trop attaché au traditionnel débat avec la peinture. La construction du livre de Renger-Patzsch est effectivement très statique, trop divisée, et reflète la conception organique des relations nature-industrie, tradition-modernité. Evans se reconnaît en revanche très facilement dans l'appel à la liberté amateur - négligence, imperfection, inachèvement- qui aboutit, dans le texte, rédigé par Franz Roh, de *foto-auge* (dont il cite de longs extraits) au rattachement de la photographie à "l'histoire mésestimée de la productivité non-professionnelle." Mais c'est au terme de l'article qu'apparaît la mention la plus positive, concernant les portraits d'August Sander: "*Antlitz der Zeit* est plus qu'un livre d'"études de types'; l'exemple d'un regard orienté avec justesse parmi les gens. C'est une des voies à venir de la photographie annoncées par Atget. C'est un découpage photographique de la société (*a photographic editing of society*), un travail clinique..."

Dans ces quelques lignes, écrites à un moment charnière de sa carrière, Evans annonce son propre programme: "*a photographic editing of society*", et il n'a cessé, ensuite, de le réaffirmer, jusqu'à la formule-limite des portraits du métro. Tout s'est joué très tôt sur l'idée de type, ou de typologie. Depuis 1928, il a produit des études d'architecture, qui se rattachent à la 'nouvelle vision' européenne, plus qu'aux exemples de Stieglitz et de Strand.[42] Il s'est essayé également, avec succès, à la photographie de rue (*street photography*), en se donnant comme règle de conduite un modèle de typologie sociale assoupli par les incertitudes de l'instantané. A ce sujet, il déclara, bien plus tard: "Je me suis laissé conduire par quelques intuitions fulgurantes. Je me suis dit que je devais saisir un type dans la rue, un 'instantané' de quelqu'un sur le bord de mer, ou une dactylo en train de déjeuner. C'était un bon filon. Je continue de l'exploiter." Il parle de la compulsion de l'artiste collectionneur.[43] Mais, comme l'indique la remarque sur Sander et comme l'ont confirmé ses projets d'édition, ce modèle de typologie instantanée, aussi stimulant fût-il, n'était pas suffisant. Il fallait une structure plus solide, qui permette d'ordonner la diversité sociale (et historique), sans la réduire à une typologie pittoresque, et sans sacrifier l'intuition à des procédures d'"étude' trop restrictives. Atget lui-même a fixé des figures types de la rue parisienne en élargissant le modèle des 'petits métiers' de la tradition pittoresque, mais il s'était donné un programme plus ambitieux, intégrant l'architecture et le mobilier urbain. D'autre part, la supériorité que Baudelaire avait reconnue à Daumier sur Henri Monnier (l'inventeur du personnage de "Monsieur Prudhomme") résume assez bien ce qui distingue Evans, dans *American Photographs* (et dans *Many Are Called*) d'un bon photographe de rue, comme il y en eut tant autour de 1940: "Plusieurs de ses *Scènes populaires* sont certainement agréables; autrement il faudrait nier le charme cruel et surprenant du daguerréotype; mais Monnier ne sait rien créer, rien idéaliser, rien arranger."[44]

Tels sont les deux bords du projet d''édition' d'Evans, tels qu'ils apparaissent dans *American Photographs*: les gens dans la ville (grande ou petite), l'architecture (vernaculaire). D'un bord à l'autre, circulent les signes (actuels et historiques). Car l'architecture elle-même, dans sa diversité typologique, caractéristique de l'éclectisme américain, est un système ou, de moins, un assemblage de signes. Editer (découper-monter), c'est mettre en ordre une collection d'images-types: types humains et architecturaux, qui vont de l'archétype au stéréotype, en passant par tous les hybrides possibles. La collection s'augmente de manière compulsive, comme les signes urbains se multiplient, mais sa réalisation (son organisation en séquences) est raisonnée, sinon constructive. L'accumulation et la richesse de l'assemblage, qui caractérisent l'environnement urbain et suburbain, doivent être ordonnés et exaltés par la rigueur du montage séquentiel.

Il existe donc une étroite relation entre le travail d'édition d'*American Photographs* et l'image de l'architecture américaine, telle qu'elle se forme dans la seconde partie de l'ouvrage. L'architecte 'pop' Robert Venturi -auquel s'est beaucoup intéressé Dan Graham depuis la fin des années soixante-dix- dira: "Main Street est presque réussie." (*Main Street is almost all right.*) Walker Evans montre déjà à quoi tient cette réussite: la combinaison rythmique de la ligne droite et des figures irrégulières (symboliques ou décoratives), résumée dans la double image des signes urbains, qui répondent à une fonction de communication et procèdent également d'intérêts moins univoques ('gratuits'). Cette combinaison est omniprésente dans le livre. L'ordre peut être très rigoureux, qu'il soit dicté par la régularité austère des *frame houses* et des alignements néoclassiques, ou par l'uniformité d'un principe de prise de vue (frontalité et faible profondeur de champ, par exemple), mais il est toujours contredit par la discordance, voire l'incongruité, des détails, et par les accélérations du montage.

On a souvent parlé du 'classicisme' d'Evans (simplicité, économie de moyens, refus du pittoresque romantique, anti-expressionisme). Il est possible que le modèle de Main Street, associé au type géorgien des *row houses*, évoque lointainement la syntaxe de l'architecture classique, où les cinq 'ordres' distincts -selon la typologie fixée à la Renaissance- sont symbolisés par des figures ornementales emblématiques: dorique, ionique, etc. Mais la complexité de l'assemblage éclectique se distingue de la simplicité, ou de la rigueur, des ordres paradigmatiques. Evans, d'autre part, a assisté à la naissance du style International aux Etats-Unis (avec l'exposition au Museum of Modern Art de New York et le livre de Philip Johnson, en 1932), mais il ne pouvait pas y adhérer, pas plus qu'il ne pouvait souscrire à l'idéal du progrès technologique sous-tendant l'universalisme de Mies van der Rohe. Sans être régionaliste, son langage est celui de l'urbanisme moyen, avec ses spécificités vernaculaires, situé entre la métropole et le monde rural, où les rares exemples de la 'grande' architecture participent de la diversité des bricolages et des styles d'emprunt: entre l'archétype, plus ou moins primitiviste (telle la fameuse hutte de Laugier mentionnée plus haut à propos de Dan Graham), et le stéréotype (historiciste et industriel). Cette situation correspondant exactement à la place de la photographie, entre les beaux-arts et les média.

En allant chercher ses modèles dans le XIXe siècle littéraire européen (Baudelaire, Flaubert), Evans a pu se dégager des divers mots d'ordre d'un modernisme utopique ou amnésique, qui transforma le cosmopolitisme des Lumières en un nationalisme fondé sur l'universalité triomphante d'un modèle de libre entreprise (comme la génération de Dan Graham l'a reconnu dans l'après-guerre). Sa première enquête conséquente, en 1930-31, commandée par Lincoln Kirstein, porta d'ailleurs sur l'architecture victorienne (Boston, Saratoga Springs, etc.). Mais il n'est pas le photographe de l'Amérique profonde, qui a ennobli l'ennui de Main Street et la misère des fermiers ruinés. La seconde section d'*American Photographs* s'ouvre et se ferme sur deux images d'ornements brisés -des 'reliques'-, malaxés comme du carton pâte ou du papier découpé. Ces ornements sont de faux vestiges de l'Antiquité, réduisant l'archétype historique au stéréotype de la désolation mélancolique. On ne peut imaginer d'images plus conformes à l'allégorie baudelairienne décrite à la même époque par Walter Benjamin, comme une ironie, exemplaire, de l'artiste collectionneur sur lui-même. Ironie exemplaire, parce qu'elle fait de la mélancolie la condition de possibilité d'une exaltation des signes modernes, dégagée des regrets nostalgiques d'une appartenance communautaire (comme, bien sûr, de toute rêverie futuriste).

A travers la citation (faussement historiciste), à l'état de déchet, les signes sont déjà en prise sur la désolation et peuvent s'en dégager comme de leur propre fond. C'est ici que se forme à son tour l'image des hommes, non pas tant sur fond d'architecture que dans le chantier de ruines des signes urbains -dont participe l'architecture-, animé et organisé en séquences par la double activité (collection-'édition') du photographe. L'humanisme de Walker Evans, comme celui de Baudelaire, peut éclater dans un moment de compassion, et d'autant plus facilement qu'il est moins enclin au "rire satanique". Mais il tient surtout à un autre *pathos,* qui se fixe sur des signes et des traces de destruction, renvoyant le collectionneur à sa propre passion.

D'où l'inflexion des vingt dernières années. Il ne s'agit plus, dans les meilleures oeuvres, du spectacle de la rue,

mais d'intérieurs où, dans l'assemblage de quelques objets-signes, se concentre l'image de ceux -absents- qui les occupent, comme un 'message' -pour reprendre le mot du livre de 1966, *Message from the Interior*- très clair mais plus ou moins déchiffrable. Evans s'était intéressé à ces 'arrangements' domestiques dès 1930, et surtout pendant la période du FSA, quand il entrait chez les fermiers. Autour de 1930, et, par la suite, parallèlement aux images du FSA, il avait parfois photographié son propre lieu de vie et de travail (notamment son laboratoire). Mais "*The Child's Room*" (1951), "*The Parlor Chairs*" (1958), "*The Home Organ*" (1968) doivent être rapportées à l'enquête sur les maisons victoriennes et au paradigme des ruines historiques, comme *Message from the Interior* l'établit clairement en associant les deux premières images mentionnées ci-dessus à des vues d'architecture abandonnée ou délabrée, d'ornements défaits, et de lieux domestiques très vétustes. Ce versant de l'oeuvre d'Evans n'est pas seulement l'indication du retrait d'un homme vieilli, fatigué, mais l'effet de la compulsion -tenue, mesurée- du collectionneur qui cherche partout, chez les autres, les signes de sa mélancolie. L'intérieur, avec ses arrangements 'décoratifs', n'est pas tant un lieu-refuge que la figure d'une histoire *retenue*, au bord de l'effacement produit par l'oubli et la fatalité du banal (de l'égalisation normalisée).

Aucun artiste, et Dan Graham pas plus que Walker Evans, ne peut, à moins de se soumettre à la mélancolie, réduire cette fatalité à un processus d'aliénation sociale, dont il serait le témoin indifférent (objectif), ou 'critique'. Le rire satanique est la solution du héros romantique. Mais celui qui ne peut pas -ou ne veut pas- se faire l'avocat du diable, est nécessairement exposé au pathos ambigü des signes individualisés (décoratifs, formalisés) du commun, surtout s'il s'interdit de recourir à un universel abstrait de ses déterminations historiques. La double lecture du Pop Art aboutit chez Dan Graham à ce pathos, que les images photographiques précipitent et tiennent à distance simultanément. Si Walker Evans a pu inventer l'image de l'Amérique, dont hérita le Pop Art, c'est parce qu'il s'était donné cette capacité de transformer sa passion mélancolique en un lyrisme attaché -à distance- au sort du commun.

1 A la demande de Jeanne Siegel qui dirigeait les programmes sur l'art de la radio newyorkaise WBAI, Lucy Lippard avait réuni le 8 mars 1970 quatre artistes - Douglas Huebler, Dan Graham, Carl Andre et Jan Dibbets - dont le point commun était d'avoir utilisé, d'une manière ou d'une autre, le langage (*"four visual artists who have used words a way or another"*). Le texte de cette rencontre a été publié par Lucy Lippard dans *Six Years: The Dematerialization of the Art Object*, New York, Praeger, 1973, pp. 155-159.

2 Dan Graham a exprimé cette idée à plusieurs reprises, en soulignant chaque fois que ses travaux pour les magazines étaient à la fois une radicalisation du Pop Art et une transformation du minimalisme par sa schématisation et sa mise en situation critique. Voir en particulier "My Works for Pages: A History of Conceptual Art", in *Dan Graham*, cat., Art Gallery of Western Australia, Perth,1985, pp. 8-11. "Si l'art 'minimal' a tiré sa signification de l'idée que la galerie constitue un support objectif, le 'pop' art, lui, a tiré la sienne des images du monde médiatique environnant. Le Pop Art voulait contester l'idée de qualité attachée aux beaux-arts, en utilisant les composants de la culture de masse. Les images du pop repassaient alors, par l'intermédiaire des magazines, dans la culture populaire, dont il devenait de ce fait même le commentaire ironique. Le pop montrait aussi qu'il était possible d'instaurer un rapport dialectique entre les médias d'information, les magazines par exemple, et le système de l'art. Autrement dit, qu' une oeuvre pouvait fonctionner à la fois comme langage artistique et comme langage populaire médiatique, en commentant et en mettant en perspective leurs hypothèses respectives. J'ai réalisé, pour des pages de magazine, des travaux qui étaient à la fois autonomes et dépendants de l'ensemble de l'information publiée dans le magazine.(...)"*Schema*" (mars 1966) reste le plus 'absolu ' ('*absolute*') de ces travaux. Plusieurs exemplaires de cette pièce ont été publiés, dans différents magazines, et toujours sous la forme d'une page isolée.(...) Les magazines d'art, traditionnellement, reproduisent en seconde main de l'art qui existe d'abord, sur le plan phénoménologique, dans les galeries. A l'inverse "*Schema*" n'existe que par sa présence dans la structure fonctionnelle du magazine, et son exposition dans une galerie n'aura de valeur que de seconde main.(...)Je voulais faire du 'pop' art qui soit littéralement accessible (ce qui figurait déjà dans l'idée de Warhol de remplacer la qualité par la quantité, selon la logique de la société de consommation). Je voulais trouver une forme artistique qui ne pourrait être ni reproduite ni exposée dans une galerie ou dans un musée, et je voulais réduire l'objet 'minimal' à une forme bidimensionnelle qui ne soit ni de la peinture ni du dessin, et pas nécessairement d'ordre esthétique: d'où l'idée de l'imprimé, qui représente de l'information reproduite à grande échelle et accessible à tout le monde." Au cours d'un entretien en 1988 avec Eugenie Tsai, in *Robert Smithson: Drawings*, cat., Münster-Sorø-München, 1989-90, pp. 8-23, Dan Graham insiste sur l'idée de l'accessible-jetable (*disposable*) dans ses premiers travaux ("*Magazine Pieces*"), comme chez les artistes (Flavin, LeWitt notamment) qu'il avait présentés dans l'éphémère John Daniels Gallery (octobre 1964-juin 1965): "A la fin de son exposition, Sol LeWitt m'avait demandé de me servir de sa pièce comme de bois à brûler; c'est une chose qu'il n'a jamais répétée depuis, mais à ce moment-là la question de la valeur ne l'intéressait absolument pas.(...) Personne ne pensait que tout ça avait la moindre valeur; on ne pensait pas comme ça, à l'époque. Une des idées-clé des années soixante, dans les vêtements, dans la mode, et aussi dans la musique rock, était cette idée de la chose qu'on prend et qu'on jette ('*disposable*'). Je me contentais donc de faire quelque chose que l'on puisse prendre et jeter; la production ne m'intéressait pas. Je n'ai jamais pensé qu'on puisse mettre ce type de travail dans un musée; j'étais totalement contre."(op. cit. p. 8).

3 Le premier essai publié de Smithson, en 1965, consacré à Judd, contient déjà cette interprétation. Voir "Donald Judd", *7 Sculptors*, cat. Institute of Contemporary Art, Philadelphia,1965, pp. 13-16, repris dans *The Writings of Robert Smithson*, anthologie établie par Nancy Holt, New York, New York University Press,1979, pp. 21-23. Smithson interprète les structures de Judd comme une spéculation sur la matière, sur la forme de la matière (*the very form of matter*) et remarque: "Judd a inversé les données de la réalité moderne (*Modern Reality*) de la même manière que les artistes maniéristes du seizième siècle avaient inversé les données de la Renaissance classique (*Classic Renaissance*). C'est ainsi que Judd a découvert une nouvelle sorte d' 'architecture', même si ce phénomène d'inversion donnait l'impression que son 'architecture' était constituée d' 'anti-matière'. Peut-être que 'matière première' et 'anti-matière' sont une seule et même chose." Dan Graham rappelle que Judd n'a pas du tout apprécié cette interprétation ("Judd n'a pas aimé le texte, il l'a détesté, même."). Smithson a "inventé Judd (dans cet essai) comme Borges invente un personnage de fiction." La divergence entre les deux artistes reflète le partage de l'art d'avant-garde américain des années soixante entre les minimalistes et conceptuels attachés à une morale puritaine, et proches de la Nouvelle Gauche, d'un côté, et les artistes pop, de l'autre, plus proches du '*rock and roll*' et de la culture '*fun*'. Smithson, selon Dan Graham, "venait beaucoup plus du pop art, et il aimait se faire l'avocat du diable. C'est là son côté maniériste, en fait, puisque les maniéristes ont adopté cette position vis à vis des valeurs de la Renaissance. Les minimalistes ne pouvaient pas comprendre; ils ne pouvaient pas être des maniéristes. Voilà où commence le désaccord de Smithson avec Judd. Il faisait entrer Judd dans un moule, et qu'il ait eu raison ou non sur le plan historique, Judd n'entendait pas les choses de cette façon et il a réagi en moraliste. Même s'il était, je dirais, de droite, il reste un idéaliste et un moraliste dans sa manière de réagir."(Entretien avec Eugenie Tsai, op. cit., note 2, p. 14.)

4 On sait qu'il en alla différemment: les éditeurs d'*Arts Magazine* substituèrent aux images de Dan Graham une photographie de Walker Evans, "*Wooden Houses, Boston*", de 1930, reproduite dans le livre de 1938, *American Photographs,* cat. Museum of Modern Art, New York, qui avait été réimprimé en 1962. *Projected Art* fut présenté en novembre 1966 au Finch College Museum of Art, New York, par Elayne Varian. Dan Graham fut, semble-t-il, dans l'exposition, le seul artiste qui projeta des diapositives. Il faudrait replacer cette initiative dans la longue histoire des usages de la diapositive (*transparency*) comme outil pédagogique - notamment dans l'étude et l'enseignement de l'architecture, depuis Frederick Henry Evans au tournant du siècle - et comme possibilité d'agrandissement d'une photographie servant de modèle pictural (Lichtenstein, Richter, les photoréalistes). Au moment de Projected Art, personne dans le milieu de l'art ne considérait plus une image diapositive couleur comme une fin en soi. Il n'en était pas ainsi au début du siècle - après l'invention des plaques autochromes par les frères Lumière - dans les cercles de la Sécession photographique américaine (Stieglitz, Steichen) et du pictorialisme international. On peut également rappeler que les photographes de la FSA (*Farm Security Administration*), dans les années trente, ont produit, avec le nouveau procédé du Kodachrome apparu en 1935, quelques centaines de diapositives en couleur, parfois comparables à celles de Dan Graham, mais qui avaient été complètement négligées jusqu'à leur redécouverte récente par Sally Stein dans les archives de la Library of Congress de Washington. A la fin des années soixante Dan Graham n'avait aucun intérêt - et n'en a pas plus aujourd'hui - pour l'histoire de la photographie, mais les autres références mentionnées ci-dessus lui étaient familières. Il associait également la projection lumineuse de diapositives aux néons de Flavin et s'intéressait, comme l'ont prouvé ses travaux ultérieurs, à l'idée de 'transparence' (du verre) contenue dans l'image projetée (*transparency*).

5 Il faut distinguer l'article de *Arts Magazine,* H o m e s f o r A m e r i c a , de l'oeuvre "*Homes for America*" réalisée ultérieurement, en 1970-1971, comme une reconstitution de la maquette originale de l'article, par l'atelier d'imprimerie du College of Art and Design de Nova Scotia, Halifax; reconstitution accompagnée de nombreuses variantes, dont le double panneau de la collection Daled, reproduit ici même page 132, où figurent des vues avec personnages prises en 1967, c'est à dire après l'article. Cette distinction est nécessaire si l'on veut tenir compte de la position anti-art dont ressortit le choix du '*disposable*' dans les "*Magazine Pieces*". Mais un tel choix était intenable, parce qu' inconciliable avec la complexité et les exigences de la fiction critique texte-images. Dan Graham voulait à l'origine publier dans un magazine comme *Esquire* et a dû se contenter d'une revue d'art qui n'a, elle-même, pas respecté son projet. En fait, dès le départ, ce projet était, par sa complexité même, irréductible à une consommation immédiate, et donc vouée à une réalisation différée, sous une forme 'artistique'. Le principe du '*disposable*' - dont participe effectivement tout article de consommation - ne pouvait être qu'un modèle pour un article de fiction critique, et un idéal intenable, fictif, pour l'artiste Dan Graham. Il faut ajouter à cela la force de la nécessité. Après 1970, au moment où il réalise "*Homes for America*", Dan Graham découvre, comme tous les artistes de la mouvance conceptuelle présentés par John Gibson à New York, que la photographie, sans se rattacher complètement aux beaux-arts, est une possible source de revenus.

6 "Judd possède une collection labyrinthique d'imprimés (*printed matter*) qu'il 'regarde' souvent, au lieu de les lire. C'est comme s'il considérait une équation mathématique qu'il pouvait traduire ensuite, visuellement, en une progression métallique d'intervalles structurés. Dans ce contexte, mieux vaut penser l'idée de l' 'imprimé' à la manière de Borges, comme 'L'univers (que d'autres appellent la bibliothèque)', ou, en d'autres termes, comme une 'bibliothèque de Babel' infinie."Holt, op. cit., note 3, p. 15.

7 Le titre original du texte était "A Tour of the Monuments of Passaic, New Jersey". Le texte est repris dans Holt, op. cit., note 3, pp. 52-57. Smithson présente ses photographies de monuments comme les images arrêtées (*stills*) d'un film. Le premier monument, un pont sur la rivière de Passaic, donne le ton: " Le soleil de midi cinéma-isait le site, donnant du pont et de la rivière une image *(picture)* surexposée. Avec mon Instamatic 400, j'avais l'impression de photographier une photographie. Le soleil est devenu comme une ampoule lumineuse monstrueuse qui aurait projeté sur ma rétine, à travers mon Instamatic, plusieurs séries distinctes d'images arrêtées *(stills)*. J'avançais sur le pont et c'était comme si je marchais sur une photographie gigantesque, de bois et d'acier, et au dessous il y avait la rivière, comme un gigantesque film , sans rien à voir que du blanc défilant sans interruption."

8 La distinction entre les deux sens du 'monument' est bien établie par Françoise Choay dans "A propos du culte et des monuments", avant-propos de la traduction française du texte de Riegl, Aloïs, *Der moderne Denmalkultus*, de 1903 (*Le culte moderne des monuments*, Paris, Editions du Seuil, 1984, p. 11: "La notion de monument historique n'est pas un invariant culturel (...) Car si le monument, c'est-à-dire, (étymologiquement) l'artefact qui nous interpelle pour nous faire ressouvenir, fait partie d'un 'art de la mémoire' universel, qu'on trouve pratiquement dans toutes les cultures, l'invention du monument historique est solidaire de celle des concepts d'art et d'histoire. Elle appartient à l'Europe post-gothique qui a élaboré ce concept au fil d'un long travail, dont la première strate peut être repérée au Quattrocento."

9 Voir l'entretien de Huebler avec Irmeline Lebeer au moment de son exposition au Kunstverein Münster (décembre 1972-janvier 1973), *Chroniques de l'art vivant*, no.38, avril 1973, pp. 21-23: "Ma principale préoccupation était alors (au moment de "*Primary Structures*") de créer des sculptures tellement grandes qu'elles ne tenaient pas à l'intérieur d'un musée. C'est pourquoi je les ai installées en plein air. Or, les structures primaires ont ceci d'intéressant qu'elles deviennent réelles: un cube est aussi réel qu'une table ou une chaise. En posant à l'extérieur ces formes d'une réalité a b s o l u e, force m'était de constater qu'elles n'entretenaient pas avec la nature les mêmes relations d'harmonie que les statues, les nus, etc...mais qu'elles fonctionnaient comme des objets réels entrant en compétition avec tous les autres objets réels du monde extérieur. Je me rendis compte qu'à moins de les intégrer dans un cadre architectonique - un environnement spécialement conçu pour les accueillir - mes sculptures ne résistaient pas à une confrontation avec les arbres, le ciel, que la nature était plus puissante. Je pouvais, bien sûr, produire des formes plus grandes, des sculptures monumentales, mais en vérité, le monde n'avait pas besoin que j'ajoute encore des objets à ceux qui existent déjà. Cette expérience m'a incité à changer fondamentalement d'orientation."

10 Au cours d'un entretien avec Daniela Salvioni, *Flash Art,* no.152 (mai-juin 1990), pp. 142-144, Dan Graham remarque: "Je ne suis pas contre la monumentalité par principe. L' art conceptuel s'était intéressé au '*disposable*', à l'idée de l' oeuvre incollectionnable, contre l'appropriation historique et permanente par le musée. Du point de vue de l'architecture, en revanche, la monumentalité désigne le lieu, l'histoire. La signification des choses est d'autant plus ouverte que leur durée historique est plus longue. Ni moi ni le public ne décidons de cette signification. Je ne dis pas qu'elle est plus juste, je dis

simplement qu'elle est plus ouverte. Cette durée peut être assez longue pour que la signification de l'oeuvre se modifie et qu'elle puisse même s'altérer. "Cet intérêt pour le monument, opposé dans sa durée aux productions éphémères destinées à la consommation rappelle l'interprétation antivitaliste (la vie est consommation) de la culture artistique traditionnelle chez Hannah Arendt, pour qui l'objet d'usage et *a fortiori* l'objet d'art se distinguent fondamentalement de l'objet de consommation. Dan Graham ne s'exprimait pas ainsi à la fin des années soixante. On ne peut pas toutefois parler d'une rupture. Cette évolution correspond à une réévaluation de l'héritage moderniste, inspiré de la méthode d'interprétation historique - et non historiciste - de Walter Benjamin, appliquée au passé récent. Le modernisme a sans doute abouti au style International du capitalisme triomphant de l'après-guerre, mais il produit, dans ses contradictions mêmes, l'écart d'une actualité critique, si on le rapporte à ses modèles utopiques du temps des Lumières.
Dès 1967, Dan Graham avait pour la première fois souligné l'ambivalence durable de ces modèles, en observant la conjonction du modèle hippie et de l'utopie pastorale (et communautaire) qui, dans l'histoire du modernisme, accompagne, comme son double, l'idéologie du progrès technologique. Voir "Eisenhower and the Hippies", publié dans le numéro d'hiver 1968-1969 de la revue *0 to 9*, et repris dans *Dan Graham Articles*, cat. Stedelijk Van Abbemuseum, Eindhoven1977, pp. 23-26. Vingt ans plus tard, au cours d'un entretien avec Birgit Pelzer (*Dan Graham*, cat. ARC, Musée de la ville de Paris, Paris, 1987, pp. 33-38) Dan Graham résume sa position actuelle: "Walter Benjamin proposait de récupérer la mémoire historique. Parce que l'idéologie présente a effacé le passé, il faut le reconstruire comme s'il rejaillissait. Le modernisme était contre les monuments. Moi, je suis tout à fait pour: les monuments marquent le temps. (...) Les monuments sont liés à la mémoire de la ville et, moi, je crois que ce qui m'intéresse le plus pour le moment, c'est de récupérer le passé récent, la mémoire historique du passé récent. Concernant les années soixante, une période que la plupart des gens en vie ont pourtant vécue, c'est comme si la mémoire collective était frappée d'amnésie. Les médias doivent continuellement effacer le passé immédiat pour fabriquer leur utopie du moment présent." C'est précisément cette utopie du moment présent que Dan Graham a toujours cherché à pervertir, d'abord en feignant de s'y conformer (modèle du *'disposable'*) puis en jouant, dans ses performances et ses installations de miroirs et de vidéos, de toutes sortes de perturbations chronologiques (*via* notamment les délais de l'enregistrement). "Le présent, dit-il à Birgit Pelzer, n'existe pas. L'impossibilité d'atteindre ce présent absolu, c'est l'échec de l'idée moderniste selon laquelle on peut faire table rase."

11 "*Yesterday/Today*" est décrite dans l'anthologie, constituée par Benjamin Buchloh, des travaux vidéo et textes sur la vidéo de Dan Graham entre 1970 et 1978, *Video-Architecture-Television*, Halifax-New York, The Press of the Nova Scotia College of Art and Design, New York University Press, 1979, p. 42. L'année précédente, en 1974, Dan Graham avait déjà réalisé plusieurs installations à diffusion vidéo retardée dans des espaces divisés ("*Time Delay Rooms*"), qui produisaient à la fois une subversion systématique des données spécifiques de la vidéo (*"a present-time medium"*, distinct du cinéma) et une altération de la co-présence du public (comme de la présence à soi-même de chaque spectateur). "*Yesterday/Today*" introduisit toutefois un nouveau paramètre dans cette structure-piège: la spécificité du lieu architectural et de l'activité quotidienne, enregistrée, qui s'y déroule. Il s'agissait désormais d'articuler les disjonctions de l'espace vécu produites par l'altération du présent vidéo avec les données de l'environnement contemporain, en choisissant comme lieux d'intervention (d'installation) des structures architecturales particulièrement significatives. Comme l'a souligné Anne Rorimer ("Dan Graham: An Introduction", *Dan Graham Pavillons*, cat. Kunstverein München, 1988, p. 24), "*Picture Window Piece*", de 1974, représente, avant "*Yesterday/Today*", le premier pas dans cette direction. C'est à ce même tournant, en 1974-75, que se place le deuxième ensemble important de photographies - après celui de 1965-67- servant de repérages ou d'amorces aux installations vidéo et pavillons ultérieurs.

12 "*Video View of Suburbia in an Urban Atrium*" est décrite par Ann Rorimer, op. cit. supra, p. 26. Cette pièce illustre parfaitement la continuité des intérêts architecturaux de Dan Graham depuis "*Homes for America.*" Il faut d'ailleurs noter que plusieurs photographies de maisons de banlieue (pour une ou deux familles) datent de 1978. Très comparables aux images de 1965-66, elles s'en distinguent par une plus grande attention portée aux maisons isolées *(detached houses)*, avec leur morphologie propre, voire un aspect physiognomonique. De 1978 également date "*Alteration of a Suburban House*". Le texte de ce projet (irréalisable) se réfère explicitement aux maisons de verre individuelles construites par Mies van der Rohe et Philip Johnson à la fin des années quarante. Toutes les facettes du modernisme se concentrent donc pour Dan Graham dans la figure de la maison suburbaine.

13 Dan Graham emploie cette formule dans un entretien avec Brian Hatton en 1991 (dépliant publié à l'occasion de l'exposition à la galerie Roger Pailhas, Marseille, en juin-juillet 1991) pour caractériser la forme de ses pavillons: "Ce sont le plus souvent des clichés de l'architecture moderne. On a pu voir de la même manière il y a dix ans, chez Pelli ou d'autres, un retour à une sorte de panthéon à la Boullée-Ledoux, des grottes et aires de jeux pour enfants jusqu' à la Foire Universelle ou aux Nations Unies. Le cinéma à 360 degrés de la Géode, à la Villette, en est un exemple. C'est donc à toutes ces formes-type que je pense. D'autre part, bien que je ne fasse pas comme Venturi qui, littéralement, "va dans le sens" *("inflects toward")*, des choses de l'environnement, je me suis toujours intéressé à cette idée de "ce qui va dans le sens" *("inflection")*, à condition d'entendre le mot un peu différemment. Les matériaux et les formes vont dans le sens des derniers développements de la ville moderne, et dans le sens des clichés historiques sur lesquels elle a pu se fonder." Ces clichés de l'architecture moderne, Dan Graham les avait déjà évoqués dans son texte de 1979, "Art in Relation to Architecture/ Architecture in Relation to Art", *Artforum*, février 1979: pp. 22-29, à propos des immeubles de verre de Mies van der Rohe et de leur fonction d'image de marque pour les sociétés multinationales et le capitalisme américain:
"Le classicisme des tours de bureaux et des immeubles d'appartements en verre de Mies est devenu le nouveau modèle de la technologie américaine, en grande partie parce que le milieu américain des grandes affaires se sentait en mesure de l'exporter dans d'autres régions du monde. Le classicisme de Mies se fondait sur une soi-disant loyauté *(trueness)* à l'égard des matériaux (les matériaux étant donnés pour ce qu'ils étaient, plutôt que masqués par l'ornement), associée à une conception idéalisée, 'universelle', et complètement abstraite de l'espace. Ces structures modernistes devinrent très vite populaires auprès des agences des sociétés internationales (multinationales) du 'monde libre'."

14 Parmi les nombreuses références historiques de ses pavillons, Dan Graham a souvent mentionné la "hutte primitive" décrite par Marc-Antoine Laugier, dans un essai de 1753, comme l'archétype de l'architecture. Ce modèle spéculatif, caractéristique du primitivisme des Lumières, correspond à l'exaltation rousseauiste de la bonté de l'homme naturel opposée aux corruptions de la civilisation urbaine. Dan Graham l'a découvert à la fin des années 1970 chez des auteurs (Manfredo Tafuri, Léon Krier) engagés dans le débat post-moderne sur l'utopie urbaine. Cf notamment "Not Post-Modernism: History as against Historicism, European Vernacular in Relation to American Commercial Vernacular, and the City as Opposed to the Individual Building." *Artforum*, décembre 1981: pp. 50-59).
Les antécédents et la fortune critique du modèle de Laugier avaient été reconstitués quelques années plus tôt par Joseph Rykwert (*On Adam's House in Paradise*, New York - Chicago, 1972), comme la figure centrale du primitivisme architectural raisonné, dont ressortit largement le modernisme, y compris chez Gropius (quand il construit en 1921, dans la banlieue de Berlin, le *Blockhaus Sommerfeld*, influencé par les maisons de la prairie de Frank Lloyd Wright.)

15 "Not Post-Modernism....", op. cit., note 14, p. 57.

16 Dan Graham parle de *"dual reading"* à propos de Lichtenstein dans "Art in Relation to Architecture/ Architecture in Relation to Art", op. cit.,note 13. Il cite, à l'appui de sa thèse, les déclarations faites par Lichtenstein à Gene Swenson en 1963 sur le Pop Art et ses relations avec la culture de masse: "Je me suis intéressé aux caractéristiques selon moi les plus inquiétantes et menaçantes de notre culture, des choses que nous avons en horreur, mais qui nous affectent en même temps de manière forte. Depuis Cézanne, l'art est devenu extrêmement romantique et irréaliste, à force de se nourrir de lui-même . Il est utopique. Il a de moins en moins à voir avec le monde, il est introspectif - néo-zen, et tout ça. Ce n'est pas une critique, mais une simple observation. C'est dehors qu'est le monde; c'est là qu'il est. Le pop art regarde le monde; il accepte l'environnement tel qu'il est. Ce n'est ni bien ni mal, c'est différent - c'est un autre état d'esprit." Et: " Les héros des bandes dessinées sont du genre fasciste, mais dans mes tableaux je ne les prends pas au sérieux . Il y a là sans doute un sens , dans ce fait de ne pas les prendre au sérieux; c'est peut-être politique. Je les utilise pour des raisons purement formelles, ce pour quoi ces héros n'étaient vraiment pas faits...La signification du pop art est immédiate, liée à l'instant (of the moment), elle est vouée à disparaître - il s'agit de choses éphémères - et le pop se sert de cette "signification" éphémère, pour détourner l'attention de son aspect formel. Je pense que le temps rendra plus clair le parti pris formel de mon travail." Dan Graham résume: " Une oeuvre de Lichtenstein peut être à la fois de "l'art pour l'art" et une forme de représentation assimilable par la culture populaire. Les deux interprétations sont possibles." Il y a , en somme, une véritable ambivalence du Pop Art à l'égard des média, irréductible à une stratégie de distanciation critique qui l' apparenterait à certaines positions brechtiennes de la Nouvelle Gauche. Cette ambivalence a toutefois une portée critique - comme la distanciation intervient nécessairement par le simple effet du procédé artistique -, si elle est replacée et développée dans un contexte historique plus large que le champ restreint des beaux-arts, c'est à dire notamment mise en relation avec les enjeux plus clairement politiques de l'architecture. Dans tous les cas, Dan Graham, ne cherche pas la vérité (dans l'histoire de l'art) du pop art; il l'interprète pour en tirer un modèle. L'entretien Lichtenstein-Swenson prit place dans la série "What is Pop Art?" publiée en deux parties dans *ARTnews* novembre 1963, février 1964, repris dans l'anthologie de Carol Anne Mahsun,,*Pop Art: The Critical Dialogue*, Ann Arbor, UMI Resaerch Press,1989, pp. 111-115.

17 Alice Weiner: "Quand on voyait les photographies de Dan à cette époque, on avait l'impression de voir celles de Walker Evans, mais sans les gens." (entretien avec Chris Dercon, le 14 avril 1992). Dan Graham se rappelle que la parenté de ses images avec celles de Walker Evans lui avait été indiquée par Mel Bochner, qui avait d'ailleurs rencontré Evans (entretien avec l'auteur, le 27 juillet 1991).

18 C'est dans la série d'entretiens, "What is Pop Art?" mentionnée ci-dessus que Jim Dine parle de Walker Evans, après avoir parlé de la beauté des panneaux publicitaires *(billboards)* qu'il avait reconnue bien avant de les prendre pour modèles: "Ce n'est pas une idée originale - Walker Evans en avait déjà photographié en 1929. Simplement, le paysage nous serre de plus en plus près , et il nous faut lui tenir tête (*stand up to it*)." op. cit., note 16, p.115. La dernière remarque de Jim Dine pourrait être une définition de la 'picturalisation' du paysage opérée par un photographe quand il en isole une portion dans son viseur.

19 Allan Kaprow remarque: "Avec sa franchise, son objectivité apparente et son indifférence aux émotions personnelles, le Pop Art (dans l'ensemble) évoque un rêve des années trente/quarante lié à l'enfance des artistes. On est très proche de l'esprit des romans de Jack Kerouac. Les affiches lacérées de Villeglé, Hains et Rotella - qui voyaient l'Amérique de loin - , avec leurs réclames et leurs déesses ringardes frappées par le temps et les intempéries, rappellent les photos de Walker Evans d'il y a quelques années; les bandes dessinées et les productions de Lichtenstein reprennent l'iconographie et le style des années quarante..." "Pop Art: Past, Present and Future", *The Malahat Review*, juillet 1967, repris dans l'anthologie de Carole Anne Mashun, op. cit., note 16, pp. 61-74.

20 Sur ce point, voir Rosenthal, Nan,"Let Us Now Praise Famous Men: Warhol as Director", *The Work of Andy Warhol*, DIA Art Foundation Discussions in Contemporary Culture no.3, Garry Garrels (ed.), Seattle, Bay Press,1989, pp. 47-50.

21 Cette exemplarité d'Evans s'est établie, à travers de nombreuses médiations, comme l'héritage accompli d'un modèle américain de la photographie documentaire, apparu au XIXème siècle. En amont d'Evans, et comme un point d'origine, Lincoln Kirstein, dans la postface d' *American Photographs*, place Mathew Brady, portraitiste de Lincoln, à côté de ses homologues européens (Nadar, Cameron, Hill). Il note également: "Walker

Evans montre la civilisation contemporaine de l'Amérique de l'Est , et des territoires attenants , comme Atget montrait le Paris d'avant la guerre et Brady la Guerre civile." Dans la revue qu'il édita au début des années 1930, *Hound and Horn*, Kirstein publia, en 1933, un article de Charles Flato qui présente les images de la guerre de Sécession de Brady comme des indications exemplaires des "immenses possibilités de la simplicité et de la franchise". Un commentateur a remarqué récemment: "Sans nommer Stieglitz ou le pictorialisme, Flato oppose implicitement l'oeuvre de Brady à l'héritage de *Camera Work*." Cf. Trachtenberg, Alan, *Reading American Photographs: Images as History, Mathew Brady to Walker Evans*, New York, Hill & Wang, 1989, pp. 231-235. Quand il parle de Brady comme " du véritable inventeur d'un style mettant à jour des valeurs éphémères et universelles" , Plato retrouve évidemment les fameuses observations de Baudelaire sur la "composition double du beau" ("un élément éternel, invariable", et "un élément relatif, circonstanciel") , dans les premières pages du *Peintre de la vie moderne*, consacré à Constantin Guys (peintre-chroniqueur, notamment de la guerre de Crimée). Trente ans après les textes de Kirstein et de ses associés, quand John Szarkowski présente au Museum of Modern Art, New York, en 1967, l'exposition *New Documents* (qui rassemble Diane Arbus, Lee Friedlander et Garry Winogrand), le modèle documentaire à l'américaine est devenu le principe fédérateur du "modernisme" en photographie. *American Photographs* reparaît l'année même où Szarkowski prend ses fonctions au Museum of Modern Art de New York. Trois ans plus tôt est paru le livre de Robert Frank, *The Americans*, dont un premier choix d'images avait été introduit par Evans dans le numéro de 1958 de *US Camera Annual*. Sous le signe commun du 'document', une solide séquence généalogique dessine désormais la ligne de crêtes d'une photographie d'auteurs, au dessus de la masse des images anonymes où s'est formée et déposée la vérité du médium. En 1966, dans la brève postface de *Message from the Interior*, Szarkowski note, avec un grand sens de la balance rhétorique: " Le style d'Evans semble avoir l'évidence et le caractère anonyme des premiers daguérreotypistes, et pourtant la nature même de son imagerie - frontale, d'une concise simplicité, dépassionnée - n'appartient indiscutablement qu'à lui."

22 Dan Graham a mentionné plusieurs fois récemment l'importance du cinéma d'après-guerre dans la formation de son intérêt pour l'architecture. Cf. notamment un entretien avec Chris Dercon en mai 1991, *Forum International*, vol.II, no.9, septembre-octobre1991,pp.73-80. La référence au néo-réalisme (Rossellini, Antonioni) est apparue à plusieurs reprises au cours de l'entretien, inédit, que nous avons eu à Los Angeles le 27 juillet 91.

23 Godard a toujours insisté sur la nécessité de fonder la fiction sur des données documentaires. "*Deux ou trois choses que je sais d'elle" (1966)* - le film que Dan Graham mentionne le plus fréquemment - est inspiré d'une enquête, dans un magazine, sur la prostitution dans les grands ensembles de logements suburbains. Mais la relation document-fiction s'ouvre aussi sur la relation réel-imaginaire. A propos de "*Vivre sa vie*" (1962), Godard déclare, au cours d'un entretien dans les *Cahiers du cinéma*, no.138, décembre 1962: "Je suis parti de l'imaginaire et j'ai découvert le réel; mais, derrière le réel, il y a de nouveau l'imaginaire."; il parle de "théâtre-vérité", de "réalisme théâtral". Enfin, Godard a toujours conçu ses films comme des "essais". Leur part documentaire porte donc d'abord sur leur propre progression. A propos de "*Deux ou trois choses que je sais d'elle*", il note: "Je me regarde filmer, et on m'entend penser. Bref, ce n'est pas un film, c'est une tentative de film et qui se présente comme telle. Ce n'est pas une histoire, cela veut être un document." Jean-Luc Godard, *2 ou 3 choses que je sais d'elle*, Paris, Seuil/Avant-Scène, 1971, p.12.

24 Dans un ouvrage collectif publié à Londres en 1967 (Studio Vista), Stig Björkman note à propos de "*Deux ou trois choses que je sais d'elle*": "Dans le film on retrouve cette nouvelle forme de réalisme qui existe dans le nouveau roman : l'économie et la précision dans le détail; une vision qui ménage une perspective extrêmement profonde grâce à un montage très rapide des gros plans et des plans généraux." Cette remarque pourrait aussi bien s'appliquer au montage de "*Homes for America*". Selon la logique documentaire auto-réflexive décrite ci-dessus, l'ensemble d'habitation où vit l'héroïne du film renvoie, comme l'indique Godard lui-même, à l'idée d'être (ou vivre) ensemble, mais aussi à l'ensemble constitué par le film lui-même. "Il s'agit de décrire un 'ensemble'." L'architecture est la métaphore du film-description. L'objet décrit est le sujet du film. "On doit tout mettre dans un film". Et ce tout doit s'organiser comme un ensemble, habité, intérieur-extérieur, sujet-objet. "Je ne peux pas éviter le fait que toutes choses existent à la fois de l'intérieur et de l'extérieur. Ceci, par exemple, pourra être rendu sensible en filmant un immeuble de l'extérieur, puis de l'intérieur, comme si l'on entrait à l'intérieur d'un cube, d'un objet. De même une personne, son visage est vu en général de l'extérieur." op. cit., note 23, p.15.

25 Dan Graham aborde cette question au cours de l'entretien avec Brian Hatton, en 1991, op. cit., note 13.

26 "The Reappearance of Photography", *Hound and Horn*, vol. 5, no.1, octobre-décembre 1931, repris dans l'anthologie de Alan Trachtenberg, *Classic Essays on Photography*, New Haven, Conn., Leete's Island Books, 1980, pp. 185-188.

27 Le livre de Bourke-White et Caldwell semble avoir constitué un véritable contre-exemple pour Agee et Evans qui voyaient l'entreprise de leurs prédécesseurs comme "un double outrage: la propagande d'abord, puis le profit tiré à la fois de la propagande et de la condition des métayers." Cité par William Stott, *Documentary Expression and Thirties America*, Chicago, The University of Chicago Press,1973, reprint 1986, p. 222.

28 William Stott, op. cit. p. 320, cite cette remarque que lui fit Evans, quand il le connut dans les dernières années de sa vie: "J'ai une faiblesse pour les déshérités, pour les pauvres gens, mais je m'en méfie. Il faut que je m'en méfie, parce que cela ne peut pas fonder l'action artistique, ou esthétique. Sinon on devient sentimental, ou on cherche à 'améliorer la société'. Je ne crois pas que le travail d'un artiste puisse aller dans cette direction."

29 Evans dit exactement (propos rapportés par W.Stott, ibid.): *"The problem is one of staying out of Left politics and still avoiding Establishment patterns."*

30 Entretien avec Paul Cummings, 13 août 71, "Archives of American Art", cité par Alan Trachtenberg, op. cit., note 21, p. 237.

31 Cette formule introduit une note rédigée par Evans pour présenter une publication de ses portraits du métro (1938-1941). Elle leur est donc postérieure. Elle est publiée dans *Walker Evans at Work*, New York, Harper and Row, p.160, ouvrage réalisé en 1982 sous la direction de l'Evans Estate. Après cette remarque introductive, le texte enchaîne sur une description du projet: "Cette collection présente au moins une sélection impure d'individus - des êtres humains en un lieu et un temps donnés - produit selon le hasard approximatif du tirage au sort." Evans insiste sur la valeur conceptuelle de ce projet, dont la réalisation est une approximation et non un accomplissement. "Le lieu des prises de vue a été choisi uniquement pour des raisons pratiques, pour la contrainte que représentaient les conditions de travail. A vrai dire, la pureté absolue de cette méthode photographique - la méthode de l'enregistrement - n'a pas été atteinte ici, mais elle est donnée comme une visée inaccomplie..." La dernière remarque établit un lieu type, la ville, une situation - des gens assis dans le métro - et une date, 1940: "Ceci est une séquence possible d'hommes et de femmes dans la ville, qui viennent effectivement s'asseoir à cet endroit, sur ce banc de métro; et ceci en 1940, environ."

32 *The Machine-Age* est l'exposition organisée en 1927 par la revue d'avant-garde de Jane Heap, *The Little Review*. Mais l'expression désigne une réalité sociale qui dépasse largement l'horizon artistique. Les organisateurs de l'exposition ne s'y sont pas trompé, puisqu'ils montraient " de vraies machines, des pièces détachées, des appareils, des photographies et des dessins de machines, d'usines, de constructions, côte à côte avec des œuvres d'architecture, des peintures, des dessins, des sculptures, des constructions et des inventions réalisés par les artistes modernes les plus importants ." (texte reproduit, anglais/français, dans *Léger et l'esprit moderne: Une alternative d'avant-garde à l'art non-objectif (1918-1931)*, cat. Musée d'art moderne de la Ville de Paris, Paris, 1982, p. 216 et 218). Dans un texte du catalogue, "The Americanization of Art", le peintre 'précisionniste' Louis Lozowick, russe immigré (très au fait du cubo-futurisme et du constructivisme européens), remarque: " L'histoire de l'Amérique est un effort opiniâtre et incessant pour maîtriser les forces de la nature (...) l'histoire de gigantesques exploits techniques et de constructions mécaniques colossales." (cité par Richard Guy Wilson, dans *The Machine Age in America, 1918-1941*, cat. The Brooklyn Museum, New York,1986, p. 30). Au début des années vingt les premiers photographes de la machine (Paul Strand, Ralph Steiner, notamment) s'en étaient tenu à une vision plus mesurée (et plus individualisée) de la machine, même si Strand avait pu la désigner dans son fameux texte de 1922 comme "The New God". L'exaltation du grandiose, du colossal, par Lozowick, ne trouva son illustration photographique qu'à partir des dernières années de la décennie, particulièrement dans les images très massives de Margaret Bourke-White. Dans ses toute premières photographies de monuments industriels - dont la célèbre "*Armco Steel, Ohio*", de 1922 - Edward Weston avait surtout utilisé ce modèle architectural pour rompre avec le pictorialisme (comme Strand avait utilisé la machine), mais sa fascination fut de courte durée. Il n'en conserva qu'un certain sens de l'emphase descriptive, appliquée à des motifs de la culture pré-industrielle, chargés de résonances érotico-cosmiques. Evans, à la fin des années 1920, contribua quelque temps à l'apologie du modernisme technologique à l'américaine, mais encore plus brièvement que Weston et sans adopter la même solution pour en sortir. Il contribua par exemple au livre du poète Hart Crane, *The Bridge*, célébrant, en 1930, la beauté symbolique du pont de Brooklyn. Mais il s'intéressait aussi à un autre spectacle urbain: les enseignes (brouillées ou cassées) de Broadway, la foule dans les rues (ou sur la plage de Coney Island). Même ses images de gratte-ciels et de rideaux d'architecture ont une valeur d'étude et d'improvisation qui les distingue des vues plus accomplies et plus distinctes produites par les disciples de Strand, en les rapprochant de la veine, expérimentale, de la 'nouvelle vision' européenne, type Bauhaus. En 1971, toutefois, il renia sa première période d'activité (1928-31) dans son ensemble, en la déclarant trop 'romantique', c'est-à-dire - interprétons - trop liée au romantisme de la machine qui avait caractérisé les années 1920 et préparé au triomphe de l'industrialisme dans les années 1930. Cf. *Walker Evans at Work*, op. cit., note 31, p. 42. Enfin, il faut préciser que les aspects de la réalité urbaine qui - en dehors de l'architecture pseudo-cubiste des blocs d'immeubles - ont le plus retenu l'attention d'Evans, n'étaient pas indifférents aux idéologues de la ville moderne et de l'industrialisation. Lewis Mumford, par exemple, avait déclaré en 1931 que le métro et les "cheap popular lunchrooms" étaient les "deux sources du modernisme d'aujourd'hui." (cité par R.G Wilson, op. cit., supra, p. 30).

33 Comme il a été précisé plus haut (note 31), la date de ce texte est incertaine. Les auteurs de *Walker Evans at Work* publient toutefois une autre note, rédigée dans la même intention, datée de 1962. Il est tentant d'utiliser ce repère chronologique pour confirmer la comparaison avec Duchamp. C'est en effet en 1961, et seulement à cette date, que Duchamp, au cours d'une table ronde organisée au Museum of Modern Art, New York, au moment de l'exposition *The Art of Assemblage*, déclara: " Il est un point que je veux établir très clairement, c'est que le choix de ces 'ready-mades' ne me fut jamais dicté par quelque délectation esthétique. Ce choix était fondé sur une réaction d'indifférence visuelle, assortie au même moment à une absence totale de bon ou mauvais goût..." Cette déclaration s'explique largement par son contexte: Duchamp, comme il l'a fait à de nombreuses autres reprises, voulait se démarquer de l'appropriation esthétique de l'objet trouvé, du déchet industriel, etc., pratiquée par les artistes de l'assemblage (Néo-dadas et Nouveaux-réalistes). Il rappelait qu'une décision artistique n'est pas un simple acte d' "appropriation du réel" célébrant la beauté du "folklore industriel" (deux formules de Pierre Restany, le théoricien des Nouveaux-Réalistes). Il est peu probable que Walker Evans, compte tenu de ses propres intérêts et de ses liens avec le Museum of Modern Art, New York, n'ait pas pris connaissance de l'exposition de William Seitz et ne se soit pas interrogé sur la problématique dégagée par Duchamp (même s'il n'a pas entendu Duchamp en parler). Pour une discussion historique du principe d'indifférence duchampien et, particulièrement, du texte de la communication de 1961, "Apropos of 'Readymades' ", voir William I. Camfield, *Marcel Duchamp: Fountain*, Houston, The Menil Collection-Houston Fine Art Press, 1989, pp. 42-47.

34 La remarque exacte d'Evans est , en réalité: " Les portraits de ce livre ont été pris avec un appareil caché, placé entre les mains d'un espion repenti et d'un voyeur apologétique. Cependant, cette invasion grossière et impudente s'est vue légèrement adoucie et en partie atténuée par les années que j'ai laissé s'écouler. Ces images ont été faites il y a vingt ans, et délibérément préservées de la publication. Evidemment vous ne verrez parmi ces gens ni le visage d'un juge, ni celui d'un sénateur ou d'un président de banque. Ce que vous voyez là est à la fois sidérant, effrayant et clair: ce sont les dames et les messieurs du jury." (*Walker Evans at Work*, op. cit., note 31). Tout ceci a l'allure d'une fable morale: l'artiste reconnaissant sa culpabilité ("un espion repenti") et s'étant déjà sanctionné lui-même en ne publiant pas ses images pendant vingt ans, reconnaît - un peu ironiquement, comme il se doit de la part d'un dandy - l'existence d'un jury populaire et, donc, d'une loi morale commune. Il s'était d'ailleurs donné comme modèle Daumier (et Dickens), c'est-à-dire une autorité esthétique, mais aussi morale et politique: "La léthargie écrasante de la vie du métro newyorkais pourrait être un jour enregistrée par un Daumier ou un Dickens modernes. Cette situation est une mine d'or sociologique en attente d'un grand artiste." Cette référence à Daumier revient en 1971 dans un entretien avec Leslie Katz (paru dans *Art in America*, mars-avril 1971): Le "Wagon de troisième classe" de Daumier est en quelque sorte un instantané *(snapshot)* qui montre des gens effectivement assis dans une voiture de chemin de fer, en France au milieu du XIXème siècle. Il n'avait pas d'appareil photographique, mais il a saisi les gens sur le vif, comme un reporter..." (Entretien repris dans l'anthologie de Vicki Goldberg, *Photography in Print: Writings from 1816 to the Present*, New York, Simon and Schuster, 1981, pp. 358-369.)

35 Baudelaire, *Mon coeur mis à nu*, dans *Œuvres complètes*, vol. I, Paris, Gallimard, Pléiade 1975, p. 697.

36 Baudelaire analyse la teneur du "rire satanique" dans "De l'essence du rire", essai théorique résumant ses observations sur la caricature. Le "rire satanique" manifeste la nature contradictoire de l'homme, partagé entre "l'idée de sa propre supériorité" et l'évidence de sa "misère": "C'est du choc perpétuel de ces deux infinis que se dégage le rire." En somme, le tragique de Pascal, de l'"humanité déchue", passé par l'héroïsme romantique. Mais ce n'est pas la France qui en a produit le plus pur exemple (Hoffmann). Molière lui-même n'est pas assez "féroce", et, finalement aucun dessinateur caricaturiste n'est mentionné. Or, c'est précisément à Molière que, dans un autre texte, "Quelques caricaturistes français", Baudelaire compare Daumier: "Sa caricature est formidable d'ampleur, mais sans rancune et sans fiel. Il y a dans toute son oeuvre un fond d'honnêteté et de bonhomie." (*Œuvres complètes*, vol. II, pp. 532-543; 556-557). Il est difficile de parler de "bonhomie" à propos d'Evans, mais c'est bien du côté de Daumier que le place la typologie baudelairienne, et qu'il se place lui-même, laissant à l'humour noir surréaliste l'héritage du rire satanique, avec, parfois, - comme en témoigne peut-être *Many Are Called* -, quelques regrets.

37 Cité par Lesley K. Baier, dans *Walker Evans at Fortune 1945-1965*, cat. Wellesley College Museum, Wellesley, Mass., 1977-78, pp.10-11. Une double page de la publication des photos de Steiner dans *Fortune* (mai 1930) est reproduite dans *Photography Rediscovered: American Photographs, 1900-1930,* cat. Whitney Museum of American Art, New York, 1979, pp. 104-105.

38 Ralph Steiner, *A Point of View,* Middletown, Wesleyan University Press, 1978, pp. 104-105.

39 Entretien avec Leslie Katz, op. cit., note 34, p. 367. Au cours du même entretien, Evans précise: "Ansel Adams et Paul Strand sont tous les deux de très grands techniciens. Quelquefois ils le montrent trop. Ce qu'ils font avec un appareil photographique est parfait, et on se dit ouh la la, c'est vraiment parfait. Mais le contenu est obscurci."

40 Walker Evans, "Photography", *Quality: Its Image in the Arts*, Louis Kronenberger, Marshall Lee (eds.), New York , 1969, repris dans Jerôme Liebling (ed.), *Photography: Current Perspectives*, Rochester, Light Impressions, 1978, pp. 16-18.

41 Il faut bien entendre le mot 'établir' (*to establish*) dans ce double sens. Walker Evans, dans l'entretien de 1971 avec Paul Cummings (op. cit., note 30, p. 238), l'utilise ainsi, quand il déclare: " Il m'a fallu du temps pour établir mon propos " ("*That took time to establish*"), parlant de sa méthode, de son 'style', puis enchaînant sur la reconnaissance institutionnelle qu'il en a reçue.

42 Nous pouvons compléter ici des observations présentées plus haut (note 32). L'image reproduite dans ce livre à l'ouverture du cahier de reproductions consacré à Walker Evans est particulièrement significative. On peut y reconnaître facilement, dans ses parti pris anti-descriptifs - la zone noire, sans détails , au centre du réseau de structures métalliques - ce qui procède de l'expressionnisme sous-jacent à l'expérimentation constructiviste européenne, distinguant les recherches d'Evans en 1929 de la rigueur descriptive d'un Weston ("*Armco Steel, Ohio*" (1922)) ou d'un Charles Sheeler photographiant les usines de Ford Plant ("*Criss Crossed Conveyors*" (1927)). Plus tard, en 1947, Evans prendra une vue de Ford Plant (*First and Last*, New York, Harper and Row, 1978 p. 173) très similaire à celle de Sheeler, car il a renié le "romantisme" de ses premières études architecturales et s'adapte, avec quelque opportunisme, à la ligne *'design'* de la *'straight photography'*. Il continue de se distinguer, au demeurant, de la tendance faussement expressionniste de l'héroïsme industriel célébré par des auteurs comme Margaret Bourke-White.

43 Entretien avec Leslie Katz, op. cit., note 34, p. 362. "L'attention du collectionneur, remarque Evans, est d'abord retenue par un certain type d'objet, puis il en tombe amoureux, et il le recherche. J'ai remarqué, dans mon travail, que pendant un certain temps je ne m'intéresse plus qu'à un certain type de visage, ou de personne. On commence à sélectionner des visages, en les enregistrant. C'est compulsif, et on ne peut plus s'arrêter. Il me semble que tous les artistes sont des collectionneurs d'images."

44 Baudelaire, op. cit., note 36, pp. 556-557.

Doppelte lesart

Jean-François Chevrier

Auf Lucy Lippards Frage am Anfang eines Rundfunkgesprächs 1970: "Dan, du wurdest für einen Poeten gehalten, für einen Kritiker und einen Photographen. Bist du jetzt ein Künstler?", antwortete Dan Graham:" Ich definiere mich nicht selbst, jedoch glaube ich, daß alles was ich mache, vom Medium definiert wird. Vor drei oder vier Jahren habe ich Gedrucktes gemacht, gedruckte Dinge für Zeitschriften, Dinge, die sich der Photographie bedienen. Ich habe Dinge in all den Bereichen gemacht, in denen andere auch gearbeitet haben, und ich glaube, sie definieren sich von selbst."[1] Diese Aussage sollte ausreichen, um von vorne herein jede überflüssige Diskussion über den 'photographischen' Charakter eines Teils von Dan Grahams Werk auszuschließen. Sobald sich die nähere Bestimmung des Künstlers aus seiner Tätigkeit ergibt, die selbst wiederum durch die benutzten Instrumente bestimmt wird , wird auch die Frage, ob Dan Graham ein richtiger Photograph ist oder nicht, überflüssig. Er ist Photograph, wenn er sich der Photographie bedient, und das, was er in diesem Bereich macht, verfügt über eine relative Autonomie, die allerdings ausreicht, um eine spezifische Untersuchung zu rechtfertigen.

Doch 1970 war die Frage der künstlerischen Definitionen durch die neuerdings immer größere Anzahl von kategorie- und gattungsübergreifenden Tätigkeiten besonders lebhaft. Die von Lucy Lippard moderierte Begegnung von Carl Andre, Douglas Huebler und Jan Dibbets spricht in diesem Punkt für sich. Die vier Künstler wurden deshalb eingeladen, weil alle "irgendwie mit Wörtern arbeiteten". Dan Graham setzt sich genau wie Carl Andre gegen die sogenannte 'Konzept'-Kunst ab: "Ich denke nicht, daß ich Konzept-Kunst mache." Er weigert sich aber auch, sich im Grenzgebiet zwischen Wort und Objekt ansiedeln zu lassen. Er ist kein Künstler, der den Objekten die Wörter vorzieht. Er lehnt die 'Dichotomie Wort-Objekt' ab und hebt dagegen den Begriff Information hervor:"Ich habe mich nie für die Wörter oder die Syntax in der Poesie interessiert, sondern vielmehr für die Information. Ich wollte, daß die von mir geschaffenen Dinge einen besonderen Platz einnehmen und in einer gegebenen Gegenwart gelesen werden. Der Kontext ist dabei sehr wichtig. Ich wollte, daß sich meine Arbeiten mit dem Ort der In-formation befassen, welcher die Gegenwart ist."

Seit H o m e s f o r A m e r i c a (*Arts Magazine*, December 1966 - January 1967) hat die Photographie einen eigenen Platz in diesem strategischen Kontext eingenommen; und zwar als visuelle Information, die mit der schriftlichen Information kombiniert ist, in einem Raum - dem Raum der Seite oder Doppelseite einer Zeitschrift - , der als Ort der Erfahrung des Lesens gilt. Die Photographie ist ein Instrument der In-Formation, der formalen Gestaltung von Erfahrung , insoweit sie als Material für Montagen dient. Soviel für das Procedere,

das man immer, wenn man unbedingt will, 'konzeptuell' nennen kann. Eigentlich wäre Dan Graham in der Post-Pop-Art anzusiedeln. Er arbeitet unmittelbar über und mit den Medien, anstatt sich deren Ikonographie oder Effekte anzueignen, wie es die Pop-Künstler getan hatten.[2]

Es ging auch darum, Kunstkritik konkret und materiell mit künstlerischer Tätigkeit gleichzustellen, und somit die durch die getrennte Rezension (a posteriori) entstandene Verschiebung aufzulösen. Diese Verschiebung sollte in die Struktur des Werkes selbst gesetzt, versetzt werden. Als er H o m e s f o r A m e r i c a veröffentlichte, brauchte Dan Graham nicht einmal richtigzustellen, daß (es) " kein Kunstwerk sei", wie es Marcel Broodthaers auf den Bildbeschriftungen der Sammlung "*Der Adler vom Oligozän bis heute*" in Düsseldorf machen mußte (*Musée d'Art Moderne. Département des Aigles, Section des Figures*, Städtische Kunsthalle Düsseldorf, Mai-Juli 1972). H o m e s f o r A m e r i c a ist ein Zeitschriftenartikel. Der Kommentar ist keine nachträgliche Überlegung zu einem separaten (und vergangenen) Werk mehr. Er spiegelt nicht mehr die Autonomie der Kunst wider. Der Kommentar ist eine Ko-Extension zum Werk, das weder verleugnet noch negiert wird. Werk und Kommentar sind in einem einzigen Warhnehmungsraum gleichzeitig präsent, im Raum der Information. Die Information ist nicht mehr Information über, sondern In-formation von. Sie ist die künstlerische Form selbst.

Am Ende der sechziger Jahre stellt sich Dan Graham mehreren kritischen Herausforderungen gleichzeitig. Er möchte die Pop-Art zurück zu ihrem Ausgangspunkt (den Medien) bringen, die künstlerische Tätigkeit an ihre kritische Rezeption anpassen und auf diese Weise den Kunstgegenstand mit seiner gesellschaftlicher Produktion identifizieren. Die gesamte formalistische Doktrin zielt dagegen darauf, ihn in einen strikten Autonomie zu isolieren - sorgfältig vom Medienbereich getrennt . Er hat schließlich erkannt, daß Minimalismus (die 'primären Strukturen') immer nur einen Hyperformalismus darstellt. So will er die typische Form des Minimalobjektes auf die Architekturmodelle zurückführen (so versteht sich die serienmäßig angewandte Kubusform der Vorstadthäuser), in denen dieses Objekt eine ideale (Donald Judd) oder negative (Tony Smith) Umsetzung darstellt, während der ganze verschleiernde Diskurs um das Kunstobjekt diese Verbindung eben negiert.

Als H o m e s f o r A m e r i c a Ende 1966 erscheint, hat Robert Smithson bereits in seinen ersten kritischen Texten, insbesondere in seiner wenig orthodoxen Interpretation der 'Architektur'-Modelle eines manieristischen Judd [3], diese Kontextualisierung des Minimalismus unternommen. Dan Grahams Strategie ist gleicher Ordnung und vielleicht radikaler, denn er ist zu dieser Zeit keineswegs versucht (er hat auch nicht die Möglichkeit) plastische Objekte herzustellen und hatte bisher nur verbale Strukturen und photographische Bilder geschaffen. Einige Monate zuvor hatte er nämlich an der

Ausstellung Projected Art teilgenommen, wo er tatsächlich Dias von Vorstadthäusern zeigte, sprich projizierte - genau diese Bilder hätten H o m e s f o r A m e r i c a illustrieren sollen.4 Nach einer Logik der Fiktion, die selbstverständlich sofort mit "Konzeptkunst" assoziiert wurde, um deren Spezifität zu reduzieren, wurde aus dem Artikel für die zeitschrift *Arts Magazine* das Werk *"Homes for America"*, als die Arbeit eines Kunstkritiker Photographen oder eines Photographen Architekturkritiker, oder noch besser eines Minimalkünstlers, der Kritiker und Photograph ist, der beschlossen hat, kein plastisches Objekt herzustellen, so wie es Architekten gibt, die beschlossen haben, nicht zu bauen.5 In "Entropy and the New Monuments", das etwa sechs Monate vor H o m e s f o r A m e r i c a veröffentlicht wurde, hatte Smithson in den Strukturen von Judd, Morris, LeWitt und Flavin die negativen Eigenschaften der Plattheit [vapidity] und Monotonie [dullness] der suburbanen Umgebung erkannt . Er stellte sie ebenfalls mit den visuellen Modellen aus der endlosen "gedruckten Materie" [printed matter] der Galaxie Gutenberg gleich, die Mc Luhan beschrieben hatte.6 Als Neoromantiker stellt Smithson das Monument (und seine Funktion des Gedenkens) auf die Probe der Zeit. Er spricht von den "instant monuments" von Flavin; seine Beschreibung der Paradoxie der "neuen Monumente" evoziert unweigerlich die photographische Aufzeichnung: "Sie sind nicht gebaut, um die Zeit zu überdauern, sondern um sich ihr zu widersetzen. Sie haben eher an einer systematischen Reduzierung der Zeit auf Bruchteile von Sekunden teil, als an der Darstellung der langen Zeiträume von Jahrhunderten. Vergangenheit und Zukunft befinden sich beide in einer objektiven Gegenwart." In dem ein Jahr später erschienenen Aufsatz "The Monuments of Passaic" (*Artforum*, December 1967) illustriert Smithson mit Photographien, die er während eines Ausfluges in seine Heimatstadt aufgenommen hatte, eine Erzählung, die eine Erinnerung an eine Große Tour in Italien parodiert.7 Er spielt hier mit der Zweideutigkeit zwischen dem historischen Monument - als Überbleibsel einer des Gedenkens würdigen kulturellen Vergangenheit - und dem breiter aufgefaßten Wert des Monuments als Werk des Gedenkens, dessen Modell die dokumentarische Photographie ausmacht, und es dennoch auf einen optischen Schein ohne Konsistenz reduziert.8

Wie Smithson und früher als er, hat Dan Graham mit der Photographie auf eine neue Definition des Monuments hingearbeitet. Zur gleichen Zeit verzichtet Douglas Huebler auf die Herstellung von Objekten und er unternimmt konzeptuelle Aktionen, bei denen die Photographie verwendet wird, nachdem er durch seine Teilnahme an der Ausstellung Primary Structures (Jewish Museum, New York,1966) zu dem Schluß gekommen ist, daß ein Kubus genau so "real" sein kann wie jeder andere Gebrauchsgegenstand - ein Tisch, ein Stuhl...-, daß er aber im Freien in monumentalem Maßstab nicht errichtet werden kann, ohne dabei einem erdrückenden Vergleich mit der Natur ausgesetzt zu sein.9 Auf diese Schwierigkeit ist Dan Graham nie gestoßen; es zog ihn auch nie zu den unberührten Plätzen einer nicht urbanisierten Natur.

Smithson hält dem Monument aus der Vergangenheit, der Verkörperung eines historischen Ideals, die Erschöpfung dieses Ideals in dem 'no man's land ' der Galerien und der para-urbanen Räume entgegen. Diese Erschöpfung aber ist grandios, sie läßt sich mit geologischen Phänomenen messen und schafft das Fundament für einen neuen Archaismus . Für Dan Graham unterlag das Monument schon immer der Reduzierung - Miniaturisierung und Entmaterialisierung -, des photographischen Bildes, das daher ein effektives Modell darstellt. Er hat also im allgemeinen nie gegen das Monument gearbeitet, auch nicht gegen das urbane Monument im Besonderen.10 Seine ersten Glaspavillons entstanden Ende der siebziger Jahre, nach den Performances, den Videoarbeiten und den Spiegelinstallationen, als eine notwendige und logische Erweiterung der kritischen Erkundung spezifischer urbaner Strukturen, die er mit der Photographie begonnen hatte.

Hier sollten wir auf die ersten Photographien zurückgreifen, die er 1965/66 außerhalb von New York, in New Jersey aufgenommen hatte. Sie weisen schon die Parameter einer Dialektik der sozio-psychologischen, auf gesellschaftlichen Einteilungen beruhenden Wahrnehmung auf, wie sie später entwickelt wurden. In einer Galerie projiziert, bringen die Dias - als Projektion - ein Draußen in den reservierten Raum eines unbefleckten, 'weißen Kubus' herein. Dieses Außen besteht aus einer spezifischen Information, die sich durch eine doppelte Verschiebung auszeichnet: an die Peripherie von New York (New Jersey), und in die unmittelbare Vergangenheit der Nachkriegszeit, in der das Bauprogramm der 'tract houses' erstellt wurde, und die auch der frühen Kindheit des 1942 geborenen Dan Graham entspricht. Das nahe Woanders - in Zeit und Raum - ist das Zeichen der photographischen (dokumentarischen) Gegenwart, die aus diesem Grunde als Vorbild für die weiteren Arbeiten galt. Es genügt in der Tat allein an die Disposition der Performances und Videos der siebziger Jahre, bei denen die Gegenwart, hic et nunc, der Aktion (oder der Rezeption) ununterbrochen verstellt wird durch das Daneben der Spiegelung und durch das unmittelbare Vergangene der Aufnahme zu denken. In *"Yesterday/Today"* von 1975 begleitet eine Tonaufzeichnung der nahen Vergangenheit (gestern) das Eindringen des Videos vom Daneben (von dem, was im Nebenraum passiert) in den aktuellen Raum des Betrachters.11 Fünf Jahre später (1979/80) führt *"Video View of Suburbia in an Urban Atrium"* wieder das nahe Woanders des Vorortes in einen privilegierten urbanen Raum ein.12

Eine andere Videoinstallation *"Edge of the City"* (1981) bezeichnet/zeigt auf genau das Verhältnis von Vorort und Stadt. Zu diesem Zeitpunkt hat sich aber der Erkundungsbereich Dan Grahams beträchtlich erweitert. War der suburbane Rand sein erstes historisches Thema, so untersucht er nun einen anderen Moment der modernistischen Utopie. Die nahe Vergangenheit hat sich verschoben: nun sind es die sechziger Jahre, die Zeit der ersten Atrien in den Glasbauten der multinationalen

Unternehmen. Während die Postmoderne im Namen aller nostalgischen 'revivals' die Geschichte der Moderne verleugnet, entwirft und baut Dan Graham Pavillons ("*Pavilions*") und bedient sich dabei der banalisiertesten, abgewerteten typologischen Modelle des internationalen Stils. Er spricht selbst von "Klischees moderner Architektur".[13]

Das Denken Dan Grahams um 1980 - wie es zwei besonders entwickelte, in *Artforum* erschienene Texte beweisen ("Art in Relation to Architecture/ Architecture in Relation to Art", Februar 1979, sowie "Not Post-Modernism...", Dezember 1981) - geht im wesentlichen von historischen Gegebenheiten aus, ohne jedoch dabei die psycho-soziologischen Modelle aufzugeben, die seine bisherigen Experimente leiteten. Von der Informations-Disposition geht er zum Architekturobjekt über, ohne dabei die axiale Frage nach der Wahrnehmung und dem Modus der Erfahrung (oder der Konstruktion) des Andersseins aus den Augen zu verlieren. Er greift - mit allem erworbenem Wissen aus Performance und Video - die historische Kontextualisierung des Minimalismus wieder auf, zu der er in "*Homes for America*" angesetzt hatte. Der offene, vervielfachte und barockisierte minimalistische Kubus wird nun mit der modernistischen Utopie der mit der Natur ausgesöhnten Stadt in Beziehung gesetzt, deren exemplarische karikaturistische Erscheinungsform im Zeitalter der Privatisierung des öffentlichen Raums eben die Atrien der Unternehmen [Corporate Atriums] sind.

Die Architektur-Plastik der "*Pavilions*", die als ein (kritisches) Monument der Utopie verstanden wird, ist eine Zusammenfassung der Fiktionen von Durchsichtigkeit (und der Spiegelungen) in der Glasarchitektur. Sie stützt sich aber auch - und vor allem - auf eine historische Analogie, die fernere Bezüge mobilisiert: der Pavillon stellt für die primitive Hütte , so wie man sie im 18. Jahrhundert erdachte - nämlich als Paradigma des originären Primitivismus der modernistischen Architektur - das dar, was das Atrium für die Tradition des malerischen Gartens, Vorbild der Stadtparks, bedeutet.[14]
Indem Dan Graham die Einteilung Stadt-Vorort wieder in die Geschichte der Dialektik Stadt-Natur aus der Zeit der Aufklärung eingliedert, erweitert er den engen Kontext des Minimalismus. Ab diesem Moment verfügt er über alle Anknüpfungspunkte, die er benötigt, um die beiden wesentlichen Bestimmungen des minimalistischen Modells konkret zu artikulieren: die modernistische Architektur, die sich in Amerika mit dem Triumph des internationalen Stil verbreitet hat, einerseits, und die Pop-Umgebung in den Vororten andererseits. Wie es "*Alteration of a Suburban House*" 1978 andeutete, reflektiert das konstruierte Kunstobjekt (der Pavillon) - sowohl im wahrsten Sinne des Wortes wie auch auf der Ebene der kritischen "Reflexion" - die zeitgenössische Umgebung und seine historischen Modelle . Die urbane Utopie der Hochhäuser mit ihren barockisierenden Geschwülsten (den Atrien) ist in der Tat ein Resümee, oder eine Reflexion im Kleinen, dieser Pop-Welt der Vororte, in denen sich ein gemischtes 'up to date' von Stadt und Natur vollzogen hat,

symbolisiert durch die wuchernden Anzeichen von Kommerz , Überfülle und Konsumgesellschaft.

In aller Logik - die Welt der uns umgebenden Pop-Zeichen bildet ja seit den sechziger Jahren den tatsächlichen Kontext der modernistischen Utopie -, hat Dan Graham das Prinzip seiner eigenen Konstruktionen anhand einer Interpretation der Pop-Art und deren kultureller Ambivalenz, bei Lichtenstein und vor allem bei dem Architekten Robert Venturi, erarbeitet. Ein Auszug aus "Not Post-Modernism..." erläutert diesen Gedanken: "Venturi hat, wie alle eher traditionell [academic] arbeitenden Pop-Künstler die Massenkultur [popular culture] nie nur in ihren eigenen Grundsätzen akzeptiert, sondern er hat sie stets mit einer formalistischen und architekturhistorischen Auffassung verbunden, die der populären Auffassung eine dialektische Perspektive gab. Ein Gebäude von Venturi, Bauch und Scott Brown kann sowohl der 'großen' Kunst wie auch den vergänglichen Produktionen der Massenkultur zugeordnet werden. Beide Lesarten sind korrekt. Wegen ihrer im Sinne des populären Codes scheinbaren Vergänglichkeit, kann solch eine Arbeit nicht unmittelbar in die akademische Architektur eingegliedert werden. Anderseits verbietet es ihre Verankerung in der 'großen' Architektur, sie der Massenkultur zuzuschreiben. Dadurch, daß das Werk sich nicht leicht einer Position zuordnen läßt, kann es beide Wertsysteme, das formale und das historische, die Massenkultur und die Architektur von innen heraus (und nicht als Gegenüberstellung) in Frage stellen." [15]

Mit denselben Wörtern beschreibt Dan Graham die Ambivalenz Lichtensteins betreffs der Massenkultur und spricht dabei von "doppelter Lesart" [dual reading]; gerade dieser 'Dualismus' - wie ihn Robert Venturi für sich in seinem 1966 erschienenen Buch *Complexity and Contradiction in Architecture* beansprucht - ermöglicht es ihm ein korrektes, da zwiespältiges Bild der Fortdauer der modernistischen Utopie in seinem degradierten, entfremdenden und unterdrückenden Gebrauch zu konstruieren.[16] Es geht nun nicht mehr darum, das modernistische Modell zu 'dekonstruieren'; es geht weder darum, mit Ironie die Zeichen der Massenkultur zu behandeln, noch, die mediatisierten Meisterwerke der Vergangenheit zu parodieren. Die kritische Korrektheit liegt in der Übersteigerung der historischen Widersprüche eines utopischen Modells, das zu einer Struktur der Entfremdung wurde. Sie rührt nicht so sehr von einer Diskriminierung (im etymologischen Sinne von Kritik), als vielmehr von der konstruktiven Dramatisierung der Zwiespältigkeit als Nebeneinander widersprüchlicher Standpunkte und Montage heterogener historischer Momente.

Die Richtigkeit und Schönheit der Photographien Dan Grahams seit 1965 haben etwas von diesen "doppelten Lesart", deren Prinzip sich aus der Pop-Art herauskristallisiert hat. Es sind gleichzeitig strenge Architekturbilder, die bis zur Abstraktion formalisiert sind und Zeitschriftenillustrationen ohne jeglichen Anspruch auf 'Kunst', vergleichbar mit der

ephemeren Produktion der Medien. Die Art, wie die Photographien heute gezeigt werden - in Form von Abzügen, die wie autonome Werke ausgestellt werden - führt dazu ihre anfängliche Zugehörigkeit zu der Pop-Kultur der Medien auszuradieren; diese Entwicklung entspricht aber der ästhetischen Forderung, die zum ersten Mal in den "Pavilions" abzulesen war, und zwar obwohl die "Pavilions"- es sollte daran erinnert werden - als "Klischees der modernen Architektur" definiert sind und somit ihre Beziehung zur Medienkultur der Markenzeichen aufrechterhalten.
Die Photographien können auch mit der Behandlung ähnlicher Themen in der zeitgenössischen 'kreativen' Photographie verglichen werden - beispielsweise mit dem dokumentarischen Geschwätz von Bill Owens in "Suburbia" (1973); dadurch wird bestätigt, daß sie tatsächlich das Merkmal ihrer doppelten Zugehörigkeit zur modernistischen Tradition (über den 'akademischen' Minimalismus) und zur Pop-Kultur beibehalten haben.

Sich 1965 für die Farbe ohne Eigenschaften des Dias zu entscheiden, setzte eine Ablehnung der Feinheiten des schönen Bildes, der koloristisch übersättigten Effekte und auch der Grauwertnuancen der Schwarz-Weiß-Photographie voraus. Dan Graham hatte damals eher die industriellen Neonröhren von Flavin im Sinne als die chromatischen Spiele der 'straight photography' in ihren verschiedenen Ausführungen (Helen Levitt, Eliot Porter, usw.), die letzten Endes alle mit dem Handwerklichen im Gegensatz zu dem Industriellen zu tun haben. Da er sich gleichzeitig der strengen Nüchternheit des Modernismus verbunden fühlte, wandte er sich ebenfalls von den überschwenglich kitschigen Bildern in den weit verbreiteten Zeitschriften à la Hollywood ab (die Überschwenglichkeit findet sich später in den Atriumbildern). Die Historiker der Photographie haben sich im Übrigen nicht geirrt, als sie ihn nicht in ihre großen geschichtlichen Übersichten aufnahmen; offensichtlich waren sie der Meinung, sein Anliegen sei auf einen unverbesserlichen Konzeptualismus zurückzuführen, d.h. auf eine Handhabung von Photographie, die sich nicht auf einen historischen Kanon reduzieren läßt, und die dennoch nicht an die typische 'Konzept-Photographie' à la Sol LeWitt erinnert.

Dan Graham hielt sich schon an das Prinzip der doppelten Lesart bevor er es benannte. Es reichte ihm aus, die Photographie streng in der Form einzusetzen, wie sie sich selbst definiert hat: zwischen den schönen Künsten und den Medien. Eine zweideutige Situation, die während der ganzen Zeit, als sich die moderne Kunst entwickelte und durchsetzte, anhielt, d.h. von 1850 bis zu den frühen sechziger Jahren, als Warhol und später Richter ihre ersten photographischen Bilder schufen. Die Zweideutigkeit wurde jedoch nicht aufgelöst. Warhol schien sich später für das Lager der Medien zu entscheiden und Richter bevorzugte allmählich das Abstrakte (behielt allerdings das photographische Modell als Kontrapunkt). Der amerikanische Photorealismus bestand allerdings darauf, mit einer zu perfekten Mechanik der Bildgestaltung, die unpersönliche Genauigkeit des photographischen Bildes zu steigern (oder zur Vollendung zu bringen). Indem Dan Graham die Photographie -auch als projiziertes Dia - als das, was sie ist, nämlich etwas zwischen dem Ausstellungsobjekt und dem Instrument der Medien, benutzte, enthüllte er die historische Stellung der Pop-Art: zwischen Modernismus - gleich der 'großen' Kunst) und Massenkultur. Genau an diesem Punkt fand er zurück zu dem Beispiel Walker Evans', der der Pop-Art vorangegangen war.

Nach aktuellen Zeugnissen scheinen die Künstler aus den Kreisen der Konzept-Kunst Ende der sechziger Jahre diese Verwandschaft erkannt zu haben.[17] Mehrere Künstler der Pop-Art oder aus ihrem Umkreis hatten allerdings schon am Anfang des Jahrzehnts Walker Evans als früheres Beispiel erwähnt, insbesondere seine Bilder von Werbeplakaten [billboards]. Jim Dine spricht davon in einem Gespräch mit Gene Swenson 1963.[18] Allan Kaprow erwähnt ihn im Zusammenhang mit den europäischen Decollagisten (Hains, Villeglé, Rotella) in einem Text, der die nostalgischen Nachklänge der Pop-Art mit ihren Bezügen auf die dreißiger und vierziger Jahre als die Jahre der Kindheit der Pop-Künstler betont.[19] Vier Jahre zuvor war die berühmte Hommage Warhols an Rauschenberg mit dem Titel "Let Us Now Praise Famous Men " des Kultbuches von James Agee und Walker Evans entstanden, in der er Familienphotos von Rauschenberg aus den dreißiger Jahren verarbeitete. [20] Letzteres Buch war übrigens 1960 neu aufgelegt worden, während American Photographs, das Katalogbuch der Evans-Ausstellung mit den von Jim Dine und Allan Kaprow zitierten Bildern im Museum of Modern Art, New York (1938), 1962 neu erschienen war.

Wenn man ergänzend hinzufügt, daß Many Are Called (Portraits aus der U-Bahn) und Message from the Interior 1966 erschienen sind, daß ebenfalls 1966/67 Garry Winogrand und Lee Friedländer gewissermaßen offiziell Evans' Erbschaft antreten durften, kann man zu dem Schluß kommen, daß die sechziger Jahre, das mit der Pop-Art eröffnete Jahrzehnt, auch jene Jahre wurden, in denen sich in der Kunst - via Photographie - ein gewisses Bild Amerikas durchsetzte, das in der reichen Kultur des Landes wurzelte, die seit den dreißiger Jahren mit Evans als leitender Figur dokumentiert wurde.[21] Gerade dies wollten die Herausgeber von Arts Magazine zum Ausdruck bringen, als sie Dan Grahams 'row houses' durch eine Reihe von Holzhäusern in Boston ersetzten, die Evans 1930 photographiert hatte das Titelbild der 1962 Ausgabe von American Photographs (Abb. S. 109)

In der zeit von 1965/66 kannte Dan Graham Walker Evans noch nicht; er ist etwas später auf ihn gestoßen, als sein Freund Mel Bochner ihm nach der Erscheinung von "Homes for America" American Photographs zeigte. Sein Interesse an der funktionalen Stadt- und Vorstadtarchitektur der Nachkriegszeit, in der die Umkehrung der modernistischen Utopie massiv in Verfremdung sichtbar wird, entstand aus einer direkten Wahrnehmung von New York und seinen Vororten. Neben dieser unmittelbaren Erfahrung spielten zwei künstlerische Modelle, die einander damals ähnlicher waren, als bei Walker Evans, eine große Rolle: der Minimalismus natürlich, aber auch der europäische Autorenfilm (Antonioni, Godard), geboren aus dem italienischen Neuen Realismus der Nachkriegszeit. Hier waren die Themen der modernen Stadt und ihrer Vororte als Stätten psychologischer Verwirrung und Heimatlosigkeit allgegenwärtig.[22] Man könnte sogar ohne weiteres den Aufbau von "Homes for America" in Zusammenhang bringen mit der dialektischen Dokumentarfiktion, die Godard systematisch einsetzte.[23]

In den Kreisen der New Yorker Avantgarde Ende der sechziger Jahre war es tatsächlich weit verbreitet, sich direkt auf den Film zu beziehen. "Deux ou trois choses que je sais d'elle" (Zwei oder drei Dinge, dich ich von ihr weiß) von Godard erschien 1966 als die Verwirklichung eines Kinos, das die Aktualität der Pop Art und des Nouveau roman mit einer dokumentarischen Dramatisierung verbindet, inspiriert vom Neuen Realismus.[24] In dieser Zeit hielt sich Walker Evans ganz von den Kreisen der Avantgarde fern. Es ist nicht nachweisbar, daß er von der Entwicklung des europäischen Films seit der Nachkriegszeit Kenntnis genommen hatte. Man darf jedoch daran erinnern, daß sein Freund James Agee von 1941 bis 1948 ein aufmerksamer Beobachter dieser Entwicklungen war. Er schrieb für die Zeitschrift der amerikanischen Linken, The Nation, Artikel über Rossellini, Vittorio de Sica oder Georges Rouquier ("Farrebique"), wie es in Frankreich André Bazin systematischer tat. Wesentlich ist ist in jedem Fall, daß es in den sechziger Jahren tatsächlich eine wirksame Übereinstimmung gab zwischen dem 'realistischen' Film von Godard und Antonioni und dem Photoprojekt von Evans. Ihr Ergebnis war die Veröffentlichung der Portraits aus der U-Bahn Ende der dreißiger Jahre als Vervollständigung der American Photographs.

In einem Kontext des Anti-Liberalismus der radikalen, marxistischen Linken als auch des Anti-Humanismus des strukturalistischen Denkens (hier schließt die Wörtlichkeit eines Robbe-Grillets an) war Evans wegen seiner Bilder von Architektur und von urbanen Zeichen besonders angesehen. Dan Graham fand - wie alle - in American Photographs das Prinzip der Reproduktion von der Reproduktion der Pop Art wieder; er erkannte aber auch im besonderen wieder, was er selbst in der unmittelbaren Umgebung von New York (in New Jersey) beobachtet hatte: das Bild der Main Street - historische Realität und Paradigma des Vorstadturbanismus - die standardisierten Reihenhäuser entlang einer Eisenbahnlinie; summa summarum, die Architektur von Kommerz und Kommunikation in ihrer mechanisierten Form, typisch für die Gesamtheit der industrialisierten Welt und unter einem nationalen Aspekt charakteristisch für Amerika. Der mit der humanistischen Ideologie der Sozialdemokratie unter Roosevelt vergleichbare Teil des Werkes von Evans wurde abgelehnt. Die Bilder aus Let Us Now Praise Famous Man waren wie jedes Portrait mit einer Spur von Empathie

belastet. Sie erschienen damit vor allem der 'Mythologie' (Barthes) zu verwandt, die Edward Steichen in Family of Man im Museum of Modern Art, New York, New York, 1955 entwickelt hatte. In den Augen von Dan Graham (und seiner Freunde) ging jede 'normale' Photographie aus den Mystifikationen des liberalen Humanismus hervor. Graham macht aber auch deutlich, daß seine Ablehnung auch eine Verdrängung war. Was er in den sechziger Jahren von sich wies, ist vor kurzem im Projekt "Children's Pavilion" zusammen mit Jeff Wall wiederaufgetaucht.[25]

In Wirklichkeit war Evans' Haltung genauso zurückhaltend oder ambivalent hinsichtlich der rhetorischen Forderungen nach einem Konsens durch das Bild. Er hat nicht an Family of Man teilgenommen. Sein Blick auf die gesellschaftliche Wirklichkeit war zu distanziert, zu moralisch (oder puritanisch) und zu dandyhaft; er konnte nicht mit der sentimentalen Betonung und den spektakulären Effekten der Bildproduktion der Allgemeinheit harmonieren. Seit 1931 hatte er, zuerst in einem Essay veröffentlicht in Hound and Horn, den Reklameästhetizismus Steichens heftig kritisiert.[26] Als er einige Jahre später (zwischen 1935 und 1938) für die Farm Security Administration (FSA) arbeitete, distanzierte er sich vom Propagandaprogramm ihrer Teilhaber; mehr noch nahm er Abstand von dramatischer Übertreibung und vom Werben um positive Gefühle, so wie Margaret Bourke-White und Erskine Caldwell sie in ihrem Bestseller You Have Seen Their Faces von 1937 praktizierten.[27] Sein Widerwille war moralischer und ästhetischer Art. Der Stil von Margaret Bourke-White, der Starphotographin von Life (sie hatte das Titelbild der ersten Ausgabe von 1936 gestaltet), war in den Medien die genaue Entsprechung der architektonischen 'Monumentalordnung', welche die offizielle Bauweise der dreißiger Jahre charakterisiert. Diese wurde als Symbol der autoritären Macht und der organische Einheit eines Volkes verstanden. Aus der Boheme hervorgegangen, wie er selbst sagt, Bewunderer von Baudelaire und Flaubert, mußte sich Evans seiner Sympathie für die Benachteiligten versichern und sich weigern zu glauben, daß Kunst "die Gesellschaft verbessern" könnte.[28] Er blieb sein ganzes Leben lang im Konflikt mit dem Dilemma des Boheme-Künstlers: er mußte sich aus den Programmen der Linken heraushalten, indem er die Kreise des 'establishment' völlig mied.[29] Er konnte weder zum Volk gehören, noch sich zu seinem aufgeklärten (oder anteilnehmenden wie Bourke-White) Fürsprecher machen.

Die künstlerische Position, die aus diesem Dilemma resultiert, ist notwendigerweise mehrdeutig. Evans hat sie mehrfach in ähnlichem Wortlaut wie Grahams Aussage über die Pop Art formuliert. In einem Interview aus dem Jahre 1971, als das Museum of Modern Art, New York ihm eine Retrospektive widmet, faßt er die doppelte Ablehnung von (photographischer) Kunst und von Kommerz zusammen. Deren Verschmelzung hatte er vor 40 Jahren bei Steichen beobachtet: "Meine Arbeit war nicht-künstlerisch und nicht-kommerziell. Ich fühlte - mit vollem Recht - ich war auf dem richtigen Wege."[30] Er war ein 'outsider'. Aber einer von denen, die ein neues Untersuchungsfeld eröffnen, und die, wenn sie anerkannt sind, riskieren, als 'establishment' angesehen zu werden. So war es ihm seit 1938 ergangen. Darauf hatte er mit den Photographien von Fahrgästen der U-Bahn, 'underground', geantwortet, mit Bildern also, die bis zu den sechziger Jahren fast unveröffentlicht bleiben sollten. Um sich ein weiteres Mal vom funktionalen (und kommerziellen) Kriterium des Informationsbildes zu befreien, forcierte er 1971 die Idee des 'dokumentarischen Stils'. Er war die magische Formel des Kompromisses zwischen der hohen Kunst und dem Bereich der Information. Er bleibt aber weiterhin bei seinem Modell der bekräftigten Ablehnung, womit er sich selbst am treuesten ist, als er erklärt: "Theoretiker schreiben dem Photoapparat nahezu alle Fähigkeiten zu, außer der negativen Tatsache [negation], daß er nicht dazu dienen kann, zu denken und die Gefühle des Photographen zu übersetzen ."[31]

Schon 1931 hatte er in "The Reappearance of Photography" geschrieben: "Amerika ist wirklich die natürliche Heimat der Photographie, wenn man die Photographie ohne den Photographen definiert." Die zuvor zitierte Aussage, die Evans Bilder von 1940 einleitet, ist radikaler. Das ist die negative Antwort auf die ideologischen Programme des vorangegangenen Jahrzehnts, die Programme des Machine Age, abgewertet wie alle Utopien, denen der Text von 1931 zuzustimmen scheinen konnte.[32] Mit der Präsentation der Portraits aus der U-Bahn formuliert Evans einen idealen Entwurf (den er nicht vollendet hat). Dieser stimmt vollkommen überein mit der Anonymität und der fehlenden ästhetischen Entscheidung, die das Duchampsche 'ready-made' definierte: "Ich wäre gerne in der Lage, einfach festzulegen, daß 62 Menschen ohne ihr Wissen in den Blickwinkel eines unpersönlichen, feststehenden Aufnahmegeräts kommen, in einem bestimmten Zeitabschnitt, und daß alle diese Individuen, die im Sucher erscheinen, photographiert werden, und zwar ohne daß irgendeine menschliche Wahl den Moment der Aufnahme bestimmt."[33] Man kann hier natürlich den Radikalismus der konzeptuellen Verfahrensweise der ausgehenden sechziger Jahre wiedererkennen. Wenn man indes die Bilder selbst betrachtet, muß man allerdings feststellen, daß ihre dramatische Resonanz nichts zu tun hat mit der von ihnen beanspruchten Gleichgültigkeit. Der Versuch vom Evans bis zum Extrem vorzudringen, bis zum Absurden, zum (blinden) Vertrauen des ursprünglichen Modernismus in die Fähigkeiten der Maschine enthüllt die dunkle Seite [the dark side] des Modernismus als Maschinenzeitalter.

Die Berliner Cineasten der zwanziger Jahre waren ihm auf diesem Weg vorangegangen: Fritz Lang besonders mit "Metropolis"(1924), aber auch mit "M. Eine Stadt sucht einen Mörder" (1931). Evans' Angabe, die Personen aus der U-Bahn seien "the ladies and gentlemen of the jury" (die Damen und Herren Geschworenen), läßt vermuten, daß er die Methode des Typeninventars der Polizeiphotographie auf den Mann aus dem Volke anwenden wollte, der Recht sprechen sollte.[34] Lang hatte

in "M. Eine Stadt sucht einen Mörder " schon eine underground-Horde von Kriminellen in ein dunkles Tribunal verwandelt. Mit Verweis auf Daumier bringt Evans all jene Spiele der Umkehrung zwischen dem 'einfachen Mann' und dem Kriminellen (in der Figur des Mannes in der Masse) in Verbindung mit den ersten Zweifel eines Künstlers an der modernen Justiz. Die unterirdische U-Bahn ist das "Kino der Straße" von Murnau ("Filme der Straße", so Kracauer). Es ist verwandelt in dieses primitivste Gericht des Unbewußten, wo Verbrecher über das Verbrechen richten. Zur Untermauerung dieser Interpretation kann man hinzufügen, daß das Beispiel, das Evans in der Straßenphotographie von Paul Strand fand, in seinen Augen im Portrait der blinden Zeitungsverkäuferin "Blind Woman" von 1916 zusammengefaßt ist.

Diese dunkle Seite des Modernismus, das Figuren - (oder Masken)- Theater des Unbewußten, hatte das Berliner Kino in Krisenzeiten in den Straßen der 'Großstadt' isoliert. Logischerweise war es New York - die moderne Stadt par excellence - wo Photographen am Rande der Kinolandschaft die ersten Hinweise hierauf gegeben haben. Hier hat auch Walker Evans am Ende einer anderen Krise die Synthese zweier historischer Momente geschaffen. Er bezog sie auf die archaische Modernität der Baudelaireschen Stadt, die von den Spuren der Sünde gezeichnet war. In einem Fragment aus "Mon coeur mis à nu" hatte Baudelaire seine 'Theorie der wahren Zivilisation' formuliert: "Sie steckt nicht in Gas oder Dampf, noch in den Drehtischen, sie steckt im Verwischen der Spuren der Erbsünde."[35] Mit der Vereinigung der Portraits aus der U-Bahn unter dem Titel Many are called (viele sind berufen...wenige aber auserwählt) gewinnt Evans die allegorische - und melancholische - Ader des Dichters der Fleurs du Mal (Die Blumen des Bösen) zurück. (Dieses Buch trug eine Zeit lang den Titel Les Limbes - Die Vorhölle.) Man muß sich letztendlich ins Gedächtnis rufen, daß Baudelaire die Karikatur als Ganzes in das 'rire satanique' (das satanische Lachen) einband, und daß er Daumier besonders bewunderte.[36]

Dies alles ist der amerikanischen Kunst der sechziger Jahre nicht fremd. Der schwarze Humor Smithsons weist Eigenschaften des 'satanischen Lachens' auf als Ventil einer Melancholie, deren allegorischen Motive die Vorstädte liefern. Da er nicht romantisch genug war, um sich so zum Advokaten des Teufels zu machen, orientierte Dan Graham sich stärker am Realismus. Dieser war Zeugnis der negativen Utopie, vollendet in der Umwelt der Vorstädte. Mit der Untersuchung der typologischen Modelle des Modernismus seit Ende der siebziger Jahre, ihrer Form und ihren neuen Transformationen, hat er indessen genau die Situation der Baudelaireschen Rückerinnerung wiedergefunden: die Vorhölle, dämmrige Stätte des Wartens, die den ganzen historischen Abfall in sich aufnahm, den die vorhandenen Utopien mitgeschwemmt hatten. In dieser Zwischenzone enthüllt die unbewegliche, gleichförmige, melancholische Zeit verneinend den utopischen

Inhalt (des Un-Ortes), das Klischee vom Wohlstand für alle. Das Baudelairesche Modell, soviel es für Evans auch hat bedeuten können, tritt so hinter dem Dandytum von Warhol hervor.

Schon vor Warhol hatte das Duchampsche Prinzip der Gleichgültigkeit bei Walker Evans tatsächlich als negative Exaltation gewirkt, und, objektiv-dramatisch via die Photographie, als Traum der amerikanischen Gesellschaft von Gleichheit. Denn diese Gleichgültigkeit ist auch und zuerst die des Dandys, der vergeblich der Boheme zu entkommen sucht, und der wie Baudelaire ein Bewunderer Daumiers ist. Durch die Einordnung in diese Genealogie trugen die Portraits aus der U-Bahn eine historische Interpretation der Modernismuskrise der dreißiger Jahre in sich. Diese trifft mit den Beobachtungen Walter Benjamins bei seiner Studie der baudelaireschen Stadt zusammen. Die von der Maschinerie der totalitären Propaganda manipulierte Masse ist das Mengenelement, in dem der Boheme-Künstler (oder der "Peintre de la vie moderne" Baudelaires) die seine Subjektivität auflöst und die Impulse für seine Tätigkeit findet. Die Kunst muß der Maschine mit der Maschine antworten; nicht durch den Modus des Medienepos (das eine Pseudo-Organität der Gemeinschaft feiert), sondern durch einen lyrischen Modus, der im Einklang mit alltäglicher Verschiedenheit ist.

Hierin ist die große Erfindung von Walker Evans in den dreißiger Jahren enthalten, wovon Dan Graham erbt: im Nationale der amerikanischen Kultur, das in seiner Verschiedenheit nicht auf modernistische Typologien reduzierbar ist. Es gibt kein amerikanisches Volk, sondern ein Schauspiel Amerikas. Reicher und komplexer als die seltenen Meisterwerke, die von einem ursprünglich europäischen Modernismus inspiriert sind, antwortet dieses Schauspiel deswegen nicht auf das Klischee einer paradiesischen, Neuen Welt, beschützt von der industriellen Zivilisation. Unter allen 'Meistern' der modernen, amerikanischen Photographie ist Walker Evans wahrscheinlich der einzige, der sich ganz von der Idee der Natur befreit hat. Er hat sich rigoros für die Zeichen und die Geschichte entschieden - um die von Barthes zur Zeit der Mythologien aufgestellte Unterscheidung wieder aufzunehmen. Er ist der einzige wahrscheinlich, der die Meisterschaft der Photographie nicht in ihrer besonderen Fähigkeit, die Natur sprechen zu lassen und geheime Botschaften aufzudecken (durch die Zauberei der Technik), begründet sah. Sein Werk begann fast mit der Krise von 1929 in New York und es ging mit ihr zu Ende. Für ihn ist das Schauspiel Amerikas dem Wesen nach urban, zwar geprägt von den Zeichen der Stadt (oder des Kommerz') und ihrem beherrschenden Einfluß, doch durch die Umwelt vergänglich. Die photographische Aufnahme soll die dauerhafte Form eines Symbols nicht isolieren ("the thing itself" von Weston), sondern muß ein Bild-Zeichen, ein Dokument-Monument bestimmen.

Für alle Photographen der zwanziger Jahre, die von Strand beeinflußt waren und mit der (anti-pikturalistischen) 'straight

photography' übereinstimmten, war die Natur simultan wie sukzessive das Modell der Idealmaschine. Aus dieser Tatsache heraus war sie einem Kunstwerk vergleichbar. Außerdem war sie die heilsame Antwort auf die negativen Auswirkungen der Technik. Man mußte von der einen wie von der anderen Seite eine 'Qualität' erwerben, die das Bild mit dem Kunstobjekt verbindet - oder wie Fernand Léger es nannte, mit dem "le bel objet" (dem schönen Objekt): dem industriellen Objekt, perfekt gestaltet, funktional, wobei das 'design' dem Plan der Natur gehorcht. Obwohl er für den Entwurf technischer Objekte empfänglich war, selbst und vor allem der gewöhnlichsten - wie es seine Publikation "Beauties of the Common Tool" in *Fortune* (1955) bestätigt - sah Evans darin hauptsächlich Beispiele einer technischen Kultur. Diese haben stärker die Eigenschaften eines anthropologischen (und historischen) Imaginären als von festen Naturgesetzen. Was auch immer sein Untersuchungsthema gewesen sein mag, seine Vorlage war in jedem Fall nicht das (natürliche oder industrielle) Objekt, sondern das Bild. Das Bild war durch Verwandtschaft und Funktion eine Verbindung mit dem gedruckten Zeichen eingegangen, dem plakatierten, zur Kommunikation benutzten Zeichen.

Der Unterschied zu seinen unmittelbaren Vorgängern ist hier ausschlaggebend. Ralph Steiner z.B., der seine Technik an ihn weitergab, hatte in den zwanziger Jahren den Reichtum des dokumentarischen Materials, das zuvor in *American Photographs* versammelt worden war, vorausgeahnt. Dies bezeugen seine Illustrationen eines Artikels in *Fortune* von 1930, am Beginn der Krisenzeit, deren Gegenstand schon genau mit dem Evansschen übereinstimmte: "Eine Aufzeichnung - nicht über das neue Amerika mit seinen Wolkenkratzern, seinen Flugzeugen und seinen Generatoren - sondern über das Amerika vor der Restauration, das unerneuert [unregenerate] bleibt, über seine Verandas und Hinterhöfe, seine Häßlichkeit und seinen Abfall."[37] Derselbe Text hat andererseits den Vorzug, daß er klar die 'mythologischen' Beweggründe in der nationalistischen Vorstellung der Herausgeber von *Fortune* formuliert. Diese erlaubten es Evans für die Zeitschrift zu arbeiten: "Im Grunde genommen ist England traurig und Amerika fröhlich. Amerika stinkt, aber Überfluß und Energie reichen aus, um das Land mit verbrauchten Überresten zu bedecken. Jede Müllhalde und jede baufällige Häuserzeile an einer Eisenbahnlinie beweist unseren grenzenlosen Reichtum. Das ist Raum, den wir nicht brauchen. Wir haben so viel." Diese Übereinstimmungen machen aber auch um so deutlicher, an welchen Stellen Evans anders dachte. Steiner hatte sich ohne Zweifel besonders früh an ein Verlangen nach kultureller Identität angepaßt, das die Ideologie des technologischen Fortschritts nicht völlig befriedigen konnte (weil sie zuviel außer acht ließ.) Aber er hatte sich zu sehr den Werten der Vollendung der traditionellen, (vorindustriellen) 'hohen Kunst' verschrieben, die Strand verkörperte, durch den er 1926/27 eine Offenbarung erlebt hatte: "Strand verblüffte mich mit seinen mexikanischen Photos. Ich war wie erschlagen. Ich hatte noch nie so reiche

Photos gesehen - mit derart echter Struktur - und so fantastischen Grauwerten."[38] Evans hat dagegen weiterhin das 'historische' Qualitätskriterium und die vollendete Ausführung zurückgewiesen, bis zu der Erklärung von 1971, als er ein weiteres Mal im Museum of Modern Art, New York ausstellte: "Ich fühle mich in einem Museum nicht mehr wohl. Ich will nicht hingehen, will nicht 'belehrt' werden, will keine 'vollendete' Kunst sehen. Mich interessiert, was man Umgangssprache nennt."[39]

Man darf dahingegen nicht die Ambiguität in Evans Position übersehen, wenn man deren künstlerischen Scharfsinn genau messen will. 1971 ist die Umgangssprache - "what's called vernacular" - eine anerkannte Spezialität im 'establishment', von dem er behauptet sich abgegrenzt zu haben. *Fortune* hatte 40 Jahre zuvor den Weg dafür geebnet, gefolgt vom Museum of Modern Art, New York. In seinen letzten Lebensjahren ist Evans selbst ein 'historischer' Künstler, ein Meister, der an der Yale Universität in New Haven unterrichtet; er erweckt den Eindruck, seine eigene Lehre zu wiederholen. 1969 entwirft er in einem Gruppenprojekt mit dem Titel *Quality: Its Image in the Arts* - ein Titel, der auf den Kommentar verzichtet - ein Modellporträt des Straßenphotographen. Er vervielfältigt die bürgerlichen Heldenfiguren, die von Moral und feiner Gesellschaft ausgeschlossen sind - den Voyeur, den Spion, das verantwortungslose Kind, so wie sie in der Romanliteratur seit dem 19.Jahrhundert (Nabakov sei an erster Stelle genannt) popularisiert worden waren. Obwohl es Stieglitz gelungen war, der Photographie den Eintritt ins Museum zu eröffnen, hat die Photographie ihren Platz "auf der Straße": "In seinen Augen das reinste Festmahl: volle Geschäfte, Schlafzimmer und Höfe, weit weg von den Hallen reicher Architektur, landschaftlicher Fülle oder überdeutlich pittoresquer Natur."[40] Dieser Gegensatz des doppelten Repertoires von 'high and low' ist offenbar zu vielsagend und hat zuviele Eigenschaften einer institutionalisierten Rhetorik, der er widersprechen will (sie aber nur negiert). Man könnte daraus leicht den Schluß ziehen, daß Evans letztendlich der "paradigmatischen Position" von Stieglitz - so seine Worte - nicht entkommen ist, bei dem er "die typische Humorlosigkeit der nachviktorianischen Boheme" wiedererkannte.

Diese Ambiguität ist aber auch die Auswirkung des erwähnten Scharfsinns. Evans hatte in Atget ein überzeugenderes Beispiel als Stieglitz (und Strand) gefunden. Aber er konnte nicht der Künstler-als-Sammler sein, der ein geheimes Werk besitzt, das er den traditionellen Institutionen und ihren Künstlern Dokumente zur Verfügung stellt. Im Amerika der zwanziger und dreißiger Jahre paßte die dokumentarische Strategie Atgets zu gut zum Programm einer Zeitschrift wie *Fortune*. Er mußte also seine Absicht 'beweisen', d.h. er mußte ihr einen institutionellen Halt außerhalb der Medien und gleichzeitig eine spezifische Form geben.[41] Genau das tat er, als er eine Ausstellung im Museum of Modern Art, New York, 1938 zur Veröffentlichung von *American Photographs* nutzte: ein Buch zwischen Zeitschrift und Ausstellung. Die Bilder wurden einfach reproduziert - und nicht wie wertvolle Werke gerahmt - aber ohne Beschriftungen, regelrecht isoliert, jedes ohne ein Gegenüber abgedruckt allein auf einer Seite. Auf diese Weise vermied er die zwei konträren, aber beide gleich irreführenden Lösungen von Stieglitz und Margaret Bourke-White. Er vermied auch die Dialektik der einfachen Propaganda, oder 'kritisch' gesagt: der Propaganda, von der die Photomontage geprägt war, welche aber weniger erfolgreich war (mit Ausnahmen wie Heartfield), zugunsten einer Angleichung der Kunst an die Techniken der Reklamekommunikation.

Wenn man von Montage spricht, bleibt diese für Evans ein filmisches, also ein synthetisches Modell des 'editing'. Besonders durch Jay Leyda kannte er die Filme von Eisenstein, von Vertov. Die Montage ist eine Art der Organisation von Bildern, deren Autonomie, so notwendig sie auch sein mag, niemals definitiv und festumrissen sein soll. Immer seine Ablehnung 'vollendeter Kunst'! Er verändert übrigens weiterhin den Bildausschnitt seiner Photos, fragmentiert sie, vergrößert Details, die er mit anderen kombiniert. Darin liegt eine Beweglichkeit mit doppelter Wirkung: sie entspricht der Praxis außerhalb der schönen Künste - den Kinos und der Presse - und ist Folge einer spezifischen Konzeption des Bild-Zeichens, als Moment eines offenen Kunstwerks.

In dem bereits zitierten Text *Hound and Horn*, der die neuen Entwicklungen (die 'Renaissance') der Photographie in Deutschland untersucht, erwähnt Evans 1931 selbstverständlich das Buch *Die Welt ist schön* von Albert Renger-Patzsch. Er würdigt es aber nur halb, denn er findet es der traditionellen Diskussion mit der Malerei zu sehr verhaftet. Der Aufbau des Buches von Renger-Patzsch ist tatsächlich sehr statisch, zu zweigeteilt, und spiegelt die organische Vorstellung der Beziehung Natur-Industrie, Tradition-Moderne. Evans erkennt sich dahingegen sehr leicht in dem Aufruf zu amateurhafter Freiheit wieder: nachlässige, unvollkommene und unfertige Bilder werden propagiert. Dieser Aufruf grenzt in dem Text von Franz Roh *foto-auge* (hieraus zitiert er lange Passagen) an die Verknüpfung der Photographie mit der "unterbewerteten Geschichte der generell nicht-professionellen Produktivität." Es ist aber im Sinne des Artikels, daß bezüglich der Portraits von August Sander folgendes am positivsten erwähnt wird: "*Antlitz der Zeit* ist mehr als nur ein Buch über 'Typenstudien'. Die Kamera blickt hier genau unter die Menschen. Dies ist einer der neuen Wege der Photographie, den Atget vorhergesagt hatte. Die Gesellschaft wird in einem klinischen Prozeß photographisch zerlegt ..."

In diesen wenigen Zeilen, geschrieben am Wendepunkt seiner Karriere, kündigt Evans sein eigenes Programm an: "die photografische Zerlegung der Gesellschaft" [a photographic editing of society]. Das hat er auch danach ununterbrochen bis zur Höchstformel der Portraits aus der U-Bahn immer wieder geltend gemacht. Sehr früh dreht sich alles um die Typenidee oder die Typologie. Seit 1928 hat er Architekturstudien gemacht, die stärker an die europäische 'neue Vision'

anknüpfen, als an die Beispiele von Stieglitz und Strand.[42]
Mit Erfolg hat er sich ebenso in der Straßenphotographie
[street photography] versucht. Hierzu macht er sich ein Modell
gesellschaftlicher Typologie zur Leitregel, aufgelockert durch
die Ungewißheit der Momentaufnahme. Zu diesem Thema
erklärte er sehr viel später: "Ich ließ mich von einigen
Geistesblitzen leiten. Ich merkte, daß ich den Typ auf der
Straße erfassen wollte, die 'Momentaufnahme' [snapshot]
von einem Mann am Strand oder einer Sekretärin beim
Mittagessen. Das war eine hervorragende Quelle. Ich schöpfe
immer noch aus ihr." Er spricht vom Zwang des Künstlers-als-
Sammler.[43] Aber wie es die Bemerkung über Sander verrät und
wie es seine Projekte der Zerlegung bestätigt haben,
war dieses Modell der Typologie des Augenblicks, so
stimulierend es auch gewesen sein mag, nicht ausreichend.
Eine solidere Struktur war vonnöten, welche es erlaubte, die
gesellschaftliche (und historische) Verschiedenheit zu ordnen,
ohne sie auf eine pittoreske Typologie zu reduzieren und
ohne die Intuition allzu restriktiven Untersuchungsverfahren zu
opfern. Selbst Atget hat Figurentypen der Pariser Straße
festgelegt, indem er das Modell des 'kleinen Handwerks' der
pittoresquen Tradition ausbaute. Er hat sich aber einem
ehrgeizigeren Programm verschrieben, das Architektur und
urbanes Mobiliar integrierte. Andererseits ist die Überlegenheit
Daumiers, die Baudelaire ihm gegenüber Henri Monnier
(Schöpfer der Kunstfigur Joseph Prudhomme) zugestanden
hatte, eine ganz gute Zusammenfassung dessen, was Evans in
American Photographs (und in *Many Are Called*) von einem
guten Photographen der Straße unterscheidet, von denen es
um 1940 so viele gab: "Einiger seiner *Scènes populaires*, seiner
volkstümlichen Szenen sind sicherlich sehr nett; wenn man
anders dächte, würde man den direkten und überraschenden
Charme der Daguerrotypie verkennen. Aber Monnier kann
nichts kreieren, nichts idealisieren und nichst arrangieren." [44]

Diese zwei Seiten des Projekts der 'Zerlegung' von Evans
erscheinen auch in *American Photographs*: das Volk in der
(großen oder kleinen) Stadt, die Architektur des Landes.
Von einer Seite zur anderen zirkulieren die (aktuellen und
historischen) Zeichen. Denn die Architektur selbst ist in ihrer
typologischen Verschiedenheit, charakteristisch für den
amerikanischen Eklektizismus, ein System oder zumindest eine
Vereinigung von Zeichen. Zu zerlegen (zu schneiden -
zu montieren) heißt eine Ansammlung von Bild-Typen in eine
Ordnung zu bringen: Menschen und Architekturen, die entlang
aller möglichen Hybriden vom Archetyp bis zur Stereotype
reichen. Die Ansammlung erweitert sich zwingend in dem
Maße, wie sich die urbanen Zeichen vervielfältigen.
Ihre Realisierung im Bild (die Organisation in Sequenzen)
ist durchdacht, wenn nicht konstruktiv. Die Akkumulation und
der Reichtum, die die städtische und vorstädtische Umwelt
charakterisieren, müssen durch die Strenge sequentieller
Montage geordnet und hervorgehoben werden.

Es besteht also eine enge Beziehung zwischen der Arbeit
der Zerlegung in *American Photographs* und dem Bild der

amerikanischen Architektur, so wie es sich im zweiten Teil des
Werkes ausformt. Der 'Pop'-Architekt Robert Venturi - für den
sich Dan Graham seit Ende der siebziger Jahre stark
interessiert - sagte: "Main Street is almost all right." Schon
Walker Evans zeigt, woraus dieser Erfolg resultiert: aus der
rhythmischen Anordnung der geraden Linie und der
unregelmäßigen (symbolischen und dekorativen) Figuren.
Diese werden zusammengefaßt im Doppelbild urbaner
Zeichen, die eine Kommunikationsfunktion erfüllen und
die auch aus weniger univoken ('zweckfreien') Interessen
herrühren. Diese Anordnung ist im Buch allgegenwärtig.
Die Ordnung kann sehr rigoros sein, sei es, daß sie von der
strengen Regelmäßigkeit der 'frame houses' und
neoklassizistischer Häuserzeilen oder daß sie von der
Uniformität eines Aufnahmeprinzips (Frontalität und geringe
Schärfentiefe) diktiert wird. Doch der Ordnung wird immer
durch das Mißverhältnis widersprochen, sogar durch
Inkongruenz der Ausschnitte und durch die schnelle
Durchführung der Montage.

Man hat bei Evans oft von 'Klassizismus' gesprochen
(Einfachheit, Sparsamkeit der Mittel, Ablehnung des
Romantisch-Pittoresquen, Anti-Expressionismus). Es ist
möglich, daß das Modell der Main Street verbunden mit den
Häusertypen der 'row houses' in Georgia entfernt an die
Syntax der klassischen Architektur erinnert. Diese kannte fünf
verschiedenen 'Ordnungen', die gemäß der Typologie
der Renaissance von ornamentalen, emblematischen Figuren
symbolisiert werden: dorisch, ionisch usw. Die Komplexität
eklektizistischer Vereinigung aber unterscheidet sich von der
Einfachheit oder Strenge solcher paradigmatischer Ordnungen.
Andererseits hat Evans die Geburt des Internationalen Stils in
den Vereinigten Staaten unterstützt (mit der Ausstellung im
Museum of Modern Art, New York und dem Buch von Philip
Johnson 1932). Er konnte ihm aber nicht zustimmen,
genausowenig wie er das Ideal des technologischen
Fortschritts, das den Universalismus Mies van der Rohes
einschloß, befürworten konnte. Obwohl kein Regionalist,
entsprach seine Ausdrucksweise dem
Durchschnittsurbanismus mit seinen umgangssprachlichen
Spezifitäten. Dieser ist zwischen der Metropole und der
ländlichen Welt angesiedelt, wo die seltenen Beispiele 'großer'
Architektur Eigenschaften von Diversität aufweisen, und zwar
von Basteleien und Leihstil: zwischen dem mehr oder weniger
primitivistischen Archetyp (wie z.B. die berühmte Hütte
Laugiers, die oben im Zusammenhang mit Dan Graham
erwähnt wurde) und der (historizistischen und industriellen)
Stereotype. Entsprechendes gilt für die Position der
Photographie zwischen den schönen Künsten und den Medien.

Indem er in der europäischen Literatur des 19.Jahrhunderts
nach seinen Modellen suchte (Baudelaire, Flaubert) konnte
Evans sich von verschiedenen Ordnungsbegriffen eines
Modernismus der Utopie und der Amnesie befreien. Er löste
sich von einer Ordnung, die das Weltbürgertum der Lumières
(also der französischen Aufklärer) umwandelte in einen

Nationalismus, der gegründet ist auf der triumphierenden Universalität eines Modells des freien Unternehmens (wie Dan Grahams Generation sie in der Nachkriegszeit wiedererkannt hat). Seine erste konsequente Untersuchung aus den Jahren 1930/1931 unter Lincoln Kirstein hatte übrigens die viktorianische Architektur zum Thema (Boston, Saratoga Springs usw.). Er ist aber nicht der Photograph des ursprünglichsten Amerikas, der die Langeweile der Main Street und das Elend der verarmten Farmer beschönigt hat. Der zweite Teil von *American Photographs* wird eröffnet und beschlossen von zwei Bildern zerbrochener Ornamente - 'Reliquien' - die aussehen als seien sie aus Papmaché oder Papierfetzen. Diese Ornamente sind falsche Überreste der Antike und reduzieren den historischen Archetyp auf die Stereotype der melancholischen Verzweiflung. Man kann sich keine Bilder vorstellen, die stärker mit der baudelaireschen Allegorie übereinstimmen. Diese beschrieb Walter Benjamin in derselben Epoche gleich einer beispielhaften Ironie des Künstlers-als-Sammler über sich selbst. Beispielhafte Ironie, weil sie aus der Melancholie die Bedingung der Möglichkeit einer Verherrlichung moderner Zeichen macht, befreit vom nostalgischen Bedauern der gemeinschaftlichen Zugehörigkeit (wie natürlich aller futuristischer Träumerei).

Quer durch das (fälschlich historische) Zitat haben die Zeichen im Zustand des Verfalls schon Zugriff auf die Verzweiflung und können sich davon lösen wie von ihrem eigenen Boden. Genau an dieser Stelle formt sich seinerseits das Bild des Menschen nicht so sehr auf der Basis der Architektur, als vielmehr auf der Baustelle der Ruinen urbaner Zeichen - woran die Architektur teilhat - durch die Doppeltätigkeit (Sammlung-'Zerlegung') des Photographen, der in Sequenzen animiert und organisiert. Der Humanismus von Walker Evans, wie der Baudelaires, kann im Moment des Mitgefühls ausbrechen. Das geschieht um so leichter, da er dem 'satanischen Lachen' weniger geneigt ist. Er legt aber insbesondere Wert auf einen anderen Pathos, der sich auf die Zeichen und Spuren der Zerstörung konzentriert und den Sammler heimschickt zu seiner wahren Leidenschaft.

Daher die Veränderungen der letzten 20 Jahre. In den besseren Werken geht es nicht mehr um ein Schauspiel der Straße, sondern um ein Schauspiel der Häuslichkeit. Hier konzentriert sich das Bild in Vereinigung einiger Objekt-Zeichen, das Bild der - abwesenden - Zeichenbesitzer. Dies erscheint wie eine mehr oder weniger lesbare Botschaft, um das Buch *Message from the Interior* von 1966 wiederaufzugreifen. Evans hatte sich seit seiner Zeit bei der FSA, als er zu den Farmern ging, für diese häuslichen 'Arrangements' interessiert. Um 1930 und später parallel zu den Bildern für die FSA hatte er manchmal seinen eigenen Arbeits- und Lebensraum (besonders seine Dunkelkammer) photographiert. "*The Child's Room*" (1951), "*The Parlor Chairs*" (1958) und "*The Home Organ*"(1968) aber müssen auf die Untersuchung über die viktorianischen Häuser und auf das Paradigma der historischen Ruinen bezogen werden. Das begründet *Message from the Interior* deutlich.

Es bringt die ersten zwei, weiter oben genannten Bilder mit denjenigen verlassener, baufälliger Architektur, mit Bildern heruntergekommener Ornamente und sehr verlebter Innenräume in Verbindung. Diese Seite im Werk von Evans ist nicht nur ein Hinweis auf den Rückzug eines alternden, müden Mannes, sondern Auswirkung des - verhaltenen, gemäßigten - Zwanges überall zu sammeln, bei anderen die Zeichen seiner Melancholie zu suchen. Das Interieur mit seinen "dekorativen" Arrangements ist genausowenig ein Zufluchtsort, wie die Figur einer in der Erinnerung lebendigen Geschichte, am Rande der Vergessenheit, aus Unachtsamkeit und dem Verhängnis des Banalen (der genormten Glätte) geschaffen.

Kein Künstler, Dan Graham so wenig wie Walker Evans, kann, wenn er nicht der Melancholie verfallen will, dieses Verhängnis auf den Prozeß einer gesellschaftlichen Verfremdung reduzieren, für den er den unbeteiligten oder kritischen (objektiven) Zeugen darstellen würde. Das satanische Lachen ist die Lösung des romantischen Helden. Wer sich aber nicht zum Advokaten des Teufels machen kann - oder will - ist notwendigerweise dem mehrdeutigen Pathos individualisierter (dekorativer, formalisierter) Zeichen der Gemeinschaft ausgesetzt. Dies gilt vor allem, wenn man es sich verbietet, Zuflucht zu nehmen zu einem universell Abstrakten der eigenen, historischen Bestimmungen. Die doppelte Lesart der Pop Art reicht bei Dan Graham bis zu diesem Pathos, den die Photographien überstürzen und gleichzeitig auf Distanz halten. Wenn Walker Evans das Bild Amerikas hat erfinden können, das die Pop Art erbte, so konnte er das, weil er sich diese Fähigkeit vermittelt hatte: die Umwandlung seiner melancholischen Leidenschaft in eine Begeisterung, die - aus der Entfernung - mit dem Schicksal der Gemeinschaft verbunden ist.

1 Im Auftrag von Jeanne Siegel, die die Kunstprogramme im New Yorker Radiosender WBAI leitete, hatte Lucy Lippard am 8. März 1970 vier bildende Künstler eingeladen, Douglas Huebler, Dan Graham, Carl Andre und Jan Dibbets , deren gemeinsamer Nenner der Gebrauch von Wörtern war ("four visual artists who have used words one way or another "). Der Text dieser Diskussion erschien in: Lippard, Lucy, *Six Years: The Dematerialization of the Art Object*, New York, Praeger, 1973, S. 155-159.

2. Dan Graham drückte wiederholt diese Idee aus und betonte dabei jedesmal, daß seine Arbeiten für Zeitschriften wegen ihrer Schematisierung und kritischer Positionierung immer sowohl eine Radikalisierung der Pop-Art als auch eine Verwandlung des Minimalismus darstellten. Siehe insbesondere "My Works for pages": A History of Conceptual Art", *Dan Graham*, Ausstellungskatalog, Art Gallery of Western Australia, Perth,1985, S. 8-11. "Wenn die Minimal Art ihre Bedeutung aus der objektiven Unterstützung der Galerie gewann, kann man Vergleichbares über die Pop Art sagen, die ihre Bedeutung aus der Bilderwelt der Medien zog. Pop wollte die Idee der Qualität der bildenden Kunst unterminieren, indem sie Inhalte der Massenkultur verwendete. Als die Pop Art ihre Bilder über die Zeitschriften wieder in die triviale Kultur einfließen ließ, war das auch ein ironischer Kommentar zur Trivialkultur selbst. Die Pop Art zeigte die Möglichkeit, Informationsmedien, wie z.B. Zeitschriften, dialektisch mit dem Kunstsystem zu benutzen. Das bedeutet, daß eine Arbeit gleichzeitig sowohl im Rahmen künstlerischer, als auch trivialer Sprache der Medien funktioniert, und zwar als Kommentar und Bezugnahme auf die jeweiligen Annahmen. Ich habe Zeitschriftenseiten gestaltet, die in sich selbst definiert sind, und die sich auch im Kontext auf die übrige Information auf den anderen Seiten beziehen...Die 'absoluteste' dieser Arbeiten ist *"Schema"* (März 1966). Jedes veröffentlichte Beispiel dieser Arbeit erscheint isoliert als Seite in verschiedenen Zeitschriften...Gewöhnlich reproduzieren Kunstzeitschriften Kunst sozusagen aus zweiter Hand, denn sie existiert in ihrer phänomenologischen Präsenz zuerst in Galerien. Im Umkehrschluß existiert *"Schema"* nur durch seine Anwesentheit in der funktionalen Struktur des Magazins, und kann allein "aus zweiter Hand" in Galerien ausgestellt werden...Ich wollte eine Art von Pop Art machen, die in einem wörtlicheren Sinne eine Wegwerfkunst war (,eine Idee, die auf Andy Warhols Idee anspielt, 'Qualität' durch 'Quantität' zu ersetzen, entsprechend der Logik der Konsumgesellschaft). Ich wollte eine Kunstform schaffen, die nicht in Galerien/Museen reproduziert oder ausgestellt werden konnte; und ich wollte eine weitere Reduktion des 'minimalen' Objektes auf eine nicht unbedingt ästhetische, zweidimensionale Form (nicht Malerei oder Zeichnung) schaffen: ein Druckerzeugnis, das Information der Massenproduktion und des Massenkonsums ist." In einem Interview mit Eugenie Tsai, veröffentlicht in *Robert Smithson: Zeichnungen*, cat., Münster-Sorø-München, 1988-90, pp. 8-23), beharrt Dan Graham auf der Idee, die Wegwerfware, sowohl in seinen frühen Zeitschriftarbeiten als auch im Werk derjenigen Künstler (besonders Dan Flavin und Sol LeWitt), die er in seiner kurzlebigen John Daniels Gallery (Oktober 1964-Juni 1965) gezeigt habe: "Als ich Sol LeWitt ausstellte, sagte er mir nach der Ausstellung, ich solle das Holz als Brennholz nehmen; er würde das nie wieder sagen, aber Wert interessierte ihn wirklich nicht ... Niemand hatte einen Sinn dafür, daß dieses Zeug einen Wert haben könnte; damals dachte man nicht in der Richtung. Eine Schlüsselidee der sechziger Jahre, was Kleidung, Mode, aber auch Rock-Musik anging, war der Einwegware. Also machte ich einfach etwas, was man wegwerfen konnte, war aber nicht daran interessiert, produzieren zu müssen. Ich dachte nie daran, daß jemand es in ein Museum stellen könnte; ich war auch dagegen." (o. Anm., S. 9).

3 Der erste veröffentlichte Aufsatz von Smithson (1965), der sich mit Judd befaßte, beinhaltet schon diese Interpretation. Siehe "Donald Judd", Ausstellungskatalog *7 Sculptors*, Institute of Contemporary Art, Philadelphia, S. 13-16, übernommen in *The Writings of Robert Smithson*, einer von Nancy Holt erstellten Anthologie, New York, New York University Press, 1979, S. 21-23. Smithson interpretiert die Strukturen Judds als eine Spekulation über Materie, über die Form der Materie ("*the very form of matter*"), und er bemerkt: "Genau wie die manieristischen Künstler des 16.Jahrhunderts die Fakten der Hochrenaissance umsetzten, hat Judd die Fakten der modernen Realität umgesetzt. So entdeckte Judd eine Art Architektur, auch wenn seine konträren Methoden seine 'Architektur' wie aus Anti-Materie gebaut erscheinen lassen. Vielleicht sind 'Primär-Materie' und 'Anti-Materie' dasselbe." , Dan Graham erinnert, daß Judd mit dieser Interpretation überhaupt nicht einverstanden war (*"Judd gefiel der Aufsatz nicht, er haßte ihn"*). Smithson "erfand (in diesem Aufsatz) einen Judd, wie Borges eine Romanfigur erfindet". Die Divergenz zwischen beiden Künstlern spiegelt die Teilung der amerikanischen Avant-Garde der sechziger Jahre wieder: die Minimal- und Konzeptkünstler , die sich der puritanischen Moral und der Neuen Linke verbunden fühlen, einerseits und die Pop-Künstler, die eher dem 'Rock-and-roll' und der 'fun'-Kultur nahestehen, andererseits. Smithson, meint Dan Graham, "kam sehr viel stärker von der Pop Art, und er spielte gerne den advocatus diaboli. Wenn Sie mal darüber nachdenken, das ist die manieristische Rolle, denn die Manieristen nahmen genau diese Position in bezug auf die Werte der Renaissance ein. Minimal-Leute konnten das nicht verstehen; sie hätten nie manieristisch sein können. Das ist der eigentliche Punkt seiner Meinungsverschiedenheit mit Judd. Er preßte Judd in ein Schema, das historisch richtig sein mag oder auch nicht, aber Judd sah das immer anders. Und Judd war ein großer Moralist, obwohl seine Position, ich würde sagen, rechts ist, er ist immer noch ein Idealist und Moralist in seiner Art, die Dinge zu sehen." (Interview mit Eugenie Tsai, o. Anm. 2, S. 17).

4 Man weiß inzwischen, daß es anders kam: Die Herausgeber von *Arts Magazine* ersetzten die Bilder Dan Grahams durch eine Photographie von Walker Evans, *Wooden Houses, Boston* aus dem Jahre 1930, die in dem Buch *American Photographs* (Ausstellungskatalog Museum of Modern Art, New York) von 1938 , das 1962 neu aufgelegtwurde, abgebildet war. Projected Art wurde im November 1966 von Elayne Varian im Finch College Museum of Art, New York, gezeigt. Es scheint, daß Dan Graham der einzige Künstler in dieser Ausstellung gewesen ist, der tatsächlich Dias projizierte. Diese Initiative gehört in die lange Geschichte der Verwendung des Diapositivs [transparency] als pädagogisches Instrument - seit Frederick Henry Evans um die Jahrhunderwende insbesondere im Architekturstudium oder -unterricht - , und als Möglichkeit des Vergrößerns einer Photographie als Malvorlage (Lichtenstein, Richter, die Photorealisten). Zum Zeitpunkt der Ausstellung Projected Art hielt im Kunstbereich niemand mehr ein Farbdiapositiv für einen Selbstzweck. Anders als in den Kreisen der photographischen Sezession in Amerika (Stieglitz, Steichen) und des internationalen Piktorialismus am Anfang des Jahrhunderts - nach der Erfindung der Autochromenplatten durch die Brüder Lumière. Es sei hier ebenfalls daran erinnert, daß die Photographen der Farm Security Administration (FSA) in den dreißiger Jahren mit dem neuen Kodachrome-Verfahren (1935), einige Hunderte von Farbdias gemacht haben, von denen einige mit denen von Dan Graham vergleichbar sind; ihnen wurde jedoch keinerlei Beachtung geschenkt, bis Sally Stein sie im Archiv der Library of Congress in Washington wiederentdeckte. Ende der sechziger Jahre hatte Dan Graham kein Interesse an der Geschichte der Photographie - im übrigen ist es heute auch nicht größer; die anderen oben erwähnten Referenzen waren ihm dennoch bekannt. Die Projektion von Licht mit Dias assoziierte er mit den Neonröhren von Flavin; wie seine späteren Arbeiten es zeigten , interessierte er sich für die Idee der "Transparenz" (des Glases), die das projizierte Lichtbild [transparency] beinhaltet.

5 Man sollte hier klar zwischen dem Aufsatz für *Arts Magazine* H o m e s f o r A m e r i c a und dem später in den Jahren 1970-71 als eine Replik des ursprünglichen Layouts des Artikels entstandenen Werk *"Homes for America"* unterscheiden; diese Replik wurde in der Druckerwerkstatt des College of Art and Design von Nova Scotia, Halifax produziert; dazu gibt es zahlreiche Varianten, darunter die Doppeltafel der Sammlung Daled (Abb. S. 132) - Ansichten mit Personen, die 1967 aufgenommen wurden -, d.h. nachdem der Artikel erschienen war. Diese Unterscheidung ist notwendig, möchte man der Anti-Kunst-Position gerecht werden, aus der die Entscheidung für das 'disposable' in den *"Magazine Pieces"* hervorgeht. Eine solche Entscheidung war aber nicht tragbar, denn sie war nicht mit der Komplexität und den Anforderungen der kritischen Fiktion Text-Bilder zu vereinbaren. Ursprünglich wollte Dan Graham in einer Zeitschrift wie *Esquire* publizieren, er mußte sich aber mit einer Kunstzeitschrift begnügen, die sein Projekt jedoch nicht respektierte. Von Anfang an konnte das Projekt aufgrund seiner eigenen Komplexität nicht auf den unmittelbaren Konsum reduziert werden und war deshalb in einer 'künstlerischen' Form zu einer zeitlich verschobenen Realisierung verurteilt. Das Prinzip des 'disposable' - das in der Tat die Grundlage für alle Artikel des normalen Konsums bildet - konnte nur als Modell für einen Artikel der kritischen Fiktion dienen und war für den Künstler Dan Graham nur ein unhaltbares, fiktives Ideal. Darüberhinaus machte sich die Macht der Notwendigkeit bemerkbar. Nach 1970, als er *"Homes for America"* realisierte, entdeckte Dan Graham wie alle Künstler der Konzept-Bewegung, die von John Gibson in New York gezeigt wurden, daß die Photographie, ohne sich ganz in die bildenden Künste einordnen zu lassen, dennoch eine mögliche Einkommensquelle sein kann.

6 "Judd hat eine labyrinthische Sammlung 'gedruckter Materie', die er teilweise eher 'betrachtet', als daß er sie liest. So könnte er z.B. eine mathematische Gleichung nehmen und sie nach Augenmaß in eine metallische, fortschreitende Struktur von Intervallen übersetzen. In diesem Zusammenhang empfiehlt es sich, 'gedruckte Materie' wie bei Borges aufzufassen, nämlich als 'Das Universum (andere nennen es die Bibliothek)', oder anders gesagt: als unendliche 'Babylonische Bibliothek'." Holt, o. Anm. 3 , S. 15.

7 Der Originaltitel des Textes war "A Tour of the Monuments of Passaic, New Jersey". Der Text befindet sich auch in Holt, o. Anm. 3, S. 52-57. Smithson bezeichnet seine Photographien von Monumenten als Standbbilder eines Filmes. Das erste Monument, a bridge over the Passaic River, gibt den Ton an:"Die Spätnachmittagssonne verwandelte den Ort in einen Film, er verwandelte die Brücke und den Fluß in ein überbelichtetes Bild. Als ich es mit meiner Instamatic 400 photographierte, war das, als ob ich ein Photo von einem Photo machte. Die Sonne wurde zu einer riesigen Glühbirne, die eine lose Serie von Standbildern durch die Instamatic hindurch auf meine Netzhaut projizierte. Als ich über die Brücke ging, war das, als ob ich über ein riesiges Photo aus Holz und Stahl lief, und unter mir der Fluß war ein riesiger Kinofilm, der nichts als ein dauerndes Nichts zeigte."

8 Die Unterscheidung zwischen den beiden Bedeutungen des Wortes 'Monument' wird von Françoise Choay in "A propos du culte et des monuments", Vorwort zur französischen Ausgabe des Textes von Alois Riegl, *Der moderne Denkmalkultus von 1903* (*Le culte moderne des monuments*, Paris, Editions du Seuil, 1984, S. 11) explizit dargelegt." Der Begriff historisches Monument ist keine kulturelle Invariante (...) Denn gehört das Monument - sprich (etymologisch) das Artefakt, das uns zur Erinnerung auffordert - zu einer universalen 'Kunst des Gedenkens', die fast in jeder Kultur zu finden ist, so haben die Erfindung des historischen Monumentes und die Erfindung der Begriffe von Kunst und Geschichte gemeinsame Wurzeln. Diese liegen in jenem Europa der Postgotik , das diesen Begriff im Laufe eines langwierigen Prozesses, dessen erste Stufe im Quattrocento anzusiedeln ist, ausgearbeitet hat."

9 Siehe dazu das Interview Hueblers mit Irmeline Lebeer anläßlich der Ausstellung im Kunstverein Münster (Dezember 1972 - Januar 1973), veröffentlicht in *Chroniques de l'art vivant* ,no.38, April 1973, S. 21-23: "Meine Hauptziel (zur Zeit der *Primary Structures*) war, Skulpturen zu schaffen, die so groß waren, das sie in kein Museum paßten. Deshalb baute ich sie draußen auf. Die primären Strukturen sind nun im Moment ihrer Realisierung interessant: ein Kubus ist genauso real wie ein Tisch oder ein Stuhl. Als ich diese absolut realen Formen draußen platzierte, hatten sie zugegebenermaßen nicht das gleiche, harmonische Verhältnis zur Natur wie eine Statue, ein Akt oder etwas Ähnliches, aber sie funktionierten als reale Objekte in Konkurrenz zu all den anderen realen Objekten in der Welt. Ich begriff, daß meine Skulpturen der Konfrontation mit Bäumen und Himmel nicht gewachsen waren, trotz Integration in einen architektonischen Rahmen - in eine Struktur, speziell entworfen, um sie aufzunehmen - war die Natur stärker. Natürlich hätte ich noch größere Formen entwerfen können, monumentale Skulpturen, in Wahrheit aber brauchte die Welt mich nicht, um noch mehr Objekte zu den bereits existierenden hinzuzufügen. Diese Erfahrung führte zu einem fundamentalen Wandel meiner Orientierung."

10 In einem Interview mit Daniela Salvioni (*Flash Art*, no.152, May-June 1990, S. 142-144) bemerkt Dan Graham:"Ich bin nicht unbedingt gegen Monumentalität. Die Konzeptkunst war am Wegwerfprodukt interessiert, an Werken, die Museen nicht sammeln konnten und die ihren permanenten, historischen Gebrauch verweigerten. Vom architektonischen Standpunkt gesehen bestimmt Monumentalität einen Ort, die Geschichte. Die Bedeutung von Dingen, die länger als eine historische Epoche Bestand haben, ist offener. Diese Bedeutung wird nicht von mir oder vom Kunstpublikum angestrengt. Ich würde nicht sagen, daß es eine bessere Bedeutung ist, sie ist einfach offener. Ein Zeitspanne, die für die Modifizierung der Werkbedeutung lang genug dauert, könnte fehlinterpretiert werden." Dieses Interesse für das Monument, dessen Dauerhaftigkeit er den für den Konsum gedachten, vergänglichen Produktionen gegenüberstellt, erinnert an die antivitalistische Interpretation der traditionellen künstlerischen Kultur bei Hannah Arendt (das Leben ist Konsum); für sie unterscheiden sich das Gebrauchsobjekt und a fortiori das Kunstobjekt grundsätzlich vom Konsumobjekt. Dan Graham drückte sich Ende der sechziger Jahre anders aus. Dennoch darf man nicht von einem Bruch sprechen. Diese Entwicklung entspricht einer Neubewertung des modernistischen Erbes, das von der historischen - und nicht historizistischen - Interpretationsmethode Walter Benjamins und deren Anwendung auf die unmittelbare Vergangenheit inspiriert. Zweifellos mündete der Modernismus in den internationalen Stil des triumphierenden Kapitalismus der Nachkriegszeit; setzt man ihn jedoch zurück in Beziehung zu seinen utopischen Modellen aus der Aufklärung, so erzeugt er - gerade durch die ihm anhaftenden Widersprüche - die Abweichung einer kritischen Aktualität. Schon 1967 hatte Dan Graham zum ersten Mal die dauerhafte Ambivalenz dieser Modelle betont und auf die Verbindung der Hippie-Friedensbewegung mit der pastoralen und gemeinschaftlichen Utopie hingewiesen, die in der Geschichte des Modernismus die Ideologie des technischen Fortschrittes immer wie ein Schatten verfolgt. Siehe "Eisenhower and the Hippies", erschienen in der Winterausgabe 1968-1969 der Zeitschrift *0 to 9*, und übernommen in *Dan Graham: Articles*, Eindhoven, Van Abbemuseum, 1977, S. 23-26. Zwanzig Jahre später faßt Dan Graham in einem Interview mit Birgit Pelzer (*Dan Graham*, Ausstellungskatalog ARC, Musée de la ville de Paris, Paris, 1987, S. 33-38) seine aktuelle Position zusammen."Walter Benjamin schlug vor, das historische Gedächtnis zurückzugewinnen. Weil die gegenwärtige Ideologie die Vergangenheit ausgelöscht hat, muß sie wieder so aufgebaut werden, als sie sie wieder aufgetaucht. Der Modernismus war gegen Monumente. Ich bin dafür: Monumente prägen die Zeit.(...)Monumente sind mit dem Bedächtnis einer Stadt verbunden; das, was mich, denke ich, im Moment persönlich am meisten interessiert, ist die nahe Vergangenheit, das historische Gedächtnis der nahen Vergangenheit zurückzugewinnen. Betreffs der sechziger Jahre, einer Zeit, die die meisten heute lebenden Menschen erlebt haben, scheint es, als sei das kollektive Gedächtnis von Amnesie befallen. Die Medien müssen ständig die nahe Vergangenheit auslöschen, um ihre Utopie des gegenwärtigen Augenblickes zu fabrizieren." Genau diese Utopie des gegenwärtigen Augenblickes wollte Dan Graham schon immer pervertieren: er tat zuerst so, als würde er sich ihr anpassen (Modell des 'disposable'), dann spielte er in seine Performances, seinen Spiegel- und Videoinstallationen mit allerlei chronologischen Störungen (besonders durch die zeitliche Verschiebung der Aufnahme). "Die Gegenwart", sagt er zu Birgit Pelzer, "existiert nicht. Die Unmöglichkeit, diese absolute Gegenwart zu erreichen, bedeutet das Scheitern der modernistischen Idee, der zufolge eine tabula rasa möglich wäre."

11 "*Yesterday/Today*" wird in der von Benjamin Buchloh zusammengestellten Anthologie der von Dan Graham zwischen 1970 und 1978 produzierten Videoarbeiten und Texten über Video beschrieben (*Video-Architecture-Television*, Halifax-New York, The Press of The Nova Scotia College of Art and Design, New York University Press, 1979, S. 42). Im Jahr zuvor (1974) hatte Dan Graham schon einige Videoinstallationen realisiert, in denen das Bild mit einer Zeitverschiebung in getrennte Räume übertragen wurde, "*Time Delay Rooms*"; solche Installationen erzeugten sowohl eine systematische Subversion der spezifischen Merkmale von Video ("a present-time medium", anders als der Kinofilm) wie auch eine Deformierung der gemeinsamen Anwesentheit des Publikums (wie auch der Präsenz jedes einzelnen Besuchers zu sich selbst). "*Yesterday/Today*" führte jedoch einen neuen Parameter in Struktur einer Falle ein: die Spezifität des architektonischen uOrtes und der aufgezeichneten alltäglichen Aktivität, die darin abläuft. Es hieß dann, die Disjunktionen des erlebten Raums, die die alterative Gegenwart des Videos produziert hatte, mit den Gegebenheiten des alktuellen Umfeldes zu verbinden, indem als Installationsort jeweils eine besonders signifikante Architekturstruktur ausgesucht wurde. Wie Anne Rorimer es betonte ("Dan Graham: An Introduction", *Dan Graham: Pavillons*, Kat. Kunstverein München, 1988, S. 24), bedeutete , noch vor "*Yesterday/Today*", "*Picture Window Piece*" (1974) den ersten Schritt in diese Richtung. Auch 1974/75, an demselben Wendepunkt, ist die zweite - nach der von 1965/67 - wichtige Serie von Photographien , die als Markierungen oder Anregungen für die späteren Videoinstallationen und Pavillons zu betrachten sind, einzugliedern.

12 "*Video View of Suburbia in an Urban Atrium*" wird von Anne Rorimer, o. Anm. 11, S. 26 beschrieben. Diese Arbeit ist eine perfekte Illustration des andauernden Interesses Dan Grahams für Architektur seit "*Homes for America*". Es sollte auch bemerkt werden, daß mehrere Bilder von Vororthäusern (Ein-oder Zweifamilienhäuser) aus dem Jahr 1978 stammen. Sie sind den Bildern von 1965/66 sehr ähnlich, unterscheiden sich jedoch dadurch von ihnen, daß er den einzeln stehenden Häusern [detached houses] mit ihrer eigenen Morphologie größere Aufmerksamkeit schenkt und sie unter einem fast physiognomonischen Aspekt betrachtet. Ebenfalls1978 entstand "*Alteration fo a Suburban House*". Der Text dieses -unrealisierbaren - Projektes bezieht sich explizit auf die individuellen Glashäuser, die Mies van der Rohe und Philip Johnson Ende der vierziger Jahre bauten. Alle Facetten des Modernismus konzentrieren sich für Dan Graham also in der Gestalt des Hauses in den Vororten.

13 Um die Form seiner Pavillons zu charakterisieren, drückt sich Dan Graham in einem Interview mit Brian Hatton 1991 wie folgt aus (Broschüre anläßlich der Ausstellung in der Galerie Roger Pailhas, Marseille, Juni-Juli 1991): "Die Formen sind meistens Klischees moderner Architektur. Genau wie vor zehn Jahren vollzog sich bei Pelli und vielen anderen eine Rückkehr zu einem Boullée-Ledoux-Pantheon, von Grotten und Kinderspielplätzen zur Weltausstellung und zu den Vereinten Nationen. La Géode, das 360°-Kino in La Vilette, war Teil davon. Ich denke nach über all diese typologischen Formen. Obwohl ich nicht das gleiche machen will wie Venturi, sich nämlich wirklich den Dingen in der Umgebung beugen, hat mich die Unbeugsamkeit immer in einem anderen Sinn interessiert. Materialien und Formen beziehen sich auf die aktuelle Phase der modernen Stadt und ebenso auf die historischen Klischees, aus denen diese hervorgehen kann." Dan Graham hatte diese Klischees der modernen Architektur, schon in seinem Text von 1979 "Art in Relation to Architecture/Architecture in Relation to Art" erwähnt (*Artforum*, February 1979, S. 22-29), und zwar im Zusammenhang mit den Glashochhäusern von Mies van der Rohe und deren Funktion als Markenzeichen für die multinationalen Unternehmen und den amerikanischen Kapitalismus: "Die Büro- und Wohnhäuser aus Glas von Mies wurden zum neuen Standard der amerikanischen Technologie, besonders weil dieser Stil sehr leicht in die anderen Teile der Welt durch die amerikanischen Geschäfte zu exportieren war. Der Klassizismus von Mies beruhte auf einer scheinbaren Treue zum Material (das Material als das gesehen, was es war, und nicht verkleidet durch das Ornament), die gepaart war mit einer idealisierten, 'universalen' und höchst abstrakten Auffassung des Raumes. Diese modernen Strukturen wurden bald populäre Verpackungen für die multinationalen Firmensitze in der 'Freien Welt'."

14 Unter zahlreichen anderen historischen Anhaltspunkten für seine Pavillons, erwähnte Dan Graham oft die "primitive Hütte" wie sie von Marc-Antoine Laugier in einem Essay von 1753 als Archetyp der Architektur beschrieben wird. Dieses spekulative Modell, das charakteristisch ist für den Primitivismus der Aufklärung, entspricht der Rousseauschen Übersteigerung der Güte des Naturmenschen, im Gegensatz zu der korrupten Kultur der Städte. Dan Graham entdeckte es Ende der siebziger Jahre bei Autoren wie Manfredo Tafuri, und Leon Krier, die in der postmodernen Debatte über die urbane Utopie einbezogen waren. Siehe unter anderem "Not Post-Modernism: History as Against Historicism, European Vernacular in Relation to American Commercial Vernacular, and the City as Opposed to the Individual Building." (*Artforum*, December 1981, S. 50-59). Die Vorgeschichte und der Erfolg des Modells von Laugier waren einige Jahre zuvor von Joseph Rykwert rekonstruiert worden (*On Adam's House in Paradise*, New York-Chicago, 1972); Laugier war die zentrale Figur des durchdachten architektonischen Primitivismus , aus der zum großen Teil der Modernismus entstand, so zum Beispiel auch bei Gropius (als er 1921 in einem Vorort von Berlin das Blockhaus Sommerfeld entwarf, das von den Präriehäusern von Frank Lloyd Wright beeinflußt war).

15 "Not Postmodernism...", o. Anm. 14, S. 57

16 Dan Graham spricht von "doppelte Lesart" [dual Reading] im Zusammenhang mit Lichtenstein in "Art in Relation to Architecture/Architecture in Relation to Art", o. Anm. 13. Er zitiert dazu die Aussagen Lichtensteins in einem Gespräch mit Gene Swenson 1963 über Pop-Art und deren Beziehungen zur Massenkultur:"Es steht in Zusammenhang mit demjenigen, was ich für die gewagtesten und bedrohlichsten Charakteristika unserer Kultur halte, Dinge, die wir hassen, die aber auch in der Konfrontation mit uns besonders stark sind. Ich glaube, daß die Kunst seit Cézanne extrem romantisch und unrealistisch geworden ist, sich von Kunst ernährt; sie ist utopisch. Sie hat immer weniger mit der Welt zu tun, blickt nach innen - Neo-Zen und all das. Dies ist weniger als Kritik gemeint, es ist viel mehr eine klare Beobachtung. Draußen ist die Welt; sie ist da. Pop Art schaut hinaus in die Welt; sie kann ihre Umwelt akzeptieren, die weder gut noch schlecht ist, sondern anders, ein anderer Geisteszustand." Und: "Die Helden der Comics sind faschistische Typen, aber ich nehme sie in meinen Bildern nicht ernst - vielleicht ist es wichtig, sie nicht ernstzunehmen, politisch wichtig. Ich benutze sie nur aus formalen Gründen, und dazu waren diese Helden sicherlich nicht gedacht...Die Pop Art hat ganz unvermittelte und aktuelle Bedeutungen, die verschwinden werden; diese Dinge sind vergänglich, und Pop zieht seinen Nutzen aus dieser 'Bedeutung', die nicht dauerhaft sein soll, indem er uns von seinem formalen Inhalt ablenkt. Ich glaube, die formale Aussage meiner Arbeit wird mit der Zeit klarer werden." Dan Graham faßt es wie folgt zusammen: "Ein Werk von Lichtenstein kann beides sein, ein 'l'art- pour -l'art'-Werk und etwas, das mit dem Sinn der Massenkultur vergleichbar wäre. Beide Lesarten sind korrekt." Es besteht also eine wirkliche Ambivalenz der Pop-Art gegenüber den Medien; sie ist nicht zu reduzieren auf eine Strategie der kritischen Verfremdung, die mit gewissen Brechtschen Stellungnahmen von Seiten der Neuen Linken verwandt wäre . Eine solche Ambivalenz besitzt jedoch eine kritische Tragweite - die Verfremdung ergibt sich notwendigerweise aus der einfachen Wirkung der künstlerischen Verfahrensweise - , wenn sie in einen breiteren historischen Zusammenhang als den beschränkten Bereich der schönen Künste eingegliedert wird, speziell wenn sie mit den eindeutiger politischen Herausforderungen der Architektur in Verbindung gesetzt wird. Auf keinen Fall sucht Dan Graham die Wahrheit (in der Kunstgeschichte) der Pop-Art; er interpretiert sie, um daraus ein Modell zu entwickeln. Das Gespräch zwischen Lichtenstein und Swenson wurde in die Reihe "What ist Pop Art?" mitaufgenommen , die in zwei Teilen in *ARTnews* (November 1963, February 1964) erschien und dann in die Anthologie von Mahsun, Carol Anne, *Pop Art: The Critical Dialogue*, Ann Arbor, Michigan, UMI Research Press, 1989, S. 111-115, übernommen wurde.

17 Alice Weiner: "Dans Photographien aus dieser Zeit zu sehen war wie Photographien von Walker Evans zu sehen, nur ohne Leute." (Gespräch mit Chris Dercon, 14. April 1992). Dan Graham erinnert sich, daß er auf die Verwandtschaft seiner Bilder mit denen von Walker Evans von Mel Bochner - der übrigens Evans begegnet war - hingewiesen wurde (Gespräch mit dem Autoren, 27.Juli 1991).

18 In der oben erwähnten Reihe "What ist Pop Art?" spricht Jim Dine von Walker Evans, nachdem er über die Schönheit der Werbeplakate [billboards] gesprochen hatte; er hatte diese Schönheit sehr früh erkannt, schon lange bevor er sie als Vorbild wählte: "Es ist keine einzigartige Idee - Walker Evans photographierte sie schon 1929. Es ist nur so, daß die Landschaft um uns herum anfängt, uns einzuschließen, und wir müssen uns dagegen erheben." o.Anm.16, S.115. Diese letzte Bemerkung von Jim Dine könnte die exakte Definition der Pikturalisierung von Landschaft sein, die ein Photograph erzeugt, wenn er im Sucher einen Ausschnitt auswählt.

19 Allan Kaprow bemerkt: "Weil sie direkt, eindeutig objektiv und frei von persönlichen Emotionen ist, ruft die Pop Art meistens eine romantische Erinnerung an die Zeit vor 20 oder 30 Jahren wach, die Zeit der Kindheit des Künstlers. Sie ähnelt stark den

Stimmungen, die man in den Romanen von Kerouac findet. Villeglés, Hains und Rotellas zerfledderte Poster sehen Amerika aus der Ferne, dessen Proklamationen und vergangene Göttlichkeit von Wetter und Alter angeschlagen ist, rufen die Erinnerung an Walker Evans' Photos von Jahren zuvor wach; Lichtensteins Cartoons und Produkte besitzen die Ikonographie und den Stil der vierziger Jahre. " ("Pop Art: Past, Present and Future", *The Malahat Review*, July 1967, in der Anthologie von Carol Anne Mahsun, o. Anm.16, S.61-74).

20 Dazu auch Rosenthal, Nan,"Let Us Now Praise Famous Men: Warhol as Art Director",*The Work of Andy Warhol*, Dia Art Foundation Discussions in Contemporary Culture, no.3, Garry Garrels (ed.), Seattle, Washington, Bay Press, 1989, S.47-50

21 Evans war auf zahlreichen Wegen zum Vorbild geworden, und zwar als die Erfüllung eines amerikanischen Modells 'dokumentarischer Photographie', die Erbe des 19.Jahrhunderts war. Im Nachwort zu *American Photographs* verweist Lincoln Kirstein zurück auf Mathew Brady, den Portraitisten Abraham Lincolns, als Ausgangspunkt für Walker Evans; Kirstein ordnet Brady seinen europäischen Kollegen zu (Nadar, Cameron, Hill). Er bemerkt außerdem: "Walker Evans führt uns die gegenwärtige Zivilisation Ost-Amerikas vor, so wie Atget uns das Paris der Vorkriegszeit und Brady uns den amerikanischen Bürgerkrieg zeigten." Kirstein publizierte 1933 in der Zeitschrift *Hound and Horn*, die er in den frühen dreißiger Jahren herausgab, einen Artikel von Charles Flato, der Bradys Photos vom Bürgerkrieg als exemplarische Anzeichen für "große Möglichkeiten von Einfachheit und Direktheit" auffaßte. Ein aktueller Kommentar zu diesem Artikel von 1933 stellte fest: "Ohne Stieglitz oder den Pikturalismus zu erwähnen, impliziert Flato den Gegensatz zwischen Brady und dem Erbe von *Camerawork*." Vgl. Trachtenberg, Alan, *Reading American Photographs: Images as History, Mathew Brady to Walker Evans*, New York, Hill & Wang,1989, S.231-235. Wenn er von Brady als "einem wahren Erfinder eines Stils, der das Vergängliche und das Universelle bezeichnet" spricht, kommt Flato ganz eindeutig zurück auf Baudelaires berühmten Beobachtungen über die "die doppelte Komposition des Schönen (aus "einem ewigen, unveränderlichen Element" und aus "einem relativen, zufälligen Element"). Dieser hatte sie auf den ersten Seiten von *Peintre de la vie moderne* entwickelt und Constantin Guys (einem Malerchronisten, insbesondere des Krim-Krieges) gewidmet. Dreißig Jahre nach den Texten von Kirstein und seiner Teilhaber, als John Szarkowski 1967 die Ausstellung *New Documents* im Museum of Modern Art, New York präsentiert (die Diane Airbus, Lee Friedlander und Garry Winograd versammelt), war das dokumentarische Modell im amerikanischen Stil zum verbindenden Prinzip im 'Modernismus' der Photographie geworden. *American Photographs* wurde im selben Jahr neu aufgelegt, als Szarkowski seine Stelle im MoMA antrat. Robert Franks Buch *The Americans* war drei Jahre zuvor erschienen; hieraus hatte Evans eine erste Auswahl in *US Camera Annual* 1958 eingeführt. Unter der gemeinsamen Parole vom 'Dokument' kennzeichnet nun eine solide, genealogische Folge(richtigkeit) die Gratlinie der Autorenphotographie, über die Masse der anonymen Bilder hinaus, die das Wesen des Mediums geformt und festgelegt hatte. 1966 merkt Szarkowski im kurzen Nachwort zu *Message from the Interior* mit einem ausgeprägten Sinn für rhetorische Ausgewogenheit an: "Evans' Stil scheint genauso zwangsläufig und anonym zu sein, wie der der frühen Daguerrotypisten, doch der Charakter seiner Bildsymbolik - frontal, exakt und deutlich, sowie wenig leidenschaftlich - ist unverkennbar sein eigener."

22 Dan Graham hat kürzlich mehrmals die Bedeutung des Nachkriegskinos für das Entstehen seines Interesses an der Architektur erwähnt. Vgl.bes. ein Interview mit Chris Dercon vom Mai 1991, publiziert in *Forum International*, vol.II,-no..9, September.-October 1991, S.73-80. Die Beziehung zum Neuen Realismus trat im Verlauf eines unveröffentlichten Interviews mit dem Autor in Los Angeles am 27.Juli 1991 zu Tage.

23 Godard hat immer auf der Notwendigkeit, die Fiktion auf dokumentarische Gegebenheiten zu stützen, bestanden. "*Zwei oder drei Dingen, die ich von ihr weiß*" (1966) - der Film, den Dan Graham am häufigsten erwähnt - wurde von einem Zeitschriftenbericht über Prostitution in den großen Wohnkomplexen der Vorstädte angeregt. Doch das Verhältnis Dokument-Fiktion hat auch Einfluß auf das Verhältnis real-imaginär. Über "*Die Geschichte der Nana S.*" ("*Vivre sa Vie*", 1962) erklärt Godard in einem Interview in *Cahiers du cinema*, no.138, decembre1962: "Ich bin vom Imaginären ausgegangen und habe das Reale entdeckt. Hinter dem Realen aber gibt es ein neues Imaginäres."; er spricht von "Theater-Wahrheit", von "theatralischem Realismus" Schließlich hat Godard seine Filme immer als Versuche ("essais") begriffen. Ihr dokumentarischer Aspekt ist deshalb in erster Linie wichtig für ihre eigene Weiterentwicklung. In Bezug auf "*Zwei oder drei Dinge, die ich von ihr weiß*" bemerkt er: "Ich sehe mich selbst beim Filmen und man hört mich denken. Kurzum, es ist kein Film, sondern der 'Versuch' eines Filmes und so stellt er sich auch dar. Er ist keine Geschichte, er will ein Dokument sein." (Godard, Jean-Luc, *2 ou 3 choses que je sais d'elle*, Paris,Seuil/Avant Scène,1971, S.12)

24 In einem Sammelband, veröffentlicht 1967 in London, sagt Stij Björkman über *"Zwei oder drei Dinge, die ich von ihr weiß"*: "Der Film spiegelt eine Art Neuen Realismus am *nouveau roman*: er ist sparsam in den Mitteln und detailgetreu. Seine filmische Darstellungsweise bietet durch die plötzlichen Wechsel zwischen Nahaufnahme und Totale eine ungewöhnliche, perspektivische Tiefe." Diese Aussage könnte man auch über die Bildmontagen in "*Homes for America*" treffen. In der dokumentarischen, selbstreflexiven Logik, die oben beschrieben wurde, steht laut Godard der Wohnkomplex, in dem die Filmheldin lebt, für die Idee des Zusammenseins (oder -lebens), aber auch für das Ensemble, das der Film selbst konstituiert. "Es geht darum, ein Ensemble zu beschreiben." Die Architektur ist die Metapher der Film-Beschreibung. Das beschriebene Objekt ist das Thema des Films. "Man sollte alles in einen Film packen." Und dieses "*tout*" (alles) sollte als komplexes Ensemble konzipiert sein, von Menschen bewohnt, als ein Innen und ein Außen, als Subjekte und Objekte. "Ich kann die Tatsache, daß alle Dinge aus einem Inneren und einem Äußeren bestehen, nicht ignorieren. Das kann z.B. dadurch sichtbar gemacht werden, daß man ein Gebäude von außen filmt, dann von innen, als ob man das Innere eines Würfels beträte, eines Objekts. Das gleiche gilt für eine Person, ihr Gesicht wird generell von außen gezeigt." Vgl. o.Anm. 23, S.15

25 Dan Graham diskutiert diese Frage 1991 im Interview mit Brian Hatton, o.Anm.13

26 "The Reappearance of Photography", in *Hound and Horn*, vol.5, no..1, October-December 1931; Reprint in Trachtenberg, Allan,*Classic Essays on Photography*, New Haven, Conn., Leete's Island Book, 1980, S.185-188.

27 Das Buch von Bourke-White und Caldwell war für Agee und Evans wohl ein abschreckendes Beispiel. Diese sahen das Vorhaben ihrer Vorläufer als "ein doppeltes Verbrechen: einerseits Propaganda und andererseits das Gewinn-Schlagen aus sowohl der Propaganda, als auch aus der Not der Farmer." Zitiert nach Stott, William, *Documentary Expression and Thirties America*, Chicago, The University of Chicago Press, 1973, 1986, S.222

28 William Stott (o.Anm. 27, S.320) zitiert diese Äußerung von Evans, den er in dessen letzten Lebensjahren kannte, die dieser ihm gegenüber gemacht hatte: "Ich habe tatsächlich eine Schwäche für die Benachteiligten, die Armen, aber dem mißtraue ich. Ich muß mißtrauisch sein, denn diese Schwäche sollte nicht das Motiv für künstlerische oder ästhetische Tätigkeit sein. Wenn sie es wäre, würden die Arbeiten entweder sentimental oder wollten sie die 'Gesellschaft verbessern'. Ich glaube nicht, daß ein Künstler so mit seiner Arbeit umgehen sollte."

29 Wörtlich sagte Evans: "The problem is one of staying out of Left politics and still avoiding Establishment patterns." ebenda.

30 Interview mit Paul Cummings vom 13.8.1971 in Archives of American Art, zitiert nach Alan Trachtenberg, o.Anm.21, S.237.

31 Diese Behauptung steht am Anfang einer undatierten Notiz, die Evans für die Einleitung einer Ausgabe der U-Bahn-Portraits (1938-1941) schrieb. Sie ist also jünger als die Portraits. Sie wurde in *Walker Evans at Work* veröffentlicht, einem Band, der 1981 unter der Leitung des Evans Estate zusammengestellt wurde (New York, S.160). Nach dieser einleitenden Bemerkung entwickelt der Text eine Beschreibung des Projekts: "Diese Sammlung ist zumindest eine unsaubere, durchschnittlich zufällige Auswahl seiner Subjekte, nämlich von Menschen, die zu einer bestimmten Zeit an einem bestimmten Ort sind." Evans betont ausdrücklich den konzeptuellen Wert des Projekts, dessen Verwirklichung eine Annäherung ist, keine Erfüllung. "Der Ort ist aus rein praktischen Gründen, wegen unumgänglicher, technischer Arbeitsvoraussetzungen gewählt worden. Die endgültige Vollendung dieser photographischen Methode - der Aufzeichnungsmethode - wurde hier nicht erreicht, aber sie ist als unerreichtes Ziel präsent..." Am Ende der Notiz nennt Evans einen Ort - die Stadt, eine Situation - Menschen in der U-Bahn und ein Datum - 1940: "Es ist eine mögliche Reihe von Menschen in der Stadt, die hier in der U-Bahn sitzen. Und es ist mehr oder weniger um 1940."

32 The Machine Age war die Ausstellung, die 1927 von Jane Heaps Avantgarde-Zeitschrift *The Little Revue* organisiert worden war. Der Ausdruck kennzeichnet aber eine soziale Realität, die weit über den künstlerischen Horizont hinausgeht. Die Organisatoren der Ausstellung von 1927 waren sich darüber völlig im klaren, denn sie zeigten "echte Maschinen, Maschinenteile, Geräte, Photos und Zeichnungen von Maschinen, Fabriken und Konstruktionen usw. in Gegenüberstellung mit Architektur, Malerei, Zeichnungen, Skulpturen, Konstruktionen und Erfindungen der bedeutensten, modernen Künstle." (Textreprint mit französischer Übersetzung in *Léger et l'esprit moderne: Une alternative d'avant-garde à l'art non-objectief (1918 - 1931)*, Kat. Musée d'art moderne de la ville de Paris, Paris, 1982, S.216 und 218) In einem Text im Katalog "The Americanization of Art" merkt der "präzisionistische" russische Maler und Immigrant Louis Lozowick (der sehr bewandert war in europäischem Kubo-Futurismus und Konstruktivismus) an: "Die Geschichte Amerikas ist die Geschichte eines sturen, unablässigen Bemühens, die Kräfte der Natur auszunutzen..., von gigantischen Ingeneursleistungen und von kollossalen, mechanischen Konstruktionen." (zitiert nach Richard Guy Wilson in *The Machine Age in America 1918 - 1941*, Kat. The Brooklyn Museum, New York, 1986, S.30) In den frühen zwanziger Jahren blieben die ersten Maschinenphotographen (besonders Paul Strand und Ralph Steiner) bei ihrer gemäßigteren (und stärker individualisierten) Vision der Maschine, auch wenn Strand sie in seinem berühmten Essay von 1922 "The New God" nennt. Lozowicks Verherrlichung des Großartigen und des Kolossalen fand seine photographische Illustration erst in den letzten Jahren des Jahrzehnts, besonders in den sehr wuchtigen Bildern von Margaret Bourke-White. In seinen ganz frühen Photos von Industriedenkmälern - darunter das gefeierte "*Armco Steel, Ohio*"- hatte Edward Weston dieses architektonische Modell vor allem dazu benutzt, um mit dem Pikturalismus zu brechen (wozu Strand die Maschine benutzt hatte); aber seine Faszination war von kurzer Dauer. Er bewahrte nur einen gewissen Sinn für Betonung durch Beschreibung, die er bei Motiven aus der vorindustriellen Kultur einsetzte. Diese vesah er mit erotisch-kosmischen Schwingungen. Ende der zwanziger Jahre trug Evans einige Zeit zur Apologie des technologischen Modernismus im amerikanischen Stil bei, aber wiederum kürzer als Weston und ohne dessen Fluchtlösung. Er leistete z.B. einen Beitrag zu einem Buch des Dichters Hart Crane mit dem Titel *The Bridge*, das 1930 die symbolische Schönheit der Brooklyn Bridge feierte. Er war aber auch an einem anderen urbanen Schauspiel interessiert: an den (undeutlichen oder zerbrochenen) Zeichen des Broadways oder an der Menschenmenge auf den Straßen (oder am Strand von Coney Island). Sogar seine Bilder von Wolkenkratzern und architektonischen Vorhängen zeigen die Werte der Studie und der Improvisation.
Das unterscheidet sie von den vollendeteren, deutlicheren Ansichten, aufgenommen von Strands Schülern, die an den experimentellen Vorstoß der "europäischen, neuen Vision" im Sinne des Bauhauses anschlossen. Jedenfalls wies Evans 1971 seine Anfangsphase des Schaffens in ihrer Gesamtheit (1928 - 1931) von sich, indem er sie für zu "romantisch" erklärt. Wenn wir interpretieren heißt das, daß sie der Maschinenromantik zu eng verbunden waren, die die zwanziger Jahre charakterisiert und den Triumph des Industrialismus der dreißiger Jahre vorbereitet hatte. Vgl. *Walker Evans at Work*, o.Anm.31, S.42. Schließlich muß deutlich gemacht werden, daß über die pseudo-kubistische Architektur der Gebäudekomplexe hinaus die Aspekte der urbanen Realität, die Evans' größte Aufmerksamkeit beanspruchten, der Ideologie der Industrialisierung und der modernen Stadt nicht gleichgültig gegenüberstanden. Lewis Mumford z.B. hatte 1931 erklärt, daß die U-Bahn und die "billigen Speiselokalen, [lunchrooms]" die "die beiden Hauptquellen des gegenwärtigen, modernen Stilst" waren (zitiert nach R.G.Wilson, o.Anm. 31, S.30).

33 Wie oben (Anm. 31) betont wurde, ist das Entstehungsdatum dieses Textes unsicher. Die Autoren von *Walker Evans at Work* haben jedoch eine andere Notiz, die sich auf denselben Anlaß bezieht, publiziert, die von 1962 datiert. Es ist verführerisch, diesen chronologischen Anhaltspunkt zu benutzen, um den Vergleich mit Duchamp zu bestätigen. Es war tatsächlich 1961, und nur dann, während einer Zusammenkunft am runden Tisch, die das MoMA zur Zeit der The Art of Assemblage organisiert hatte, daß Duchamp erklärte: "Ich möchte unbedingt betonen, daß die Auswahl der' readymades' zu keiner Zeit von ästhetischen Vorlieben bestimmt war. Die Auswahl basierte auf der Reaktion auf visuelle Gleichgültigkeit und gleichzeitig auf der völligen Abwesenheit von gutem oder schlechtem Geschmack." Diese Erklärung versteht sich größtenteils aus ihrem Kontext: Duchamp wollte sich, so wie er es schon bei zahlreichen Gelegenheiten getan hatte, abgrenzen von der ästhetischen Aneignung des l'objet trouvé, des industriellen Abfallprodukts usw., wie sie die Assemblage-Künstler (Neo-Dadaisten und Neue Realisten) praktizierten. Er erinnerte daran, daß eine künstlerische Entscheidung nicht nur ein simpler Akt der "Aneignung des Realen" ist, der die Schönheit "industrieller Folklore" zelebriert (zwei Formulierungen von Pierre Restany, dem Theoretiker schlechthin der Neuen Realisten). Angesichts seiner eigenen Interessen und seiner Verbindungen zum Museum of Modern Art, New York ist es unwahrscheinlich, daß Walker Evans der Ausstellung von William Seitz keine Beachtung schenkte, und daß er sich nicht mit der von Duchamp aufgedeckten Problematik auseinandersetzte, (auch wenn er Duchamp selbst nicht darüber hat sprechen hören.) Vgl. für eine historische Diskussion über das Prinzip der Duchampschen Indifferenz und im besonderen über den Inhalt des Gesprächs "Apropos of Readymades' von 1961: Camfield,William I. , The Menil Collection-Housten Fine Art Press, *Marcel Duchamp: Fountain*, Houston, 1989, S.42-47

34 Tatsächlich lautet Evans genaue Anmerkung: "Die Portraits auf diesen Seiten sind mit einer versteckten Kamera aufgenommen worden, von einem reuigen Spion, einem schuldbewußten Voyeur. Das grobe und unverschämte Eindringen wurde jedoch sorgfältig abgeschwächt und durch geplante, zeitliche Distanz gemildert. Diese Photos wurden vor 20 Jahren gemacht und absichtlich nicht veröffentlicht. Wie man sieht, findet man die Gesichter von Richtern, Bankdirektoren und Senatoren nicht. Was man sieht, ist sofort ernüchternd, überraschend und eindeutig: dies sind die Damen und Herren Geschworenen." (*Walker Evans at Work*, o.Anm. 32) All dies erweckt den Eindruck einer moralischen Fabel: der Künstler bekennt sich schuldig ("reuiger Spion") und sanktioniert sich selbst, indem er seine Bilder 20 Jahre lang unter Verschluß hält; er erkennt - mit leichter Ironie, wie es dem Dandy sich schuldig ist - die Existenz von Geschworenen aus dem Volk und damit die einer allgemeinen moralischen Gesetzgebung an. Er hatte sich außerdem Daumier (und Dickens) als Vorbild ausgesucht, d.h. eine ästhetische Autorität, die gleichzeitig moralisch und politisch ist: "Die fürchterliche Anti-Euphorie der New Yorker U-Bahn wird vielleicht eines Tages von einem modernen Dickens oder Daumier aufgezeichnet werden. Der Schauplatz ist eine soziologische Goldmine, die auf einen herausragenden Künstler wartet." Dieser Bezug auf Daumier taucht 1971 wieder auf in einem Interview mit Leslie Katz (erschienen in *Art in America*, March-April 1971): "Daumiers *Wagon de troisième class* ist eine Art Momentaufnahme von echten Menschen, die in einem Eisenbahnabteil im Frankreich des 19.Jahrhunderts sitzen. Obwohl er keine Kamera benutzte, skizzierte er die Menschen an Ort und Stelle, wie ein Reporter." Reprint in der Anthologie von Goldberg, Vicki, *Photography in Print: Writings from 1816 to the Present*, New York, Simon and Schuster, 1981, S.358-369.

35 Baudelaire, *Mon coeur mis à nu*, in: *Oeuvres complètes*, vol.1, Paris, Gallimard, Pléiade, 1975, S.697.

36 Baudelaire analysiert den Gehalt des 'satanischen Lachen' in seiner theoretischen Abhandlung *De l'essence du rire*, die seine Beobachtungen zur Karikatur zusammenfaßt. Das "satanische Lachen" ist der Ausdruck des widersprüchlichen Wesens des Menschen, hin und her gerissen zwischen "l'idee de se propre supériorité", der Idee seiner eigenen Überlegenheit und der Augenscheinlichkeit seiner "misère", seines Elends: "Es ist der unaufhörliche Schock dieser zwei unendlichen Größen, aus denen sich das Lachen befreit." Zusammengefaßt also die Tragik Pascals, der "humanité déchueu", der verwirkten Menschlichkeit, die vom romantischen Heldentum überholt wird. Aber es ist nicht Frankreich, das dafür das reinste Beispiel hervorbringt (E.T.A. Hoffmann). Molière seinerseits ist nicht "féroce" (unbarmherzig) genug, und schließlich wird kein weiterer Karikaturist erwähnt. Folglich ist es auch Molière, mit dem Baudelaire Daumier in einem anderen Text, *Quelques caricaturistes français*, vergleicht: "Seine Karikatur ist von überragender Größe, aber sein Groll ist ohne Gehässigkeit. Sein ganzes Werk ist im Grunde genommen anständig und gutmütig." (*Oeuvre complètes*, vol.2, S.532-543 und S.556-557) Es fällt schwer, bei Evans von "Gutmütigkeit" zu sprechen, aber im Sinne der Baudelaireschen Typologie würde er tatsächlich neben Daumier eingeordnet werden. Das tut er ja auch selbst. Er läßt dabei dem schwarzen, surrealistischen Humor die Nachfolge des 'satanische Lachen', nicht ohne von Zeit zu Zeit ein leises Bedauern zu zeigen - wie es vielleicht *Many Are Called* bezeugt.

37 Zitiert nach Lesley K. Baier in *Walker Evans at "Fortune" 1945 -1965*, Kat. Wellesley College Museum, Wellesley, Mass., 1977-1978, S.10-11. Eine Doppelseite der Veröffentlichung von Steiners Photos in *Fortune* (Mai 1930) ist reproduziert in *Photography Rediscovered: American Photographs, 1900 - 1930*, Kat. Whitney Museum of American Art, New York, 1979, S.104-105.

38 Steiner, Ralph, *A Point of View*, Middeltown,m Wesleyan University Press, 1978, S.104-105.

39 Interview mit Leslie Katz, o.Anm.34, S.367. Im Verlauf dieses Interviews bestimmt Evans näher: "Anselm Adams und Paul Strand waren beide wirklich hervorragend in ihrer Technik. Manchmal waren sie zu gut. Sie schaffen die Perfektion mit der Kamera und man bricht in Rufe des Erstaunens aus: Ooh! und Aah! und Wie perfekt!. Doch dann erfährt man den Inhalt nicht richtig."

40 Evans, Walker "Photography", *Quality: Its Image in the Arts*, Louis Kronenberger, Marshall Lee, (eds.), New York, Atheneum, 1969, Reprint in Liebling, Jerôme,*Photography: Current Perspectives*, Rochester, Light Impressions, 1978, S.16-18.

41 Der Begriff 'to establish' (hier übersetzt als 'begründen') muß in dieser seiner doppelten Bedeutung verstanden werden. Walker Evans benutzt ihn so in einem Interview mit Paul Cummings 1971 (o.Anm. 30, S.238) als er erklärt: "That took time to establish." Er spricht hier von seiner Methode, seinem "Stil", dabei an die institutionelle Anerkennung anknüpfend, die er dadurch gefunden hat.

42 Wir können an dieser Stelle die in o.Anm. 32 vorgestellten Beobachtungen vervollständigen. Das Bild, das in diesem Buch am Anfang des Abbildungsteils, der Walker Evans gewidmet ist, wiedergegeben wird, ist von außergewöhnlicher Bedeutsamkeit. Hier in seiner anti-deskriptiven Haltung - die schwarzen Zone, ohne Details, im Geflecht metallischer Strukturen - kann man leicht wiedererkennen, was aus dem Expressionismus hervorgeht. Der Expressionismus liegt den europäischen, konstruktiven Experimenten zugrunde und die Recherchen von Evans aus dem Jahr 1929 von der deskriptiven Unnachgiebigkeit eines Weston ("Armco Steel, Ohio", 1922) oder eines Charles Sheeler unterscheidet, welcher die Ford Plant-Werke photographierte ("Criss Crossed Conveyors", 1927). Später, im Jahre 1947, sollte Evans eine Ansicht von Ford-Plant aufnehmen (*First and Last*, New York, Harper and Row, 1978, S.173), die derjenigen Sheelers sehr ähnelte, denn er hat den "Romantizismus" seiner ersten architektonischen Studien abgelegt und paßt sich nun, mit gewissem Opportunismus der 'Design-Linie' der 'Straight Photography' an. Er wird von nun an konsequent die Haltung beibehalten, sich von der fälschlich expressionistischen Richtung des industriellen Heldentums, zelebriert von Autoren wie Margaret Bourke-White, abzuheben.

43 Interview mit Leslie Katz, o.Anm. 34, S.362. Evans bemerkt: "Dem Sammler wird eine bestimmte Art von Objekt ganz übermäßig bewußt, er verliebt sich in es und verfolgt es. Ich merke, daß ich mich in meiner Arbeit eine Zeit lang für nichts anderes als eine bestimmte Art von Gesicht, Typ oder Person interessiere. Man beginnt, mit der Kamera Menschen zu sammeln. Es ist wie ein Zwang und man kann nicht damit aufhören. Ich glaube, alle Künstler sind Sammler von Bildern."

44 Baudelaire, o.Anm. 36, S.556-557.

Dubbele Lezing

Jean-François Chevrier

Op de vraag van Lucy Lippard aan het begin van een radio-ontmoeting in 1970: "Dan, je bent als dichter, als criticus en als fotograaf beschouwd. Ben je nu beeldend kunstenaar?" antwoordde Dan Graham: "Ik definieer mezelf niet, maar alles wat ik doe wordt, volgens mij, gedefinieerd door het medium. Zo'n drie tot vier jaar geleden was ik bezig met drukwerk. Dingen in druk, dingen voor tijdschriften, dingen waar fotografie bij gebruikt wordt. Ik heb op alle terreinen waarop andere mensen werkzaam waren dingen gedaan en ik vind dat ze zichzelf definiëren."[1] Deze verklaring zou voldoende moeten zijn om elke zinloze discussie over het 'fotografische' karakter van een deel van het werk van Dan Graham op slag uit de weg te ruimen. Vanaf het moment dat de kunstenaar wordt gedefinieerd door zijn activiteiten, die op hun beurt worden gedefinieerd door de gebruikte werktuigen, wordt het zinloos om ons af te vragen of Dan Graham nu wel of niet een echte fotograaf is. Hij is fotograaf omdat hij de fotografie gebruikt, en wat hij op dat terrein doet bezit voldoende autonomie om een specifiek soort onderzoek te rechtvaardigen.

In 1970 was het probleem van de artistieke definities echter verscherpt door de recente toename van activiteiten die dwars door de geïnstitutionaliseerde categorieën en genres heenliepen. De op instigatie van Lucy Lippard georganiseerde ontmoeting met Carl Andre, Douglas Huebler en Jan Dibbets spreekt op dit punt boekdelen. De vier kunstenaars zijn bijeengebracht omdat het "vier beeldend kunstenaars zijn die alle vier op de een of andere manier woorden hebben gebruikt." Net als Carl Andre, distantieert Dan Graham zich van de zogenaamde 'conceptuele' kunst: "Ik geloof niet dat ik conceptuele kunst maak." Maar hij weigert evenzeer om zichzelf in een soort deelgebied tussen de woorden en de objecten te situeren. Hij verwerpt de 'dichotomie woord-object', en plaatst het begrip informatie op de voorgrond. Hij preciseert: "Ik ben nooit geïnteresseerd geweest in woorden of syntaxis in poëzie, maar veel meer in informatie. Ik wilde dat de dingen die ik deed een specifieke plek innamen en in een specifiek heden werden gelezen. De context is heel belangrijk. Ik wilde dat mijn werken over plekken gingen als in-formatie die in het heden aanwezig is."

Sinds H o m e s f o r A m e r i c a (*Arts Magazine*, December 1966 - January 1967) heeft de fotografie haar plaats gevonden in deze strategische context, als visuele informatie die wordt gecombineerd met geschreven informatie, in een ruimte - de pagina, of de dubbele tijdschriftpagina - die de plek van een leeservaring vormt. De fotografie is een in-formatie instrument, een instrument om ervaring mee vorm te geven, voor zover zij montagemateriaal is. Dat wat de gebruikte procedure betreft, die men, als men per se wil, natuurlijk altijd 'conceptueel' kan noemen. In werkelijkheid echter neemt Dan Graham vooral de positie in van een post-pop kunstenaar, die rechtstreeks op en met de media werkt, in plaats van zich er de iconografie en de effecten van toe te eigenen, zoals de pop-kunstenaars deden.[2]

Het ging er ook om de kunstkritiek concreet en materieel in de artistieke activiteit te verdisconteren, om zo de zijsprong van het geïsoleerde oordeel (a posteriori) te absorberen. Deze uitweiding moest binnen de structuur van het werk zelf worden geplaatst. Toen hij H o m e s f o r A m e r i c a publiceerde had Dan Graham zelfs geen behoefte aan preciseringen in de trant van "Dit is geen kunstwerk", zoals Marcel Broodthaers niet veel later nog deed op de etiketten van de collectie "*Der Adler vom Oligozän bis heute*", die hij in Düsseldorf presenteerde (*Musée d'Art Moderne. Département des Aigles, Section des Figures*, Städtische Kunsthalle, Düsseldorf, mei-juli 1972). H o m e s f o r A m e r i c a is een tijdschriftartikel. Het commentaar is geen secundaire reflectie meer over een geïsoleerd (en voorbij) kunstwerk. Het is geen weerspiegeling meer van de autonomie van de kunst. Het commentaar valt samen met het werk (dat niet geloochend of ontkend wordt). Het werk en het commentaar zijn samen en naast elkaar aanwezig in één en dezelfde waarnemingsruimte, die de ruimte van de informatie is. Dat is geen informatie meer over; het is informatie van. Het is de artistieke vorm zelf.

Aan het eind van de jaren zestig legt Dan Graham zich tegelijkertijd toe op verschillende kritische taken. Hij wil de Pop Art terugbrengen tot de plek waar zij ontstaan is (de media), de artistieke activiteit naar het moment van haar kritische perceptie verschuiven en zo het kunstvoorwerp met zijn sociale vorming vereenzelvigen, terwijl de formalistische doctrine er juist toe neigt het in een strikte autonomie (zorgvuldig onderscheiden van de sfeer van de media) te isoleren. Tenslotte heeft hij ingezien dat het minimalisme (de 'primaire structuren') nooit anders dan een hyperformalisme kan zijn, en hij wil de karakteristieke vorm van het minimale object tot de architectonische modellen terugbrengen - zoals de in serie vervaardigde kubus van de voorstedelijke paviljoenen - waarvan dat object de ideale (Donald Judd) of negatieve (Tony Smith) transformatie is, al wordt die relatie ontkend door heel de haar omringende mystificerende discours.

Als H o m e s f o r A m e r i c a eind 1966 verschijnt is Robert Smithson deze contextualisering van het minimalisme al begonnen in zijn eerste kritische teksten en, met name, in zijn weinig orthodoxe interpretatie van de 'architectonische' modellen van een maniëristische Judd.[3] De strategie van Dan Graham is van dezelfde orde en wellicht nog radikaler, want hij heeft op dat moment geen enkele zin (en ook geen enkele mogelijkheid) om plastische objecten te maken en heeft tot dan toe uitsluitend verbale structuren en fotografische beelden vervaardigd. Hij had inderdaad een paar maanden daarvoor aan een tentoonstelling met de titel Projected Art meegedaan, en toen daadwerkelijk diabeelden van voorstedelijke woningen geprojecteerd, en het zijn deze beelden die H o m e s f o r A m e r i c a hadden moeten illustreren.[4] Volgens een fictionele logica - die men onmiddellijk in verband zal brengen met de 'conceptuele' kunst om het bijzondere karakter te reduceren - werd het aan het tijdschrift *Arts Magazine* gegeven artikel het werk "*Homes for America*" van een kunstcriticus die ook fotograaf is, of van een fotograaf die ook architectuurcriticus is, of liever nog, van een minimaal kunstenaar die ook criticus en fotograaf is, die ervoor gekozen heeft om geen plastische objecten te maken, zoals er architecten zijn die ervoor gekozen hebben om niet te bouwen.[5]

In "Entropy and the New Monuments", zo'n zes maanden gepubliceerd voor H o m e s o f A m e r i c a, had Smithson in de structuren van Judd, Morris, LeWitt en Flavin de negatieve kwaliteiten (geestloosheid en monotonie) [vapidity, dullness], van de voorstedelijke omgeving herkend. Hij vergeleek ze eveneens met de visuele modellen die waren verschaft door de onnoembare hoeveelheid 'drukwerk' [printed matter] van de door McLuhan beschreven Gutenberg Galaxy.[6] Neoromanticus als hij is, onderzoekt Smithson in hoeverre het monument (en zijn herdenkingsfunctie) bestand is tegen de tand des tijds. Hij heeft het over de "instant monuments" van Flavin en beschrijft de paradox van de "nieuwe monumenten" in termen die onweerstaanbaar aan de fotografische opname doen denken: "Ze zijn niet vóór, maar juist tegen alle tijden gebouwd. Ze hebben deel aan een systematische reductie van tijd tot in fracties van seconden toe, in plaats van de enorme uitgestrektheden van de eeuwen te vertegenwoordigen. Zowel verleden als toekomst worden in een objectief heden geplaatst." In een het jaar daarop gepubliceerd essay, "The Monuments of Passaïc" (*Artforum*, December 1967), illustreert Smithson een verhaal dat de herinneringen aan een Grand Tour door Italië parodieert met foto's die hij tijdens een tochtje door zijn geboortestad had gemaakt.[7] Hij speelt hier met de dubbelzinnige relatie tussen het historische monument (overblijfsel van een gedenkwaardig cultureel verleden) en de veel grotere waarde van het monument als werk van het geheugen, waarvan de documentaire fotografie het model samenstelt maar dat door haar tegelijk wordt gereduceerd tot een optische verschijningsvorm zonder duurzaamheid.[8]

Net als Smithson en zelfs vóór hem, heeft Dan Graham met de fotografie gewerkt aan een nieuwe definitie van het monument. In dezelfde periode ziet Douglas Huebler af van de vervaardiging van objecten en onderneemt hij conceptuele acties waarbij de fotografie gebruikt wordt, na uit zijn deelneming aan de tentoonstelling Primary Structures (Jewish Museum, New York, 1966) geconcludeerd te hebben dat een kubus net zo 'echt' kan zijn als willekeurig welk gebruiksvoorwerp - een tafel, een stoel -, maar niet in de open lucht op een monumentale schaal kan worden opgericht zonder te worden blootgesteld aan een verpletterende vergelijking met de natuur.[9] Deze moeilijkheid is bij Dan Graham nooit opgekomen, omdat hij de aantrekkingskracht van de ongerepte ruimten van een natuur zonder verstedelijking nooit heeft gevoeld. Smithson stelt tegenover het monument uit het verleden, dat de belichaming is van een

historisch ideaal, die uitputting van dat ideaal in het 'no man's land' van de galerieën en para-stedelijke ruimten. maar deze uitputting is grandioos, zij heeft de maat van geologische fenomenen en legt het fundament voor een nieuw archaïsme. Voor Dan Graham heeft het monument altijd al de reductie (miniaturisatie en dematerialisering) van het fotografische beeld ondergaan, dat dientengevolge een doeltreffend model samenstelt. Daarom heeft hij nooit tegen het monument in het algemeen gewerkt, en zelfs niet, in het bijzonder, tegen het stedelijke monument.[10] Zijn eerste glazen paviljoenen verschenen aan het eind van de jaren zeventig, na de performances, de videowerken en de spiegelopstellingen, als een noodzakelijke en logische uitbreiding van het met de fotografie verrichte kritische onderzoek van specifieke stedelijke structuren.

In dit verband moet gewezen worden op de eerste foto's die in 1965-66 buiten New York in New Jersey zijn genomen. Want zij produceren reeds de parameters van een dialectiek van de socio-psychologische waarneming, gebaseerd op sociale onderscheidingen, zoals die later is ontwikkeld. Geprojecteerd in een galerie, introduceren (projecteren) de dia's een buitenwereld in de geprivilegieerde ruimte van de onbevlekte 'witte kubus'. Deze buitenwereld is samengesteld uit specifieke informatie, die wordt gekenmerkt door een dubbele verplaatsing: naar de periferie van New York (New Jersey) en naar het nabije verleden van de periode na de oorlog, waaruit het bouwprogramma van de 'tract houses' dateert en die overeenkomt met de kindertijd van Graham (geboren in 1942). Het nabije 'elders' - in de ruimte en in de tijd - is het merkteken van het fotografische (documentaire) heden, dat om die reden het model van de daarop volgende werken zal behelzen. We hoeven maar te denken aan de opstellingen van de performances en de video's van de jaren zeventig, waarin het heden, hic et nunc, van de actie (of van de receptie) voortdurend veranderd wordt door de nabijheid van de weerkaatsing in de spiegel en door het onmiddellijke verleden van de opname. In "*Yesterday/Today*" uit 1975 bijvoorbeeld, is er sprake van een begeleidende geluidsopname, die met een nabij verleden (gisteren) het via video binnendringen van de nabijheid (datgene wat in het belendende vertrek plaatsvindt) in de feitelijke, actuele ruimte van de toeschouwer begeleidt.[11] Vijf jaar later, in 1979-80, introduceert "*Video View of Suburbia in an Urban Atrium*" opnieuw het nabije 'elders' van de buitenwijk in een geprivilegieerde stedelijke ruimte.[12]

Een andere video-installatie, "*Edge of the City*", uit 1981, bepaalt nauwkeurig de relatie van de buitenwijk tot de stad. Maar in die periode is het onderzoeksterrein van Dan Graham aanzienlijk uitgebreid. Als de stedelijke marge zijn eerste historische onderwerp is geweest, dan onderzoekt hij voortaan een ander moment van de modernistische utopie. Het nabije verleden is verplaatst: het zijn nu de jaren zestig, de periode van de eerste atria onderin de glazen flatgebouwen van de multinationale ondernemingen. Terwijl het postmodernisme volop bezig is om, uit naam van alle nostalgische 'revivals', de geschiedenis van het modernisme te ontkennen, bedenkt en bouwt Dan Graham paviljoenen ("Pavilions"), en gebruikt daarbij de meest gebanaliseerde, meest gedevalueerde typologische modellen van de Internationale Stijl. Hij heeft het zelf over "clichés of modern architecture".[13]

Zoals blijkt uit twee omstandig uitgewerkte teksten die zijn gepubliceerd in *Artforum* ("Art in relation to Architecture/ Architecture in Relation to Art", februari 1979, en "Not Post-Modernism...", in december 1981), spreekt het denken van Dan Graham zich in essentie uit over historische gegevens, zonder daarbij echter af te zien van de psycho-sociologische modellen die de richting van zijn vroegere experimenten hadden bepaald. Van de informatie-opstelling gaat hij over op het object van de architectuur, zonder daarbij het kernprobleem van de perceptie en de modaliteiten van de ervaring (of de constructie) van het 'ergens anders' zijn uit het oog te verliezen. Hij hervat - met alle verworvenheden van de performance en de video - de historische contextualisering van het minimalisme die hij in *"Homes for America"* had ondernomen. De open en vertraagde, barok gemaakte minimalistische kubus wordt nu in verband gebracht met de modernistische utopie van de met de natuur verzoende stad, waarbinnen de multinationale atria [corporate atriums] de voorbeeldige en karikaturale manifestatie zijn van een privatisering van de openbare ruimte.

Bedacht als een kritisch monument van de utopie, vat de sculptuur-architectuur van de *"Pavilions"* de ficties van transparantie (en de spiegelspelen) van de architectuur van glas samen. Maar ze is ook en vooral gebaseerd op een historische analogie die de verder verwijderde verwijzingen mobiliseert: het paviljoen is ten opzichte van de aan de fantasie van de 18e eeuw ontsproten primitieve hut - paradigma van het oorspronkelijke primitivisme van de modernistische architectuur - wat het atrium is ten opzichte van de traditie van de pittoreske tuin, model van de stedelijke parken.[14] Door de onderverdeling stad-buitenwijk opnieuw een plaats te geven in de geschiedenis van de dialectiek stad-natuur van de Lumières, vergroot Dan Graham de nauwe context van het minimalisme. Hij beschikt voortaan over alle instrumenten die hem in staat stellen de twee essentiële bepalingen van het minimalistische model concreet onder woorden te brengen: het architectonische modernisme, zoals dat in Amerika is verbreid met de triomf van de Internationale Stijl, en de Pop Art-omgeving van de buitenwijken. Zoals *"Alteration of a Suburban House"* in 1978 al aankondigde, weerspiegelt het gebouwde kunstwerk (het paviljoen), zowel letterlijk als op het niveau van de kritische 'reflectie', de eigentijdse omgeving en haar historische modellen. De stedelijke utopie van de flatgebouwen, met hun barok aandoende uitwassen (de atria), is gewoon de samenvatting, of de reflectie in het klein, van de Pop Art-omgeving van die buitenwijken waarin een 'up to date' vermenging is verwezenlijkt van de stad en de natuur, gesymboliseerd door de exuberantie van tekens die getuigen van commercie, overvloed en consumptie.

Omdat de omgeving van Pop Art-tekens sinds de jaren zestig overduidelijk de doeltreffende context van de modernistische utopie is geweest, heeft Dan Graham volkomen logisch, via zijn interpretaties van de Pop Art en haar culturele dubbelzinnigheid bij Lichtenstein en vooral bij de architect Robert Venturi, het principe van zijn eigen constructies uitgewerkt. Een passage uit "Not Post-Modernism..." spreekt op dit punt boekdelen: "Venturi heeft, net als de meer traditionele [academic] pop kunstenaars, de populaire cultuur nooit kunnen accepteren voor wat ze was, maar haar altijd in verband gebracht met formalistische en architectonisch-historische interpretaties die populaire interpretaties in een dialectisch perspectief plaatsen. Een gebouw van Venturi, Rauch en Scott Brown kan zowel geïnterpreteerd worden vanuit een 'hoog' architectonisch schema als vanuit een schema dat verenigbaar is met populaire, vluchtige interpretaties. Beide interpretaties of lezingen zijn correct. Door zijn schijnbare vluchtigheid in termen van de populaire code, kan zo'n werk niet onmiddellijk worden opgenomen binnen de academische architectuur: omgekeerd kan het werk ook niet onmiddellijk worden opgenomen en ingelijfd door de massa-cultuur, omdat het nu eenmaal in de 'hoge' architectuur wortelt. Het feit dat het niet zomaar kan worden opgenomen zorgt ervoor dat het werk beide posities in twijfel kan trekken, maar vanuit (en niet in tegenspraak met) de formele en historische waardesystemen van de populaire cultuur en de architectuur."[15]

Wanneer hij de dubbelzinnigheid van Lichtenstein met betrekking tot de populaire cultuur in dezelfde termen beschrijft, heeft Dan Graham het over 'dubbele lezing' [dual reading], en het is precies dit 'dualisme' - zoals Robert Venturi dat voor zich opeiste in zijn boek uit 1966, *Complexity and Contradiction in Architecture* - dat hem de gelegenheid biedt een juist, want dubbelzinnig beeld te construeren van de duurzaamheid van de modernistische utopie in haar gedegradeerde, vervreemdende en onderdrukkende procedures.[16] Vanaf dat moment gaat het er niet meer om het modernistische model te 'deconstrueren' en evenmin om de tekens van de populaire cultuur ironisch te behandelen of de door de media overgeleverde meesterwerken uit het verleden zelfs maar te parodiëren. De kritische juistheid bestaat in de verheerlijking van de historische contradicties van een utopisch model, dat veranderd is in een vervreemdende structuur. Ze komt niet zozeer voort uit een onderscheidende actie (volgens de etymologische betekenis van het woord kritiek) als wel uit een constructieve dramatisering van de dubbelzinnigheid in de vorm van een naast elkaar bestaan van tegenstrijdige gezichtspunten en een montage van heterogene historische momenten.

Van deze 'dubbele lezing', waarvan het principe zich van de Pop Art heeft losgemaakt, zijn de juistheid en de schoonheid van de vanaf 1965 vervaardigde foto's doordrongen. Het zijn tegelijk rigoreuze architectonische beelden, tot in de abstractie geformaliseerd, en tijdschriftillustraties zonder 'kunst' pretenties, die passen binnen het vluchtige produktiekader van de media. Hun feitelijke presentatie, in de vorm van als autonome werken gepresenteerde afdrukken, neigt ertoe het feit dat ze oorspronkelijk tot de popcultuur van de media behoren uit te vlakken, maar deze ontwikkeling correspondeert met de esthetische aanspraken waar de paviljoenen blijk van geven, die desalniettemin - het moet worden gememoreerd - als 'clichés van de moderne architectuur' worden gedefinieerd en zo hun relatie met de via de media overgeleverde cultuur van beeldmerken behouden. We kunnen deze foto's ook vergelijken met de behandeling van soortgelijke onderwerpen in de hedendaagse 'creatieve fotografie' - neem bijvoorbeeld de documentaire vrijblijvendheid van Bill Owens in *"Suburbia"*, verschenen in 1973 - om na te gaan of de kenmerkende hoedanigheid van hun dubbele identiteit, het feit zowel tot de modernistische traditie (overgeleverd door het 'academische' minimalisme) als tot de popcultuur te behoren, intact is gebleven.

In 1965 opteren voor de kwaliteitsloze kleur van de dia veronderstelde een weigering van de verfijnde nuances van het mooie beeld, zowel van de koloristische verzadigingseffecten als van de waardeschakeringen van zwart en wit. Dan Graham dacht destijds meer aan de industriële neonbuizen van Flavin dan aan de chromatische spelen van de 'straight photography', in haar vele verschillende versies (Helen LeVitt, Eliot Porter, etc.), die uiteindelijk allemaal tot de tegen de industrie opponerende ambachtelijkheid behoren. Tegelijkertijd gehecht aan de sobere strengheid van het modernisme, wendde hij zich eveneens af van de kitsch-overdaad van de illustraties à la Hollywood welke in tijdschriften met gigantische oplagen verschenen (deze overdaad zou bij hem later verschijnen, met de beelden van atria). De historici van de fotografie hebben zich overigens niet vergist: ze hebben hem niet opgenomen in hun panoramas en zijn ontegenzeggelijk van mening dat zijn onderneming deel uitmaakt van een niet terug te vorderen conceptualisme, dat wil zeggen van een gebruik van de fotografie dat niet is terug te voeren op historische canons en dat evenmin het typische gezicht van de 'conceptuele fotografie' à la Sol LeWitt vertoont.

Dan Graham heeft zich geschikt naar het principe van de dubbele lezing nog voor hij het had geformuleerd. Hij kon volstaan met het rigoureuze gebruik van de fotografie in haar standaardfunctie, tussen de schone kunsten en de media. Een dubbelzinnige situatie, die de hele periode waarin de moderne kunst zich heeft ontwikkeld en gemanifesteerd is volgehouden, vanaf 1850 tot aan het begin van de jaren zestig, toen Warhol en vervolgens Richter hun eerste fotografische schilderijen vervaardigden. De dubbelzinnigheid was toen overigens nog niet opgelost. Warhol leek tenslotte de 'camp' van de media te kiezen en Richter bevoorrechtte langzaam maar zeker de abstractie (waarbij hij echter het contrapunt van het fotografische model handhaafde). Het Amerikaanse fotorealisme hield, op zijn beurt, hardnekkig vol om, binnen een te perfecte picturale mechaniek, de onpersoonlijke

nauwgezetheid van het fotografische beeld te verheerlijken. Door de fotografie op die manier te gebruiken, in haar gestandaardiseerde hoedanigheid, tussen expositie-object (zelfs in de vorm van geprojecteerde dia's) en instrument van de media in, openbaarde Dan Graham de historische situatie van de Pop Art: tussen het modernisme (opgenomen in de 'grote' kunst) en de populaire cultuur. Precies op dit punt keerde hij terug naar het voorbeeld van Walker Evans, met andere woorden bij de oorsprong van de Pop Art.

Volgens de getuigenissen die we anno nu kunnen verzamelen hadden de kunstenaars van de conceptuele kring deze verwantschap aan het eind van de jaren zestig onderkend.[17]. Maar al vanaf het begin van het decennium hadden verschillende popkunstenaars of kunstenaars die dicht bij de Pop Art stonden het precedent van Walker Evans genoemd, en in het bijzonder zijn beelden van reclameborden [billboards]. Jim Dine heeft het erover in een gesprek met Gene Swanson in 1963.[18] In 1967 roept Allan Kaprow hem voor de geest naar aanleiding van de Europese décollagisten (Hains, Villeglé, Rotella) in een tekst die de nadruk legt op de nostalgische resonanties van de Pop Art, met haar verwijzingen naar de jaren dertig-veertig, de kinderjaren van de popkunstenaars.[19] Vier jaar eerder had Warhol zijn fameuze hommage aan Rauschenberg, *"Let Us Now Praise Famous Men"*, vervaardigd, waarin hij familiefoto's van Rauschenberg (genomen in de jaren dertig) gebruikte, en waaraan hij de titel van het cultboek van James Agee en Walker Evans gaf.[20] Dit boek had overigens in 1960 een herdruk beleefd. En *American Photographs*, de catalogus van de Evans-tentoonstelling in het Museum of Modern Art, New York, in 1938, waarin de door Dine en Kaprow genoemde beelden staan, was in 1962 opnieuw verschenen.

Als we hier nog aan toevoegen dat in 1966 *Many Are Called* (de metroportretten) en *Message from the Interior* verschenen, en dat eveneens in 1966-67 Garry Winogrand en Lee Friedlander in zekere zin officieel de erfenis van Evans te beheren kregen, kunnen we concluderen dat de jaren zestig, de door de Pop Art ontsloten jaren, ook de jaren waren waarin zich in de kunst, via de fotografie, een bepaald beeld van Amerika ging manifesteren, dat gebaseerd was op de rijkdom van de sinds de jaren dertig gedocumenteerde alledaagse cultuur, waarvan Evans als de sleutelfiguur kon worden beschouwd.[21] Dat wilden de redacteuren van *Arts Magazine* te kennen geven toen ze de 'row houses' van Dan Graham vervingen door een rij houten huizen in Boston, gefotografeerd door Evans in 1930: de afbeelding werd gereproduceerd op de omslag van de editie van 1962 van *American Photographs* (p.109).

In 1965-66 was Dan Graham nog niet bekend met Walker Evans. Hij ontdekte die pas later, toen zijn vriend Mel Bochner hem, na de verschijning van *"Homes for America"*, *American Photographs* liet zien. Zijn belangstelling voor de stedelijke en voorstedelijke functionele architectuur van na de oorlog -

waarin zich de omkering van de modernistische utopie in een vervreemdende structuur massaal manifesteert - kwam voort uit zijn directe contact met New York en haar buitenwijken, en, buiten deze rechtstreekse waarnemingen om, uit twee artistieke modellen die - in de tijd - veel nabijer waren dan Walker Evans: natuurlijk het minimalisme, maar ook een uit het Italiaanse neorealisme van na de oorlog voortgevloeide filmkunst van Europese auteurs (Antonioni, Godard), waarin de thema's van de moderne stad en haar buitenwijken, als plekken van psychologische verbijstering en existentiële omzwervingen, alomtegenwoordig waren.[22] De structuur van "*Homes for America*" zou zelfs zonder meer in verband gebracht kunnen worden met de dialektiek van document en fictie die door Godard systematisch is aangewend.[23]

Deze verwijzingen naar de film waren in het Newyorkse avant-garde milieu aan het eind van de jaren zestig in feite schering en inslag. "*Deux ou trois choses que je sais d'elle*" van Godard, die "*Made in USA*" completeerde, kwam uit in 1966 en betekende de verwezenlijking van een filmkunst die de actualiteit van de Pop Art en de nouveau roman verbond met een door het neorealisme geïnspireerde documentaire dramatisering.[24] In deze periode hield Walker Evans zich geheel buiten de avant-garde milieus, en het is niet bekend of hij kennis genomen heeft van de ontwikkeling van de Europese filmkunst van na de oorlog. We kunnen evenwel herinneren aan het feit dat zijn vriend James Agee deze filmtraditie van 1941 tot 1948 aandachtig gevolgd heeft toen hij voor de krant van links Amerika, *The Nation*, artikelen schreef over Rosselini, Vittorio de Sica of Georges Rouquier ("*Farrebique*"), zoals André Bazin in Frankrijk, overigens veel systematischer, deed. Maar essentieel blijft de overeenkomst die zich in de jaren zestig daadwerkelijk voordeed tussen een geschiedenis van de 'realistische' cinema, die naar Godard en Antonioni leidt, en het fotografische project van Evans, dat destijds zijn voltooiing vond toen de publicatie van de metroportretten uit het eind van de jaren dertig *American Photographs* ging completeren.

In een context die in sterke mate gekenmerkt werd door enerzijds een anti-liberalisme van marxistische georiënteerd radikaal links en anderzijds een anti-humanisme van het structuralistische denken - waar het litteralisme van Robbe-Grillet bij aansloot - werd Evans vooral geacht om zijn beelden van stedelijke architectuur en tekens. Net als iedereen, vond Dan Graham in *American Photographs* het principe van de reproductie van de reproductie van de Pop Art terug, maar ook, meer in het bijzonder, wat hij zelf in de onmiddellijke buitenwijken van New York (New Jersey) had waargenomen: het beeld van Main Street - historische werkelijkheid en paradigma van suburbane stedebouw - de in rijen langs een spoorlijn gerangschikte gestandaardiseerde huizen; de architectuur, kortom, van commercie en communicatie, in haar gemechaniseerde vorm, die in gelijke mate karakteristiek is voor de gehele industriële wereld, en in een specifieke alledaagse visuele hoedanigheid, eigen aan Amerika.

Het deel van het oeuvre van Evans dat paste in de humanistische ideologie van de Rooseveltiaanse sociaal-democratie was terzijde geschoven. De beelden van *Let Us Now Praise Famous Men* bleken net als elk van het minste geringste inlevingsvermogen getuigende portret, vooral te dicht bij de door Edward Steichen in The Family of Man in het Museum of Modern Art, New York, in 1955 ontwikkelde 'mythologie' (Barthes) te staan. In de ogen van Dan Graham (en van zijn vrienden) vloeide elke 'normale' foto voort uit de mystificaties van het liberale humanisme. Hij preciseert echter dat deze verwerping ook een verdringing was en dat wat hij in de jaren zestig verwierp recentelijk opnieuw is opgedoken in het samen met Jeff Wall ondernomen project "*Children's Pavilion*".[25]

In werkelijkheid stond Evans zelf niet minder gereserveerd of ambivalent tegenover het van het beeld uitgaande retorische beroep op gemeenschap(pelijkheid). Hij had niet meegedaan aan Family of Man. Zijn visie op de sociale realiteit was te afstandelijk, te moreel (of puriteins) en te dandyesk om in te kunnen stemmen met de sentimentele gezwollenheid en spectaculaire effecten van een prentenfabriek van de universele gemeenschap. Vanaf 1931 had hij, in een door Lincoln Kirstein in *Hound and Horn* gepubliceerd essay, de publicitaire esthetica van Steichen heftig bekritiseerd.[26] Enkele jaren later, toen hij voor de Farm Security Administration (FSA) werkte (tussen 1935 en 1938), verzette hij zich tegen het propaganda-programma van zijn vennoten en in nog sterkere mate tegen de dramatische heftigheid en de ronseling van gezonde sentimenten zoals Margaret Bourke-White en Erskine Caldwell die in hun bestseller uit 1937, *You Have Seen Their Faces*, praktiseerden.[27] Zijn afkeer was moreel en esthetisch. De stijl van Margaret Bourke-White, topfotografe van *Life* (waarvan ze het omslag voor het eerste nummer in 1936 had gemaakt), vertegenwoordigde het exacte equivalent in de media van de 'monumentale orde' die de officiële architectuur van de jaren dertig karakteriseert, opgevat als het symbool van een autoritaire macht die de organische eenheid van een volk belichaamt. Voortgekomen, zoals hij het zelf zegt, uit de bohème, lezer van Baudelaire en Flaubert, moest hij zijn sympathie met de kansarmen bekennen en tegelijk weigeren te geloven dat de kunst in staat was "de maatschappij te verbeteren".[28] Hij bleef zijn hele leven geconfronteerd met het dilemma van de bohemiaanse kunstenaar: hij diende zich buiten de politieke programma's van links te houden, en tegelijk de patronen van het establishment volstrekt te vermijden.[29] Hij kon zo niet tot het volk behoren maar zich er ook niet de verlichte (of à la Bourke-White geïnteresseerde) woordvoerder van maken.

De artistieke positie die uit dit dilemma resulteert is noodzake-lijkerwijs dubbelzinnig. Evans heeft zich er herhaaldelijk over uitgelaten in soortgelijke termen als Dan Graham gebruikt met betrekking tot de Pop Art. In de loop van een gesprek uit 1971, op het moment dat het Museum of Modern Art, New York. Een overzichtstentoonstelling aan hem wijdt, vat hij de dubbele weigering van de (fotografische) kunst en de commercie samen, waarvan hij, veertig jaar eerder, de koppeling bij Steichen had waargenomen: "Ik deed niet-artistiek en niet-commercieel werk. Ik had het gevoel - en terecht - dat ik op het juiste spoor zat." [30] Hij was een 'outsider', één van degenen die een nieuw onderzoeksterrein openen en die, wanneer ze erkend worden, het risico lopen door het establishment te worden opgeslokt, zoals hem vanaf 1938 was overkomen (waarop hij had gereageerd door 'underground' metropassagiers te gaan fotograferen, wat beelden opleverde die tot de jaren zestig vrijwel onuitgegeven bleven). In 1971 distantieerde hij zich opnieuw van het functionele (en commerciële) criterium van het informatieve beeld, en bracht hij het idee naar voren van de 'documentaire stijl', magische formule van een compromis tussen de grote kunst en het informatiemétier. Maar het is toch met betrekking tot het model van 'de bevestiging van de ontkenning' dat hij zichzelf het meeste trouw blijft wanneer hij verklaart: "De theoretici schrijven het fototoestel alle mogelijke vermogens toe, behalve het negatieve feit [negation] dat het niet kan denken en de emoties van de fotograaf niet kan vertalen." [31]

Hij had in 1931 al in "The Reappearance of Photography" geschreven: "Amerika is werkelijk het natuurlijke domein van de fotografie als je dat tenminste definieert zonder aan de fotograaf te denken." De formule uit 1940 is radikaler. Het is de negatieve reactie op de ideologische programma's van het afgelopen decennium, en tegelijk op alle gedegradeerde utopieën van de 'Machine Age', waaraan de tekst van 1931 nog haar goedkeuring lijkt te hechten.[32] Met zijn presentatie van de metroportretten articuleert Evans een ideaal project (dat hij niet heeft voltooid), volmaakt conform het onpersoonlijke en de afwezigheid van esthetische keuzes, die de Duchampiaanse 'ready made' definieerden: "Ik zou het liefst gewoon willen zeggen dat tweeënzestig mensen binnen een bepaald tijdsinterval in beeld verschenen bij een onpersoonlijk en onbeweeglijk opnameapparaat, en dat al deze individuen gefotografeerd werden, maar dan zonder enige menselijke ingreep zolang ze aan de lens werden blootgesteld."[33]
We kunnen hierin zonder meer het radikalisme van de conceptuele procedures van het eind van de jaren zestig herkennen. Maar als we de beelden zelf in aanmerking nemen moeten we toch constateren dat hun dramatische resonantie geen deel heeft aan de opgeëiste onverschilligheid. Door te proberen het (blinde) vertrouwen van het eerste modernisme in de vermogens van de machine in absurde mate tot het uiterste door te voeren, heeft Evans de schaduwzijde [the dark side] van het modernisme als tijdperk van de machine aan het licht gebracht.

De Berlijnse cineasten van de jaren twintig waren hem op deze weg voorgegaan: Fritz Lang, met name, met "*Metropolis*" (1924) maar ook met "*M.*" (1931). Wanneer Evans aangeeft dat de metropersonages "de dames en heren van de jury" zijn, kunnen we concluderen dat hij de typologische inventarisatiemethode van de politiefotografie op de man uit

het volk, die de uitoefening van de rechtspraak is beloofd, heeft willen toepassen.[34] Lang had, in "*M.*", een 'underground' menigte van criminelen al veranderd in een duister tribunaal. Door Daumier als referentie op te voeren, brengt Evans de allereerste argwaan van een kunstenaar met betrekking tot de moderne rechtspraak in verband met alle mogelijke omkeringsspelletjes waarbij de 'massa' en de misdadiger in de gestalte van de mens in de menigte van identiteit wisselen. De ondergrondse metro is 'de cinema van de straten' van Murnau ("street films" zegt Kracauer), veranderd in dit 'volks'-tribunaal van het onbewuste, waarbinnen de misdaad wordt berecht door de misdadiger. Ter ondersteuning van deze interpretatie kunnen we hier nog aan toe voegen dat het door Evans in de straatfotografie van Paul Strand gevonden model zich voor hem toespitste op het portret van de blinde krantenverkoopster, "*Blind Woman*", uit 1916.

Deze schaduwzijde van het modernisme, dit theater van figuren (of maskers) van het onbewuste, was door de Berlijnse cinema, in de crisistijd, geïsoleerd uit het straatleven van de 'grote stad' [Großstadt]. Het ligt voor de hand dat New York - de moderne stad bij uitstek - vervolgens de plaats is waar fotografen, er, in de marge van de filmkunst, de eerste tekens van gaven en waar Walker Evans, aan het eind van een andere crisis, de synthese produceerde van de twee historische momenten, door ze in verband te brengen met het archaïsche moderne karakter van de Baudelairiaanse stad, gekarakteriseerd door de stigmata van de zonde. In een fragment uit *Mon coeur mis à nu*, had Baudelaire zijn 'theorie van de ware beschaving' geformuleerd: "Ze bevindt zich niet in het gas, niet in de damp, niet in de ronddraaiende tafels, zij bevindt zich in de vermindering van de sporen van de erfzonde."[35] Door de metroportretten te verzamelen onder de titel *Many Are Called* (velen zijn geroepen...maar weinigen uitverkoren), herneemt Evans de allegorische - en melancholieke inspiratie van de dichter van *Les Fleurs du Mal* (de bundel die een tijdlang *Het Voorgeborchte* zou gaan heten). Tenslotte moet eraan herinnerd worden dat Baudelaire de karikatuur in haar totaliteit in verband bracht met de 'satanische lach' en dat hij met name Daumier bewonderde.[36]

Dit alles is niet vreemd aan de Amerikaanse kunst van de jaren zestig. De zwarte humor van Smithson heeft deel aan de 'satanische lach' als uitlaatklep voor een melancholie waarvoor de buitenwijken allegorische motieven verschaffen. Omdat hij niet romantisch genoeg was om zich in diezelfde krant als 'de advocaat van de duivel' te manifesteren, heeft Dan Graham zich realistischer opgesteld, en wel door te constateren dat de negatieve utopie in de voorstedelijke omgeving verwezenlijkt werd. Door sinds het eind van de jaren zestig de typologische modellen van het modernisme - hun vorming en hun recente veranderingen - te bestuderen, heeft hij echter precies de situatie van de Baudelairiaanse herinneringsmethodiek teruggevonden: het voorgeborchte, het schemergebied van het (ver)wachten, dat alle door de officiële utopieën meegevoerde historische afvalprodukten in zich opneemt. In dit tussengebied onthult de onbeweeglijke, gelijkblijvende tijd van de melancholie op een negatieve manier de utopische inhoud (de niet-plek) van de clichés van geluk voor iedereen. Het Baudelairiaanse model, zoals dat voor Evans heeft kunnen gelden, duikt aldus opnieuw op achter het Warholiaanse dandyisme.

Ver voor Warhol heeft het principe van de Duchampiaanse onverschilligheid inderdaad voor Evans gegolden als de negatieve en objectief dramatische verheerlijking, via de fotografie, van de gelijkheidsdroom van de Amerikaanse samenleving. Want deze onverschilligheid is ook en in de eerste plaats die van de dandy die tevergeefs probeert te ontsnappen aan de bohème en, net als Baudelaire, Daumier bewondert. Door hun plaats binnen deze genealogie in te nemen behelzen de metroportretten een historische interpretatie van de crisis in het modernisme in de jaren dertig, die overeenstemt met de uit de bestudering van de Baudelairiaanse stad afgeleide observaties van Walter Benjamin. De menigte, gemanipuleerd door de machinerie van een totalitaire propaganda, vertegenwoordigt het aantal waarin de bohemiaanse kunstenaar (of de 'schilder van het moderne leven') zijn subjectiviteit ontbindt en de impulsen voor zijn activiteit vindt. De kunst moet op de machine reageren door middel van de machine, niet op de manier van het via de media overgeleverde epos (dat een pseudo-organische gemeenschap verheerlijkt) maar op een lyrische manier, die de diversiteit van het gewone benadrukt.

Dat is de grote uitvinding van Evans in de jaren dertig, waarvan Dan Graham een der erfgenamen is: het inheemse van de Amerikaanse cultuur, in een diversiteit die niet herleidbaar is tot modernistische typologieën. Er is geen Amerikaans volk maar een Amerikaans schouwspel. Rijker en complexer dan de zeldzame door een van oorsprong Europees modernisme geïnspireerde meesterwerken, beantwoordt zijn werk desondanks niet aan het cliché van een Nieuwe paradijselijke wereld, beschermd door de industriële beschaving. Van alle 'meesters' van de Amerikaanse fotografie, is Walker Evans zonder enige twijfel de enige die zich volkomen heeft losgemaakt van het idee van de Natuur, die rigoureus de kant heeft gekozen van de tekens en van de geschiedenis - om het door Barthes ten tijde van de *Mythologies* gemaakte onderscheid te gebruiken -; de enige die niet heeft geprobeerd een fotografisch meesterschap te baseren op het vermogen om de natuur aan het woord te laten of om er via de magie van de techniek de geheime boodschappen van te onthullen. Op enkele werken na, is zijn oeuvre begonnen met de crisis van 1929, in New York, en is daar ook mee geëindigd. Voor hem is het Amerikaanse schouwspel in essentie stedelijk, gekenmerkt door de tekens van de stad (of van de commercie) en hun heftige maar vluchtige invloed op de omgeving. De opname moet niet de vorm van een symbool ("the thing itself" van Weston) isoleren maar een beeld-teken vastleggen, een document-monument.

Voor alle fotografen van de jaren twintig die door Strand waren beïnvloed en de anti-picturalistische 'straight photography' beoefenden, was de natuur tegelijk, of achtereenvolgens, het model van de ideale machine - en zo vergelijkbaar met en opneembaar in een kunstwerk - en het heilzame antwoord op de negatieve effecten van het tijdperk van de mechanisering. Ze moesten in beide gevallen een 'kwaliteit' zien te verkrijgen die het beeld verenigt met het kunstvoorwerp of wat Fernand Léger "het schone object" noemde: het industriële object, volmaakt ontworpen, functioneel, waarvan het 'design' gehoorzaamt aan het ontwerp van de natuur. Hoewel hij gevoelig was voor de projectietekening van technische objecten, zelfs en vooral de meest gewone - zoals blijkt uit zijn publicatie in *Fortune* in 1955, "Beauties of the Common Tool" - zag Evans er in essentie de voorbeelden in van een technische cultuur die eerder deel heeft aan een antropologische (en historische) denkbeeldigheid dan aan de constante wetten van de natuur. Wat verder ook zijn voorwerp van studie was, zijn model was nooit en te nimmer het (natuurlijke of industriële) object maar het op grond van verwantschap en functie met de gedrukte, aangeplakte en voor de communicatie gebruikte tekens verbonden beeld

Het verschil met zijn onmiddellijke voorgangers is op dit punt beslissend. Ralph Steiner bijvoorbeeld, die hem zijn techniek overdraagt, had in de jaren twintig de enorme rijkdom van het later in *American Photographs* bijeengebrachte documentaire materiaal gezien. Daarvan getuigen zijn illustrates bij een artikel in *Fortune* uit 1930, aan het begin van de crisis, waarvan de opzet al exact die van Evans was: "Een constatering: niet het recente Amerika, met zijn wolkenkrabbers, zijn vliegtuigen en zijn generatoren, maar een onveranderlijk [unregenerate] Amerika, met zijn veranda's en achtererven, zijn lelijkheid en zijn rotzooi."[37] Dezelfde tekst heeft overigens de verdienste uiterst helder de in de nationalistische verbeelding van de redacteuren van *Fortune* bestaande 'mythologische' redenen te formuleren, die Evans de gelegenheid zouden geven voor dit tijdschrift te gaan werken: "In wezen is Engeland triest en Amerika vrolijk. Ze voelt zich niet goed, maar ze heeft voldoende exuberantie en energie om het land te bezaaien met versleten en aan hun lot overgelaten spullen. Iedere vuilnisbelt, iedere rij gammele huizen langs een spoorlijn, is het bewijs van onze grenzeloze rijkdom. Dit is ruimte die we niet nodig hebben. We hebben voldoende." Maar deze overeenkomsten maken des te tastbaarder waarin Evans verschilt. Steiner had zich ongetwijfeld al zeer vroeg geschikt naar een behoefte aan culturele identiteit die door de ideologie van de technologische vooruitgang niet geheel kon worden bevredigd (omdat ze teveel dingen buiten beschouwing liet). Maar hij was te veel gehecht aan de waarden die de perfectionering van de traditionele (pre-industriële) 'grote kunst' met zich meebracht, die hem in 1926-27 via Strand, het grote voorbeeld ervan, was geopenbaard. "Strand heeft me zijn Mexicaanse foto's laten zien. Ik was er kapot van: nog nooit had ik zulke rijke afdrukken gezien - met zo'n tastbare structuur - en zo'n magnifieke tonaliteit."[38] Evans daarentegen is dit criterium van 'historische' kwaliteit en perfectionering in de uitvoering altijd blijven verwerpen, en verklaarde zelfs nog in 1971, toen hij weer een keer in het Museum of Modern Art, New York, exposeerde: "Ik voel me niet langer op mijn gemak in een museum. Ik wil er niet meer heen, wil helemaal niks geleerd worden, wil geen 'volmaakte' kunst zien. Ik ben geïnteresserd in wat ze het inheemse noemen." [39]

Toch moeten we de dubbelzinnige aspekten van de positie van Evans niet over het hoofd zien, als we een exact beeld willen hebben van zijn artistieke luciditeit. In 1971 is het inheemse - "wat ze het inheemse noemen"- een specialiteit die wordt onderkend door het establishment, waartegen hij gekant beweerd te zijn. *Fortune* had, veertig jaar eerder, de weg gebaand, gevolgd door het Museum of Modern Art, New York. In de laatste jaren van zijn leven is Evans zelf een 'historisch' kunstenaar, een meester, die doceert aan de universiteit van Yale; hij maakt de indruk zijn eigen lessen te herhalen. In 1969 schetst hij in een collectief werk met de titel *Quality: Its Image in the Arts* - een titel die geen commentaar behoeft - een straatfotograaf-achtig portret, en levert daarmee een zoveelste variant op de van moraal en fatsoen gespeende burgelijke held - de voyeur, de spion, het onverantwoordelijke kind -, zoals die is gepopulariseerd door de romanliteratuur sinds de 19e eeuw (Nabokov wordt overigens geciteerd). Hoewel Stieglitz erin slaagde de fotografie het museum in te krijgen, is de plaats van de fotografie 'op straat': "Een rauw feest voor het oog: veelgebruikte winkels, slaapkamers en achtererven, ver van de ruimten vol grootse architectuur, landschappelijke pracht, of de meer gewoon pittoreske natuur." [40] Deze tegenstelling van de beide 'high and low' repertoires is duidelijk te welsprekend en heeft deel aan dezelfde gevestigde retoriek die ze wil tegenspreken (en slechts ontkent). We zouden ietwat gemakkelijk kunnen concluderen dat Evans uiteindelijk niet is ontsnapt aan de "paradigmatische positie" - in zijn eigen woorden - van Stieglitz, bij wie hij "de afwezigheid van humor die zo karakteristiek is voor de post-Victoriaanse bohème" herkende.

Maar deze dubbelzinnigheid is ook het effect van de luciditeit. Evans had in Atget een overtuigender voorbeeld gevonden dan Stieglitz (en Strand). Maar hij kon niet de kunstenaar-collectionneur zijn die een heimelijk oeuvre aanlegt door instituten en academische kunstenaars documenten te verschaffen. In het Amerika van de jaren twintig en dertig stemde de documentaire strategie van Atget maar al te zeer overeen met het programma van een tijdschrift als *Fortune*. Hij moest zijn 'onderneming' dus 'vestigen', dat wil zeggen haar tegelijk een institutionele ondersteuning en een specifieke vorm geven, buiten de media om. [41] Dat deed hij toen hij in 1938 gebruik maakte van een tentoonstelling in het Museum of Modern Art, New York, om *Americain Photographs* te publiceren: een boek, tussen tijdschrift en galeriewand in, waarbinnen de beelden eenvoudigweg zijn gereproduceerd - en niet ingelijst, als kostbare werken -, maar zonder bijschriften, met regelmatige onderlinge afstanden,

elk afzonderlijk gepubliceerd op een pagina zonder beeld ertegenover. Hij omzeilde op deze manier de twee tegengestelde maar in gelijkmatige mystificerende oplossingen van Stieglitz en Margaret Bourke-White. Hij omzeilde ook de schoolmeester- achtige aanpak (van de simpele of meer 'kritische' propoganda) die de fotomontage kenmerkte maar die minder goede resultaten opleverde (op uitzonderingen als Heartfield na) dan de aanpassing van de kunst aan de communicatie-technieken van de reclame.

Over montage gesproken, deze blijft voor Evans een cinematografisch, dus syntactisch, model van 'editing'. Door bemiddeling van met name Jay Leyda kende hij de films van Eisenstein, en van Vertov. De montage is een manier om beelden te organiseren waarvan de autonomie, hoe noodzakelijk ook, nooit definitief, uiteindelijk mag zijn. Steeds weer zijn weigering van geperfectioneerde kunst! Hij blijft overigens voortdurend bezig de montage van zijn foto's te veranderen, ze te fragmentariseren, er details aan te onttrekken die hij combineert met weer andere. Zo is er sprake van een mobiliteit met een dubbele resonantie: ze komt overeen met technieken - de film en de pers - buiten de schone kunsten om, en ze komt voort uit een specifieke opvatting van het beeld-teken, als een moment binnen een open werk.

In 1931 maakt Evans, in de al geciteerde tekst uit *Hound and Horn*, die de recente ontwikkelingen (de 'renaissance') van de fotografie in Duitsland verkent, weliswaar gewag van het boek *Die Welt is schön* van Albert Renger-Patzsch, maar hij is er maar half over te spreken, want hij vindt het te sterk betrokken op het traditionele debat met de schilderkunst. De structuur van het boek van Renger-Patzsch is inderdaad buitengewoon statisch, te opgesplitst, en weerspiegelt de organische opvatting van de relatie tussen natuur en industrie, traditioneel en modern. Evans herkende zich daarentegen sterk in het appèl aan de amateuristische vrijheid - onverschilligheid, onvolkomenheid, onvoltooidheid - die er, in de door Franz Roh geregideerde tekst van *foto-auge*, toe leidt dat de fotografie in verband wordt gebracht met de 'onderschatte geschiedenis van de niet-professionele produktiviteit'. Maar pas aan het eind van het artikel verschijnt de meest positieve vermelding, met betrekking tot de portretten van August Sander: "*Antlitz der Zeit* is meer dan een boek met typologische studies; het is een voorbeeld van een camera die haar blik precies in de goede richting op mensen richt. Dit is een van de door Atget aangekondigde nieuwe wegen in de fotografie. Het is een fotografische montage van de samenleving [a photographic editing of society], een klinisch proces..."

In die paar regels, geschreven op een keerpunt van zijn carrière, kondigt Evans zijn eigen programma aan: "a photographic editing of society", en hij heeft dat programma vervolgens niet anders dan steeds opnieuw bevestigd, tot de uiterste formule van de metroportretten toe. Alles draaide al heel vroeg om het idee van type of typologie. Vanaf 1928 vervaardigde hij architectuurstudies, die eerder aansluiten bij de Europese 'nieuwe visie' dan bij de voorbeelden van Stieglitz en van Strand.[42] Hij waagde zich ook, en met succes, aan de straatfotografie [street photography], waarbij hij als gedragsregel een door de onzekerheden van de momentopnamen versoepelde sociale typologie in acht nam. Hierover verklaarde hij heel veel later: "Ik heb me laten leiden door een paar plotselinge vooruitziende invallen. Ik voelde dat ik een bepaald type op straat wilde vastleggen, een 'snapshot' van iemand aan de waterkant, of een stenograaf die aan het lunchen is. Dat was een hele goeie ader. Die boor ik nog steeds aan." Hij heeft het over de dwangmatigheid van de kunstenaar-collectioneur.[43] Maar, zoals blijkt uit de opmerking over Sander en zoals zijn montage-projecten hebben bevestigd, was dit model van 'snapshot'-gewijze typologie, hoe stimulerend ook, niet bevredigend. Er was een meer solide structuur nodig, die hem in staat zou stellen de sociale (en historische) diversiteit te ordenen, zonder haar tot een pittoreske typologie te reduceren, en zonder de intuïtie aan de beperkende 'studie'-procedures op te offeren. Atget zelf heeft de typische figuren van het Parijse straatleven vastgelegd en daarmee het model van de 'kleine ambachten' van de pittoreske traditie verruimd, maar hij had zichzelf een veel ambitieuzer programma opgelegd, dat de intergratie van architectuur en stadsmeubilair inhield. Anderzijds vat de manier waarop Baudelaire de voorkeur gaf aan Daumier boven Monnier (de bedenker van het personage van 'Monsieur Prudhomme') tamelijk goed samen wat Evans, in *American Photographs* (en in *Many Are Called*) onderscheidt van een goede straatfotograaf, waarvan er rond 1940 zoveel waren: "Verscheidene van zijn *Scènes populaires* zijn zeker aangenaam; anders zou men de wrede en verassende charme van de daguerrotype moeten ontkennen; maar Monnier weet niets te creëren, niets te idealiseren, niets te arrangeren." [44]

Dit zijn de twee oevers van het montage-project van Evans, zoals ze verschenen in *American Photographs*: de mensen in de (grote of kleine) stad, de (alledaagse) architectuur. Van de ene oever naar de andere, over en weer, bewegen zich de (actuele en historische) tekens. Want de architectuur zelf, in haar typologische diversiteit, karakteristiek voor het Amerikaanse eclectisme, is een systeem of, op zijn minst, een assemblage van tekens. 'Editing', monteren betekent het ordenen van een collectie beeld-typen: menselijke en architectonische typen, die van archetype tot stereotype variëren, via alle mogelijke bastaardvormen. De collectie neemt op een dwangmatige manier toe, net zoals de stedelijke tekens zich vermenigvuldigen, maar de methode volgens welke ze verwezenlijkt wordt (haar organisatie in sequenties) is beredeneerd, zo niet synthetisch. De accumulatie en de rijkdom van de assemblage, die de stedelijke en voorstedelijke omgeving karakteriseren, moeten geordend en in zekere zin verheerlijkt worden door de gestrengheid van de montage in sequenties.

Er bestaat dus een nauwe samenhang tussen de montage-arbeid van *American Photographs* en het beeld van de

Amerikaanse architectuur, zoals dat in het tweede deel van het werk wordt ontwikkeld. De 'pop'-architect Robert Venturi - in wie Dan Graham vanaf het eind van de jaren zeventig sterk geïnteresseerd is - zal zeggen: "Main Street is bijna o.k." [Main Street is almost all right.] Walker Evans laat reeds zien waar dit welslagen op stoelt: de ritmische combinatie van de rechte lijn met onregelmatige, symbolische of decoratieve figuren, samengevat in het dubbele beeld van de stedelijke tekens, die een communicatiefunctie vervullen en tegelijk voortkomen uit de minder ondubbelzinnige ('gratuite') belangen. Deze combinatie is alomtegenwoordig in het boek. De ordening kan uiterst rigoureus zijn, of ze nu gedicteerd wordt door de strenge regelmatigheid van de 'frame houses' en de neoklassieke rijvormige rangschikkingen, of door de uniformiteit van een bepaald opnameprincipe (frontaliteit en nauwelijks benadrukte diepte van het gezichtsveld, bijvoorbeeld), maar ze wordt altijd tegengesproken door de wanklank, ja zelfs de ongepastheid van de details, en door de versnellingen van de montage.

Er is vaak gesproken over het 'classicisme' van Evans (eenvoud, bescheiden gebruik van middelen, afwijzing van het romantisch pittoreske, anti-expressionisme). Het is mogelijk dat het model van Main Street, verbonden met het Georgische type van de 'row houses', in de verte de syntaxis van de klassieke architectuur oproept, waarin de vijf afzonderlijke 'ordes' -volgens de in de renaissance vastgelegde typologie - gesymboliseerd worden door zinnebeeldige ornamentale figuren: dorisch, ionisch, etc. Maar de complexiteit van de eclectische assemblage onderscheidt zich van de eenvoud, of gestrengheid, van de paradigmatische ordes. Evans heeft, aan de andere kant, de opkomst bijgewoond van de Internationale Stijl in de Verenigde Staten (met de expositie in het Museum of Modern Art, New York, en het boek van Philip Johnson, in 1932), maar hij kon er niet mee instemmen, en hij kon evenmin het ideaal van de technologische vooruitgang, dat ten grondslag lag aan het universalisme van Mies van der Rohe, onderschrijven. Zonder regionaal te zijn, is zijn taal die van de gemiddelde stadscultuur, met haar alledaagse bijzonderheden, gesitueerd tussen de metropool en de wereld van het platteland, waarbinnen de zeldzame voorbeelden van de 'grote' architectuur deelhebben aan de diversiteit van de bricolages en ontleende schijn-stijlen: tussen het min of meer primitivistische archetype (zoals de hiervoor met betrekking tot Dan Graham genoemde fameuze hut van Laugier) en het historische en industriële stereotype. Deze situatie komt exact overeen met de plaats van de fotografie, tussen de schone kunsten en de media.

Door zijn modellen in de negentiende-eeuwse Europese literatuur te zoeken, heeft Evans zich kunnen losmaken van de diverse wachtwoorden van een utopisch of aan geheugenverlies lijdend modernisme, dat het kosmopolitisme van de Lumières zou veranderen in een nationalisme dat was gebaseerd op de triomfantelijke universaliteit van een model van vrije onderneming (zoals de generatie van Dan Graham dat in de na-oorlogse periode zag gebeuren). Zijn eerste coherente documentaireproject in 1930-31, opgedragen door Lincoln Kirstein, betrof overigens de Victoriaanse architectuur (Boston, Saratoga Springs, etc.). Maar het is niet de fotograaf van het hart van Amerika, die de ennui van Main Street en de ellende van geruïneerde pachters heeft veredeld. De tweede sectie van *American Photographs* opent en sluit met twee afbeeldingen van verbrijzelde ornamenten - 'relikwieën' - gekneed als papier-maché of uitgeknipt papier. Deze ornamenten zijn valse overblijfsels van de Oudheid, en reduceren het historische archetype tot het stereotype van de melancholieke verslagenheid. Men kan zich nauwelijks afbeeldingen voorstellen die sterker overeenkomen met de Baudelairiaanse allegorie, zoals die in diezelfde periode is beschreven door Walter Benjamin als een voorbeeldige ironische attitude van de kunstenaar-collectioneur met betrekking tot zichzelf. Voorbeeldige ironie, omdat ze van de melancholie de voorwaarde maakt voor de mogelijkheid van een verheerlijking van de moderne tekens, vrij van het nostalgische terugverlangen naar een gemeenschapsgevoel (en in feite van elke futuristische dromerij).

Via (valselijk historicistische) citaten staan de tekens "in de hoedanigheid van afval" al bloot aan vernietiging en kunnen ze zich er van losmaken als van hun eigen basis. Op dit punt vormt zich op zijn beurt het beeld van de mensen, niet zozeer tegen een architectonische achtergrond als wel temidden van de bouwval van de stedelijke tekens - waaraan de architectuur deelheeft: het beeld ontstaat, gestimuleerd en in sequenties georganiseerd door de dubbele activiteit (verzamelen, monteren) van de fotograaf. Het humanisme van Walker Evans kan, net als dat van Baudelaire, uitbreken in een moment van medelijden, en wel des te gemakkelijker naarmate hij minder geneigd is tot de 'satanische lach'. Maar hij zweert vooral bij een ander 'pathos', dat zich richt op tekens en sporen van destructie, waarmee de collectionneur met zijn eigen passie wordt geconfronteerd.

Vandaar de koerswijziging van de laatste twintig jaar. Het gaat, in zijn beste werk, niet meer om het schouwspel van de straat, maar om interieurs, waar zich in de assemblage van enkele objecten-tekens, het beeld concentreert van degenen - afwezigen - die ze bewonen, als een hele heldere maar min of meer ontcijferbare boodschap - om de term van het boek uit 1966, *Messages from the Interior,* weer eens te gebruiken. Evans was geïnteresseerd in deze huiselijke 'arrangementen' sinds de periode van de FSA, toen hij bij de pachters over de vloer kwam. Eerder, rond 1930, en later, parallel met de beelden van FSA, had hij een enkele keer zijn eigen woon- en werkplek (met name zijn werkplaats) gefotografeerd. Maar "*The Child's Room* "(1951), "*The Parlor Chair* "(1958), "*The Home Organ*"(1968) moeten in verband worden gebracht met het project met betrekking tot de Victoriaanse huizen en met het paradigma van de historische ruïnes, zoals *Messages from the Interior* duidelijk vaststelt door de eerste twee hierboven vermelde beelden te associëren met beelden van verlaten of bouwvallige gebouwen, van versleten ornamenten, en van volstrekt vervallen huiselijke plekken. Deze kant van het oeuvre van Evans is niet alleen de indicatie van de retraite van een oude, vermoeide man, maar het effect van de aangehouden, afgemeten dwangmatigheid van de collectionneur die overal, bij de anderen, de tekens van zijn melancholie zoekt. Het interieur, met zijn 'decoratieve' arrangementen, is niet zozeer een toevluchtsoord als wel de vorm van een achtergehouden geschiedenis, die op het punt staat te worden uitgewist door de vergetelheid en de noodlottigheid van het banale (van de genormaliseerde gelijkschakeling).

Geen enkele kunstenaar, en Dan Graham net zomin als Walker Evans, kan, tenzij hij zich onderwerpt aan de melancholie, deze noodlottigheid herleiden tot een proces van sociale vervreemding, waarvan hij de onverschillige of 'kritische' getuige is. De satanische lach is de oplossing van de romantische held. Maar wie zich niet de advocaat van de duivel kan - of wil - laten maken, wordt noodzakelijkerwijs blootgesteld aan het dubbelzinnige pathos van de geïndividualiseerde, decoratieve, geformaliseerde tekens van het gewone, vooral als hij weigert zijn toevlucht te nemen tot een universele werkelijkheid, geabstraheerd uit historische determineringen. De dubbele lezing van de Pop Art mondt bij Dan Graham uit in dit pathos, dat door de fotografische beelden tegelijk versneld en op afstand gehouden wordt..
Als Walker Evans het door de Pop Art medegeërfde beeld van Amerika heeft kunnen uitvinden, dan was dat omdat hem het vermogen was gegeven om zijn melancholieke passie te transformeren in een lyriek die - op afstand - verbonden was met het lot van de massa.

1 Op verzoek van Jeanne Siegel die de kunstprogramma's van de Newyorkse radiozender WBAI leidde, had Lucy Lippard op 8 maart 1970 vier kunstenaars - Douglas Huebler, Dan Graham, Carl Andre en Jan Dibbets - bijeengebracht die gemeen hadden dat ze alle vier op de een of andere manier de taal hadden gebruikt ["four visual artists who have used words a way or another"]. De tekst van deze ontmoeting is gepubliceerd in Lippard, Lucy, *Six Years: The Dematerialization of the Art Object*, New York, Praeger, 1973, pp. 155-159.

2 Dan Graham heeft dit idee herhaaldelijk onder woorden gebracht, waarbij hij iedere keer benadrukte dat zijn werken voor de tijdschriften tegelijk een radikalisering van de Pop Art was en een transformatie van het minimalisme door zijn schematisering en zijn situering van het werk in een kritische context. Zie in het bijzonder "My Works for Pages: A History of Conceptual Art", in *Dan Graham*, cat. Art Gallery of Western Australia, Perth, 1985, pp. 8-11. "Als de 'minimale' kunst haar betekenis heeft ontleend aan het idee dat de galerie een objectieve steun betekent, heeft de Pop Art de hare ontleend aan de beelden van de haar omgevende wereld van de media. De Pop Art wilde het aan de schone kunsten toegekende kwaliteitsidee bestrijden door de componenten van de massacultuur te gebruiken.
De beelden van de Pop werden via de tijdschriften teruggevoerd in de populaire cultuur, waar zij zo zelf het ironische commentaar op werd. Wat Pop aantoonde was dat de informatiemedia, zoals tijdschriften, dialectisch binnen het kunstsysteem konden worden gebruikt. Dat wil zeggen dat een werk tegelijkertijd kon functioneren in termen van zowel de kunsttaal als de populaire taal van de media, waarbij het de veronderstellingen van beide becommentarieerde en in een perspectief plaatste. Ik ontwierp werken voor tijdschriftpagina's die tegelijk autonoom waren en via de context verband hielden met de hen omgevende informatie op de andere bedrukte pagina's. (...). "*Schema*" (maart 1966) is het meest 'absolute' van deze werken. Elk gepubliceerd voorbeeld van dit werk verschijnt als een geïsoleerde pagina in verschillende tijdschriften. (...) Normaal gesproken reproduceren kunsttijdschriften tweedehands kunst die eerst, als tastbare aanwezigheid, in galerieën wordt geëxposeerd. Door dit om te keren, bestaat "*Schema*" uitsluitend bij de gratie van zijn aanwezigheid in de functionele structuur van het tijdschrift en kan alleen in tweedehands vorm in een galerie worden tentoongesteld. (...) Ik wilde Pop Art maken die in letterlijke zin beschikbaar en wegwerpbaar zou zijn (een idee waarop gezinspeeld werd in Warhols idee om 'kwaliteit' door 'kwantiteit' te vervangen, de logica van een consumptiemaatschappij). Ik wilde een kunstvorm maken die niet kon worden gereproduceerd of tentoongesteld in een galerie/museum, en ik wilde een verdere reductie van het 'minimale' object tot een niet noodzakelijkerwijs esthetische twee-dimensionale vorm (die niet geschilderd of getekend mocht zijn): drukwerk dat massaal geproduceerde en massaal beschikbare/wegwerpbare informatie is." In de loop van een gesprek in 1988 met Eugenie Tsai, in *Robert Smithson: Drawings*, cat., Münster-Sorø-München, 1989-90, pp. 8-23, benadrukt Dan Graham het idee van het beschikbare/wegwerpbare [disposable] in zijn eerste werken ("*Magazine Pieces*"), net als bij de kunstenaars (met name Flavin, LeWitt) die hij in de kortstondige John Daniels Gallery (oktober 1964-juni 1965) had gepresenteerd: "Toen ik Sol LeWitt exposeerde, was zijn opdracht aan mij na afloop om het hout als brandhout te gebruiken; hij zou dat daarna nooit meer zeggen maar hij was op dat moment volstrekt niet geïnteresseerd in het probleem van de waarde. (...) Niemand had werkelijk ook maar enig benul dat deze dingen een bepaalde waarde konden hebben; zo dacht je toen gewoon niet. Een sleutelidee van de zestiger jaren, in kleding, mode, en ook in rockmuziek, was dat van dingen die even beschikbaar zijn en vervolgens weggeworpen worden ('disposable'). Dus deed of maakte ik iets dat weggeworpen kon worden, de produktie ervan interesseerde me niet. Ik dacht er nooit aan dat iemand het in een museum zou kunnen plaatsen; daar was ik volkomen tegen." op. cit. p.8.

3 Het eerste essay van Smithson, uit 1965, gewijd aan Judd, bevat deze interpretatie reeds. Zie "Donald Judd", *7 sculptors*, cat. Philadelphia, Institute of Contemporary Art, 1965, pp. 13-16, herdrukt in *The Writings of Robert Smithson*, bloemlezing bezorgd door Holt, Nancy, New York University Press, 1979, pp. 21-23. Smithson interpreteert de structuren van Judd als een speculatie over de materie, over de vorm van de materie ("the very form of matter") en merkt op: "Net zoals de maniëristische kunstenaars van de zestiende eeuw de feiten van de klassieke renaissance herschikten, zo heeft Judd de feiten van de Moderne Werkelijkheid herschikt. Op die manier heeft Judd een nieuw soort 'architectuur' ontdekt, terwijl zijn omkeringsmethoden zijn 'architectuur' juist de indruk gaven opgebouwd te zijn uit 'anti-materie'. Misschien zijn 'primaire materie' en 'anti-materie' wel identiek."
Dan Graham herinnert eraan dat Judd deze interpretatie volstrekt niet op prijs stelde ("Judd didn't like the essay, he hated it."). Smithson heeft "Judd (in dat essay) verzonnen zoals Borges een fictief personage verzint." De divergentie tussen de beide kunstenaars weerspiegelt de verdeeldheid van de Amerikaanse avant-garde kunst van de zestiger jaren tussen enerzijds de aan een puriteinse moraal gehechte minimalisten en conceptualisten, verwant aan Nieuw Links, en anderzijds de popkunstenaars, die dichter bij de 'rock and roll' en de 'fun'-cultuur stonden. Smithson "behoorde veel meer tot de Pop Art", volgens Dan Graham, "en hij hield ervan de advocaat van de duivel te spelen. Dat is in feite zijn maniëristische kant, want de maniëristen hebben deze positie ingenomen tegenover de waarden van de renaissance. De minimalisten konden dat niet begrijpen; ze konden geen maniëristen zijn. Op die manier is het meningsverschil tussen Smithson en Judd ontstaan. Hij stopte Judd in een mal die al of niet historisch juist kan zijn, maar Judd zag het zo nooit. Judd stelde zich altijd heel moralistisch op, en ook al is hij volgens mij gewoon rechts, reageert hij nog steeds idealistisch en moralistisch." (Gesprek met Eugenie Tsai, op. cit., noot 2, p. 14.)

4 We weten dat het anders ging: de redacteuren van *Arts Magazine* vervingen de afbeeldingen van Dan Graham door een foto van Walker Evans, "*Wooden Houses, Boston*", uit 1930, gereproduceerd in het boek uit 1938, *American Photographs*, cat. Museum of Modern Art, New York, dat in 1962 herdrukt was. Projected Art werd gepresenteerd in november 1966 in het Finch College Museum of Art, New York, door Elayne Varian.
Dan Graham was, lijkt het, de enige kunstenaar in deze expositie die dia's projecteerde. We moeten dit initiatief opnieuw in de lange geschiedenis van het gebruik van de dia [transparancy] als pedagogisch instrument plaatsen - met name in de studie en het onderwijs van architectuur, sinds Frederick Henry Evans omtrent de eeuwwisseling - en als mogelijkheid om een foto die als picturaal model dient te vergroten (Lichtenstein, Richter, de fotorealisten). Op het moment dat Projected Art plaatsvond, beschouwde niemand in het kunstmilieu een kleurendia als een doel op zich. Dat was heel anders aan het begin van de eeuw - na de uitvinding van de fotografische plaat door de gebroeders Lumière - in de kringen van de Amerikaanse Secessie-fotografen (Steiglitz, Steichen) en van het internationale picturalisme. We kunnen er ook aan herinneren dat de fotografen van de Farm Security Administration (FSA), in de jaren dertig, met het nieuwe procédé van de in 1935 op de markt gekomen Kodachrome, enige honderden kleurendia's hebben vervaardigd, soms vergelijkbaar met die van Dan Graham, maar volkomen verontachtzaamd tot hun recente herontdekking door Sally Stein in de archieven van het Library of Congress in Washington. Aan het eind van de jaren vijftig had Dan Graham - net als nu overigens - geen enkele belangstelling voor de geschiedenis van de fotografie, maar de andere hierboven genoemde verwijzingen waren hem bekend. Hij associeerde de lichtgevende projectie van dia's eveneens met de neons van Flavin en interesseerde zich, zoals blijkt uit zijn latere werken, voor het idee van 'transparantie' (van het glas) in het geprojecteerde beeld ('transparancy')

5 We moeten onderscheid maken tussen het artikel in *Arts Magazine*, H o m e s f o r A m e r i c a , en het werk "*Homes for America*" dat later werd gerealiseerd, in 1970-71, als een reconstructie van de oorspronkelijke maquette van het artikel, door de drukkerij van het College of Art and Design van Nova Scotia, Halifax; een door talloze varianten begeleide reconstructie, waaronder het dubbele paneel van de collectie Daled, hier gereproduceerd op pagina 132, waarin foto's met personages voorkomen die zijn genomen in 1967, dat wil zeggen na het artikel. Dit onderscheid is noodzakelijk als we rekening willen houden met de anti-kunst houding waaruit de keuze van de 'disposable' in de "*Magazine Pieces*" voortvloeit. Maar een dergelijke keuze was onhoudbaar, want onverenigbaar met de complexiteit en veeleisendheid van de kritische fictie van tekst-beelden. Dan Graham wilde aanvankelijk in een tijdschrift als *Esquire* publiceren en moest zich tevreden stellen met een kunsttijdschrift dat zijn project zelf niet eens heeft gerespecteerd. In feite was dit project vanaf het begin, juist door zijn complexiteit, niet herleidbaar tot een vorm die onmiddellijk geconsumeerd kon worden, en dus gedoemd tot een uitgestelde (en veranderde) verwezenlijking, in een 'artistieke' vorm. Het principe van de 'disposable' - waaraan elk consumptieartikel daadwerkelijk deelheeft - kon slechts een model zijn voor een produkt van kritische fictie, en, voor de kunstenaar Dan Graham, een onhoudbaar, fictief ideaal. Hier komt de macht van de noodzaak nog eens bij. Na 1970, op het moment dat hij "*Homes for America*" realiseert, ontdekt Dan Graham, net als alle andere kunstenaars van de door John Gibson in New York gepresenteerde conceptuele beweging, dat de fotografie een bron van inkomsten kon zijn, zonder zich daarmee ondergeschikt te maken aan de schone kunsten.

6 "Judd heeft een labyrintische collectie 'drukwerk', waarvan een deel door hem 'bekeken' in plaats van gelezen wordt. Zo kan hij bijvoorbeeld een wiskundige vergelijking nemen, en die visueel vertalen in een metalen reeks gestructureerde intervallen. In deze context kan je 'drukwerk' het beste opvatten op de manier van Borges, als 'Het Universum' (dat anderen de bibliotheek noemen) - met andere woorden als een nooit eindigende 'bibliotheek van Babel'." Holt, op. cit., noot 3, p. 15.

7 De oorspronkelijke titel van de tekst was 'A Tour of the Monuments of Passaic, New Jersey'. De tekst is herdrukt in Holt, op. cit., noot 3, pp. 52-57. Smithson presenteert zijn foto's van monumenten als de stilstaande beelden [stills] van een film. Het eerste monument, een brug over de rivier de Passaic, geeft de toon aan: "De middagzon maakte de plek tot cinema, en veranderde de brug en de rivier in een overbelicht beeld [picture]. Als ik het fotografeerde met mijn Instamatic 400 leek het net of ik een foto fotografeerde. De zon werd een monsterachtige gloeilamp die een afzonderlijkee reeks 'stills' via mijn Instamatic in mijn ogen projecteerde. Als ik over de brug liep was het net of ik op een reusachtige foto liep die van hout en staal was gemaakt, en beneden me bevond zich de rivier als een enorme film die niets dan een continu blanco liet zien."

8 Het onderscheid tussen de twee betekenissen van 'monument' is goed geanalyseerd door Françoise Choay in "A propos du culte et des monuments", voorbericht bij de Franse vertaling van de tekst van Aloïs Riegl, *Der moderne Denkmalkultus*, uit 1903 (*Le culte moderne des monuments*, Paris, Editions du Seuil, 1984, p. 11): "Het begrip historisch monument is niet een nooit variërend cultureel gegeven (...) Want als het monument, dat wil zeggen, (etymologisch) het artefact dat ons aanroept om ons iets te doen herinneren, deel uitmaakt van een universele 'geheugenkunst', die men in praktisch alle culturen aantreft, dan houdt de uitvinding van het historische monument rechtstreeks verband met die van de begrippen kunst en geschiedenis. Ze behoort tot het post-gothische Europa dat dit concept heeft uitgewerkt in de loop van een lange arbeid, waarvan de eerste aardlaag kan worden ontdekt in het Quattrocento."

9 Zie het gesprek met Huebler met Irmeline Lebeer op het moment van zijn expositie in de Kunstverein Münster (december 1972-januari 1973), *Chroniques de l'art vivant*, no. 38, april 1973, pp. 21-23: "Mijn voornaamste preoccupatie was toen (op het moment van de "*Primary Structures*") om zulke grote sculpturen te maken dat ze niet in het interieur van een museum pasten. Daarom heb ik ze in de open lucht opgesteld. Nu is het zo dat de primaire structuren interessant zijn omdat ze werkelijk worden: een kubus is even werkelijk als een tafel of een stoel. Door deze vormen van een absolute werkelijkheid buiten op te stellen, werd ik gedwongen te constateren dat ze met de natuur niet dezelfde harmonische relaties aangingen als de standbeelden, de naakten, etc. ... maar dat ze als werkelijke objecten functioneerden die gingen wedijveren met alle andere werkelijke objecten van de buitenwereld. Ik gaf me er rekenschap van dat, tenzij ik ze in een architectonisch kader zou integreren - een omgeving die speciaal was ontworpen om ze op te nemen -, mijn sculpturen de confrontatie met de bomen, de hemel niet aankonden, dat de natuur machtiger was. Ik kon natuurlijk nog grotere vormen maken, monumentale sculpturen, maar in feite had de wereld er geen behoefte aan dat ik nog meer objecten toevoegde aan de al bestaande. Deze ervaring heeft me aangespoord een totaal andere richting uit te gaan."

10 In de loop van een gesprek met Daniela Salvioni (*Flash Art*, no. 152, May-June

1990, pp. 142-144), merkt Dan Graham op: "Ik ben niet per se tegen monumentaliteit. De conceptuele kunst was geïnteresseerd in de 'disposable', het wegwerpbare, niet door het museum verzamelbare werk, dat een duurzame historische toeëigening weigerde.
Vanuit een architectonisch gezichtspunt daarentegen markeert monumentaliteit plaats, geschiedenis. De betekenis van dingen die langer dan een historisch tijdsbestek duren is opener. Het is niet een betekenis die door mij of een kunstpubliek zo maar eventjes kan worden vastgesteld. Ik zeg niet dat het een betere betekenis is, ze is gewoon opener.
Een tijdsduur die lang genoeg is om het mogelijk te maken dat de betekenis van het werk wijzigingen ondergaat, misschien wel verkeerd geïnterpreteerd wordt." Deze interesse voor het monument, dat tijdens zijn duur tegengesteld is aan de voor de consumptie bestemde efemere produkties herinnert aan de antivitalistische interpretatie (het leven is consumptie) van de traditionele artistieke cultuur bij monde van Hannah Arendt, voor wie het gebruiksvoorwerp en a fortiori het kunstvoorwerp zich wezenlijk onderscheiden van het consumptievoorwerp. Dan Graham drukte zich aan het eind van de jaren zestig niet in die trant uit. Toch kunnen we niet van een breuk spreken. Deze evolutie komt overeen met een re-evaluatie van het modernistische erfgoed, geïnspireerd door de historische - en niet historicistische - interpretatiemethode van Walter Benjamin, maar dan toegepast op het recente verleden. Het modernisme is zonder enige twijfel uitgemond in de Internationale Stijl van het triomfantelijke naoorlogse kapitalisme, maar het produceert binnen zijn eigen tegenstrijdigheden de zijsprong van een kritische actualiteit, als men het in verband brengt met zijn utopische modellen uit de tijd van de Lumières. Al in 1967 had Dan Graham voor de eerste keer de duurzame dubbelzinnigheid van zijn modellen onderstreept, door het samenvallen te constateren van het hippie-pacifisme en de pastorale (en op de gemeenschap georiënteerde) utopie die, in de geschiedenis van het modernisme, als een soort dubbelganger de ideologie van de technologische vooruitgang begeleidt.
Zie "Eisenhower and the Hippies", gepubliceerd in het winternummer 1968-69 van het tijdschrift *0 to 9*, en herdrukt in *Dan Graham Articles*, cat. Stedelijk Van Abbemuseum, Eindhoven1977, pp. 23-26. Twintig jaar later vat Dan Graham, in de loop van een gesprek met Birgit Pelzer (*Dan Graham*, cat. ARC, Musée de la ville de Paris, Paris, 1987, pp. 33-38), zijn huidige positie samen: "Walter Benjamin stelde voor het historische geheugen terug te winnen. Omdat de ideologie van nu het verleden heeft uitgewist, moeten we het reconstrueren alsof het wordt teruggekaatst. Het modernisme was tegen de monumenten. Ik zelf ben er helemaal voor: de monumenten markeren de tijd. (...) De monumenten zijn verbonden met het geheugen van de stad en wat mijzelf op dit moment het meeste interesseert is om het recente verleden terug te winnen, het historische geheugen van het recente verleden. Wat de jaren zestig betreft, een periode die het merendeel van de mensen die nu leven toch heeft meegemaakt, is het net of het collectieve geheugen door amnesie is getroffen. De media moeten het onmiddellijke verleden onophoudelijk uitwissen om hun utopie van het huidige moment te kunnen fabriceren." Het is precies deze utopie van het huidige moment die Dan Graham steeds heeft proberen te vervalsen, eerst door net te doen alsof hij zich eraan conformeerde (model van de 'disposable'), vervolgens door er, in zijn performances en zijn spiegel-videoinstallaties, door middel van alle mogelijke chronologische verstoringen (via met name de vertragingen van de opname), mee te spelen. "Het heden", zegt hij tegen Birgit Pelzer, "bestaat niet. De onmogelijkheid om dit absolute heden te bereiken, dat is het echec van het modernistische idee dat zegt dat je schoon schip kunt maken."

11 "*Yesterday/Today*" wordt beschreven in de door Benjamin Buchloh samengestelde anthologie van videowerken en teksten op video van Dan Graham tussen 1970 en 1978, *Video-Architecture-Television*, Halifax/New York, The Press of the Nova Scotia College of Art and Design, New York University Press, 1979, p. 42. Het jaar daarvoor, in 1974, had Dan Graham al verschillende installaties met vertraagde video's in onderverdeelde ruimten ("*Time Delay Rooms*") gerealiseerd, die tegelijk een systematische omverwerping van de grondslagen van de video ("a present-time medium"), totaal verschillend van de film en een wijziging van de mede-aanwezigheid van het publiek (en ook van de aanwezigheid van iedere toeschouwer ten opzichte van zichzelf) bewerkstelligde. "*Yesterday/Today*" introduceerde in elk geval een nieuwe parameter in deze valstrik-structuur: de specificiteit van de architectonische plek en van de geregistreerde dagelijkse activiteit, die zich er afspeelt. Het ging er voortaan om de door de wijziging van het video-heden teweeggebrachte scheidingen binnen de leefruimte met de gegevenheden van de hedendaagse omgeving uit te drukken, door uiterst veelbetekenende architectonische structuren te kiezen als plekken voor de interventie (installatie). Zoals Anne Rorimer heeft onderstreept ("Dan Graham: An Introduction", *Dan Graham Pavillons*, cat. Kunstverein München, 1988, p. 24), is "*Picture Window Piece*", uit 1974, de eerste stap in deze richting, nog voor "*Yesterday/Today*". Op ditzelfde keerpunt, in 1974-75, valt de tweede belangrijke verzameling foto's - na die van 1965-67 - die dienst doen als herkenningstekens of oriëntatiepunten voor de latere video-installaties en paviljoenen.

12 "*Video View of Suburbia in an Urban Atrium*" is beschreven door Anne Rorimer, op. cit., supra, p. 26. Dit werk is een volmaakte illustratie van de continuïteit van de architectuur-interesses van Dan Graham sinds "*Homes for America*". Overigens dient opgemerkt te worden dat verschillende foto's van huizen uit buitenwijken (voor één of twee gezinnen) uit 1978 dateren. Zeer goed vergelijkbaar met de beelden uit 1965-66, onderscheiden zij zich daarvan door een veel grotere aandacht voor de geïsoleerde huizen [detached houses], met hun geheel eigen morfologie, en zelfs fysionomische uitstraling. Eveneens uit 1978 dateert "*Alteration of a Suburban House*". De tekst van dit (onrealiseerbare) project verwijst expliciet naar de door Mies van der Rohe en Philip Johnson aan het eind van de jaren veertig gebouwde afzonderlijke glazen huizen.
Alle facetten van het modernisme concentreren zich dus voor Dan Graham in de vorm van het voorstedelijke huis.

13 Dan Graham gebruikt deze formulering in een gesprek met Brian Hatton in 1991 (vouwblad, gepubliceerd ter gelegenheid van de expositie in de galerie Roger Pailhas, Marseille, in juni-juli 1991) om de vorm van zijn paviljoenen te karakteriseren: "De vormen zijn doorgaans clichés van de moderne architectuur. Net als tien jaar geleden toen er bij Pelli en vele anderen een terugkeer was naar een Boullée-Ledoux-achtig pantheon, van grotten en kinderspeelplaatsen tot de Universele Kermis of de Verenigde Naties.
De Geode, de 360 graden bioscoop in La Villette maakte daar ook deel van uit. Ik denk dus aan al die typologische vormen. Daarnaast, hoewel ik niet doe wat Venturi doet, dat is zich letterlijk buigen naar dingen in de omgeving, ben ik altijd geïnteresseerd geweest in ombuigingen [inflection] in een andere betekenis van het woord. De materialen en vormen buigen zich naar de meest recente fase van de moderne stad en tegelijk naar het soort historische clichés waar ze misschien wel op gebaseerd is." Deze clichés van de moderne architectuur waren door Dan Graham al eerder aan de orde gesteld in zijn tekst uit 1979, "Art in Relation to Architecture/Architecture in Relation to Art", (*Artforum*, February 1979: pp. 22-29, naar aanleiding van de glazen flats van Mies van der Rohe en hun functie als beeldmerk voor de multinationale ondernemingen en het Amerikaanse kapitalisme:
"De klassieke glazen kantoor- en woontorens van Mies werden de nieuwe standaard van de Amerikaanse technologie, vooral toen zijn stijl door de Amerikaanse big business werd geëxporteerd naar andere delen van de wereld. Het classicisme van Mies was gebaseerd op een schijnbare eerlijkheid [trueness] ten opzichte van de materialen (die gezien werden voor wat ze waren, in plaats van vermomd door het gebruik van ornamenten), gekoppeld aan een geïdealiseerde, 'universele' en uiterst abstracte opvatting van ruimte. Deze modernistische structuren werden al gauw populaire packages voor internationale (multinationale) bijkantoren in de 'Vrije Wereld'."

14 Onder de talrijke historische verwijzingen met betrekking tot zijn paviljoenen, heeft Dan Graham vaak gewag gemaakt van de 'primitieve hut' die door Marc-Antoine Laugier, in een essay uit 1753, als het archetype van de architectuur is beschreven.
Dit speculatieve model, karakteristiek voor het primitivisme van de Lumières, komt overeen met de Rousseauïstische verheerlijking van de goedheid van de natuurlijke mens die zich verzet tegen de verdorvenheden van de stedelijke beschaving. Dan Graham heeft hem aan het eind van de jaren '70 ontdekt bij de auteurs (Manfredo Tafuri, Léon Krier) die verwikkeld waren in het post-moderne debat over de stedelijk utopie. Cf, met name "Not Post-Modernism: History as against Historicism, European Vernacular in Relation to American Commercial Vernacular, and the City as Opposed to the Individual Building", *Artforum* December 1981, pp. 50-59. De antecedenten en het kritische lot van het model van Laugier zijn enkele jaren eerder gereconstrueerd door Rykwert, Joseph, *On Adam's House in Paradise*, New York - Chicago, 1972, als de centrale vorm van het beredeneerde architectonische primitivisme, waar het modernisme grotendeels uit voortkwam, inclusief dat van Gropius (als hij in 1921, in het voorstedelijke Berlijn, het "*Blockhaus Sommerfeld*" bouwt, beïnvloed door de prairiehuizen van Frank Lloyd Wright).

15 "Not Post-Modernism ...", op. cit., supra, p. 57.

16 Dan Graham heeft het over "dual reading" met betrekking tot Lichtenstein in "Art in Relation to Architecture/Architecture in Relation to Art", op. cit., noot 13. Hij citeert, ter ondersteuning van zijn stelling, de uitspraken die Lichtenstein in een gesprek met Gene Swenson in 1963 deed over de Pop Art en haar releaties met de massacultuur: "Het is een betrokkenheid bij wat volgens mij de meest schaamteloze en bedreigende kenmerken van onze cultuur zijn, dingen die we haten, maar die ook een enorme invloed op ons uitoefenen. Volgens mij is de kunst sinds Cézanne buitengewoon romantisch en onrealistisch geworden, kunst die zich met kunst voedt; ze is utopisch. Ze heeft steeds minder met de wereld van doen, ze kijkt naar binnen neo-Zen en wat dies meer zij. Dit is geen kritiek, maar een simpele constatering. Buiten is de wereld; daar is het. Pop Art kijkt naar buiten, naar die wereld; ze lijkt tenminste haar omgeving te accepteren, die goed noch slecht is, maar gewoon anders - een andere gemoedstoestand." En: "De in stripverhalen afgebeelde helden zijn fascistische types, maar ik neem ze niet serieus in die schilderijen - misschien is het van betekenis om ze niet serieus te nemen, van politieke betekenis. Ik gebruik ze om strikt formele redenen, en daar zijn die helden niet voor bedoeld... Pop Art heeft hele directe en ogenblikkelijke [of the moment] betekenissen die weer zullen verdwijnen - dat soort dingen is heel vluchtig - en Pop buit deze 'betekenis', die verondersteld wordt niet lang te duren, uit om ons van de formele inhoud ervan af te leiden. Ik denk dat het formele aspekt in mijn werk mettertijd duidelijker zal worden". Dan Graham resumeert: "Een werk van Lichtenstein kan zowel 'kunst om de kunst' zijn als iets dat populaire culturele betekenissen kan aannemen. Beide interpretaties zijn correct". Er is, kortom, een werkelijke dubbelzinnigheid van de Pop Art ten opzichte van de media, die niet te herleiden is tot een kritische distantiëringsstrategie zoals die bijvoorbeeld bepaalde Brechtiaanse standpunten van Nieuw Links aankleeft. Deze dubbelzinnigheid heeft echter een kritische betekenis - omdat de distantiëring tot stand komt door het simpele effect van het artistieke procédé - wanneer ze wordt gesitueerd en ontwikkeld binnen een grotere historische context dan het beperkte gebied van de schone kunsten, en met name als ze in betrekking wordt gebracht met de in politiek opzicht veel helderder betrokkenheden van de architectuur. Hoe het ook zij, Dan Graham zoekt niet de waarheid van de Pop Art (in de geschiedenis van de kunst); hij interpreteert haar om er een model aan te ontlenen. Het gesprek tussen Lichtenstein en Swenson vond plaats in het kader van de serie 'What is Pop Art', gepubliceerd in twee delen in *ARTnews* (November 1963, February 1964), opnieuw opgenomen in de anthologie van Mahsun, Carol Anne, *Pop Art: The Critical Dialogue*, Ann Arbor, Michigan, UMI Research Press, 1989, pp. 111-115.

17 Alice Weiner: "Als je in die periode de foto's van Dan zag was het net of je naar foto's van Walker Evans keek, maar dan zonder mensen." (gesprek met Chris Dercon, 14 april 1992). Dan Graham herinnert zich dat hij op de verwantschap van zijn beelden met die van Walker Evans attent was gemaakt door Mel Bochner, die Evans trouwens ontmoet had (gesprek met de auteur, 27 juli 1991).

18 Het is in de hierboven genoemde reeks gesprekken "What is Pop Art?" dat Jim Dine het over Walker Evans heeft, na lang te hebben gesproken over de schoonheid van de reclameborden [billboards] die hij ver voordat hij ze als model nam onderkend had: "Het is geen uniek idee - Walker Evans fotografeerde ze al in 1929. Het is gewoon zo dat het landschap om je heen op je af begint te komen en je het moet trotseren". op. cit., noot 16, p.115. De laatste opmerking van Jim Dine zou een definitie kunnen zijn van de 'picturalisering' van het landschap, zoals dat wordt teweeggebracht door een fotograaf als hij er in zijn zoeker een gedeelte van isoleert.

19 Allan Kaprow merkt op: "Op grond van haar directheid, haar ogenschijnlijke objectiviteit en onverschilligheid tegenover persoonlijke emoties, roept de meeste Pop Art een romantisch beeld van de periode van zo'n twintig tot dertig jaar geleden op, de tijd van de kinderjaren van de kunstenaars. Ze heeft heel veel weg van de sfeer die we aantreffen in de romans van Jack Kerouac. Villeglé's, Hains' en Rotella's aan flarden gescheurde affiches, waarin Amerika als het ware van verre wordt gezien, en waarvan de reclameteksten en achterhaalde godinnen door het weer en de tijd zijn verweerd, doen denken aan Walker Evans' foto's van jaren geleden; Lichtenstein's cartoons en produkten hebben een iconografie en stijl van de jaren veertig ..." ("Pop Art: Past, Present and Future", *The Malahat Review*, July 1967, opnieuw opgenomen in de anthologie van Carole Anne Mahsun, op. cit., noot 16, pp. 61-74).

20 Zie hierover Rosenthal, Nan, "Let Us Now Praise Famous Men: Warhol as Director", *The Works of Andy Warhol,* Dia Art Foundation Discussions in Contemporary Culture no. 3, Garry Garrels (ed.), Seattle, Washington, Bay Press, 1989, pp. 47-50.

21 Deze voorbeeldigheid van Evans is zich, via talrijke mediabemiddelingen, als het eersterangs erfgoed van een Amerikaans model van de in de 19e eeuw opgekomen 'documentaire fotografie', gaan manifesteren. Boven Evans, als een punt van oorsprong, plaatst Lincoln Kirstein, in het voorwoord van *American Photographs*, de figuur van Mathew Brady, die Lincoln portretteerde, naast diens Europese evenknieën (Nadar, Cameron, Hill). Hij noteert ook: "Walker Evans laat de hedendaagse beschaving van Oost-Amerika, en de aangrenzende gebieden, zien, zoals Atget het Parijs van voor de oorlog en Brady de Burgeroorlog lieten zien." In het tijdschrift *Hound and Horn,* dat hij aan het begin van de jaren '30 uitgaf, publiceerde Kirstein in 1933 een artikel van Charles Flato die de beelden van de secessieoorlog van Brady als voorbeeldige aanwijzingen van de 'reusachtige mogelijkheden van de eenvoud en van de vrijheid' presenteert. Een commentator heeft recentelijk opgemerkt: "Zonder Steiglitz of het picturalisme te noemen, stelt Flato het oeuvre van Brady impliciet tegenover het erfgoed van *Camerawork.*" Cf. Trachtenberg, Alan, *Reading American Photographs: Images and History, Mathew Brady to Walker Evans,* New York, Hill & Wang, 1989, pp. 231-235. Als hij het over Brady heeft als over "de waarachtige uitvinder van een stijl die efemere en universele waarden aan het licht brengt", komt Flato vanzelf uit bij de fameuze opmerkingen van Baudelaire over de "dubbele compositie van het schone" ('een eeuwig, onveranderlijk element' en 'een betrekkelijk, van de omstandigheden afhangend element'), uit de eerste bladzijden van *Peintre du la vie moderne*, gewijd aan Constantin Guys (schilder-chroniqueur, met name van de Krim-oorlog). Dertig jaar na de teksten van Kirstein en van zijn compagnons, wanneer John Szarkowski in het Museum of Modern Art, New York in 1967, de tentoonstelling New Documents (die Diana Arbus, Lee Friedlander en Garry Winogrand bijeenbrengt) presenteert, is het Amerikaanse documentaire model het verbindende principe van het 'modernisme' in de fotografie geworden. *American Photographs* verschijnt opnieuw in hetzelfde jaar als waarin Szarkowski voor het Museum of Modern Art, New York gaat werken. Drie jaar eerder is het boek *The Americans* van Robert Frank verschenen, waarvan een eerste keuze aan beelden door Evans was ingeleid in het nummer uit 1958 van *US Camera Annual.* Onder het gemeenschappelijke teken van 'document' bepaalt een hechte genealogische opeenvolging voortaan de nieuwe categorie van een fotografie van auteurs, naast en boven een massa anonieme beelden waarin de waarheid van het medium is gevormd en bezonken. In 1966 merkt Szarkowski in het korte nabericht bij *Messsage from the Interior* met een groot gevoel voor retorisch evenwicht op: "De stijl van Evans lijkt de onaantastbaarheid en het anonieme karakter te bezitten van de eerste daguerrotypisten, en toch is de aard van zijn eigen beeldspraak - frontaal, van een bondige simpelheid, van hartstocht bevrijd - ontegenzeggelijk de zijne".

22 Dan Graham heeft recentelijk verschillende malen het belang van de naoorlogse filmkunst voor de vorming van zijn interesse in de architectuur genoemd. Cf. met name een gesprek met Chris Dercon in mei 1991, *Forum International*, vol. 11, no. 9, sept./okt. 1991, pp. 73-80. De verwijzing naar het neorealisme (Rossellini, Antonioni) valt verschillende malen in de loop van het onuitgegeven gesprek op 27 juli 1991 met de auteur in Los Angeles.

23 Godard heeft altijd de noodzaak benadrukt om de fictie op documentaire gegevens te baseren. "*Deux ou trois choses que je sais d'elle*" (1966) - de film die door Dan Graham het meest wordt genoemd - is geïnspireerd door een enquête, in een tijdschrift, over prostitutie in de grote voorstedelijke wooneenheden. Maar de relatie document-fictie strekt zich ook uit tot de relatie werkelijk-imaginair. Naar aanleiding van "*Vivre sa vie*" (1962) verklaart Godard, in de loop van een gesprek in *Cahiers du cinéma*, no. 138, décembre 1962, "Ik ben uitgegaan van het imaginaire en ik heb het werkelijke ontdekt; maar achter het werkelijke is er weer opnieuw het imaginaire"; hij heeft het over 'theater-waarheid', over 'theatraal realisme'. Godard heeft zijn films, kortom, altijd opgevat als 'essays'. Hun documentaire aspect steunt dus allereerst op hun eigen progressie. Naar aanleiding van "*Deux ou trois choses que je sais d'elle*", merkt hij op: "Ik zie mezelf filmen, en men hoort mij denken. Met andere woorden, het is geen film, het is een poging tot een film die zich als zodanig presenteert. Het is geen geschiedenis, het wil een document zijn." (Jean-Luc Godard, *2 ou 3 choses que je sais d'elle,* Paris, Seuil/Avant-Scène, 1971, p. 12).

24 In een collectief werk, gepubliceerd in Londen in 1967 (Studio Vista), merkt Stig Björkman naar aanleiding van "*Deux ou trois choses que je sais d'elle*" op: "In de film vindt men die nieuwe vorm van realisme terug die in de 'nouveau roman' bestaat: de economie en de precisie van het detail; een visie die een buitengewoon diep perspectief bewerkstelligt dankzij een razendsnelle montage van close-ups en long-shots". Deze opmerking zou net zo goed op de montage van "*Homes for America*" toegepast kunnen worden. Volgens de hierboven beschreven auto-reflexieve documentaire logica verwijst de wooneenheid waarin mensen min of meer samenwonen en waarin de heldin van de film woont naar het idee van samen zijn (of wonen), maar ook naar de door de film zelf samengestelde eenheid, zoals Godard zelf aangeeft. "Het gaat om de beschijving van een 'eenheid'." De architectuur is de metafoor van de film-beschrijving. Het beschreven object is het subject/thema van de film. "Je moet alles in een film stoppen." En dat alles moet worden georganiseerd als een eenheid, bewoond, interieur-exterieur, subject-object. "Ik kan niet om het feit heen dat alle dingen tegelijk van binnen en van buiten bestaan. Dat kan bijvoorbeeld tastbaar gemaakt worden door een flat van buiten te filmen, vervolgens van binnen, alsof je de binnenkant van een kubus, van een object binnenkomt. Dat geldt ook voor een persoon, zijn of haar gezicht wordt in het algemeen van buiten gezien." op. cit., supra, p. 15.

25 Dan Graham snijdt dit probleem aan in de loop van het gesprek met Brian Hatton, in 1991, op. cit., noot 13.

26 "The Reappearance of Photography", *Hound and Horn,* vol. 5, no. 1 (October-December, 1931), opnieuw opgenomen in de anthologie van Trachtenberg, Alan, *Classic Essays on Photography*, New Haven, Conn.,Leete's Island Books, 1980, pp. 185-188.

27 Het boek van Bourke-White en Caldwell lijkt een onvervalst tegen-voorbeeld te zijn geweest voor Agee en Evans die de onderneming van hun voorgangers zagen als 'een dubbele smaad: allereerst de propaganda, vervolgens het profijt dat zowel uit de propaganda als uit de omstandigheden van de pachters getrokken werd". Geciteerd door Stott, William, *Documentary Expression and Thirties America,* Chicago,The University of Chicago Press,1973, 1986, p. 222.

28 William Stott, op. cit. p. 320, citeert deze opmerking die Evans in een van zijn laatste levensjaren tegen hem maakte: "Ik heb een zwak voor de achtergestelden, voor oude mensen, maar tegelijk wantrouw ik dat gevoel. Ik moet wel, omdat dat niet het motief voor artistieke of esthetische actie mag zijn. Als dat wel het geval is, dan is je werk of sentimenteel of gericht op het 'verbeteren van de maatschappij', om het zomaar te zeggen. Ik geloof niet dat het werk van een kunstenaar die richting uit kan gaan."

29 Evans zegt letterlijk (uitspraken opgetekend door W. Stott, ibid.): "The problem is one of staying out of Left politics and still avoiding Establishment patterns".

30 Onderhoud met Paul Cummings, 13 augustus. 1971, "Archives of American Art", geciteerd door Alan Trachtenberg, op. cit., noot 21, p. 237.

31 Deze formulering leidt een door Evans geredigeerde aantekening ter presentatie van een publicatie van zijn metroportretten (1938-1941) in. Ze dateert dus van na die portretten. Ze is gepubliceerd in *Walker Evans at Work,* New York, Harper and Row, 1982, p. 160, een onder leiding van de Evans Estate in 1982 gerealiseerd boekwerk, Na deze inleidende opmerking, gaat de tekst over op een beschrijving van het project: "Deze collectie presenteert op zijn minst een onzuivere selectie van individuen - menselijke wezens op een bepaalde plek binnen een gegeven tijd - geproduceerd volgens een toeval dat de loting benadert." Evans benadrukt de conceptuele waarde van dit project, waarvan de verwezenlijking een benadering is en geen voltooid werkstuk. "De plaats van de opnamen is uitsluitend gekozen om praktische redenen, gedwongen door werkcondities. In feite is de absolute zuiverheid van deze fotografische methode - de methode van de opname - hier niet echt bereikt, maar ze is aanwezig als een niet verwezenlijkt doel..." De laatste opmerking geeft een bepaald soort plek aan, de stad, een situatie - mensen die in de metro zitten - en een datum, 1940: "Dit is een doorsnee reeks van mannen en vrouwen in de stad, die daadwerkelijk op deze plek gaan zitten, op deze metrobank; en dat in 1940, ongeveer."

32 The Machine-Age is de in 1927 door *The Litle Review*, het avant-garde tijdschrift van Jean Heap georganiseerde expositie. Maar de uitdrukking geeft een sociale werkelijkheid aan die de artistieke horizon ruimschoots overschrijdt. De organisatoren van de expositie hebben zich daar niet op verkeken, want ze toonden "echte machines, losse onderdelen, apparaten, foto's en tekeningen van machines, fabrieken, gebouwen, zij aan zij met architectonische werken, schilderijen, tekeningen, sculpturen en door de belangrijkste moderne kunstenaars gerealiseerde uitvindingen". . (Tekst, in het frans/engels herdrukt in *Léger et l'esprit moderne: Une alternative d'avant-garde à l'art non-objectif (1918-1931),* cat. Musée d'art moderne de la ville de Paris, Paris, 1982, p. 216 en 218). In een tekst van de catalogus "The Americanization of Art" merkt de 'precisionistische' schilder Louis Lozowick, Russische immigrant (zeer goed op de hoogte van het Europese cubo-futurisme en constructivisme) op: "De geschiedenis van Amerika is een koppige en aanhoudende poging meester te worden over de krachten van de natuur (...) de geschiedenis van gigantische technische heldendaden en kolossale mechanische constructies." (geciteerd door Richard Guy Wilson, in *The Machine Age in America*, 1918-1941, cat. The Brooklyn Museum, New York,1986, p.30). Aan het begin van de jaren twintig waren de eerste fotografen van de machine (Paul Strand en Ralph Steiner met name) gehouden aan een veel gematigder (en individueler) visie op de machine, zelfs al kon Strand haar in zijn fameuze tekst uit 1922 aanduiden als "The New God". De verheerlijking van het grandioze, van het kolossale, door Lozowick, kreeg haar fotografische pendant pas vanaf de laatste jaren van het decennium, met name in de uiterst massieve beelden van Margaret Bourke-White. In zijn allereerste foto's van industriële monumenten - waaronder het beroemde "*Armco Steel, Ohio*", uit 1922 - had Edward Weston dit architectonische model vooral gebruikt om te breken met het picturalisme (zoals Strand, met hetzelfde doel, de machine had gebruikt), maar zijn fascinatie was van korte duur. Hij hield er slechts een bepaald soort beschrijvende gezwollenheid aan over, toegepast op motieven uit de pre-industriële cultuur, geladen met erotisch-kosmische resonanties. Evans droeg, aan het eind van de jaren '20, enige tijd zijn steentje bij aan de verdediging van het Amerikaanse technologische modernisme , maar nog korter dan Weston en zonder dezelfde oplossing aan te voeren om er weer aan te ontsnappen. Hij droeg bijvoorbeeld bij aan het boek *The Bridge* van de dichter Hart Crane, dat, in 1930, de symbolische schoonheid van de brug van Brooklyn verheerlijkte. Maar hij interesseerde zich ook voor een ander stedelijk schouwspel: de (verfletste of kapotte) uithangborden van Broadway, de menigte in de straten (of op het strand van Coney Island). Zelfs zijn beelden van wolkenkrabbers en huizenrijen hebben hun waarde als studie en improvisatie die hen onderscheidt van de door de leerlingen van Strand vervaardigde meer geacheveerde en helderder opnamen, omdat hij er de experimentele trant mee benadert van de Europese 'nieuwe visie', type Bauhaus. In 1971 zwoer hij zijn eerste periode van activiteiten (1928-31) echter in haar geheel af, en verklaarde dat ze te 'romantisch' was, dat wil zeggen - zo luidt een mogelijke uitleg - te zeer verbonden met de romantiek van de machine die de jaren '20 had gekenmerkt en de triomf van het industrialisme in de jaren '30 had voorbereid. Cf. *Walker Evans at Work,* op. cit., noot 31, p. 42. Tenslotte moet worden gepreciseerd dat de aspecten van de stedelijke werkelijkheid die - buiten de pseudo-kubistische architectuur van de flatblokken - de aandacht van Evans het meest hebben opgeëist, door de ideologen van moderne stad en van de industrialisatie bepaald niet zijn verontachtzaamd. Lewis Mumford bijvoorbeeld verklaarde in 1931 dat de metro en de "cheap popular lunchrooms" de "twee bronnen van het huidige modernisme" waren. (Geciteerd door R.G. Wilson, op. cit., supra, p. 30).

33 Zoals hierboven (noot 31) al is gepreciseerd, is de datering van deze tekst onzeker. De auteurs van *Walker Evans at Work* publiceren in elk geval nog een andere aantekening, met dezelfde bedoeling opgesteld, die uit 1962 dateert. Het is verleidelijk om dit chronologische houvast te gebruiken voor een bevestiging van de vergelijking met Duchamp. Het is inderdaad in 1961, en alleen dàn, dat Duchamp, tijdens een in het Museum of Modern Art, New York georganiseerd rondetafelgesprek ter gelegenheid van de expositie The Art of Assemblage, zal verklaren: "Er is een punt waar ik heel duidelijk over wil zijn, en dat is dat de keuze van deze ready-mades me nooit door een of ander esthetisch genot is gedicteerd. Deze keuze was gebaseerd op een reactie die visuele onverschilligheid inhield, en op hetzelfde moment gekoppeld was aan een totale afwezigheid van goede of slechte smaak ..." Deze verklaring laat zich grotendeels door haar context verklaren: Duchamp wilde zich, net als bij zovele andere gelegenheden, ontdoen van de esthetische toeëigening van het objet trouvé, van het industriële afvalprodukt, etc, door de assemblage-kunstenaars (neo-dadas en nouveau realisten). Hij herinnerde eraan dat een artistieke beslissing niet een simpele "toeëigening van het reële" is die de schoonheid van de 'industriële folklore' verheerlijkt (twee formuleringen van Pierre Restany, de theoreticus van de Nouveau Realisme). Het is niet erg waarschijnlijk dat Walker Evans, met zijn rekening houden met zijn eigen interesses en met zijn binding met het Museum of Modern Art, New York, niet op de hoogte is geweest van de expositie van William Seitz, en zich niet heeft beziggehouden met het door Duchamp naar voren gebrachte probleem (zelfs als hij Duchamp er niet over heeft horen spreken). Voor een historische bespreking van het Duchampiaanse onverschilligheidsprincipe en, in het bijzonder, de tekst van het gesprek uit 1961, "Apropos of 'Readymades'", zie Camfield, William I., *Marcel Duchamp: Fountain*, Houston, The Menil Collection Houston Fine Art Press, 1989, pp. 42-47.

34 De exacte opmerking van Evans was, in feite: "De portretten in dit boek zijn genomen met een verborgen camera, geplaatst in de handen van een berouwvolle spion en van een zich verontschuldigende voyeur. Toch is deze brute en onbeschaamde invasie in geringe mate verzacht en gedeeltelijk afgezwakt door de jaren die ik heb laten voorbijgaan. Deze beelden zijn twintig jaar geleden gemaakt en opzettelijk achtergehouden voor publicatie. Natuurlijk ziet u tussen deze mensen niet het gezicht van een rechter en ook niet van een senator of een bankdirecteur. Wat u daar ziet is tegelijkertijd verbijsterend, beangstigend en duidelijk: het zijn de dames en heren van de jury." (*Walker Evans at Work*, op. cit., supra). Dit alles heeft de allure van een morele fabel: de kunstenaar die zijn schuld bekent ('een berouwvolle spion') en na zichzelf te hebben gesanctioneerd door zijn beelden gedurende twintig jaar niet openbaar te maken vervolgens - enigszins ironisch, zoals verwacht mag worden van de kant van een dandy - het bestaan van een volksjury en daarmee van een gemeenschappelijke morele wet onderkent. Als model had hij overigens Daumier (en Dickens) aangenomen, dat wil zeggen een esthetische maar ook een morele en politieke autoriteit: "De verpletterende lethargie van het leven in de Newyorkse metro zou een keer door een moderne Daumier of Dickens moeten worden geregistreerd. Deze situatie is een sociologische goudmijn die op een groot kunstenaar ligt te wachten". Deze verwijzing naar Daumier keert in 1971 terug in een gesprek met Leslie Katz (verschenen in *Art in America* (March-April, 1971): De 'Derde klas wagon' van Daumier is in zekere zin een momentopname [snapshot] die inderdaad in een spoorrijtuig gezeten mensen toont, in het Frankrijk van het midden van de 19e eeuw. "Hij had geen fototoestel, maar hij heeft de mensen naar het leven getekend, als een reporter ..." (Gesprek, opnieuw opgenomen in de anthologie van Goldberg, Vicki, *Photography in Print: Writings from 1816 to the Present*, New York, Simon and Schuster, 1981, pp. 358-369).

35 Baudelaire, *Mon coeur mis à nu*, in *Oeuvres complètes*, vol. 1, Paris, Gallimard, Pléiade, 1975, p. 697.

36 Baudelaire analyseert de portée van de 'satanische lach' in "De l'essence du rire", theoretisch essay dat zijn opmerking over de karikatuur samenvat. De 'satanische lach' demonstreert de tegenstrijdige natuur van de mens, verdeeld tussen "het idee van zijn eigen superioriteit" en de zekerheid van zijn "ellende": "En uit de onophoudelijke botsing van deze twee oneindigheden komt de lach vrij." De tragiek van Pascal, kortom, van de 'gevallen mensheid', waar de romantische heroïek aan voorbij is gegaan. Toch heeft Frankrijk er niet het meest zuivere voorbeeld van voortgebracht (Hoffmann). Molière zelf is niet 'wreed' genoeg, en uiteindelijk wordt geen enkele karikatuurtekenaar genoemd. Maar het is juist Molière die door Baudelaire in een andere tekst, "Quelques caricaturistes français", met Daumier wordt vergeleken: "Zijn karikatuur is formidabel van omvang, maar zonder rancune en zonder gal. Er is in zijn hele werk een kern van rechtschapenheid en van goedhartigheid." (*Oeuvres complètes*, vol. II, pp. 532-543; 556-557). Het valt niet mee om het in verband met Evans over 'goedhartigheid' te hebben, maar toch is het een plaats naast Daumier die de Baudelairiaanse typologie hem toekent, en die hij zichzelf toekent, waarbij hij de erfenis van de satanische lach aan de surrealistische zwarte humor laat, met soms - zoals wellicht uit *Many Are Called* blijkt - wat spijt en smart.

37 Geciteerd door Lesley K. Baier, in *Walker Evans at Fortune 1945-1965*, cat. Wellesley College Museum, Wellesley, Mass., 1977-78, pp. 10-11. Een dubbele pagina van de publicatie van foto's van Steiner in *Fortune* (May 1930) is gereproduceerd in *Photography Rediscovered: American Photographs, 1900-1930*, cat. Whitney Museum of American Art, New York,1979, pp. 104-105.

38 Steiner, Ralph, *A Point of View*, Middletown, Connecticut, Wesleyan University Press, 1978, pp. 104-105.

39 Gesprek met Leslie Katz, op. cit., noot 34, p. 367. In de loop van hetzelfde gesprek preciseert Evans: "Ansel Adams en Paul Strand zijn allebei grote technici. Soms laten ze dat te veel zien. Wat ze met een fototoestel doen is volmaakt, en je zegt oh en ah, wat volmaakt. Toch komt niet helder genoeg door waar het over gaat."

40 Evans, Walker, "Photography", *Quality: Its Image in the Arts*, Louis Kronenberger, Marshall Lee (ed.), New York Atheneum, 1969, opnieuw opgenomen in Liebling,

Jerôme (ed.), *Photography: Current Perspectives*, Rochester, Light Impressions, 1978, pp. 16-18.

41 Hier is het woord 'establish' vertaald als 'vestigen' Het is nodig om de dubbele betekenis van dit werkwoord te benadrukken. Walker Evans gebruikt het in die trant in het gesprek met Paul Cummings uit 1971 (op. cit., noot 30, p. 238), als hij verklaart: "That took time to establish" met betrekking tot zijn methode, zijn 'stijl', en vervolgens de institutionele erkenning die hij ermee heeft verworven.

42 We kunnen het hierboven gepresenteerde overzicht nu completeren (noot 32). De in dit boek, aan het begin van het aan Walker Evans gewijde katern, afgebeelde reproducties zijn bijzonder veelzeggend. We kunnen in hun anti-descriptieve vooronderstellingen - de zwarte zone, zonder details, in het centrum van het netwerk van metaalachtige structuren - gemakkelijk de uitvloeisels herkennen van het aan de Europese constructivistische experimenten ten grondslag liggende expressionisme, waarbij we onderscheid maken tussen het project van Evans in 1929 en de beschrijvende strengheid van een Weston ("*Armco Steel, Ohio*", 1922) of van een Charles Sheeler als hij de fabrieken van Ford Plant fotografeert ("*Criss Crossed Conveyors*", 1927). Veel later, in 1947, zal Evans een opname van Ford Plant maken (*First and Last*, New York, Harper and Row, 1978, p. 173) die sterk lijkt op die van Sheeler, want hij heeft de 'romantiek' van zijn eerste architectonische studies afgezworen, en richt zich, niet geheel onopportunistisch, maar de 'design'-lijn van de 'straight photography'. Hij blijft zich overigens onderscheiden van de valselijk expressionistische tendens van het door auteurs als Margaret Bourke-White gevierde industriële heroïsme.

43 Gesprek met Leslie Katz, op. cit., noot 34, p. 362. "Een verzamelaar", verklaart Evans, "wordt zich in hevige mate bewust van een bepaald soort object, wordt er verliefd op, maakt er vervolgens jacht op. Ik merk dat in mijn werk gedurende een bepaalde tijd uitsluitend in een bepaald soort gezicht of type mens geïnteresseerd ben. Je begint mensen te selecteren met je camera. Het is dwangmatig en je kunt nauwelijks ophouden. Ik denk dat alle kunstenaars verzamelaars van beelden zijn."

44 Baudelaire, op. cit., noot 36, pp. 556-557.

The bibliographical indications refer to reproductions
published in books and catalogues that are mentioned
in the selected bibliography. As a precaution,
the photographs which are not reproduced in these
volumes are indicated as "Unpublished (?)".

Les mentions bibliographiques se réfèrent aux
reproductions publiées dans les livres et les catalogues
cités dans la bibliographie sélective. Les photographies qui
n'ont pas été reproduites dans ces ouvrages figurent,
par précaution, sous la mention: "Unpublished (?)".

Die bibliographischen Anmerkungen beziehen sich auf
Reproduktionen in den in der Bibliographie-Auswahl
aufgeführten Büchern und Katalogen. In diesen
Publikationen nicht enthaltene Photographien tragen -
sicherheitshalber - den Vermerk "Unpublished (?)".

De bibliografische aanduidingen verwijzen naar
reprodukties in de boeken en catalogi die genoemd staan
in de geselecteerde bibliografie. De foto's die niet in de
publicaties staan afgebeeld kregen zekerheidshalve de
aanduiding: "Unpublished (?)".

r. = Reproduced in/Reproduitdans/
    Reproduziertin/Gereproduceerd in

v.= Variant/Variante/Variante/Variant

WALKER EVANS

Selected Photographs/Un choix de photographies/Eine Auswahl von Photographien/Een Selectie van Foto's

1928-1968

1

Part One/Première partie/Teil Eins/Deel Een

**The City, People and Signs/La ville, les gens, les signes/
Die Stadt, Menschen und Zeichen/ De Stad, Mensen en Tekens**

Untitled (Industrial Elevators)
ca. 1929
Gelatin-silver print
22 cm x 16,5 cm

r. Walker Evans at Work, 1982, p. 39

Collection particulière, Paris

Untitled (Building with Metal Gate)
ca. 1928
Gelatin-silver print
6,3 x 3,8 cm

r. Walker Evans at Work, 1982, p. 27

Collection The Museum of Modern Art, New York

Gift of Dr. Iago Galdtson 71.77

Copyright Estate of Walker Evans ©

Untitled (New York)
ca. 1929
Gelatin-silver print
18,5 x 22 cm

r. Walker Evans at Work, 1982, p.27

Collection particulière, Paris

Copyright Estate of Walker Evans ©

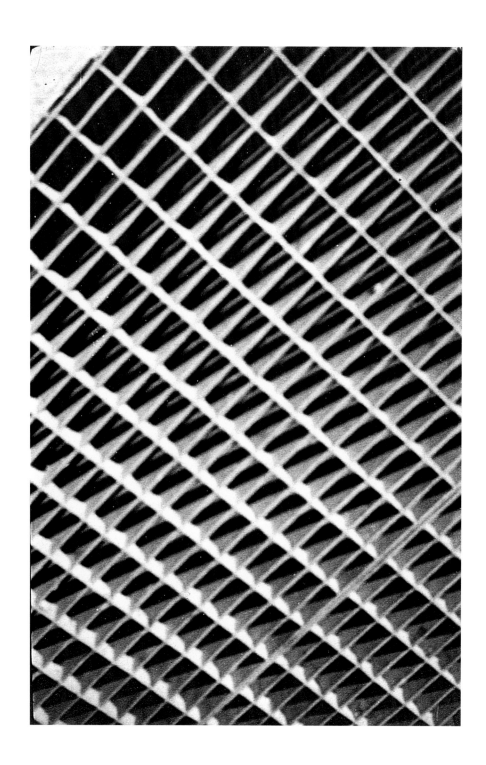

Untitled (Metal Grid)
ca. 1929
Gelatin-silver print
23,5 cm x 15 cm

Unpublished (?)

Collection particulière, Paris

Untitled (New York Buildings)
ca. 1929
Gelatin-silver print
13,2 x 22,6 cm

Unpublished (?)

Collection particulière, Paris

Untitled (Chicago)
ca. 1946
Gelatin-silver print
22 cm x 27,5 cm

Unpublished (?)

Collection particulière, Paris

Untitled (People in the Street - Chicago)
ca. 1946
Gelatin-silver print
20,5 cm x 20,5 cm

Unpublished (?)

Collection particulière, Paris

Subway Portraits
1939-1940
Gelatin-silver print
11,2 cm x 16,5 cm

r. Many Are Called, 1966, p. 110 (v.), p. 128 (v.), Walker Evans, Subways and Streets,1991, p. 97 (v.)

Collection particulière, Paris

Subway Portraits
1939-1940
Gelatin-silver print
11,5 cm x 16 cm

r. Walker Evans, Subways and Streets, p. 90 (v.)

Collection particulière, Paris

Untitled (Independence Day, Terra Alta, West Virginia)
1935
Gelatin-silver print
20 cm x 21 cm

r. Walker Evans, Photographs for the Farm Security Administration 1935-1938, 1973, no. 26 (v.)

Collection particulière, Paris

Subway Portraits
1939-1940
Gelatin-silver print
10,7 cm x 15,3 cm

r. Many Are Called, 1966, p.44 (v.)

Collection particulière, Paris

New York Lunch Bar
ca. 1937
Gelatin-silver print
15,7 cm x 23,9 cm

r. Walker Evans at Work, 1982, p. 47, Amerika, 1990, p. 246

Subway Portraits
1939-1940
Gelatin-silver print
11 cm x 16 cm

r. Many Are Called, p. 116 (v.)

Collection particulière, Paris

Untitled (Three Men Seated on a Wall)
ca. 1932
Gelatin-silver print
15,8 cm x 21,7 cm

Unpublished (?)

Collection particulière, Paris

Former collection of James Agee

Copyright Estate of Walker Evans ©

Untitled (Men Seated in Front of Coca-Cola Sign - Mississippi)
ca. 1936
Gelatin-silver print
11,5 cm x 18, 5 cm

Unpublished (?)

Collection particulière, Paris

Sidewalk in Vicksburg, Mississippi
1936
Gelatin-silver print
14 cm x 13,5 cm

r. Walker Evans American Photographs, 1938, Part I, p. 24, Let Us Now Praise Famous Men, 1941, n.p(v), Walker Evans, Photographs for the Farm Security Administration 1935-1938, 1973, no. 130 (v.),

Walker Evans at Work, 1982, p. 140 (v.), Amerika, 1990, p.254 (v.)

Collection The Museum of Modern Art, New York

Purchase, 297.63

Shoe Shine Sign in a Southern Town
1936
Gelatin-silver print
14 cm x 16,5 cm

r. Walker Evans, 1971, p. 122, Walker Evans, Photographs for the Farm Security Administration 1935-1938, 1973, nos. 389, 390 (v.), Amerika, p. 71(v.)

Collection particulière, Paris

Sidewalk in Vicksburg, Mississippi
1936
Gelatin-silver print
19,5 cm x 24,5 cm

r. Walker Evans American Photographs, 1938, Part I, p. 24 (v.), Let Us Now Praise Famous Men, 1941, n.p. (v.)Walker Evans, Photographs for the Farm Security Administration 1935-1938,

1973, No. 130 (v.), Walker Evans at Work, 1982, p. 140 (v.), Amerika, 1990, p.254 (v.)

Collection particulière, Paris

Billboard, Birmingham, Alabama
1936
Gelatin-silver print
19,1 cm x 23,9 cm

r. Walker Evans, Photographs for the Farm Security Administration 1935-1938, 1973, no. 230 (v.), Walker Evans,

1971, p. 137 (v.), First and Last, 1978, p. 92 (v.), Amerika, 1990, p. 74 (v.)

The Metropolitan Museum of Art, New York

Purchase, The Horace W. Goldsmith Foundation Gift 1990. (1990.1169)

Torn Movie Poster
1930
Gelatin-silver print
15,7 x 10,7 cm

r. Walker Evans American Photographs, 1938, Part I, no. 13, First and Last, 1978, p. 67

Gift of Mrs. James Ward Thorne, 1962.151

2

Part Two/Deuxième partie/Teil Zwei/Deel Twee

**Houses, Ornaments and Interiors/Architectures, ornements et intérieurs/
Häuser, Ornamente und Interieurs/Huizen, Ornamenten en Interieurs**

West Virginia Coal Miner's House (Scott's Run)
1936
Gelatin-silver print
22,4 x 19 cm

r. First and Last, 1978, p. 113, Walker Evans American Photographs, Part I, 1938, no. 23 (v.),

Walker Evans, Photographs for the Farm Security Administration 1935-1938, 1973, no. 15 (v.), Amerika, 1990, p. 29 (v.)

Photography Purchase Account, 1973.430

Main Street Block, Selma, Alabama
1936
Gelatin-silver print
16,8 cm x 23 cm

r. Walker Evans American Photographs,1938, Part II, no. 30, Walker Evans, Photographs for the Farm Security Administration 1935-1938, 1973, no. 203, Amerika, 1990, p. 57

Collection The Museum of Modern Art, New York

Gift of Willard van Dyke 1463.68

Houses and Billboard in Atlanta
1936
Gelatin-silver print
16,4 cm x 23,2 cm

r. Walker Evans American Photographs, 1938, Part I, no. 47, Walker Evans, Photographs for the Farm Security Administration 1935-1938, 1973, no. 163, First and Last, 1978, p. 119, Amerika, 1990, p. 52

Collection The Museum of Modern Art, New York

Purchase. 303.63

Frame Houses in Virginia
1936
Gelatin-silver print
15,9 x 19,7 cm

r. Walker Evans American Photographs, 1938, Part II, no. 22

The Minneapolis Institute of Arts

The William Hood Dunwoody Fund, 75.26.10

Millworkers' Houses in Willimantic, Connecticut
1931
Gelatin-silver print
23,1 cm x 32,8 cm

r. Walker Evans American Photographs, 1938, Part II, no. 21, Walker Evans at Work, 1982, p. 21

The Minneapolis Institute of Arts

Gift of D. Thomas Bergen, 76.82.2

Frame Houses in Virginia
1936
Gelatin-silver print
14,4 x 20,5 cm

r. Walker Evans American Photographs, 1938, Part II, no. 23

Gift of Mrs. James Ward Thorne, 1962.173

Company Houses, West Virginia
1935
Gelatin-silver print
15,4 x 17,2 cm

r. Walker Evans American Photographs, 1938, Part II, no. 13, Walker Evans, Photographs for the Farm Security Administration 1935-1938, 1973, no. 14

The Minneapolis Institute of Arts

The William Hood Dunwoody Fund, 75.26.9

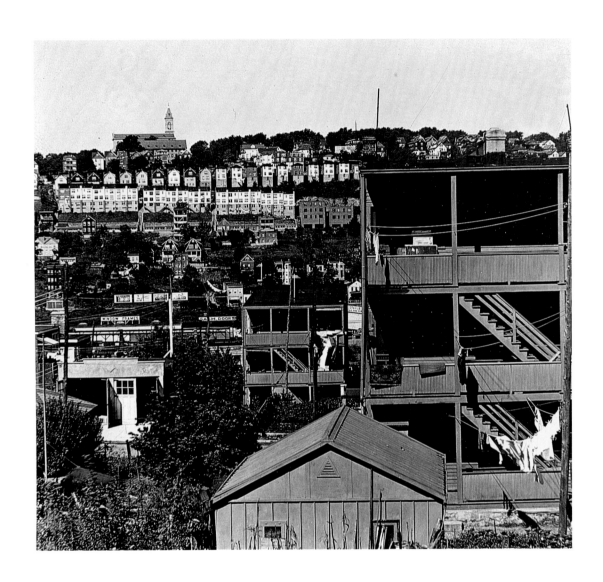

Untitled (Bethlehem, Pennsylvania)
1936
Gelatin-silver print
17,8 cm x 20,7 cm

Unpublished (?)

Collection particulière, Paris

Former collection of James Agee

Untitled (Detail of View of Easton, Pennsylvania)
1935
Gelatin-silver print
8,6 cm x 13,7 cm

r. Walker Evans American Photographs, 1938, Part II, no. 2 (v.),Walker Evans at Work, 1982, p. 120

The Metropolitan Museum of Art,

Purchase, The Horace W. Goldsmith Foundation Gift, 1991 (1991.1076)

Wooden House in Ossining, New York
1930
Gelatin-silver print
14,6 cm x 14,3 cm

Unpublished (?)

Collection The Museum of Modern Art, New York

Purchase, 404.38.17

Copyright Estate of Walker Evans ©

a. Detail of Frame Houses in Virginia; b. Detail of Church Steeple
1936;1936
Gelatin-silver print
13,3 cm x 8,5 cm; 13,3 cm x 8,5 cm

r. (a)Walker Evans American Photographs, 1938, Part II, no. 22,

r.(b)Walker Evans American Photographs, 1938, Part II, no. 19, First and Last, 1978, p. 48 (v.), Amerika, 1990, p. 53 (v.)

Collection The Museum of Modern Art, New York

Anonymus Fund, 404.38.11; Anonymus Fund 404.38.12

Copyright Estate of Walker Evans ©

Wooden Houses, Boston
1930
Gelatin-silver print
11,1 x 14,7 cm

r. Walker Evans American Photographs, 1938, Part II, no. 27, Walker Evans at Work, 1982, p. 53

The Minneapolis Institute of Arts

Gift of Arnold H. Crane, 75.42.5

Sidewalk Scene, Selma, Alabama
1935
Gelatin-silver print
18,2 x 23,2 cm

r. Walker Evans, Photographs for the Farm Security Administration 1935-1938, 1973, no. 210

Collection particulière, Paris

Untitled (Saratoga Springs)
1931
Gelatin-silver print
16 x 19 cm

Unpublished (?)

Collection particulière, Paris

Houses in Negro Quarter of Tupelo, Mississippi
1936
Gelatin-silver print
14 cm x 17,8 cm

r. Walker Evans American Photographs, 1938, Part I, no. 21, Walker Evans, Photographs for the Farm Security Administration 1935-1938, 1973, no.125

Collection The Museum of Modern Art, New York

Purchase, 296.63

House in French Quarter, New Orleans
1935
Gelatin-silver print
18,1 cm x 15,5 cm

r. Walker Evans American Photographs, 1938, Part II, no. 36

Collection The Museum of Modern Art, New York.

Anonymous Fund, 404.38.24

Houses, Nuhant
1932
Gelatin-silver print
10,4 cm x 15,5 cm
Unpublished (?)
Collection The Museum of Modern Art, New York
Gift of Lincoln Kirstein, 5.33
Copyright Estate of Walker Evans ©

Gothic Gate Cottage near Poughkeepsie, New York
1931
Gelatin-silver print
10,4 cm x 15,5 cm

r. Walker Evans American Photographs, 1938, Part II, no. 28

Collection The Museum of Modern Art, New York.

Gift of Lincoln Kirstein, 58.33

Jigsaw House at Ocean City, New Jersey
1931
Gelatin-silver print
14,6 x 12,5 cm

Unpublished (?)

Gift of Mrs. James Ward Thorne, 1962.175

Houses, Ginger Bread, Cambridge
1932
Gelatin-silver print
10,4 cm x 15,5 cm

Unpublished (?)

Collection The Museum of Modern Art, New York

Gift of Lincoln Kirstein, 38.33

Copyright Estate of Walker Evans ©

The Parlor Chairs, Oldwick, New Jersey
1958
Gelatin-silver print
29,2 cm x 24,7 cm

r. Walker Evans, 1971, p. 170, Message from the Interior, 1966, pl. 8

Collection The Museum of Modern Art, New York

Purchase, 76.71

The Child's Room, Stockbridge, Massachusetts
1951
Gelatin-silver print
19 cm x 18,4 cm

r. Walker Evans, 1971, p. 169, Message from the Interior, 1966, pl. 10

Collection The Museum of Modern Art, New York

Purchase, 73.71

The Home Organ, Chester, Nova Scotia
1968
Gelatin-silver print
17,5 x 17,5 cm

r. Walker Evans, 1971, p. 173

Collection particulière, Paris

Walker Evans (1903-1975)

Chronology

1903	Born in St. Louis, Missouri.
1922-1923	Graduates from the Phillips Academy, Andover, Massachusetts. Attends Williams College, Williamstown, Massachusetts, for one year.
1926	Travels in Europe. Stays in Paris and attends classes at La Sorbonne.
1927-1931	Makes abstract formal photographs, influenced by European avant-garde photography. Illustrates the American poet Hart Crane's *The Bridge*. Makes street photographs, influenced by Ben Shahn with whom he shares a studio. Meets Lincoln Kirstein, chief editor of *Hound and Horn*, where Evans publishes "The Reappearance of Photography". Travels with Kirstein to photograph Victorian houses. Shows at the Jonh Becker Gallery, April-May 1931, with Ralph Steiner and Margaret Bourke-White.
1932	Shows at the Julien Levy Gallery with George Platt Lynes.
1933	Travels to Cuba. Illustrates Carleton Beals' *Crime of Cuba*. First exhibition at The Museum of Modern Art, New York: Walker Evans: Photographs of 19th Century Houses.
1934	First publication in *Fortune* magazine: "The Communist Party".
1935	477 photographs are published in the catalogue of the exhibition African Negro Art at The Museum of Modern Art, New York. Shows at Julien Levy Gallery with Cartier-Bresson and Alvarez Bravo. Travels to New Orleans. Starts to work for the Farm Security Administration (FSA).
1936-1938	Travels south on assignment for the FSA. Works in Alabama with James Agee on what will become *Let Us Now Praise Famous Men*. Solo exhibition at The Museum of Modern Art, New York: American Photographs, curated by Lincoln Kirstein.
1938-1941	With a hidden camera takes photographs in the subway. Receives a Guggenheim fellowship to record contemporary american subjects. *Let Us Now Praise Famous Men* is published.
1943-1945	Staff writer for *Time* magazine.
1945	Becomes associate editor for *Fortune* magazine.
1948	Exhibition at the Art Institute of Chicago. Publishes in *Vogue*.
1956	Shows with Alvarez Bravo, Sander and Strand at The Museum of Modern Art, New York: Diogenes with a Camera, curated by Edward Steichen.
1958	Publishes in *Architectural Forum*.
1959	Receives a Guggenheim fellowship.
Early 60s	Photographs in Nova Scotia, Canada, Maine, Virginia and New Hampshire.
1961-1962	Publishes in *Architectural Forum* and *Harper's Bazaar*. Solo exhibition at The Museum of Modern Art, New York: Walker Evans: American Photographs.
1964	Becomes Professor of Photography at Yale University, School of Art and Architecture, New Haven, Connecticut.
1965	Stops his collaboration with *Fortune* magazine.
1966	Publishes *Many Are Called* (Subway photographs 1939-1941), and *Message from the Interior*. Solo exhibition at The Museum of Modern Art, New York: Walker Evans, Subway Photographs. Shows at the Robert Shoelkopf Gallery.
1971	Major retrospective at The Museum of Modern Art, New York : travelling exhibition in the US). Catalogue with an essay by John Szarkowski.
1974	Professor Emeritus, Yale University.
1975	Dies in New Haven, Connecticut.

Chronologie

1903	Naît à St. Louis, Missouri.
1922-1923	Diplômé de la Phillips Academy, Andover, Massachusetts. Entre au Williams College, Williamstown, Massachusetts, où il ne reste qu'un an.
1926	Voyage en Europe. Séjourne à Paris, où il suit des cours à la Sorbonne.
1927-1931	Retourne à New York. Fait des photographies inspirées par l'abstraction formelle de l'avant-garde européenne. Illustre le livre du poète Americain Hart Crane, *The Bridge*. Ainsi que des photographies de rue, à l'instigation de Ben Shahn avec qui il partage un appartement dans Greenwich Village. Rencontre Lincoln Kirstein, rédacteur en chef de la revue *Hound and Horn*, dans laquelle Evans publie "The Reappearance of Photography". Photographie des maisons victoriennes, accompagné de Kirstein. Expose à la galerie John Becker, en Avril-Mai 1931, avec Ralph Steiner et Margaret Bourke-White.
1932	Expose à la galerie Julien Levy, avec George Platt Lynes.
1933	Se rend à Cuba, pour illustrer le livre de Carleton Beals, *Crime of Cuba*. Première exposition au Museum of Modern Art de New York: Walker Evans: Photographs of 19th Century Houses.
1934	Publie pour la première fois dans le magazine *Fortune*: "The Communist Party".
1935	Expose chez Julien Levy Gallery, avec Cartier-Bresson et Alvarez Bravo. Publie 477 reproductions dans le catalogue de l'exposition African Negro Art au Museum of Modern Art de New York. Séjourne à New Orleans. Commence à travailler pour la Farm Security Administration (FSA).
1936-1938	Voyage dans le Sud pour la FSA. Se rend en Alabama avec James Agee, pour travailler au projet de *Let Us Now Praise Famous Men*. Rétrospective au Museum of Modern Art de New York: American Photographs. Commissaire de l'exposition et auteur du livre: Lincoln Kirstein.
1938-1941	Fait des photographies dans le métro avec un appareil caché. Obtient une bourse du Guggenheim pour rendre compte de sujets contemporain saméricains. Publication de *Let Us Now Praise Famous Men*.
1943-1945	Entre au comité de rédaction de *Time*.
1945	Devient rédacteur adjoint de *Fortune*.
1948	Exposition personnelle à l'Art Institute of Chicago. Publie dans *Vogue*.
1956	Participe à l'exposition Diogenes with a Camera, au Museum of Modern Art de New York, avec Alvarez Bravo, Sander et Strand. Commissaire: Edward Steichen.
1958	Publie dans *Architectural Forum*.
1959	Obtient une bourse du Guggenheim.
Début 60's	Fait des photographies en Nova Scotia, Canada, Maine, Virginia et New Hampshire.
1961-1962	Publie dans *Architectural Forum* et *Harper's Bazaar*. Expose au Museum of Modern Art de New York: Walker Evans: American Photographs.
1964	Devient Professeur de Photographie à l'Ecole d'Art et d'Architecture de Yale, New Haven, Connecticut.
1965	Interrompt sa collaboration à *Fortune*.
1966	Publication de *Many Are Called* (photographies prises dans le métro entre 1939 et 1941) et *Message from the Interior*. Expose au Museum of Modern Art de New York: Walker Evans: Subway Photographs. Expose à la galerie Robert Shoelkopf.
1971	Rétrospective au Museum of Modern Art de New York (exposition itinérante, aux Etats-Unis). Commissaire de l'exposition et auteur du catalogue: John Szarkowski.
1974	Nommé Professeur Emérite à l'Université de Yale.
1975	Meurt à New Haven, Connecticut.

Chronologie

1903   Geboren in St. Louis, Missouri.

1922-1923   Abschluss an der Philips Academy, Andover, Massachusetts. Besucht ein Jahr lang das Williams College, Williamstown, Massachusetts.

1926   Reist durch Europa. Bleibt in Paris und besucht Kurse an der Sorbonne.

1927-1931   Kehrt nach New York zurück. Es enstehen von der formalen Abstraktion der europäischen Avantgarde inspirierte Photos. Illustriert das Buch *The Bridge* des amerikansichen Dichters Hart Crane. Erste Straßenphotographien, auf Anregung von Ben Shahn, mit dem er ein Appartment in Greenwich Village teilt. Lernt Lincoln Kirstein kennen, Chefredakteur der Zeitschrift *Hound and Horn*, in der Evans "The Reappearance of Photography" publiziert. Photographiert, in Begleitung von Kirstein, viktorianischer Häuser. Stellt im April/Mai 1931, zusammen mit Ralph Steiner und Margaret Bourke-White, in der Galerie John Becker aus.

1932   Stellt, mit George Platt Lynes, in der Galerie Julien Levy aus.

1933   Reist nach Kuba. Illustriert Carleton Beals' *Crime of Cuba*. Erste Austellung im Museum of Modern Art, New York: Walker Evans Photographs of 19th Century Houses.

1934   Publiziert erstmals in der Zeitschrift *Fortune*: "The Communist Party".

1935   Im Katalog der Ausstellung African Negro Art im Museum of Modern Art, New York, werden 477 Photographien veröffentlicht. Stellt, zusammen mit Cartier-Bresson und Alvarez Bravo, in der Galerie Julien Levy aus. Reist nach New Orleans. Beginnt seine Arbeit für die Farm Security Administration (FSA).

1936-1938   Reist im Auftrag der FSA in die Südstaaten. Arbeiten in Alabama mit James Agee an dem späteren *Let Us Now Praise Famous Men*. Einzelausstellung im Museum of Modern Art, New York: American Photographs, organisiert von Lincoln Kirstein.

1938-1941   Photographiert in der U-Bahn mit versteckter Kamera. Erhält ein Guggenheim-Stipendium für eine Dokumentation zeitgenössischer amerikanischer Themen. Veröffentlichung von *Let Us Now Praise Famous Men*.

1943-1945   Fester Mitarbeiter *Time*.

1945   Wird Redaktionsmitgleid von *Fortune*.

1948   Einzelausstellung am Art Institute of Chicago. Publiziert in *Vogue*.

1956   Stellt zusammen mit Alvarez Bravo, Sander und Strand in der von Edward Steichen organisierten Ausstellung: Diogenes with a Camera im Museum of Modern Art, New York aus.

1958   Publiziert im *Architectural Forum*.

1959   Erhält Guggenheim-Stipendium.

Anfang 60er   Photographiert in Nova Scotia, Canada, Maine, Virginia, New Hampshire.

1961-1962   Publiziert im *Architectural Forum* und in *Harpers's Bazaar*. Ausstellung im Museum of Modern Art, New York: Walker Evans: American Photographs.

1964-1965   Ernennung zum Professor für Photographie an der School of Art and Architecture, Yale University, New Haven, Connecticut.

1965   Beendet seine Zusammenarbeit mit *Fortune*.

1966   Publiziert *Many Are Called* (U-Bahn Photos aus 1939-1941) und *Message from the Interior*. Ausstellung im Museum of Modern Art, New York: Walker Evans: Subway Photographs. Stellt in der Galerie Robert Shoelkopf aus.

1971   Retrospektive im Museum of Modern Art, New York (Wanderausstellung, nur in den USA gezeigt). Ausstellung und Katalogtext: John Szarkowski.

1974   Emeritierung als Professor der Yale University.

1975   Stirbt in New Haven, Connecticut.

Chronologie

1903   Geboren in St.Louis, Missouri.

1922-1923   Eindexamen aan de Phillips Academy, Andover, Massachusetts. Studeert een jaar verder aan het Williams College, Williamstown, Massachusetts.

1926   Reist door Europa. Blijft in Parijs en volgt colleges aan de Sorbonne.

1927   Terugkeer naar New York. Maakt foto's, geïnspireerd door de formele abstractie van de Europese avantgarde. Illustreert het boek *The Bridge* van de Amerikaanse dichter Hart Crane. Eerste straatfoto's, daartoe aangespoord door Ben Shahn met wie hij een appartement deelt in Greenwich Village. Maakt kennis met Lincoln Kirstein, de hoofdredacteur van *Horn and Hound* en publiceert daarin "The Reappearance of Photography". Fotografeert onder begeleiding van Kirstein victoriaanse huizen. In april-mei 1931 expositie in John Becker Gallery, samen met Ralph Steiner en Margaret Bourke-White.

1932   Expositie in Julien Levy Gallery, samen met George Platt Lynes.

1933   Reist naar Cuba. Bijdrage aan Carleton Beals' *Crime of Cuba*. Eerste tentoonstelling in het Museum of Modern Art, New York: Walker Evans Photographs of 19th Century Houses.

1934   Publiceert voor de eerste keer in het tijdschrift *Fortune*: "The Communist Party".

1935   In de catalogus van de tentoonstelling African Negro Art in het Museum of Modern Art, worden 477 foto's afgebeeld. Expositie met Cartier-Bresson en Alvarez Bravo in Galerie Julien Levy. Reist naar New Orleans. Begint te werken voor de Farm Security Administration (FSA).

1936-1938   Reist in opdracht van de FSA naar de Zuidelijke Staten. Werkt in Alabama met James Agee aan het later te verschijnen boek *Let Us Now Praise Famous Men*. Solo-expositie in Museum of Modern Art, New York: American Photographs, samengesteld door Lincoln Kirstein.

1938 - 1941   Fotografeert met verborgen camera in de metro. Ontvangt Guggenheim-beurs voor een documentatie van hedendaagse Amerikaanse thema's. Publicatie van *Let Us Now Praise Famous Men*.

1943-1945   Vaste medewerker bij *Time*.

1945   Wordt redacteur bij *Fortune*.

1948   Solotentoonstelling in het Art Institute of Chicago. Publiceert in *Vogue*.

1956   Groepstentoonstelling met Alvarez Bravo, Sander en Strand in de door Edward Steichen samengestelde expositie: Diogenes with a Camera in het Museum of Modern Art, New York.

1958   Publiceert in *Architectural Forum*.

1959   Ontvangt Guggenheim-beurs.

Begin '60   Fotografeert in Nova Scotia, Canada, Maine, Virginia, New Hampshire.

1961-1962   Publiceert in *Architectural Forum* en *Harper's Bazaar*. Tentoonstelling in Museum of Modern Art, New York:: Walker Evans: American Photographs.

1964   Benoeming tot hoogleraar fotografie aan de School of Art and Architecture, Yale University, New Haven, Connecticut.

1965   Beëindigt zijn werkzaamheden bij *Fortune*.

1966   Publiceert *Many Are Called* (metrofoto's uit 1939-1941) en *Message from the Interior*. Tentoonstelling in het Museum of Modern Art, New York: Walker Evans: Subway Photographs. Tentoonstelling in Robert Shoelkopf Gallery.

1971   Retrospectief in het Museum of Modern Art, New York (Reizende tentoonstelling, alleen in de VS). Tentoonstelling en catalogus: John Szarkowski.

1974   Emeritaat als hoogleraar aan de Yale University.

1975   Overlijdt in New Haven, Connecticut.

Selected Bibliography/Bibliographie sélective
Bibliographie (Auswahl)/Geselecteerde Bibliografie

Books and catalogues published before 1975
Livres et catalogues publiés avant 1975
Vor 1975 veröffentlichten Bücher und Kataloge
Vóór 1975 gepubliceerde boeken en catalogi

1930
Crane, Hart, *The Bridge*, Paris/New York , Black Sun Press, (3 rep. W. Evans).

1931
Beals, Carleton, *The Crime of Cuba*, Philadelphia/London, J.B. Lippincott Company, (31 rep. W. Evans).

1935
African Negro Art, cat.The Museum of Modern Art, New York (477 rep.W. Evans).

1938
Kirstein, Lincoln, *Walker Evans: American Photographs*,
cat. The Museum of Modern Art, New York (87 rep. W. Evans).
Reprint 1963, with foreword by Monroe Wheeler.
Reprint 1988, with note by Peter Galassi.

1941
Agee, James, Walker Evans, *Let Us Now Praise Famous Men*,
Boston, Houghton Mifflin, (31 rep. W. Evans).
Reprint 1960, foreword by Walker Evans, (62 rep. W. Evans).
Reprint 1966, New York, Ballantine Books.
Reprint 1988, foreword by John Hersey.

Wheaton College Photographs, Norton, Massachusetts, Wheaton College,
(24 rep. W. Evans). Foreword by J. Edgar Park.

1942
Bickel, Karl, *The Mangrove Cost*, New York , Coward Mc Cann, (32 rep. W. Evans).

1952
Radin, Paul, James Johnson Sweeney, *African Folktales and Sculpture*, New York,
Pantheon Books, (113 rep. W. Evans).
Reprint 1964, 1970, Princeton, Princeton University Press.

1966
Agee, James, *Many Are Called*, Boston, Houghton Mifflin, (89 rep. W. Evans).
Introduction by James Agee (first published in *Cambridge Review March 1956*).
Reprint 1978, Liebling, Jerome (ed.), *Photography: Current Perspectives*, Rochester,
Light Impressions.
Szarkowski, John, *Message from the Interior*, New York , Eakin Press,
(12 rep. W. Evans).

1971
Szarkowski, John, *Walker Evans*, cat. The Museum of Modern Art, New York
(100 rep. W.Evans).

1973
Walker Evans, Photographs for the Farm Security Administration, 1935-1938,
New York, Da Capo Press. Introduction by Jerald C. Maddox.

Texts and Interviews/Entretiens et textes
Texte und Interviews/Teksten en Interviews

1931
Evans, Walker, "The Reappearance of Photography", *Hound and Horn*,
Lincoln Kirstein (ed.).
Reprint 1980 in: Trachtenberg, Alan (ed.),*Classic Essays on Photography*,
New Haven, Connecticut , Leete's Island Books.

1958
Evans, Walker, "Robert Frank", *US Camera Annual*.

1960
Evans, Walker, "James Agee in 1936", *Atlantic Monthly*, July.

1969
Evans, Walker, "Photography", *Quality: Its Image in the Arts*, Louis Kronenberger,
Marshall Lee (eds.), New York, Atheneum.

1971
Katz, Leslie, "Interview with Walker Evans", *Art in America*, March-April.
Reprint 1981 Goldberg, Vicki (ed.), *Photography in Print-Writings from 1816 to the
Present*, New York, A Touchstone Book.

1974
"The Thing Itself is Such a Secret and so Unapproachable", Interview with Yale
students, *Yale Alumni Magazine*, February.

1976
Caplan, Lincoln (ed.)," Walker Evans on himself, A Discussion with
Harvard Students in April 1975", *New Republic*, 11 November.
Bunnell, Peter," An Introduction to Evans' Work and his Recollections",
New Republic, 11 November.

1977
Ferris, Bill, "A Visit with Walker Evans", *Images of the South: visits with Eudora
Welty and Walker Evans*, Memphis, Tennessee, Center for Southern Folklore.

1980
Newhall, Beaumont (ed.), "Walker Evans, Visiting Artist: a Transcript of his
Discussion with the Students of the University of Michigan, 1971",
Photography: Essays and Images, Beaumont Newhall (ed.), New York,
The Museum of Modern Art.

Texts and Photographs in Magazines
Textes et photographies publiés dans des magazines
Texte und Photographien in Zeitschriften
Teksten en Foto's in Tijdschriften

Architectural Forum
Color Accidents, I 1958.
The London Look, IV 1968.
Primitive Churches, XII 1961.
The American Warehouse, IV 1962.
Come on Down, VII 1962.

Architectural Record
Photographic Studies, IX 1930.

Architectural Review (London)
Middletown and Main Street, V 1939.
Man made America, XII 1950.

Review
Rapid Transit, III 1956.

Creative Art
Mr. Walker Evans Records a City's Scene, XII 1930.

Dance Index
Criticism of Edwin Denby, II 1946.

Du (Zürich)
Amerikanische Architektur gestern: 12 Schwarz-weissaufnahmen, VI 1964.

Hound and Horn
New York City, X-XII 1930.
Cuba Libre, VII-IX 1934.

Fortune
The Communist Party, IX 1934.
Six Days at Sea, IX 1937.
In Bridgeport's War Factories, IX 1941.
The Small Shop, XI 1945.
The Boom in Ballet, XII 1945.
Collins Co., Collinsville, Connecticut , I 1946.
Adventures of Henry and Joe in Autoland, III 1946.
Homes of Americans, IV 1946.
The Yankees, VI 1946.
Labor Anonymous, XI 1946.
Chicago: A Camera Exploration, II 1947.
One Newspaper Town, VIII 1947.
Is the Market Right, IV 1948.
Main Street Looking North from Courthouse Square, V 1948.
In the Heart of the Black Belt, VIII 1948.
Summer North of Boston, VIII 1949.
The Gentle Truckers, V 1950.
Along the Right-of-Way, IX, 1950.
Clay: the Commonest Industrial Raw Material, I 1951.
The Wreckers, V 1951.
Chicago River: the creek that made a city grow, VIII 1951.
Imperial Washington, II 1952.
U.N. Capitol, V 1952.
The U.S. Depot, II 1953.
Vintage Office Furniture. VIII 1953.
The Twilight of American Woolen, III 1954.

Over California, III 1954.
Text Exposures, VII 1954 (Ansel Adams, Paul Strand, Charles Sheeler, Charles Abott, Edward Weston).
October's Game, X 1954.
Beauties of the Common Tool, VII 1955.
The Congressional, XI 1955.
These Dark Satanic Mills, IV 1956.
Downtown: a Last Look Backward, X 1956.
Before they Disappear, III 1957.
The Stones of duPont, V 1957.
The Last of Railroad Steam, IX 1958.
And That is That, X 1958.
Summer at Harbor Point, VII 1960.
On the Waterfront, XI 1960.
People and Places in Trouble, III 1961.
When Downtown was a Beautiful Mess, I 1962.
The Auto Junkyard, IV 1962.
The Athenian Reach, VI 1964.
American Masonry, IV 1965.
NB.
• Certain issues of Fortune published just one photograph by Evans. They are not mentioned here. A list of them can be found in *Walker Evans at Fortune, 1945-1965*.
• Fortune a publié, dans certains numéros, une seule image de Walker Evans. Ces images isolées n'ont pas été réportoriées ici. On peut en trouver la liste dans le catalogue *Walker Evans at Fortune, 1945-1965*.
• Einige Ausgaben von Fortune enthalten nur eine Photographie van Evans und sind hier nicht aufgenommen. Eine Liste von diesen steht in *Walker Evans at Fortune, 1945-1965*.
• In een aantal nummers van Fortune staat slechts één foto van Evans. Deze zijn hier niet vermeld. Een complete lijst is afgedrukt in *Walker Evans at Fortune, 1945-1965*.

Harper's Bazaar
Walker Evans: the Unposed Portrait, III 1962.
Those Little Screens, II 1963.

Mademoiselle
Collectors' Items, V 1963.

Life
A Heritage Must be Saved, VII 1963.
Gallery, VIII 1970.

US Camera Annual
Corner of State and Randolph Streets, Chicago, 1949.

Vogue
Faulkner's Mississippi, X 1948.

Books and Catalogues Published after 1975
Livres et catalogues publiés après 1975
Nach 1975 veröffentlichte Bücher und Kataloge
Na 1975 gepubliceerde boeken en catalogi

1977
Baier, Leslie K., *Walker Evans at Fortune 1945-1965*, cat. Wellesley College Museum, Wellesley, Massachusetts.

1978
Walker Evans, First and Last, New York, Harper and Row,1978.
Walker Evans, cat. Sidney Janis Gallery, New York, 1978.

1979
Walker Evans, New York, The Aperture History of Photography.

1981
Papageorge, Tod, *Walker Evans and Robert Frank: An Essay on Influence*, cat. Yale University Art Gallery, New Haven, Connecticut.

1982
Thompson, Jerry (ed.), *Walker Evans at Work*, New York, Harper and Row.

1983
Rosenheim, Jeff, et.al, *Walker Evans 1903-1975*, cat. IVAM Centre Julio Gonzales, Valencia.

1987
Travis, David, *Walker Evans: Leaving Things as They Are*, cat. Art Institute of Chicago, Chicago.

1989
Mora, Gilles, *Walker Evans, Havana*, Paris, Contrejour.

1990
Walker Evans, Centre National de la Photographie, Paris, 1990.
Brix, Michael, et. al. *Walker Evans-Amerika: Bilder aus den Jahren der Depression*, Kat. Städtische Galerie im Lembachhaus, München, Schirmer und Mosel, München. English edition, édition française.

1991
Rosenheim, Jeff, *Walker Evans and Jane Ninas in New Orleans 1935-1936*, cat. The Historic New Orleans Collection, New Orleans, Louisiana.
Greenough, Sarah, *Walker Evans, Subways and Streets*, cat. National Gallery of Art, Washington D.C.

Selected Articles and Essays on Walker Evans
Articles et essais sur Walker Evans (sélection)
Artikel und Essays über Walker Evans (Auswahl)
Artikelen en essays over Walker Evans (selectie)

1938
Mabry, Thomas Dabney, "Walker Evans' Photographs of America", *Harper's Bazaar*, November.
MacCausland, Elizabeth, "Rural Life in America as the Camera Shows it", *Springfield Republican*, September 11.
Williams, William Carlos, "Sermon with a Camera", *New Republic*, October 12.

1956
Soby, James Thrall, "Walker Evans", *Saturday Review of Literature*, February 18.

1957
Kozloff, Max, "Photos within Photographs", *Artforum*, February.
Kirstein, Lincoln, "Photographs by Walker Evans", *Print*, February/March.

1962
Soby, James Thrall, "The Muse was not for Hire", *Saturday Review*, September 22.

1966
Soby, James Thrall, "Art of Seeing", *The New Yorker*, December 24.

1967
Tillim, Sidney, "Walker Evans: Photography as Representation", *Artforum*, March.

1968
Sylvester, David, "Walker Evans, a World of Stillness and Silence", *The Sunday Times Magazine*, March 31.

1971
Lanes, Jerrold, "Walker Evans: the Image as Process and as Subject", *Artforum*, June.
Sobieszek, Robert, "Another Look at Walker Evans", *Art in America*, November-December.

1973
Stott, William, *Documentary Expression and Thirties America*, New York, Oxford University Press.
Reprint in 1986, Chicago, The University of Chicago Press.

1974
Stott, William, "Visions of America", *Harper's Magazine*, February.
Stott, William, "Walker Evans, Robert Frank and the Landscape of Dissociation", *Artscanada*, December.

1978
Trachtenberg, Alan, "The Presence of Walker Evans", *Atlantic Monthly*, September.

1981
Baier, Leslie, "Visions of Fascination and Despair: the Relationship between Walker Evans and Robert Frank", *Art Journal*, vol 41, no. 1, Spring.
Papageorge, Tod, "From Walker Evans to Robert Frank: a Legacy Received, Embraced and Transformed", *Artforum*, April.

1988
Trachtenberg, Alan, "From Image to Story: Reading the File", *Documenting America, 1935-1943*, Carl Fleishhauer, Beverly W. Brannan (eds.), Berkeley.

1989
Kirstein, Lincoln, "Walker Evans: American Photographs", *USA Today*, March.
Kozloff, Max, "Walker Evans' American Photographs", *Artforum*, April.
Trachtenberg, Alan, "The Book Nearly Anonymous", *Reading American Photographs: Images as History - Matthew Brady to Walker Evans*, New York, Hill & Wang.

Dan Graham originally took, and continues to take, photographs with Kodachrome slide film. On occasion he used Kodacolor print film. From the 1970s on, when he began to show the photographs, Graham reprinted the originals from internegatives as c-prints, with the exception of a few which were produced as Cibachromes.
The titles of the photographs are meant only as descriptions, each photograph being given an alphabetical and numerical code. The croppings, in the case of the double-mounted photographs, are simply edge adjustments. Some of the photographs were cropped directly on the slide film.
In the case of the double-mounted photographs, the same photograph may be used several times, but in different combinations so that each combination is, in principle, unique.

Les photographies de Dan Graham ont toutes été prises avec de la pellicule diapositive couleur Kodak (hormis quelques-unes, faites avec de la pellicule négative couleur). Dès les années 1970, à l'époque où il commence à exposer ses photographies, Dan Graham a refait des tirages en C-print (et quelques-uns en Cibachrome) à partir d'internégatifs réalisés d'après les originaux.
Les titres donnés aux photographies ont une simple fonction de description; un code alphabétique et numérique a été attribué à chacune d'elles. Les recadrages, dans le cas des diptyques, ne correspondent qu'à des ajustements techniques. Certaines photographies ont été recadrées en coupant directement dans les diapositives.En ce qui concerne les diptyques, une image a pu être utilisée plusieurs fois, combinée chaque fois différement avec une autre, de manière à ce que chaque combinaison soit, en principe, unique.

Dan Graham fotografierte ursprünglich und fotografiert auch heute noch mit Kodachrome-Dia Film, mit Ausnahme einiger Fotos, die mit Kodacolor-Print Film aufgenommen wurden. Abgesehen von einigen Fotos, die als Cibachrome hergestellt wurden, reproduziert Graham seit den 70er Jahren, als er anfing, seine Fotos auszustellen, die Originale von Internegativen als c-prints.
Die Titel der Fotos sind lediglich als Beschreibung gedacht, jedes Foto ist mit einer Buchstaben-Zahlen-Kombination bezeichnet. Die Beschneidungen im Fall der im Sandwich-Verfahren hergestellten Fotos sind lediglich Randbegleichungen. Bei einigen Fotos wurde der Dia-Film direkt beschnitten. Im Fall dieser Sandwich-Fotos kann dasselbe Foto mehrmals verwendet sein, jedoch in unterschiedlichen Kombinationen, so daß jede Kombination prinzipiell ein Unikat darstellt.

Dan Graham fotografeert vanaf het begin met Kodachrome dia-film, een enkele keer fotografeerde hij met Kodacolor negatief-film. Vanaf de jaren '70, toen hij begon te exposeren, maakte hij met behulp van tussennegatieven nieuwe afdrukken van de originelen als c-prints, later werden enkele Cibachromes afgedrukt.
De titels van de foto's zijn slechts bedoeld als beschrijvingen, elke foto is zowel alfabetisch als numeriek gecodeerd. In het geval van dubbele montages zijn de uitsneden formaataanpassingen. Soms werden uitsneden direct op de dia-film gemaakt.
Bij de dubbele montages kunnen foto's meerdere keren gebruikt worden, maar altijd in verschillende combinaties, zodat elke combinatie in principe uniek is.

DAN GRAHAM

Selected Photographs/Un choix de photographies/Eine Auswahl von Photographien/Een Selectie van Foto's

1965-1991

1

Part One/Première partie/Teil Eins/Deel Een

"Homes for America"

Homes for America

D. GRAHAM

Belleplain
Brooklawn
Colonia
Colonia Manor
Fair Haven
Fair Lawn
Greenfields Village
Green Village
Plainsboro
Pleasant Grove
Pleasant Plains
Sunset Hill Garden

Garden City
Garden City Park
Greenlawn
Island Park
Levitown
Middleville
New City Park
Pine Lawn
Plainview
Plandome Manor
Pleasantside
Pleasantville

"The Serenade" - Cape Coral unit, Fla.

THE SERENADE
Three Bedrooms,
Two Baths,
Enclosed Garage,
Screened Porch

Set-back, Jersey City, New Jersey

Each house in a development is a lightly constructed 'shell' although this fact is often con-
cealed by fake (half-stone) brick walls. Shells
can be added or subtracted easily. The standard
unit is a box or a series of boxes, sometimes con-
temptuously called 'pillboxes'. When the box
has a sharply oblique roof it is called a Cape Cod.
When it is longer than wide it is a 'ranch'. A

The logic relating each sectioned part to the entire plan follows a systematic plan. A development contains a limited, set number of house
models. For instance, Cape Coral, a Florida project, advertises eight different models:

A The Sonata
B The Concerto
C The Overture
D The Ballet
E The Prelude
F The Serenade
G The Nocturne
H The Rhapsody

Large-scale 'tract' housing 'developments' constitute the new city. They are located every-
where. They are not particularly bound to existing communities; they fail to develop either regional characteristics or separate identity. These
'projects' date from the end of World War II
when in southern California speculators or 'operative' builders adapted mass production techniques to quickly build many houses for the de-
fense workers over-concentrated there. This
'California Method' consisted simply of determining in advance the exact amount and lengths
of pieces of lumber and multiplying them by the
number of standardized houses to be built. A
cutting yard was set up near the site of the project to saw rough lumber into those sizes. By
mass buying, greater use of machines and factory
produced parts, assembly line standardization,
multiple units were easily fabricated.

Two Entrance Doorways, 'Two Home Homes', Jersey City, N.D.

Center Court, Entrances, Development, Jersey City

two-story house is usually called 'colonial'. If it
consists of contiguous boxes with one slightly
higher elevation it is a 'split level.' Such stylistic
differentiation is advantageous to the basic structure (with the possible exception of the split level
whose plan simplifies construction on discontinuous ground levels).

There is a recent trend toward 'two home homes'
which are two boxes split by adjoining walls and
having separate entrances. The left and right
hand units are mirror reproductions of each other. Often sold as private units are strings of
apartment-like, quasi-discrete cells formed by
subdividing laterally an extended rectangular
parallelopiped into as many as ten or twelve separate dwellings.

In addition, there is a choice of eight exterior
colors:
1 White
2 Moonstone Grey
3 Nickle

LAWN GREEN

4 Seafoam Green
5 Lawn Green
6 Bamboo
7 Coral Pink
8 Colonial Red

Housing Development, rear view, Bayonne, New Jersey

Housing Development, front view, Bayonne, New Jersey

Developers usually build large groups of individual homes sharing similar floor plans and
whose overall grouping possesses a discrete flow
plan. Regional shopping centers and industrial
parks are sometimes integrated as well into the
general scheme. Each development is sectioned
into blocked-out areas containing a series of iden-
tical or sequentially related types of houses all of
which have uniform or staggered set-backs and
land plots.

As the color series usually varies independent
of the model series, a block of eight houses util-
izing four models and four colors might have
forty-eight times forty-eight or 2.304 possible arrangements.

Dan Graham

Homes for America
(2 panels)
1965-1970
mixed media
102 cm x 77 cm (x 2)
Collection Daled, Bruxelles

Interior of Model Home, Staten Island, N.Y.

The 8 color variables were equally distributed among the house exteriors. The first buyers were more likely to have obtained their first choice in color. Family units had to make a choice based on the available colors which also took account of both husband and wife's likes and dislikes. Adult male and female color likes and dislikes were compared in a survey of the homeowners:

'Like'

Male	Female
Skyway	Skyway Blue
Colonial Red	Lawn Green
Patio White	Nickle
Yellow Chiffon	Colonial Red
Lawn Green	Yellow Chiffon
Nickle	Patio White
Fawn	Moonstone Grey
Moonstone Grey	Fawn

'Split-Level', 'Two Home Homes', Jersey City, N.J.

ach block of houses is a self-contained sequence - there is no development -- selected from the ossible acceptable arrangements. As an ex- mple, if a section was to contain eight houses of which four model types were to be used, any of hese permutational possibilities could be used:

Bedroom of Model Home, S.I., N.Y.

AABBCCDD	ABCDABCD
AABBDDCC	ABDCABDC
AACCBBDD	ACBDACBD
AACCDDBB	ACDBACDB
AADDCCBB	ADBCADBC
AADDBBCC	ADCBADCB
BBAADDCC	BACDBACD
BBCCAADD	BCADBCAD
BBCCDDAA	BCDABCDA
BBDDAACC	BDACBDAC
BBDDCCAA	BDCABDCA
CCAABBDD	CABDCABD
CCAADDBB	CADBCADB
CCBBDDAA	CBADCBAD
CCBBAADD	CBDACBDA
CCDDAABB	CDABCDAB
CCDDBBAA	CDBACDBA
DDAABBCC	DACBDACB
DDAACCBB	DABCDABC
DDBBAACC	DBACDBAC
DDBBCCAA	DBCADBCA
DDCCAABB	DCABDCAB
DDCCBBAA	DCBADCBA

Two Family Units, Staten Island, N.Y.

'Ground-Level', 'Two Home Homes', Jersey City, N.J.

'Dislike'

Male	Female
Lawn Green	Patio White
Colonial Red	Fawn
Patio White	Colonial Red
Moonstone Grey	Moonstone Grey
Fawn	Yellow Chiffon
Yellow Chiffon	Lawn Green
Nickle	Skyway blue
Skyway Blue	Nickle

Although there is perhaps some aesthetic pre- cedence in the row houses which are indigenous to many older cities along the east coast, and built with uniform façades and set-backs early this century, housing developments as an archi- tectural phenomenon seem peculiarly gratuitous. They exist apart from prior standards of 'good' architecture. They were not built to satisfy in- dividual needs or tastes. The owner is complete- ly tangential to the product's completion. His home isn't really possessable in the old sense; it wasn't designed to 'last for generations', and out- side of its immediate 'here and now' context it is useless, designed to be thrown away. Both ar- chitecture and craftsmanship as values are' sub- verted by the dependence on simplified and easily duplicated techniques of fabrication and standardized modular plans. Contingencies such as mass production technology and land use economies make the final decisions, denying the architect his former 'unique' role. Develop- ments stand in an altered relationship to their environment. Designed to fill in 'dead' land areas, the houses needn't adapt to or attempt to withstand Nature. There is no organic unity connecting the land site and the home. Both are without roots — separate parts in a larger, pre- determined, synthetic order.

Basement Doors, Home, New Jersey

Car Hop, Jersey City, N.J.

Kitchen Trays, 'Discount House', New Jersey

'Discount Store', Sweaters on Racks, New Jersey

A given development might use, perhaps, four of these possibilities as an arbitrary scheme for different sectors; then select four from another scheme which utilizes the remaining four unused models and colors; then select four from another scheme which utilizes all eight models and eight colors; then four from another scheme which utilizes a single model and all eight colors (or four or two colors); and finally utilize that single scheme for one model and one color. This serial logic might follow consistently until, at the edges, it is abruptly terminated by pre-existent high- ways, bowling alleys, shopping plazas, car hops, discount houses, lumber yards or factories.

ARTS MAGAZINE/December 1966-January 1967.

Untitled (Family in New Highway Restaurant, Jersey City, N.J.; Row of Tract Houses, Bayonne, N.J.)
1967; 1966
Kodacolor; c-print
29,7 cm x 39,5 cm; 26,8 cm x 34,4 cm

Privatbesitz, Köln

135

Court Steps, New York City; Side Facade of Suburban House, Westfield, N.J.
1966;1965
c-prints
23,9 cm x 26,5 cm; 22,8 cm x 25,6 cm

Courtesy Marian Goodman Gallery, New York

Entrance "Two Home Home", Brick Facade, Staten Island, New York City
1978
c-print
27,7 cm x 35,3 cm

Privatbesitz Köln, Courtesy Le Case d'Arte, Milano

Trucks, New York, N.Y.

Trucks, New York, N.Y.
1966
cibachrome
24 cm x 34,3 cm

Courtesy Marian Goodman Galery, New York

Top: Tract Houses, Bayonne, N.J. 1966   Bottom: New Housing, Vancouver, B.C., Canada, 1974

Tract Houses, Bayonne, N.J.; New Housing, Vancouver, B.C., Canada
1966;1974
c-prints
26,8 cm x 35 cm; 27,8 cm x 35,5 cm

Top: Row of New Tract Houses, Bayonne, N.J. Bottom: New Highway Restaurant Opening, Jersey City, N.J. 1967
1966

Row of New Tract Houses, Bayonne, N.J.; New Highway Restaurant Opening, Jersey City, N.J.
1966;1967
c-prints
22,2 cm x 32,2 cm; 24,6 cm x 32 cm
Courtesy Marian Goodman Gallery, New York

Hrnslng Project Under Construction   Staten Island, N.y —   Dan Graham 1978

Housing Project under Construction, Staten Island, N.Y.
1978
cibachrome
22,4 cm x 31,5 cm

Courtesy Marian Goodman Gallery, New York

Top: World War II Housing Project, Vancouver, Canada; Bottom: Show window of Store selling Kitchen Goods, Bayonne, New Jersey 1969
1974

World War II Housing Project, Vancouver, Canada; Show Window of Store selling Kitchen Goods, Bayonne, New Jersey
1974;1969
c-prints
32,5 cm x 48,5 cm; 32,5 cm x 48,5 cm

Top: Housing Development, Bayonne, N.J. 1966   Warehouse in 'Neo-Colonial Style'
                                                Westfield, N.J. 1978

Housing Development, Bayonne, N.J.; Warehouse in 'Neo-Colonial Style' Westfield, N.J.
1966;1978
c-print; cibachrome
27,9 cm x 35,5 cm; 23 cm x 34 cm

Courtesy Marian Goodman Gallery, New York

Row of New "Tract" Houses; Row of "Tract" House with Backyard Fence, Jersey City, N.J.
1966;1966
c-prints
27,7 cm x 35,5 cm; 27,7 cm x 35,5 cm
Collection Mac Adams, New York

2

Part Two/Deuxième partie/Teil Zwei/Deel Twee

**Houses and People/L'architecture et les gens/
Häuser und Menschen/Huizen en Mensen**

Staten Island House   1978

Staten Island House
1978
c-print
32,5 cm x 49 cm

149

Two Home Home, Staten Island, New York City
1981
c-print
32 cm x 22 cm
Courtesy Galerie Durand-Dessert, Paris

150

Top: "Two Home Housing For Two Families, Staten Island, N.Y., 1978 Bottom: Family in Backyard, Staten Island, N.Y. 1969 *[signature]*

Two Home Housing for Two Families, Staten Island, N.Y.; Family in Backyard, Staten Island
1978;1969
c-prints
23,2 cm x 35 cm; 24,2 x 35 cm

Backyards with Corner Garden of Housing Project, Staten Island, N.Y.
1978
c-print
23,5 cm x 35 cm
Courtesy Marian Goodman Gallery, New York

Mother and Son in Backyard, Bayonne, N.J.
1969
c-print
22,6 cm x 33,8 cm

Apartment House, Cement Steps Entrance, Vancouver, B.C., Canada
1975
c-print
25,1 cm x 30,5 cm
Courtesy Marian Goodman Gallery, New York

Top: People in Highway Restaurant, Jersey City, N.J. 1967   Bottom: Two Families in Front of Housing Development, Staten Island, New York City, 1967

People in Highway Restaurant, Jersey City; Two Families in Front of Housing Development, Staten Island, New York
1967; 1967
c-prints
35,5 cm x 27,5 cm; 35 cm x 29 cm

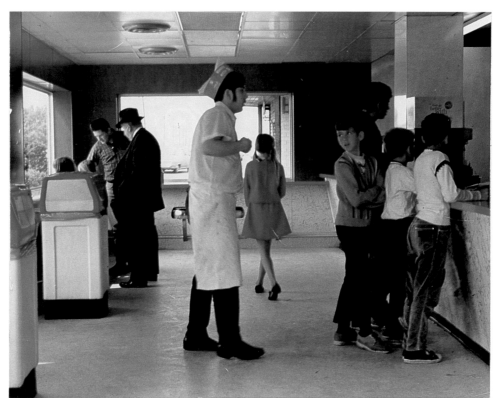

First Day Opening of Highway Restaurant, Jersey City, N.J.
1967
c-print
26,7 cm x 34,2 cm

Cue in front of 'Telethon Home', Perth, Australia; Tract Houses Under Construction, Bayonne, N.J.
1988;1982
c-prints
20,1 cm x 30,5 cm; 20,2 cm x 29,8 cm

3

Part Three/Troisième partie/Teil Drei/Deel Drie

The City/La ville/Die Stadt/De Stad

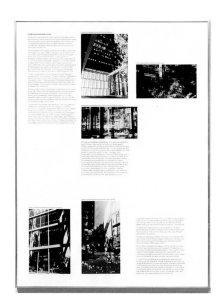

Private "Public" Space: Corporate Park Atriums
1987
mixed media
101,6 cm x 76,2 cm (x 6)
Collaboration with Robin Hurst

Courtesy Marian Goodman Gallery, New York

'Ziggurat' Skyscraper, New York, N.Y.; Two-way Mirror Building, The Hague, Holland
1967; 1974
c-prints
27,8 cm x 35 cm; 27,8 cm x 35,7 cm

Right: "Two Way Mirror" Glass Office Building, Los Angeles, Ca. 1975

Left: View Through Office Building, Toronto, Ontario, Canada, 1976

"Two-Way Mirror" Glass Office Building, Los Angeles, Ca.; View Through Office Building, Toronto, Ontario, Canada
1975;1976
c-prints
20,9 cm x 31,3 cm; 27,8 cm x 31 cm
Courtesy Marian Goodman Gallery, New York

Corporate Office Building in Two Way Mirror, Los Angeles, Ca.; Corporate Office Building, Water St., New York, N.Y.
1974; 1974
c-prints
31,7 cm x 21,1 cm; 32 cm x 22,8 cm
Courtesy Marian Goodman Gallery, New York

Pink Kitchen Trays in Discount, Bayonne, N.J.; Low Income Public Housing, Bronx, New York, N.Y.
1966; 1967
c-prints
26,3 cm x 35,4 cm; 23,5 cm x 35,4 cm

Left: 'Tombs' Prison Building, New York, N.Y. 1965   *Right: Two Housing Projects, New York, N.Y. 1966*

'Tombs' Prison Building, New York, N.Y.; Two Housing Projects, New York, N.Y.
1965; 1966
c-print; cibachrome
31,1 cm x 22,5 cm; 31,1 cm x 18,1 cm

Collection The Carnegie Museum of Art, Pittsburgh

A.W. Mellon Acquisition Endowment Fund

Top: Parking Lot and Factory, Union City, N.J. 1967 Bottom: Employees in Chicago Office Building, Chicago Ill. 1971

Parking Lot and Factory, Union City, N.J.; Employees in Chicago Office Building, Chicago, Ill.
1967; 1971
c-print; b/w-print
27,7 cm x 35,2 cm; 25,7cm x 34,8 cm

Courtesy Marian Goodman Gallery, New York

Showcase Window, Chicago
1969
Kodacolor
39,8 cm x 26,8 cm

Collection of Benjamin H.D. Buchloh, New York

Employees' Dining Area, Chemcourt Building, N.Y.
1986
c-print
27,8 cm x 35,3 cm
Collaboration with Robin Hurst

4

Part Four/Quatrième partie/Teil Vier/Deel Vier

**Interiors and Ornaments/Intérieurs et ornements/
Interieurs und Ornamente/Interieurs en Ornamenten**

High School Corridor, Westfield, New Jersey
1965
c-print
27,7 cm x 35,5 cm

Collezione Pasquale Leccese, Courtesy Le Case d'Arte, Milano

177

Mirror in Children's Bedroom of Model Home; Reflection of Model Home Interior and Other New Houses seen through Front Door of
Model Home, Staten Island, New York City
1975; 1975
c-prints
32 cm x 22 cm; 32 cm x 22 cm
Sammlung Dr. Susanna Hegewisch-Becker, Hamburg

Diner on Highway, Staten Island, N.Y.; View from Window of Highway from Restaurant, Jersey City, N.J.
1967; 1969
c-prints
27,6 cm x 34 cm; 22,3 cm x 34 cm
Courtesy Marian Goodman Gallery, New York

Top: Highway Restaurant, Seattle, 1974 Bottom: Bedroom Suite, Model House, Staten Island, N.Y., 1967 Dan Graham

Highway Restaurant, Seattle; Bedroom Suite, "Model House", Staten Island, N.Y.
1974; 1967
c-prints
27,3 cm x 34,4 cm; 24 cm x 34,8 cm

Courtesy Marian Goodman Gallery, New York

Row of Houses, Bayonne, N.J.; Hall of "Model Home", Staten Island, N.Y.
1966;1967
c-prints
24,6 cm x 29,3 cm; 23,6 cm x 29 cm

Courtesy Galerie Micheline Szwajcer, Antwerpen

Backyards of New Housing Development, Staten Island, New York, N.Y. Dan Graham 1974

Backyards of New Housing Development, Staten Island, New York, N.Y.
1974
c-print
21,4 cm x 33,5 cm
Courtesy Marian Goodman Gallery, New York

Top: 'Baroque' Bedroom, 'Model Home', Staten Island, N.Y.   Bottom: Motel, San Francisco   1982 [signature]
1967

Children behind Chain-link Fence, Jersey City, N.J.; Dracula Sign, Times Square, New York City
1969; 1975
c-prints
27,7 cm x 35,5 cm; 25,7 cm x 35,5 cm

Courtesy Marian Goodman Gallery, New York

184

Top: Children Behind Chain Link Fence, Jersey City, N.J., 1969 Bottom: Dracula Sign, Times Square, New York City, 1975

'Baroque' Bedroom, 'Model Home', Staten Island, N.Y.; Motel, San Francisco
1967; 1982
c-prints
23,6 cm x 35,6 cm; 23,6 cm x 35,5 cm

'Split-Level' Two Home Houses, Jersey City, N.J.; Wendy's Restaurant, Vancouver, Canada
1966;1974
c-prints
24 cm x 36,5 cm; 27,8 cm x 35,5 cm

Courtesy Galerie Roger Pailhas, Marseille/Paris

Dan Graham (1942, Urbana, Illinois)

**Selected Bibliography/Bibliographie sélective
Bibliographie (Auswahl)/Geselecteerde Bibliografie**

In the context of this book we thought that a selection of the texts and writings by Dan Graham would suffice. The photographs of Dan Graham are often mentioned and reproduced herein. In most cases the titles also refer to exhibitions of the artist.

Nous avons pensé, dans le contexte de ce livre, qu'une sélection des écrits de Dan Graham suffirait. Ses photographies ont été mentionnées et reproduites à l'intérieur de ces textes. Les titres sont souvent les mêmes que ceux des expositions de Dan Graham.

Im Zusammenhang dieses Buches hielten wir eine Auswahl von Texten und Schriften von Dan Graham für ausreichend. Grahams Photographien sind darin häufig erwähnt und publiziert. In den meisten Fällen beziehen sich die Titel auch auf Ausstellungen des Künstlers.

In de context van dit boek hebben we gemeend te kunnen volstaan met een selectie van teksten en geschriften van en over Dan Graham. De foto's van Dan Graham werden vaak hierin vermeld en gepubliceerd. De titels duiden in de meeste gevallen ook de tentoonstellingen van de kunstenaar aan.

Texts by/Textes de/Texte von/Teksten van Dan Graham

1966
"Homes for America", *Arts Magazine*, December-January (1967).
"Schema", Brian O'Doherty (ed.), *Aspen magazine*, no. 5,6.
"Detumescence", *National Tatler*.

1967
"Muybridge Moments", *Arts Magazine*, February.
"Carl Andre", *Arts Magazine*, no. 3.
"The Book as Object", *Arts Magazine*, May.
"Dan Flavin", cat. *Dan Flavin*, Museum of Contemporary Art, Chicago.

1968
"Oldenburg's Monuments", *Artforum*, January.
"Eisenhower and the Hippies", *0 to 9*, Winter.

1969
"Two Parallel Essays, Photographs of Motion, Two Related Projects for Slide Projectors", *Artists & Photographs*, New York , Multiples, Inc..
"Poem-schema", *Art-Language*, vol. 1, no. 1, May.
"Dean Martin/Entertainment as Theater", *Fusion*, Autumn.
"Some Implications and Observations", *Art & Language*, no. 7.

1970
Editorial note and contribution, *Aspen magazine*, no. 9.
Various pieces, *Interfunktionen*, no. 5.
"Thoughts On Two Structures", cat. *Sol LeWitt*, Haags Gemeentemuseum.
"Eleven Sugar Cubes", *Art in America*, May-June.

1971
"Homes for America", *Interfunktionen* no. 7.
"Performance as a Perceptual Process", *Interfunktionen* no. 7.
"TV Camera/Monitor Performance", *Radical Software*, Fall.
"Subject Matter", *arTitudes*, no. 1, octobre.

1972
"Film Pieces: Visual Field", *Interfunktionen*, no. 8.
"Eight Pieces by Dan Graham", *Studio International*, May.

1973
Various pieces, *Interfunktionen*, no. 9.
"Intention Intentionality Sequence", *Arts Magazine*, April.
"Dan Graham I/Eye", con Tommaso Trini, *Domus*, febbraio.
"Scheme (1965)", *Schema Informazione*, Firenze.
"Magazine/Ads", Deurle.

1974
"Two Consciousness Projection(s)", *Arts Magazine*, December.
"The Book as Object", *Interfunktione*n, no. 11.
"Notes on Income (Outflow) Piece", *Interfunktionen*, no. 11.

1975
"#7, Performance/Audience Sequence, Notes on 'Income Piece'",
Control Magazine no. 9.

1976
"The Glass Divider, Light and Social Division, Video Feedback",
+ - o (Revue d'art contemporain), no. 14, septembre.

"Interior Space/Exterior Space", *Video Art*, Ira Schneider, Beryl Korot (eds.), New York, Harcourt, Brace, Jovanovich.
"Elements of Video/Elements of Architecture, *Video by Artists*, Peggy Gale (ed.), Toronto, Art Metropole.

1977
"Dean Martin, Entertainment as Theatre", *Tracks,* vol. 3, nos. 1, 2.
"Public Space/Two Audiences", *Skira Annuel 1977*, Genève, Art Actuel.
Response to query by Philippe Sers on "What Does Duchamp Mean to You Today? Do You Consider Him to Already Belong to the Past?", *Connaissance des arts*, no. 299, janvier.

1978
"Notes on Public Space/Two Audiences", *Aspects,* no. 5, Winter 1978/79.

1979
"Art in Relation to Architecture/Architecture in Relation to Art", *Artforum*, February.
"Punk-politische Pop/Punk als Propaganda", *Überblick*, Teilen 1,2,3.
"The Lickerish Quartet", *12 Films*, Barbara Bloom (ed.), Amsterdam, De Appel.
"'Punk': Political 'Pop'", *LAICA Journal*, no. 22, March-April.
"Video-Arbeit für Schaufenster", *Zweitschrift*, nos. 4,5.
"Dan Graham a Milano: Architectural Models and Photographs", con Lisa Licitra Ponti, *Domus*, no.594, maggio.

1980
"Impermanent Art and Seventies Audience", *Artforum*, January.
two untitled pages, *Artforum*, February.
The Destroyed Room of Jeff Wall", *Real Life Magazine*, March.
"L'Espace de la Communication", *Skira Annuel 1980*, Genève, Art Actuel.
"Larry Wayne Richards' Projects for 'Conceptual Projects'", *Larry Richards, Works, 1977-80*, Halifax, Library of Canadian Architecture, Nova Scotia Technical College.
"Video-Architecture-Television", *Video El Temps i L'Esprit*, cat. Collegi d'Arquitectes de Catalunya, Barcelona .

1981
"Signs", *Artforum*, April.
"New Wave Rock en het Feminiene", *Museumjournaal*, no. 1.
"Bow Wow Wow", *Real Life Magazine*, Summer.
"Cinema, 1981", *A.E.I.O.U.*, no.4.
"The End of Liberalism", *ZG*, no.5.
"Not Post-Modernism: History as Against Historicism, European Archetypal Vernacular in Relation to American Commercial Vernacular, and City as Opposed to the Individual Building", *Artforum*, December.
"Video-Performance-Architecture", *Art Present*, no. 9.
"Pavilion/Sculpture for Park Setting", *Performance Text(e)s & Documents*, Chantal Pontbriand (ed.), Montreal, Parachute.
"Untitled", *Just Another Asshole*, New York.

1982
"McLaren's Children (We're Only in it for the Manet)", *ZG*, no. 7.
"Semio-Sex: New Wave and the Feminine", *Live*, no. 6,7.
"Bioscoop", *Museumjournaal*, no. 5,6 .
"My Religion", *Museumjournaal*, no. 7.
"Rock Religion", *Scenes and Conventions in Architecture by Artists*, cat. ICA, London.
"The End of Liberalism (Part II)", *The Unnecessary Image*, Peter D'Agostino, Antonio Muntadas (eds.), New York, Tanam Press.

1983
"Theatre, Cinema, Power", *Parachute*, Summer.
"Sur Gordon Matta-Clark", *Art Press*, Special Architecture, juin-juillet-août.
"Europäischer Archetypos und Amerikanischer Kommerzialismus", *Kunstforum*, Bd. 65, September.
"Rock Religion", *Just Another Asshole*, no.6, New York.

1984
"On John Knight's Journals Work", John Knight Catalogue, *LAICA Journal*, vol. 4, no. 40.
"Gordon Matta-Clark's Projects", *Flykepunkter-Vanishing Points*, cat. Moderna Museet, Stockholm.

1985
"Darcy Lange: Work and Music", *New Observations*, no. 29.
"An American Family", TV Guides, Barbara Kruger (ed.), *New Observations*, no. 31.
"My Works for Pages/A History of Conceptual Art", *Dan Graham*, cat. Art Gallery of Western Australia, Perth.
"Two Adjacent Pavilions", *Dan Graham*, cat. Art Gallery of Western Australia, Perth.
"Alteration to a Suburban House,1978", *Doch Doch*, cat. Klapstuk '85, Arenberginstituut, Leuven.
"Cinema 1981", *Doch Doch*, cat. Klapstuk '85, Arenberginstituut, Leuven.

1986
"Urban/Suburban Projects", *Zone*, no. 1/2, New York.
"Gordon Matta-Clark", *Parachute*, no. 2, May-June.

"Public Space/Two Audiences", *Museumjournaal*, nos. 3, 4.
"Kunst als Design/Design als Kunst", *Museumjournaal*, nos. 3, 4.
"Rock My Religion", *Video by Artists II*, Elke Town (ed.), Toronto, Art Metropole.
"Chamberlain's Couches", *Interior Design for Space Showing Videotapes*, cat. Kijkhuis, Den Haag.
"Pavilion/Sculpture Works", *Chambres d'Amis*, cat. Museum voor Hedendaagse Kunst, Gent.

1987
"Dan Graham, d'apres un entretien avec Birgit Pelzer", *Dan Graham*, cat. ARC, Musée d'art moderne de la ville de Paris.
"Design Comme Art/Art Comme Design", *Des Arts*, no. 5, Hiver 1986-87.
"Corporate Arcadias", with Robin Hurst, *Artforum*, December.
"Dean Martin/Entertainment as Theater", *Blasted Allegories: An Anthology of Writings by Contemporary Artists*, Brian Wallis (ed.), New York/Cambridge, Mass., London, England, The New Museum of Contemporary Art/The MIT Press.
"Legacy of Critical Practice in the 1980's", *Dia Art Foundation*, no. 21.

1988
"Pavilions, Stagesets and Exhibition Designs, 1983-1988", *Dan Graham Pavillons*, cat. Kunstverein München.
"Malcolm McLaren and the Making of Annabella", *Impresario: Malcolm McLaren & the British New Wave,* New York/Cambridge, Mass., London, England, The New Museum of Contemporary Art/The MIT Press.

1989
"The Children's Pavilion", with Jeff Wall, *Parkett Magazine*, no. 22 .
"El jardín como teatro como museo", *Teatrojardin Bestiarium*, cat. Junta de Andalucia, Consejeria de Cultura, Sevilla.
"Le Jardin comme Théâtre, comme Musée", *Bestiarium Jardin-Theatre*, cat. Entrepot-Galerie du Confort Moderne, Poitiers.
"Théâtre, Cinema, Pouvoir", *Bestiarium Jardin-Theatre*, cat. Entrepot-Galerie du Confort Moderne, Poitiers.

1990
"Garden as Theater as Museum", *Theatergarden Bestiarium*, Long Island City, New York/Cambridge, Mass., London, England, The Institute for Contemporary Art, P.S. 1 Museum/The MIT Press.
"Video in Relation to Architecture, Illuminating Video", New York, *Aperture/BAVC* 1991.
"Cinema '81", *Splinter*, no. 4.

1992
"De Tuin als Theater als Museum", *Allocaties/Allocations*, cat. Floriade, Zoetermeer.

Catalogues & Publications
Catalogues & publications
Kataloge & Publikationen
Catalogi & Publicaties

1969
End Moments, New York, Dan Graham.

1970
Some Photographic Projects, New York, John Gibson.
1966, New York, John Gibson.
Performance, New York , John Gibson.

1971
Sonsbeek 71, cat. Sonsbeek buiten de perken, Arnhem.
Prospect, cat. Städtische Kunsthalle Düsseldorf.

1972
Selected Works, 1965-1972, New York, Köln/London, König Brothers/Lisson Publications.
documenta 5, cat. Kassel.

1974
Textes, Paris/Bruxelles, Galerie 17/Editions Daled.
Kunst bleibt Kunst: Projekt '74, Kunstverein Köln

1975
For Publication, Otis Art Institute, Los Angeles.

1976
Dan Graham, cat. Kunsthalle Basel.
Ambiente Arte, cat. Biennale di Venezia.

1977
Dan Graham Articles, cat. Stedelijk Van Abbemuseum, Eindhoven.
Films, Genève, Éditions Centre d'Art Contemporain & Écart Publications.
Time, Philadelphia College of Art, Philadelphia.

1979
Video-Architecture-Television, Buchloh, Benjamin H.D. (ed.), Halifax/New York, The Press of the Nova Scotia College of Art and Design/The New York University Press.

1981
Buildings and Signs, cat.The Renaissance Society at the University of Chicago/Museum of Modern Art, Oxford.
Westkunst. cat. Museen der Stadt Köln, Laszlo Glozer (ed.),Köln, DuMont Buchverlag.

1982
Dan Graham, Bruxelles, Editions Daled.
Dan Graham, Theatre, Gent, Anton Herbert.
documenta 7, cat., Kassel.
'60-'80 attitudes/concepts/images, cat. Stedelijk Museum, Amsterdam
Rock Religion: Architecture by Artists, cat. ICA, London.

1983
Dan Graham Pavilions, cat. Kunsthalle, Bern.

1984
Tijd/L'Art et le Temps, cat. Paleis voor Schone Kunsten/Palais des Beaux-Arts, Brussel/Bruxelles.

1985
Dan Graham, cat. The Art Gallery of Western Australia, Perth.
Doch Doch, cat. Klapstuk '85, Arenberginstituut, Leuven.

1986
<<op.cit.>> citeren in de kunst, cat. Beursschouwburg, Brussel.
Chambres d'Amis, cat. Museum voor Hedendaagse Kunst,Gent.
Sonsbeek 86, cat. Sonsbeek buiten de perken, Arnhem.

1987
Dan Graham, cat. ARC, Musée d'art moderne de la ville de Paris.
Dan Graham, cat. Centro de Arte Reina Sofia, Madrid.
Flykepunkter-Vanishing Points, cat. Moderna Museet, Stockholm.
Dan Graham, Art as Design - Design as Art, Fruitmarket Gallery, Edinburgh.
Skulptur Projekte in Münster, cat., Köln, DuMont Buchverlag.
Non in Codice, cat. American Academy, Galleria Pieroni, Rome.
L'époque, la mode, la morale, la passion, cat. Musée d'Art Moderne Centre Georges Pompidou, Paris.

1988
Dan Graham, cat. Kunsthalle Kiel.
Dan Graham Pavillons, cat. Kunstverein München.
The New Urban Landscape, New York, Reichert Associates.

1989
Dan Graham, Jeff Wall, Children's Pavilion, Collection FRAC Rhône-Alpes.
A Guide to the Children's Pavilion, Santa Barbara Contemporary Arts Forum.
L'art conceptuel, une perspective, cat. ARC, Musée d'art moderne de la ville de Paris.
Architectuur en Verbeelding/Architecture and Imagination, Jan Brand, Han Janselijn (eds.), Zwolle, Waanders.
Bestiarium Jardin-Theatre, cat. Entrepot-Galerie du Confort Moderne, Poitiers.

1990
Theatergarden Bestiarium, Long Island City, New York/Cambridge, Mass.,London, England, The Institute for Contemporary Art, P.S. 1 Museum/The MIT Press.
Dan Graham: Drawings 1965-1969, Bleich-Rossi Galerie, Graz.
Dan Graham, cat. Yamaguchi Perfectural Museum of Art, Yamaguchi.
Some Detached Houses, cat. Contemporary Art Gallery Vancouver.
A New Necessity, First Tyne International, Newcastle.

1991
Pavillons, sculptures, Fondation pour l'Architecture, Bruxelles.
A Dialogue about Recent American and European Photography, cat. The Museum of Contemporary Art, Los Angeles.
For Publication, Otis Art Institute, Los Angeles. Reprint 1991 Marian Goodman Gallery, New York.
Carnegie International, The Carnegie Museum of Art, Pittsburgh.

1992
Càmeres indiscretes, Centre d'Art Santa Monica, Barcelona.
Electronic Arts Intermix: Video, Lori Zippay (ed.), New York, Electronic Arts Intermix.
documenta 9, cat., Kassel.
transForm, cat. Kunstmuseum Basel.

Articles, Reviews & Documentation
Articles, critiques & documentation
Artikel, Kritiken & Dokumentation
Artikelen, Recensies & Documentatie

1966
Smithson, Robert, "Quasi-Infinities and the Waning of Space", *Arts Magazine*, November.
Bochner, Mel, "Less and Less", *Art and Artists*, December.

1967
LeWitt, Sol, "Some Paragraphs on Conceptual Art", *Artforum*, June.
Bochner, Mel, "The Serial Attitude", *Artforum*, November.
Flavin, Dan, "Some Other Remarks", *Artforum*, December.

1968
Atkinson, Terry, "Introduction", *Art-Language*, vol. 1, no. 1.
Battock, Gregory, *Minimal Art*, New York, Dutton.
Smithson, Robert, "A Museum of Language in the Vicinity of Art", *Art International*, March.

1970
Antin, David, ""Dan Graham", *Studio International*, vol. 180, July.

1971
Pacquement, Alfred, "Art conceptuel", *Connaissance des arts*.

1972
Townsend, Charlotte, "The Mezzanine: Nova Scotia College of Art", *Artscanada,* Spring.
Meyer, Ursula, "Conceptual Art", New York, Dutton.

1973
Lebeer, Irmeline, "Le corps materiel perceptuel", *L'art vivant*, no. 41, juillet.
Lippard, Lucy, *Six Years, The Dematerialization of the Art Object*, New York, Praeger.

1974
Borgeaud, Bernard, *Pariscope*, no. 309, mars.
Herzogenrath, Wulf, Marlis Grüterich, "Video", *Magazine Kunst,* no. 4.

1975
Goldberg, Roselee, "A Space, a Thousand Words", *Architecural Design*, May.
Kozloff, Max, "Pygmalion Reversed", *Artforum*, November.

1977
Graevenitz, Antje von, "Dingen gebeuren binnen het gezichtsveld", *Museumjournaal*, no.2.
Buchloh, Benjamin H.D., "Augenblicke der Geschichte in der Arbeit von Dan Graham", *Dimitrijevic, Graham, Kawara, Opalka*, Galerie René Block, Berlin/DAAD.
Buchloh, Benjamin H.D., "Moments of History in the Work of Dan Graham", *Dan Graham Articles*, cat. Stedelijk Van Abbemuseum, Eindhoven.

1978
Buchloh, Benjamin H.D., "Process, Sculpture and Film in Richard Serra's Work", *Richard Serra, Works 1966-77*, Clara Weyergraf (ed.), cat. Kunsthalle Tübingen, Kunsthalle Baden-Baden.
Francis, Mark, *Dan Graham*, Aspects, no. 5, Winter 1978/1979.

1979
Rorimer, Anne, introduction, *73rd American Exhibition*, cat. The Art Institute of Chicago, Chicago.
Morgan, Robert, "Conceptual Art and the Continuing Quest for a New Social Context", *LAICA Journal*, no. 23, June-July.
Pelzer, Birgit, "Vision in Process", *October*, no. 10, Fall.

1980
Goldberg, Roselee, *Performance Art*, London, Thames and Hudson.

1981
Payant, Rene, "Dan Graham L'effet-méduse mis en scène", *Art Press*, no. 47, avril
Buchloh, Benjamin H.D., "Michael Asher and the conclusion of Modernist Sculpture", *Performance Text(e)s & Documents*, Chantal Pontbriand (ed.), Montreal, Parachute.

1982
Buchloh, Benjamin H.D., "Documenta 7: a Dictionary of Received Ideas", *October*, no. 22, Fall.

1983
Duve, Thierry de, "Dan Graham und die Kritik der künstlerischen Autonomie/Dan Graham et la Critique de l'Autonomie Artistique", *Dan Graham Pavilions*, cat. Kunsthalle Bern.
Hatton, B., "Artists and Architects at the ICA, London", *Architectural Review*, no. 174, March.

Gintz, Claude, "Dan Graham à Berne", *Art Press*, mars.
Gintz, Claude, "A Pierre et Marie", *Cover*, Fall.

1984
Moffarts, Eric de, "Dan Graham: le présent ou l'indice du temps", *Artistes*, mars
Jochimsen, Margarethe, "Le Temps dans l'Art d'Aujourd'hui Entre La Borne et L'Infini"/"Tijd tussen Ontgrenzing en Begrenzing van de Beeldende Kunst Nu", *Art et le Temps/Tijd, de Vierde Dimensie in de Kunst*, cat. Palais des Beaux-Arts/Paleis voor Schone Kunsten, Bruxelles/Brussel.
Herzogenrath, Wulf, "Le Temps chez Dan Graham et Nam June Paik"/"Tijd bij Dan Graham en Nam June Paik", *Art et le Temps/Tijd, de Vierde Dimensie in de Kunst* cat. Palais des Beaux-Arts/Paleis voor Schone Kunsten, Bruxelles/Brussel.
Lawson, Thomas, "Ken Lum, Conversation between Thomas Lawson and Ken Lum", *Flash Art*, no. 17, April-May.

1985
Lyotard, Jean François, "Les Immatériaux", *Art and Text*, no. 17, April.
Kuspit, Donald, "Dan Graham: Prometheus Mediabound", *Artforum,* May.
Gale, Peggy, "A Tableau Vivant", *Parachute*, June-August.
Wall, Jeff, "Dan Graham's Kammerspiel, part 1/ part 2", *Real Life Magazine*, nos. 14,15.
Wall, Jeff, "Dan Graham's Kammerspiel", *Dan Graham*, cat. Art Gallery of Western Australia, Perth.
Mot, Jan, "Doch, Doch", *Metropolis M*, no.6.
Kirshner, Judith Russi "Non-Uments", *Artforum*, October .
Fol, Jac," Dan Graham: L'artiste à distance", *Des Arts*, no. 2.
Linker, Kate, "Cinemaobjects", *Artforum*, December.
Buchloh, Benjamin H.D., "From Gadget Video to Agit Video: Some Notes of Four Recent Video Works", *Art Journal*, no. 45, Fall.

1986
Dreher, Thomas, "Dan Graham, Ausenwelt im Kubus", *NIKE*, no. 13, Mai/Juni.
Tazzi, Pier Luigi, Annelie Pohlen, Paul Groot, "Sculpture in Review, Critics and Curators, What is Today's Sculpture? Three Views", *Artforum*, September.
Wall, Jeff, "Dan Grahams Kammerspiel", *Museumjournaal*, nos. 5,6.

1987
Wall, Jeff, "Dan Grahams Kammerspiel", *Museumjournaal*, nos. 1,2,3.
Bos, Saskia, "Dan Graham", *De Appel*, no. 2.
Miller, John, "In The Beginning There Was Formica", *Artscribe International*, March/April.
Soutif, Daniel, "Le point virgule sur le Minimal", *Libération*, avril 13.
Wood, Paul, "Dan Graham", *Artscribe* no. 66, November-December .
Vandermarliere, Katrien, "Dan Graham in Gesprek (Gent, 1986)", *Vlees en Beton*, no. 8.

1988
Groot, Paul, "Bolwerken zijn houdbaar, illusies niet: Over onder meer het pittoreske; of de rehabilitatie van een verloren gewaand genre", *Museumjournaal*, no. 5/6.
Reeve, Charles, "Dan Graham's Homes for America", *Parachute*, December 1988.
Wall, Jeff, "Kammerspiel de Dan Graham", Bruxelles, Editions Daled-Goldschmidt.

1989
Dreher, Thomas, "Dan Graham: Plastische Modelle als Betretbare Geschichtsmethaphern", *Artefactum*, vol.5, no. 30, september/oktober.
Duguet, Anne-Marie, "Dispositifs", *Vidéo, Communications*, no. 48 .
Tsai, Eugenie, "Interview with Dan Graham by Eugenie Tsai, New York, October 27, 1988", *Robert Smithson Zeichnungen - Drawings*, cat. Westfälisches Landesmuseum für Kunst und Kulturgeschichte, Münster,Vestjællands Kunstmuseum Sorø, Kunstraum München.

1990
Salvioni, Daniela, "Dan Graham, I'll call myself a conceptual artist, though I don't like conceptual art", *Flash Art*, no.152, May-June.
Chevrier, Jean-François, "Entre les beaux-arts et les médias", *Galeries Magazine*, no. 37, juin/juillet.

1991
Wall, Jeff, "Dan Graham's Kammerspiel", *Art Metropole*, Toronto.
Van den Boogerd, Dominic, "De architectuur van het kinderspel", *Archis*, juni, no. 6.
Francis, Mark, "New York, Dia Center for the Arts, Brice Marden, Dan Graham", *Burlington Magazine*, February.
Ardenne, P., A. Barak, "Dan Graham, Fondation pour l'Architecture", *Art Press*, juillet/août.
Dercon, Chris, "Dan Graham, I Enjoy that Closeness, Where I Take Two Things that Are Very Close and Just Slightly Overlap", *Forum International*, no. 9, September-October.
Hatton, Brian, "Conversation with Dan Graham", *Galeries Magazine*, decembre.
Hatton, Brian," Dan Graham: Present Continuous", *Artscribe*, Winter.

1992
Buchloh, Benjamin, *De l'esthétique d'aministration à la critique institutionelle (aspects de l'art conceptuel, 1962-1969)*, Essais historiques II , Lyon, art édition.

Walker Evans and
The Police

Allan Sekula

... When rationalism claims to be the universal method by
which to obtain knowledge of the whole of existence ... the
necessary correlation with the principle of irrationality becomes
crucial: it erodes and dissolves the whole system.

Georg Lukács, 1923

1

How might we chart a pattern of tensions, intersections,
and divergences between the lineages of 'fine art' photography
and 'applied' photography, between the often awkward,
sometimes pathetic, only intermittently successful aspiration
for an autonomous art of photography and the existing
multitude of practical realism?

The question lingers, despite the recent effort by John
Szarkowski to view nineteenth century industrial photographs
from the Krupp archives as a kind of inchoate modernism
'avant la lettre'. Szarkowski's Photography until Now offers
a triumphalist but also rather mournful crypto-Hegelian
teleology: photography's project of self-development,
the 'Bildungsroman' of this 150 year old adolescent, entails an
escape from the realm of necessity (applied photography)
into the realm of freedom (art photography). The realm of
freedom (like the Prussian state) is 'now' immediately at hand,
coinciding most fully with Szarkowski's tenure as Director of
the Department of Photography at the Museum of Modern Art.
The pictorial spirit that slumbered innocently in slavishly
mimetic photographs depicting nineteenth century machines
and factories would awaken like a sleeping beauty within early
modernism, and 'now', in a period of late modernism, turn
dystopian and elegiac, and even a bit apocalyptic. In the
process, a certain 'muscularity' gets lost. This is the price of
self-consciousness and the outcome of freedom. The Prince
retires. [1]

And so the discourse of photography continues its blind
oscillation between what Georg Lukács, speaking of the limits
of modern rationalist philosophy, termed the "antinomies of
bourgeois thought". Rationalism yields to irrationalism,
and then reasserts itself only by an act of sheer idealist faith.
Human agents can "think" the totality, but they cannot grasp it
practically, despite enormous and increasing technical power
over the "details" of social existence. [2]

In the little world of photography, the art of "details" (derided
as such by Lukács for both anti-modernist and anti-naturalist
reasons), objectivist and subjectivist claims are made in the
same breath. Scientific instrumentalism and aestheticism work
out a deal. The old myth of photographic truth and the newer
myth of photographic untruth stage a summit meeting.
Neo-'Neue Sachlichkeit' and neo-'Subjektive Photographie' in
one pot? Why not? Somehow the desire for denotative
certainty, for clarity and precise descriptive limits, peacefully
coexists with the desire for semantic multiplicity, ambiguity
and irreducible uncodable excess. Everyone wants to have it
both ways.

2

A good place to begin to sort out this mess is with the attempt
to contain one particular figure of irrationality and excess:
the figure of the criminal. Symbolically, the criminal is the
exteriorization of the principle of bourgeois self-interest.
Furthermore, the criminal subjectivizes the everyday egoism
and chancy opportunism of economic activity in a capitalist
society. Criminals give the 'inexorable laws' of capitalism a
fleeting and distorted human face. (This is what makes the
moral outcry over looting such an interesting phenomenon.)

Pictorially, the problem of the criminal collides with the
problem of the portrait, the pictorial genre that sought in
the nineteenth century to contain the optimistic plentitude of
the bourgeois self. Honorific and repressive modes constituted
the functional extremes of routine portrait practice from the
1860s on. In the first instance, the photographic portrait sought
to individuate an idealized propertied subject. In the second,
the portrait individuated the subject of medico-legal regulation
and surveillance. Physiognomy, which constituted a powerful
hermeneutic paradigm throughout the nineteenth century,
served to unify these two modes of visual construction of the
self. Following work by Georges Canguilhem and Michel
Foucault on the genesis and logic of the bio-social sciences,
we can argue that the 'normal' and 'respectable' self is
produced only on the basis of a simultaneous construction:
that of the 'pathological' and 'deviant' other. Although the
proliferation of physiognomy and photographic portraiture
threatened to dissolve social distinctions into an
undifferentiated and continually shifting mass, both could be
used in proto-technocratic fashion to reintroduce order and
hierarchy into the body politic. The key to this latter promise
lay in the precise fixing of the image of the criminal, both as an
individual and as a type. But the pursuit of the criminal body
ran afoul of the problem of categorization and retrieval. How
were sense and order to be made of an unprecedented number
of images?

Roughly between 1885 and 1900, an institutional model of
photographic meaning was invented: the model of the archive.
This model answered the need to assemble and order vast
functional collections of photographs. Nowhere was the
archival model more urgently and rigorously pursued than in
a number of new, related and intercommunicating 'sciences' of
social regulation and control: in criminology, practical police
work (criminalistics), and eugenics.

However, contrary to the commonplace understandings of the mug shot as the rather disreputable exemplar of a powerful, wholly denotative visual empiricism, these early archival uses of photography were systematized on the basis of an acute recognition of the inadequacies and limitations of ordinary procedures for the visual identification and typing of criminals. The anarchy of the camera's prolific production had to be tamed by the filing cabinet. This project entailed a diminishing of the epistemological prestige of optics, and a corresponding increase in the prestige of statistics. Enlightenment notions of physiognomic insight into human character were devalued.

How did this happen? Two novel systems of description of the criminal body emerged in the 1880s, both founded on the attempt to salvage the value of physiognomic evidence through recourse to more abstract statistical methods. In effect, the contingency of optics was made to submit to the regularity of statistics. Both projects relied upon the central conceptual category of social statistics: the mathematical notion of the average man ("l'homme moyen") proposed by the Belgian astronomer and mathematician Adolphe Quetelet in the 1830s. The Paris police official Alphonse Bertillon invented the first modern system of criminal identification, first, by combining standardized front-and-profile photographic portraits with a numerical anthropometrical series of nine bodily measurements on a single 'fiche'; and second, by organizing these cards in a massive filing system based on their relative positions in a statistical distribution. The English psychologist and founder of eugenics, Francis Galton, invented a method of composite portraiture ("pictorial statistics") in an attempt to produce actual photographic impressions of abstract, statistically defined bio-social types. He was especially concerned with the isolation of a distinctive criminal type engendered by heredity.

Bertillon's practical nominalism and Galton's theoretical essentialism constitute the two methodological poles of positivist attempts to define and regulate social deviance. Their notions of the proper relation between image and archive were diametrically opposed, but complementary within a division of intellectual labor that distinguished criminology from practical police forensics. Bertillon sought to efficiently and unerringly embed the image within the archive. Galton sought to embed the archive within a single generic image. Although their projects were specialized and idiosyncratic, they mapped out general epistemological parameters for the bureaucratic handling of visual documents. Between 1895 and 1910 this broader, more encyclopedic project was pursued by a number of international congresses on the rationalization of library science and the refinement of methods of photographic documentation. [3]

3

If we reject Szarkowski's metaphysical pictorial teleology, what connections can be traced between the archival mode of photography and the emergence of photographic modernism?

To what degree did self-conscious modernist practice accommodate itself to the model of the archive? To what degree did modernists consciously or unconsciously resist or subvert the model of the archive, which tended to relegate the individual photographer to the status of a detail worker, providing fragmentary images for an apparatus beyond his or her control? A few provisional lines of investigation can be charted.

The proto-modernism of the Photo Secession and its affiliated movements, extending roughly to 1916, can be seen as an attempt to resist the archival mode through a strategy of avoidance and denial based on craft production. The elegant 'few' were opposed to the mechanized 'many', in terms both of images and authors. This strategy required the ostentatious display of the "honorific marks of hand labor", to borrow the phrase coined by the American sociologist Thorstein Veblen in 1899. The second vector of resistance to the archival mode emerged from the attempt to situate the pictorial photograph within an anti-positivist philosophical discourse, drawing variously on Bergsonian intuitionalism, symbolism, and Swedenborgian mysticism. After 1916, however, aesthetically ambitious photographers abandoned painterly techniques and embraced pictorial rhetorics much closer to those already operative within the instrumental realist and archival paradigms. It is tempting to argue that the triumph of statistics over optics had the effect of 'liberating' the optical image for 'purposeless' aesthetic purposes, but the philosophical shifts were less clear and direct than that.

I want to return to the question of the portrait, and to the possibility that physiognomy passes into a kind of twilight within modernism, neither exhausted nor suffused with the same glowing Enlightenment optimism that fueled the realism of Balzac and Nadar. Certainly we can identify a formal and semantic crisis of the portrait, emerging from cubism, but we can also identify a new monumentalization and revalorization of the silently expressive face in the cinematic close-up. We need to remember also that physiognomy reached a new level of official murderousness within the 'reactionary modernist' program of National Socialism. But for the moment my interest is in the situation as it unfolded in the United States, where politics, especially the politics of race and class, is so commonly boiled down into a discourse on crime.

The critical language used within the Stieglitz Circle to describe portraits made after 1915 by Paul Strand and by Stieglitz is marked by reference to pathology, deviance, and criminal transgression and detection, as if animated by the ghost of Zola. There is Camera Work's 1917 reference to the "brutality" of Strand's clandestine New York street portraits, and Charles Sheeler's review of Stieglitz's 1923 Anderson Gallery exhibition of portraits "which hover so near the realm of pathology, that so slight a disturbance as the vibration of a passing truck might send them over the borderline." [4]

This American modernist 'neo-naturalism' coincided with a broad popular legitimation of rationalized police methods centering on the documentary evidence offered by police photographs. These were reproduced or imitated in a new genre of detective magazine which had begun to appear by the early 1920s. In *True Detective*, a pulp magazine published by the physical-culture entrepreneur Brennar Macfadden, police photographs and reproductions of fingerprint cards had by 1924 almost entirely replaced posed photographic tableaux as the primary illustrations for crime stories. This 'documentary' turn itself coincided with the formation of the Federal Bureau of Investigation and the tabloid glamorization of J. Edgar Hoover's machine-gun toting G-men. I would argue that the emergence of a dominant documentary aesthetic in the United States, so commonly traced to the 1930s, actually emerges within mass culture a decade earlier in the photographically illustrated crime pulps and reader-authored 'confessional' magazines published by Macfadden, *True Detective* and *True Confessions*. By the late 1930s, the fetish of the archival document had reached extraordinary proportions. A series of expensive detective novels were published in limited folio editions which dispensed almost entirely with the pretense of narrative, aiming instead for the convincing simulation of police dossiers, complete with tipped-in glassine envelopes containing human hairs, as well as eight by ten inch glossy prints of the crime scene. But this ostentious 'archivalism' sought a different audience from that reached by the cheap halftones of the pulps. The latter lived much closer to the choice between criminality and joining the police.

While in France the surrealists were clearly fascinated with the operational manuals of the police, and the work of forensic criminologists, as evidenced both in *La Révolution Surréaliste* and *Minotaure,* it is likely that American artists came to know the iconography of police work, if at all, exclusively through the pulps and tabloids.

Thus if the archive and the police photograph served as a convenient 'bad objects' for early modernist art photographers, constituting a brute realism that 'art' must transcend, both also exerted a seductive appeal. This seductive appeal was akin to that animating detective fiction, a fascination with the possibility of subjectivizing the forensic detail, winning it over for a realist poetics of the criminal demiurge underlying capitalist social relations.

4
The most extreme and wily response to this ambiguous situation within the Stieglitz Circle, the most corrosive in its amalgam of anti-positivism and anti-romanticism, and thus in its rejection of any physiognomics whatsoever, can be found not surprisingly in the work of Marcel Duchamp, in his offhanded 1924 wanted-poster 'self portrait.'

Short of Duchamp's calculated dismissal of physiognomic identity, the most complicated and intellectual sophisticated

response to the model of the police archive was that of Walker Evans. Evan's response begins in 1931 with an omnibus book review published in Lincoln Kirstein's *Hound and Horn*. The young photographer was reviewing a number of recent photographic books, including August Sander's *Antlitz der Zeit*, Carl Sandburg's *Steichen the Photographer*, the French edition of *Atget*, Albert Renger-Patzsch's *Die Welt ist schön*, and *foto-auge* by Franz Roh and Jan Tschichold.

Evans begins with a complaint about the "dishonesty of vision" of the still pervasive pictorialist aesthetics of camera club photographers, linking this without mentioning names to a brutally succinct catalogue of Edward Steichen and Clarence White photographs published in early numbers of *Camera Work*: "pictures of misty October Lanes, snow scenes, reflets dans l'eau, young girls with crystal balls." From the pictorialist camera clubbers "arises the loud and suspicious protest about photography being an art. So there is in one of the anthologies under review a photo of a corpse in a pool of blood *'because you like nice things'*. Suddenly there is a difference between a quaint evocation of the past and an open window looking straight down a stack of decades."

The sudden description of the police photograph functions as a dadaist shock device, profoundly shifting the target of Evans' attack. The literary strategy is rapid-fire verbal montage, a mockery of advertising copy. The brutal description collides not only with the antiquarian aestheticism of the pictorialists, but also implicitly with the "slick", "parvenue"."note (of) money" of Steichen's more recent advertising photographs of beds and cigarette lighters reproduced in the opulently printed vanity monograph *Steichen the Photographer*. Since Evans hadn't yet gotten around to voicing these complaints about this later stage of Steichen's career, the move is one of telepathic anticipation, a strategy he would repeat later in the photographic sequencing of his 1938 book *American Photographs*. In this small bit of writing Evans actually demonstrates a way of cutting, all at once, through the "stack of decades".[5]

The police photograph that Evans briefly describes here was reproduced near the end of *foto-auge*. Taken from the archives of the Stuttgart police, it was captioned "murder in times of peace", and placed opposite a photograph from German government archives depicting a live trio of soldiers and a dead horse on a shelled bridge, captioned "murder in times of war". (The police photo would later be appropriated by John Heartfield for inclusion in an anti-fascist montage.) [6]

Brutal and tendentious as the juxtaposition in *foto-auge* was, it was only a pale reflection of the obsessive archival documentation pursued by the anarchist and pacifist militant Ernst Friedrich in the wake of the First World War. Starting in 1924, Friedrich published several editions of a book entitled *Krieg dem Kriege* (War Against War). With a text in German, French, English and Dutch, the book was illustrated with photographs of the most horrific human carnage, and with medical 'portraits' of living men whose faces had been destroyed by bullets and shrapnel. Friedrich can be said to have been most deeply obsessed with the brutally transformative physiognomics of modern warfare. Innocent of any notion of the death instinct, he believed, as did also the Weimar police who persistently censored his work, that such images could provide the positive pedagogical groundwork for pacifism. Friedrich's central slogan was a virtual inversion of the hygienic futurist cult of war: "War is pestilence-and soldiers are the bacilli".[7]

If in Germany the police photograph was rechanneled into the fight against war and fascism, in the United States Evans redirected it against art photography and commerce. This direction was not dissimilar to that taken by Duchamp in his wanted poster of 1924. In both cases the image of crime is a means to another end.

Evans retained an emphatic interest in police photography into the middle of the 1930s and beyond. Perhaps inspired most by what he had described in his book review as the "clinical process" of August Sander's "photographic editing of society", Evans constructed a terse topical list of subjects for a photographic study of "New York society in the 1930's". The list contains a central, telegraphic, underlined inscription: "*This project get police cards*".[8]

Later, in 1938 and again in 1941, Evans embarked on the compilation of an archive of clandestine subway portraits, taken with a camera hidden in his coat. This was his closest approach to the methods of the detective police and the FBI. But this work was only completed as an organized ensemble of pictures much later, with the 1966 book *Many Are Called*. In effect, what Evans both discovers and enacts in this project is the Sartrean logic of serialized social relations. Sartre defined seriality as the "plurality of isolations" in the modern city, seeing its most characteristic manifestation in the bus queue.[9] Evans' camera follows the subway in producing a grouping of humans existing in relations of mutual otherness, rather than reciprocity. The group exists as such only by virtue of being organized by the subway machine and the camera machine. In his written notes and drafts for this project, written between 1942 and 1966, Evans was drawn to the curiously abstracted, contingent and randomized character of this fluid ensemble. His "unfulfilled aim" was "to be able to state flatly that sixty-two people came unconsciously into range before an impersonal fixed recording machine during a certain time period, and that all these individuals who came into the film frame were photographed, and photographed without any human selection for the moment of lens exposure." As another note put it: "These people are everybody. Their pictures have been selected and arranged, of course, but the total result of the
line-up has claim to some kind of chance-average."[10]

If Evans' strategy can be traced back to Duchamp (and forward to Cage), it also touches on the underlying thematic of the detective novel, the idea of economic life as a gamble, a throw of the dice, something seized and controlled only fleetingly and partially, irritationally.

Optics and statistics collide again, but this time the encounter is subjectivized through the figure of a watchful but willfully almost powerless artist, the dandy-gambler-voyeur, master of the "documentary style". Though Walter Benjamin had proposed that "no matter what trail the flâneur may follow, every one of them will lead him to a crime", Evans avoided this final rendez-vous, stressing the important difference between his "documentary style" and the "literal document", such as "a police photograph of a murder scene".[11]

But once touched, the stain of the crime scene is hard to erase. The subway project was Evans' great effort to bring optical detection up against the law of averages, thus recapitulating in art the philosophical and practical problem tackled sixty years earlier by Bertillon, who also was annoyed by the idea of an 'art' of photography. But Evans, in his imagined flat, mechanical passivity, like Sartre's voyeur peering through the keyhole and realizing that he is being watched from the other side, manages to reverse the field of power: "As it happens, you don't see among them the face of a judge or a senator or a bank president. What you do see is at once sobering, startling, and obvious: These are the ladies and gentlemen of the jury." Even so, as Evans wrote here for the readers of *Harper's Bazaar*, this "sobering" final thought owes more to LeBon than to Sartre or even to Jefferson. The subway is the revenge of "l'homme moyen" against those who "like nice things".[12]

Los Angeles May 1992

1 See Szarkowski, John, *Photography until Now*, Museum of Modern Art, New York, 1989.

2 Lukács, Georg, *History and Class Consciousness: Studies in Marxist Dialectics*, trans. Rodney Livingston, Cambridge, Mass., 1971, pp. 110-148.

3 For a more complete version of the argument summarized here, see: Sekula, Allan, "The Body and the Archive", *October*, no. 39, winter 1986, pp. 3-64.

4 Sheeler, Charles, "The Recent Photographs of Alfred Stieglitz", *The Arts*, May 1923, p. 345.

5 Evans, Walker, "The Reappearance of Photography", *Hound and Horn*, no. 5, October-December 1931, p. 126-127.

6 Roh, Franz, Jan Tschichold (Hrsg.), *foto-auge*, Stuttgart, 1929, pl. 73-74.

7 Friedrich, Ernst, *Krieg dem Kriege*, Berlin, 1926.

8 Reproduced in: Thompson, Jerry (ed.), *Walker Evans at Work*, New York, 1982, p. 107.

9 Sartre, Jean-Paul, *Critique of Dialectical Reason*, trans. Alan Sheridan-Smith, London, 1976, pp. 256-269.

10 Evans, Walker, "Unposed Photographic Record of People", in: Sarah Greenough, *Walker Evans: Subways and Streets*, Washington D.C., 1991, p. 126. Evans, Walker, undated handwritten draft, Department of Photographs, J. Paul Getty Museum, Santa Monica, California.

11 Benjamin, Walter, *Charles Baudelaire: A Lyric Poet in the Era of High Capitalism*, trans. Harry Zohn, London, 1983, p. 41. Katz, Leslie, "Interview with Walker Evans", *Art in America* no. 2, March-April 1971, p. 87.

12 Evans, Walker, "The Unposed Portrait", *Harper's Bazaar*, no. 95, March 1962, p. 120.

Walker Evans et la police

Allan Sekula

"Si le rationalisme revendique de représenter la méthode universelle pour la connaissance de l'ensemble de l'être ... la question de la corrélation nécessaire avec le principe irrationnel acquiert une importance décisive, dissolvante et désintégrante pour tout le système."

Georg Lukács, 1923

1

Comment décrire les réseaux de tensions, de correspondances et de divergences qui existent entre les familles de photographie dite 'artistique' et 'appliquée'? Entre le désir - maladroit, pathétique même, et le plus souvent vain - que la photographie soit reconnue comme un art autonome, et la multitude de ses applications empiriques et réalistes?

La question est restée sans réponse, malgré l'effort de John Szarkowski pour considérer les photographies industrielles des archives Krupp, au dix-neuvième siècle, comme l'apparition d'une forme de modernisme avant la lettre. Son exposition, *Photography until Now* propose une téléologie crypto-hegelienne triomphaliste, mais plutôt lugubre: le projet d'un développement autonome de la photographie, le '*Bildungsroman*' de ce vieil adolescent de 150 ans, ont pour conséquence l'abandon du royaume de la nécessité (la photographie appliquée) pour le royaume de la liberté (la photographie d'art). Le royaume de la liberté (comme l'état Prussien) est alors (*Now*) à portée de la main, puisque Szarkowski dirige le Département de Photographie du Museum of Modern Art de New York. L'esprit pictural qui sommeillait en toute innocence dans les photographies bassement mimétiques de machines et d'usines du dix-neuvième siècle, s'est réveillé comme une belle au bois dormant au début du modernisme; aujourd'hui (*Now*), en cette fin de modernisme, il semble déplacé, élégiaque, et légèrement apocalyptique. Dans cette histoire, une certaine "énergie musculaire" s'est perdue. C'est le prix de la complaisance et le fruit de la liberté. Le Prince se retire.[1]

Le discours de la photographie continue donc son oscillation aveugle entre ce que Georg Lukács, parlant des limites de la philosophie rationaliste moderne, appelle les "antinomies de la pensée bourgeoise". Le rationalisme cède à l'irrationalisme, et ne peut se réaffirmer que dans un acte de pure foi idéaliste. Les être humains peuvent "penser" la totalité, mais ils ne peuvent pas s'en saisir concrètement, malgré une puissance technique de plus en plus considérable mise au service des "petits faits" de l'existence sociale.[2]

Dans le petit monde de la photographie, l'art des "petits faits" (dont Lukács se moque pour des raisons à la fois anti-modernistes et anti-naturalistes) et les revendications objectivistes et subjectivistes se manifestent dans le même élan. L'instrumentalisme scientifique et l'esthétisme ont passé un accord. Le vieux mythe de la vérité photographique, et le nouveau mythe du mensonge photographique organisent une rencontre au sommet. Neo-*Neue Sachlichkeit* et neo-*Subjektive Photographie* dans le même panier? Pourquoi pas? D'une certaine manière l'exigence d'une certitude explicite, d'une clarté et d'une précision descriptive, cohabite pacifiquement avec celle d'une multiplicité sémantique, d'une ambigüité et d'une forme d'excès irréductible un code. On voudrait garder toutes les options.

2

Pour organiser ce désordre, il faudrait d'abord essayer de circonscrire une figure particulière de l'irrationalité et de l'excès: la figure du criminel. Le criminel incarne, symboliquement, le principe de l'intérêt bourgeois, l'égoïsme quotidien et l'opportunisme aventureux de l'économie capitaliste. Les criminels prêtent aux lois 'inexorables' du capitalisme leur visage flou et retors. (Et ceux qui s'indignent au nom de la morale ne peuvent que fermer les yeux sur un phénomène aussi intéressant).

La figuration du criminel est confrontée au problème du portrait, genre par excellence dans lequel s'exprime, au dix-neuvième siècle, l'optimisme satisfait de l'individualité bourgeoise. Dans la pratique quotidienne du portrait depuis 1860, la représentation oscillait entre deux extrêmes: honorer et réprimer. Dans le premier cas, il s'agissait de distinguer dans le modèle le sujet idéalisé et possédant. Dans le deuxième cas de ficher ce sujet dans le cadre d'un contrôle et d'une règlementation médico-légale. La physiognomonie, qui a constitué un puissant paradigme herméneutique pendant tout le dix-neuvième siècle, a servi à unifier ces deux modes de construction visuelle de l'identité. Après les travaux de Georges Canguilhem et de Michel Foucault sur la genèse et la logique des sciences biosociales, on peut affirmer que l'individu 'normal' et 'respectable' ne peut se concevoir qu'en prenant simultanément en compte l'autre, 'pathologique' et 'déviant'. Bien que les pratiques de la physiognomonie et du portrait photographique, en se développant, aient menacé de dissoudre les distinctions sociales en une masse indifférenciée et continuellement mouvante, elles auraient pu représenter l'une et l'autre une manière de réintroduire de l'ordre et de la hiérarchie dans le corps politique. Cette hypothèse dépendait de la mise en place précise de l'image du criminel, en tant qu'individu et en tant que type. Mais l'identification du criminel posait le problème de la typologie et de la recherche documentaire. Comment organiser de manière significative une telle quantité d'images ?

Entre 1885 et 1900 environ, l'institution inventa le modèle de l'archive pour pouvoir rassembler et ordonner les importantes

collections administratives de photographies. Ce modèle ne fut nulle part appliqué avec autant de rigueur et d'efficacité que dans certaines 'sciences' récentes, qui avaient en commun de traiter de la régulation sociale et du contrôle: la criminologie, le travail de la police en matière criminelle et l'eugénisme. Contrairement à l'idée que l'on se faisait communément de la 'photo criminelle', d'une image un peu crapuleuse témoignant d'une expérience visuelle forte, chargée de sens, les premières utilisations des archives photographiques ont été systématisées en prenant précisément en compte les inadéquations et les limites des procédures ordinaires d'identification visuelle et typologique des criminels. Il fallait maîtriser l'anarchie et l'abondance de la production photographique par un système de classement.
La conséquence de ce projet fut de diminuer le prestige épistémologique de l'optique et inversement, d'accroître celui des statistiques. Les idées des Lumières en matière de physiognomonie humaine furent dévaluées.

Comment cela s'est-il produit? Deux nouveaux systèmes de description du corps criminel apparurent dans les années 1880, pour réhabiliter la physiognomonie en recourant à des méthodes statistiques plus abstraites. Du fait de son caractère arbitraire l'optique devait finir par se plier à la norme des statistiques. Ces deux projets dépendaient de la catégorie conceptuelle centrale des statistiques sociales: la théorie mathématique de "l'homme moyen" proposée par l'astronome et mathématicien belge Adolphe Quetelet dans les années 1830. Le commissaire de police de Paris Alphonse Bertillon inventa le premier système moderne d'identification criminelle: on combinait sur une seule fiche des portraits photographiques, standardisés, de face et de profil, avec une série chiffrée de neuf mensurations anthropométriques et on classait ensuite ces cartes selon une méthode rigoureuse fondée sur leurs positions relatives dans une configuration statistique. Le psychologue anglais et fondateur de l'eugénisme, Francis Galton, inventa une méthode de portrait composite ("statistique pictural") pour représenter photographiquement les caractéristiques réelles de différents types biosociaux, abstraits et statistiquement définis. Galton s'est surtout appliqué à distinguer un certain type criminel engendré par hérédité.

Le nominalisme pratique de Bertillon et l'essentialisme théorique de Galton constituaient les deux pôles méthodologiques des tentatives positivistes pour définir et réguler la déviance sociale. Leurs conceptions de la relation entre image et archive étaient diamétralement opposées, mais complémentaires, à l'intérieur d'une division du travail intellectuel qui distingue la criminologie de la pratique des services médico-légaux de la police. Bertillon a cherché à inscrire, avec efficacité et précision, l'image à l'intérieur de l'archive. Galton, lui, a cherché à inscrire l'archive à l'intérieur de l'image unique et générique. Bien que leurs projets fussent spécifiques et singuliers, ces deux chercheurs ont défini les paramètres épistémologiques généraux du traitement

bureaucratique des documents visuels. Entre 1895 et 1910 ce projet fut développé de manière plus large et plus encyclopédique dans plusieurs congrès internationaux portant sur la rationalisation de la bibliothéconomie et le raffinement des méthodes de documentation photographique.[3]

3
Quels liens établir entre la photographie d'archive et l'apparition d'un modernisme photographique, si l'on rejette la téléologie picturale et métaphysique de Szarkowski? A quel degré une pratique moderniste, repliée sur elle-même, s'accomode-t-elle du modèle de l'archive? Ce modèle tendait à reléguer le photographe individuel au statut d'un travailleur du "petit fait", qui fournit des images fragmentaires à un appareil sur lequel il n'a pas de prise. A quel degré les modernistes ont-ils, consciemment ou inconsciemment, résisté ou subverti ce modèle? On peut esquisser quelques réponses provisoires.

On peut considérer le protomodernisme de la Photo Sécession et des mouvements qui lui sont affiliés, autour de 1916, comme une tentative de résister au modèle de l'archive par une stratégie d'évasion et de déni, fondée sur une production artisanale. On opposa un petit nombre d'élégants à la masse mécanisée, en termes d'images comme d'auteurs. Cette stratégie supposait une exhibition des "marques honorifiques du travail manuel", pour reprendre la formule employée en 1899 par le sociologue américain Thorstein Veblen.
Le deuxième facteur de résistance au modèle de l'archive apparut avec la tentative de situer la photographie pictorialiste à l'intérieur d'un discours philosophique anti-positiviste, diversement inspiré de l'intuition bergsonienne, du symbolisme, et du mysticisme à la Swedenborg. Cependant, après 1916, les photographes qui avaient une ambition esthétique abandonnèrent les techniques du pictorialisme et adoptèrent une rhétorique picturale beaucoup plus proche de celle déjà à l'œuvre dans les paradigmes instrumentaux et réalistes du procédé de l'archive. Il serait tentant d'en conclure que le triomphe des statistiques sur l'optique a eu pour effet de libérer l'image à des fins 'purement' esthétiques; mais sur un plan philosophique un tel glissement est loin d'être aussi clair.

Revenons maintenant à la question du portrait, et à l'hypothèse selon laquelle la physiognomonie aurait décliné à l'époque du modernisme, sans sombrer tout à fait, ni se laisser éblouir par l'optimisme des Lumières, dont le réalisme de Balzac et de Nadar s'était alimenté. On assiste sans aucun doute, après le cubisme, à une crise formelle et sémantique du portrait; mais on assiste également, à travers le gros plan cinématographique, à une nouvelle monumentalisation et revalorisation du visage silencieusement expressif. Il ne faut pas oublier que la physiognomonie fut appliquée à un autre niveau de criminalité, dans le cadre du programme 'moderniste réactionnaire' du National Socialisme. Mais je me limite ici à la situation particulière des Etats-Unis, où la politique, et plus précisément la politique raciale et sociale est si communément ramenée à un discours sur le crime. Le langage critique utilisé à l'intérieur du cercle de Stieglitz pour décrire ses portraits et ceux de Paul Strand d'après 1915 se caractérisait par la référence à la pathologie, la déviance, la transgression et la détection criminelle, comme si le fantôme de Zola leur était apparu. Un numéro de *Camera Work* de 1917 faisait référence à la "brutalité" des portraits pris clandestinement par Strand dans les rues de New York. Dans son article sur l'exposition de Stieglitz en 1923 à la Anderson Gallery, Charles Sheeler écrivait à propos de ces portraits qu'ils "rôdent si près du domaine de la pathologie, qu'une légère perturbation, la vibration d'un camion, suffirait à les projeter dans la folie."[4]

Ce 'néo-naturalisme' moderniste américain coïncidait avec la légitimation populaire des méthodes policières organisées et fondées sur la preuve documentaire que constituaient les photographies policières. Celles-ci étaient reproduites ou imitées dans un nouveau type de magazine détective apparu au début des années 1920. Dans le magazine à sensation *True Detective*, publié par le propriétaire de gymnases Brennar Macfadden, les histoires de crime étaient illustrées principalement par des photographies policières et des reproductions de cartes d'empreintes digitales. Elles avaient, dès 1924, presque entièrement remplacé les photographies mises-en-scène. Cette 'documentarisation' coïncidait avec la formation du *Federal Bureau of Investigation* et la popularisation naïve des hommes (les "*G-men*") de J. Edgar Hoover avec leurs mitraillettes. On date généralement des années 1930 l'affirmation de l'esthétique documentaire aux Etats-Unis. Elle fit plus probablement son apparition à l'intérieur d'une culture de masse une dizaine d'années auparavant, à travers des magazines de crimes à sensation illustrés par des photographies, comme *True Detective* et à travers des magazines de courrier des lecteurs, du genre 'confidence', comme *True Confessions*, également publié par Macfadden. A la fin des années 1930, le fétiche du document d'archive atteignait des proportions extraordinaires. Une série de romans policiers à gros budget, d'où la narration avait presque entièrement disparu, fut publiée dans des éditions folio à tirage limité. L'idée était de simuler les dossiers de police avec des enveloppes vitrifiées contenant des cheveux humains, et des images sur papier brillant 20 x 25 représentant la scène du crime. Mais cet 'archivisme' sophistiqué visait un public différent de celui des petits magazines à sensation qui hésitaient à prendre le parti du criminel ou celui de la police.

Tandis qu'en France les surréalistes étaient, on le sait, fascinés par les fiches de police et les recherches des criminologues légistes, comme en témoigne *La Révolution Surraliste* et *Minotaure*, il est probable que les artistes américains prirent connaissance de l'iconographie policière à travers les magazines bon-marché et la presse à scandale.

Les artistes photographes du début du modernisme ont vu les photographies d'archive et les photographies policières

comme des 'objets un peu crapuleux' dont l'art devait transcender le réalisme brutal. Ces objets exerçaient également une séduction qui tenait à la force de suggestion de la fiction policière, à la possibilité pour le lecteur de s'identifier au détail juridique et au triomphe de la poésie réaliste du démiurge criminel, figure centrale des relations sociales dans le système capitaliste.

4

Comme on pouvait s'y attendre c'est dans le travail de Marcel Duchamp, avec son 'auto-portrait' provocateur, l'avis de recherche de 1924, que l'on trouve la réponse la plus extrême et la plus astucieuse à cette attitude ambiguë du cercle de Stieglitz. La plus corrosive, aussi, dans son mélange d'anti-positivisme et d'anti-romantisme, et donc dans son rejet définitif de la physiognomonie.

Mis à part Duchamp, la réponse au modèle de l'archive de police la plus complexe et la plus sophistiquée sur le plan intellectuel, fut celle de Walker Evans, comme en témoigne déjà en 1931 son texte critique publié dans la revue de Lincoln Kirstein *Hound and Horn*. Ce texte était un commentaire de livres de photographie récents, *Antlitz der Zeit* d'August Sander, *Steichen the Photographer* de Carl Sandburg, l'édition française d'Atget *Die Welt ist schön* de Renger-Patszch et *foto-auge* de Franz Roh et Jan Tschichold.

Dès les premières lignes Evans accusait la "malhonnêteté de la vision" de l'esthétique pictorialiste encore en vigueur dans les photo clubs. Il faisait ainsi référence, sans citer de noms, à un port-folio de photographies d'Edward Steichen et Clarence White publié dans les premiers numéros de *Camera Work*: "images de ruelles brumeuses en octobre, scènes de neige, 'reflets dans l'eau' [en français dans le texte], jeunes filles avec des boules de cristal." On entend la voix des pictorialistes, "on entend leur plaidoyer véhément et suspicieux pour que la photographie soit reconnue comme un art. Et dans une de ces anthologies, on trouve la photo d'un cadavre qui baigne dans un mare de sang, '*parce que vous aimez les jolies choses*'. Une distinction apparaît brusquement, entre l'évocation désuète du passé et la confrontation directe avec les décénnies qui viennent de s'écouler".

La description brutale de la photographie policière agit comme un dispositif de choc dadaïste, et permet à Evans de changer de cible. Il utilise une stratégie littéraire de montage ultra-rapide, une parodie de message publicitaire. La description brutale ne vise pas seulement l'esthétisme d'antiquaire des pictorialistes; elle vise aussi, implicitement, le côté "lisse, "parvenu" et "intéressé" des photographies publicitaires de Steichen, les lits et les briquets à cigarettes reproduits dans sa monographie prétentieuse et somptueusement imprimée: *Steichen the photographer*. C'était la première fois qu'Evans avait l'occasion de dire ce qu'il pensait de cette dernière période de la carrière de Steichen; et il employait déjà ce style télégraphique qui caractérisera le rythme de la séquence des images de son livre de 1938, *American Photographs*. Il donnait déjà l'exemple, à travers ces quelques lignes, de ce qu'il appelait une "confrontation directe avec le passé".[5]

La photographie policière décrite ici brièvement par Evans était reproduite vers la fin de *foto-auge*. Elle était tirée des archives de la police de Stuttgart et portait le titre de "meurtre civil". Une image des archives du gouvernement allemand représentant trois soldats vivants et un cheval mort sur un pont bombardé, était placée en vis à vis, avec la légende "meurtre de guerre". (La photographie des archives de Stuttgart sera utilisée plus tard par John Heartfield dans un de ses montages anti-fascistes.)[6]

Aussi brutale et tendancieuse que pouvait apparaître la juxtaposition dans *foto-auge*, elle n'était encore qu'un pâle reflet de la documentation d'archive obsessionnelle entreprise par le militant anarchiste et pacifiste Ernst Friedrich après la première guerre mondiale. A partir de 1924, Friedrich publia plusieurs éditions d'un livre intitulé *Krieg dem Kriege*. Le livre était accompagné d'un texte en allemand, français, anglais et hollandais, et illustré de photographies d'un monstrueux carnage humain, ainsi que de 'portraits' médicaux d'hommes vivants, défigurés par des balles et des éclats d'obus. Il semble que Friedrich ait été très frappé par les défigurations violentes dues à la guerre moderne. Complètement étranger à la notion d'instinct de mort, il croyait, comme la police de Weimar qui censura systématiquement son travail, que de telles images pouvaient fournir le point de départ pédagogique et positif d'une propagande pour la paix. Le grand slogan de Friedrich était une inversion virtuelle du culte futuriste et hygiénique de la guerre: " La guerre est la peste -- et les soldats sont les bacilles."[7]

Si, en Allemagne, la photographie policière fut mise au service du combat contre la guerre et le fascisme, aux Etats-Unis Evans la dirigea contre la photographie d'art et le commerce. Duchamp adoptait la même attitude dans son affiche d'avis de recherche de 1924. Dans les deux cas l'image du crime était détournée de son sens initial.

Evans continua de s'intéresser à la photographie policière pendant toutes les années 1930, et plus tard. Sans doute inspiré par ce qu'il avait décrit dans son article comme le "procédé clinique" de "découpage photographique de la société" d'August Sander, il établit une liste précise de sujets d'actualité, en vue d'une étude photographique de "la société New Yorkaise des années 30". Au milieu de cette liste il a noté et souligné: "*Pour ce projet, obtenir des cartes de police.*"[8]

Plus tard, en 1938, puis de nouveau en 1941, Evans fit clandestinement une série de portraits dans le métro, un appareil caché dans son manteau. C'est avec ce travail qu'il s'est le plus approché des méthodes de la police et du FBI. Mais ce travail ne fut achevé, organisé en une séquence

d'images, que beaucoup plus tard, en 1966, avec la parution de *Many Are Called*. Evans découvrait et reproduisait en même temps dans ce projet la logique sartrienne des relations sociales "sérialisées": ce que Sartre appelait "la pluralité des solitudes", dans la ville moderne, et dont il voyait la manifestation la plus caractéristique dans les files d'attente aux arrêts d'autobus.[9] L'appareil photographique, comme le métro, révélait un groupe d'individus existant à travers des relations d'altérité mutuelle, plutôt que de réciprocité. Le groupe, en tant que tel, n'existait que par ce qu'il était produit par le mécanisme du métro et par celui de l'appareil photographique. Dans ses notes et brouillons pour ce projet, rédigés entre 1942 et 1966, Evans insiste sur le caractère curieusement abstrait, contingent et hasardeux de cet ensemble mouvant. Son "projet inaccompli" était "de pouvoir établir clairement le fait que soixante deux personnes sont venues, sans le savoir et pendant une période déterminée, se placer devant un appareil d'enregistrement impersonnel et fixe, et que tout ceux qui sont passés dans ce cadre ont été photographiés, et photographiés sans qu'aucune décision humaine n'intervienne au moment de l'exposition". Comme une autre note le précise: "Ces gens sont tout le monde. Ces images sont bien entendu le résultat d'un choix et d'un montage, mais l'ordre de la séquence, tel qu'il se présente maintenant, ne prétend dépendre que du hasard le plus courant."[10]

Si la stratégie d'Evans remontait à Duchamp (et annonçait Cage), elle ressortissait également de la thématique implicite du roman policier, de l'idée que la vie économique est un jeu de hasard, un coup de dés, quelque chose que l'on saisit et contrôle fugitivement, partiellement, irrationnellement. L'optique et la statistique étaient confrontées une nouvelle fois, mais la confrontation s'exprimait ici par la voix d'un artiste attentif et volontairement désarmé, le dandy-joueur-voyeur, maître du "style documentaire". Malgré la proposition de Walter Benjamin: "quelque trace que le flâneur puisse suivre, chacune le conduira vers un crime", Evans renonçait à cette issue en insistant sur la différence entre son "style documentaire", et "le document au sens strict" que représente la "photographie policière d'une scène de meurtre ".[11]

Mais une fois qu'on y a goûté, la saveur du crime persiste. Dans son projet du métro Evans s'était efforcé d'opposer l a détection optique à la loi des moyennes; c'était une manière de reprendre dans l'art le problème pratique et philosophique abordé soixante ans plus tôt par Bertillon, également réticent à l'idée d'un "art" de la photographie. Mais Evans, dans la situation du voyeur de Sartre qui regarde à travers le trou de la serrure et voit qu'il est observé, réussit à inverser le rapport de force. Grâce à son idée d'un enregistrement passif et neutre, il donne l'avantage à celui qui est observé: "Evidemment vous ne trouverez pas parmi eux le visage d'un juge, ni celui d'un sénateur, ni celui d'un président de banque. Ce que vous voyez là est la fois sidérant, effrayant et clair: ce sont les dames et les messieurs du jury."

Pourtant, telle que Walker Evans l'exprime ici pour les lecteurs d'*Harper's Bazaar*, cette pensée définitive et sidérante doit plus à Gustave Le Bon qu'à Sartre ou même à Jefferson.
Le métro est la revanche de l'homme moyen sur ceux qui "aiment les jolies choses." 12

Los Angeles Mai 1992

1 Voir John Szarkowski, *Photography until Now*, Museum of Modern Art, New York, 1989.
2 Georg Lukács, *Histoire et conscience de classe*, Traduction de Kostas Axelos et Jacqueline Bois, Paris, 1960, p.146.
3 Pour plus de précision, voir Allan Sekula, "The Body and the Archive", *October*, no. 39, hiver 1986, pp. 3-64.
4 Charles Sheeler, "The recent Photographs of Alfred Stieglitz", *The Arts*, mai 1923, p.345.
5 Walker Evans, "The Reappearance of Photography", *Hound and Horn*, no. 5, octobre-décembre 1931, p. 126-127.
6 Franz Roh, Jan Tschichold, *foto-auge*, Stuttgart, 1929, p. 73-74.
7 Ernst Friedrich, *Krieg dem Kriege*, Berlin, 1926.
8 Reproduit dans: Jerry Thompson (ed.), *Walker Evans at Work*, , New York, 1982, p.107.
9 Jean-Paul Sartre, *Critique de la Raison Dialectique*, Paris,1960.
10 WalkerEvans, "Unposed Photographic Record of People", in: Sarah Greenough, *Walker Evans: Subways and Streets*, cat. National Gallery of Art, Washington, 1991, p.126. Walker Evans, brouillon rédigé à la main, non-daté, Department of Photographs, J. Paul Getty Museum, Santa Monica, California.
11 Walter Benjamin, *Charles Baudelaire: Un Poète lyrique à l'apogée du capitalisme*, trad. Jean Lacoste, Paris, Payot, 1982, p.63. Katz, Leslie, "Interview with Walker Evans", *Art in America* no. 2, March-April 1971, p. 87.
12 Walker Evans, "The Unposed Portrait", *Harper's Bazaar*, no. 95, March 1962, p. 120.

Walker Evans und Die Polizei

Allan Sekula

(...)Wenn der Rationalismus mit dem Anspruch, die Universalmethode des gesamten Seins vorzustellen, auftritt ... erlangt die Frage der notwendigen Korrelation des irrationellen Prinzips eine entscheidende, das ganze System auflösende und zersetzende Bedeutung.

Georg Lukács, 1923

1

Wie könnten wir ein Muster der Spannungskurven, Schnittpunkte und Abweichungen zwischen den Abstammungs-linien der 'Kunst'-Photographie und der 'angewandten' Photographie, zwischen dem oft merkwürdigen, manchmal mitleiderregenden, nur hin und wieder erfolgreichen hochgesteckten Ziel einer autonomen Kunst der Photographie und der bestehenden Vielzahl praktischer Realismen darstellen?

Trotz der jüngsten Bemühungen von John Szarkowski, die Industrie-Photographie des 19. Jahrhunderts aus den Krupp-Archiven als eine Art unausgeformter Moderne avant la lettre zu sehen, bleibt diese Frage bestehen. Szarkowskis Photography until Now bietet eine triumphale, aber auch etwas klägliche krypto-hegelianische Teleologie: das Projekt Selbstentwicklung der Photographie, der Bildungsroman dieser hundertfünfzigjährigen Jugendlichen bringt eine Flucht aus dem Reich der Notwendigkeit (angewandte Photographie) in das Reich der Freiheit (Kunstphotographie) mit sich. Das Reich der Freiheit ist (wie der Preußische Staat) 'jetzt' unmittelbar vorhanden, fällt vollständig mit Szarkowskis Amtszeit als Direktor der Abteilung für Photographie am Museum of Modern Art zusammen. Der bildhafte Geist, der in sklavisch nachzeichnenden Photographien, die Maschinen und Fabriken des 19. Jahrhunderts abbilden, unschuldig schlummerte, wacht wie ein Dornröschen in der frühen Moderne auf und wird 'jetzt', in einer Phase der Spätmoderne, dystopisch und elegisch und sogar ein bißchen apokalyptisch. In diesem Prozeß geht eine gewisse 'Muskularität' verloren. Das ist der Preis des Selbstbewußtseins und das Ergebnis der Freiheit. Der Prinz zieht sich zurück.[1]

Und so fährt der Diskurs der Photographie fort, zwischen dem, was Georg Lukács, als er von den Grenzen der modernen rationalistischen Philosophie sprach, die "Antinomien des bürgerlichen Denkens" genannt hat, blind hin- und herzuschwanken. Der Rationalismus beugt sich dem Irrationalismus, um sich dann allein durch einen Akt reinen idealistischen Glaubens wieder zu behaupten. Menschliche Wesen können, trotz enormer und zunehmender technischer Macht über die "Details" sozialer Existenz, die Totalität "denken", aber nicht praktisch begreifen.[2]

In der kleinen Welt der Photographie, der Kunst der "Details" (die Lukács in seiner Ablehnung der Moderne wie auch des Naturalismus als solche verspottete), werden objektivistische und subjektivistische Ansprüche in einem Atemzug erhoben. Wissenschaftlicher Instrumentalismus und Ästhetizismus handeln ein Abkommen aus. Der alte Mythos der photographischen Wahrheit und der neuere Mythos photographischer Unwahrheit inszenieren ein Gipfeltreffen. Neo-Neue Sachlichkeit und Neo-Subjektive Photographie in einem Topf? Warum nicht? Irgendwie existiert der Wunsch nach denotativer Gewißheit, nach Klarheit und präzisen, deskriptiven Grenzen friedlich neben dem Wunsch nach semantischer Vielfalt, Mehrdeutigkeit und nichtreduzierbarem, nichtkodierbarem Exzeß. Jeder möchte beides haben.

2

Ein guter Ansatz, mit dem Aussortieren dieses Durcheinanders zu beginnen, ist der Versuch, eine ganz besondere Figur von Irrationalität und Exzeß zu fassen: die Figur des Kriminellen. Symbolisch gesehen ist der Kriminelle das nach außen gekehrte Prinzip des bürgerlichen Eigeninteresses. Darüber hinaus subjektiviert der Kriminelle den täglichen Egoismus und den riskanten Opportunismus wirtschaftlicher Aktivitäten in einer kapitalistischen Gesellschaft. Kriminelle geben den 'unumstößlichen Gesetzen' des Kapitalismus ein flüchtiges und verzerrtes menschliches Gesicht. (Das ist es, was den moralischen Aufschrei angesichts von Plündereien zu einem so interessanten Phänomen macht.)

Bildlich gesehen kollidiert das Problem des Kriminellen mit dem Problem des Portraits, jenem Bildgenre, das im 19. Jahrhundert die optimistische Fülle des bürgerlichen Selbst zu fassen suchte. Ehrerbietige und repressive Modi konstituierten die funktionalen Extreme der Routine-Portraits seit den 60er Jahren des 19. Jahrhunderts. In erster Linie suchte das photographische Portrait ein idealisiertes, besitzendes Subjekt zu individualisieren. In zweiter Linie individualisierte das Portrait das Objekt medizinisch-rechtlicher Regulierung und Überwachung. Die Physiognomik, die das ganze 19. Jahrhundert hindurch ein mächtiges hermeneutisches Paradigma darstellte, diente dazu, diese beiden Formen der visuellen Konstruktion des Selbst zu vereinen. In Anlehnung an die Arbeiten von Georges Canguilhem und Michel Foucault über die Genese und Logik der biosozialen Wissenschaften können wir behaupten, daß das 'normale' und 'respektable' Selbst nur auf der Basis einer simultanen Konstruktion entsteht: der des 'pathologischen' und 'abweichenden' Anderen. Obwohl das Umsichgreifen der Physiognomik und der Portraitphotographie soziale Unterschiede zu einer undifferenzierten und sich permanent verschiebenden Masse aufzulösen drohte, konnten beide in einer proto-technokratischen Art und Weise dazu benutzt werden, wieder Ordnung und Hierarchie in das Staatswesen einzuführen. Der Schlüssel zu diesem letzteren Versprechen lag in der präzisen Fixierung des Bildes des Kriminellen, und zwar als Individuum wie auch als Typus. Aber die Verfolgung

Krimineller geriet in Konflikt mit dem Problem des Kategorisierens und Wiederfindens. Wie war in eine noch nie dagewesene Anzahl von Bildern Sinn und Ordnung zu bringen?

Etwa zwischen 1885 und 1900 wurde ein institutionelles Modell photographischer Bedeutung erfunden: das Modell des Archivs. Dieses Modell war die Antwort auf das Bedürfnis, enorme funktionale Sammlungen von Photographien zusammenzutragen und zu ordnen. Nirgendwo wurde das Archivieren eiliger und rigoroser betrieben als in einer Reihe von neuen, miteinander verwandten und der untereinander austauschenden 'Wissenschaften' der sozialer Regulierung und Kontrolle: in der Kriminologie, der praktischen Polizeiarbeit (Kriminalistik) und der Eugenik.

Im Gegensatz zum allgemein üblichen Verständnis des Verbrecherphotos als eher anrüchigem Beispiel einer mächtigen, völlig denotativen, visuellen Empirie jedoch wurde diese frühe archivierende Nutzung der Photographie auf der Grundlage der scharfsinnigen Erkenntnis der Unzulänglichkeiten und Grenzen gewöhnlicher Verfahren der visuellen Identifizierung und Typisierung von Kriminellen systematisiert. Die Anarchie der übergroßen Produktivität der Kamera mußte durch den Aktenschrank gezähmt werden. Dieses Vorhaben hatte ein Abnehmen des epistemologischen Prestiges der Optik und ein dementsprechendes Anwachsen des Prestiges der Statistik zur Folge. Vorstellungen aus der Zeit der Aufklärung über Einsichten, die die Physiognomie in den menschlichen Charakter gewährt, verloren an Wert.

Wie kam es dazu? In den 80er Jahren des 19. Jahrhunderts tauchten zwei neuartige Systeme der Beschreibung Krimineller auf, die beide auf dem Versuch basierten, den Wert physiognomischer Beweisführung durch Rückgriff auf abstraktere statistische Methoden zu retten. Der Effekt war, daß die Möglichkeiten der Optik den Regelmäßigkeiten der Statistik unterworfen wurden. Beide Projekte verließen sich auf die zentrale konzeptuelle Kategorie sozialer Statistik: die mathematische Vorstellung vom Durchschnittsmenschen ("l'homme moyen"), wie sie der belgische Astronom und Mathematiker Adolphe Quetelet in den 30er Jahren des 19. Jahrhunderts vorgeschlagen hatte. Der Pariser Polizeibeamte Alphonse Bertillon erfand das erste moderne System der Identifizierung Krimineller, indem er zunächst standardisierte Frontal- und Profilportraitphotos und eine numerische, anthropometrische Reihe von neun Körpermaßen auf einer einzigen 'fiche' zusammenfaßte und diese Karteikarten dann in einem riesigen Registratursystem auf der Basis ihrer relativen Position in einer statistischen Verteilung organisierte. Der englische Psychologe und Eugeniker Francis Galton erfand bei dem Versuch, Photoabzüge von abstrakten, statistisch definierten biosozialen Typen zu produzieren, eine Methode des zusammengesetzten Portraitphotos ("Bildstatistik"). Ihn beschäftigte vor allem die Isolierung eines charakteristischen, durch Vererbung hervorgebrachten kriminellen Typus.

Bertillons praktischer Nominalismus und Galtons theoretischer Essentialismus stellen die beiden methodologischen Pole positivistischer Versuche dar, abweichendes Sozialverhalten zu definieren. Ihre Vorstellungen eines angemessenen Verhältnisses zwischen Bild und Archiv waren einander diametral entgegengesetzt, ergänzten sich jedoch innerhalb einer Aufteilung intellektueller Arbeit, die die Kriminologie von praktischer polizeilicher Spurensicherung unterscheidet. Bertillon suchte das Bild innerhalb des Archivs effizient und unfehlbar zu verankern. Galton suchte das Archiv innerhalb eines einzigen Gattungsbildes zu verankern. Und obwohl beide Vorhaben spezialisiert und außerordentlich eigenständig waren, legten sie allgemeine, erkenntnistheoretische Parameter für die bürokratische Handhabung visueller Dokumente fest. Zwischen 1895 und 1910 war dieses breiter angelegte, mehr enzyklopädische Projekt Gegenstand einer Reihe internationaler Kongresse über die Rationalisierung der Bibliothekswissenschaft und die Verbesserung der Methoden photographischer Dokumentation.[3]

3

Wenn wir Szarkowskis metaphysische Bildteleologie ablehnen, welche Verbindungen können dann zwischen dem Archivierungsmodus von Photographie und dem Aufkommen der photographischen Moderne gefunden werden? Bis zu welchem Grad paßte sich die ihrer selbst bewußte moderne Praxis dem Modell des Archivs an? Bis zu welchem Grad widerstanden Anhänger der Moderne bewußt oder unbewußt dem Modell des Archivs oder untergruben dieses Modell, das dazu neigte, den einzelnen Photographen auf den Status des Detail-Arbeiters zu verweisen, der fragmentarische Bilder für einen Apparat liefert, der außerhalb seiner Kontrollmöglichkeiten liegt? Ein paar vorläufige Forschungslinien können nachgezeichnet werden.

Der Protomodernismus der Photo-Sezession und der ihr angeschlossenen Bewegungen, der bis etwa 1916 dauert, kann als Versuch gesehen werden, dem Archivierungsmodus durch eine Strategie von Vermeidung und Leugnung zu widerstehen, die auf handwerklicher Produktion basierte. Die eleganten Wenigen standen den mechanisierten Vielen gegenüber, sowohl was die Bilder als auch was die Autoren betrifft. Diese Strategie erforderte das ostentative Zurschaustellen der "ehrwürdigen Spuren der Handarbeit", um den von dem amerikanischen Soziologen Thorstein Veblen 1899 geprägten Ausdruck zu übernehmen. Der zweite Vektor des Widerstandes gegenüber dem Archivierungsmodus entstand aus dem Versuch, die bildhafte Photographie innerhalb eines anti-positivistischen philosophischen Diskurses anzusiedeln, wobei man sich verschiedentlich auf den Bergsonschen Institutionalismus, den Symbolismus und den Swedenborgschen Mystizismus stützte. Nach 1916 jedoch gaben ästhetisch ambitionierte Photographen malerische Techniken auf und ergriffen bildhafte Rhetoriken, die jenen, welche innerhalb der instrumentellen Realismus- und Archivparadigmen bereits wirksam waren, sehr viel näher

kamen. Es ist verlockend zu behaupten, daß der Triumph der Statistik über die Optik den Effekt der 'Befreiung' des optischen Bildes zu 'zweckfreien' ästhetischen Zwecken hatte, aber die philosophischen Verschiebungen waren weniger klar und direkt.

Ich möchte an dieser Stelle auf das Problem des Portraits zurückkommen und auf die Möglichkeit, daß die Physiognomik in eine Art Dämmerlicht innerhalb der Moderne geriet, weder erschöpft, noch mit demselben glühenden Optimismus der Aufklärung erfüllt, der den Realismus von Balzac oder Nadar antrieb. Sicherlich können wir eine formale und semantische Krise des Portraits feststellen, die aus dem Kubismus entstand, aber wir können auch eine Monumentalisierung und neue Wertfestsetzung des still expressiven Gesichts in der filmischen Nahaufnahme feststellen. Auch müssen wir uns daran erinnern, daß die Physiognomik im 'reaktionär modernen' Programm des Nationalsozialismus ein neues Niveau offiziellen Mordenstums erreichte. Im Moment gilt mein Interesse jedoch der Situation, wie sie sich in den Vereinigten Staaten entwickelt hat, wo die Politik, speziell die Rassen- und Klassenpolitik, gemeinhin auf einen Diskurs über Kriminalität hinausläuft.

Die innerhalb des Stieglitz-Kreises benutzte kritische Sprache zur Beschreibung von Portraits, die Paul Strand und Stieglitz nach 1915 aufnahmen, ist gekennzeichnet durch Bezüge zu Pathologie, abweichendem Verhalten und kriminellen Verstößen und Aufdeckungen, als wäre sie vom Geist Zolas beseelt. In *Camera Work* findet sich 1917 der Verweis auf die "Brutalität" von Strands heimlichen New Yorker Straßenportraits sowie Charles Sheelers Besprechung der Ausstellung von Stieglitz 1923 in der Galerie Anderson mit Portraits, "die so nah am Reich der Pathologie schweben, daß eine so leichte Störung wie die Vibration eines vorbeifahrenden LKWs sie über die Grenze schicken könnte."[4]

Dieser moderne amerikanische 'Neo-Naturalismus' fiel mit einer in der breiten Bevölkerung akzeptierten Legitimation rationalisierter Polizeimethoden zusammen, die sich auf die durch die Polizeiphotos eröffnete Möglichkeit der dokumentarischen Beweisführung konzentrierten. Diese Photos wurden in einem neuen Genre von Krimi-Heften, die Anfang der 20er Jahre dieses Jahrhunderts erstmals erschienen, reproduziert oder imitiert. In *True Detective*, einer Groschenheftreihe, die der Körperkultur-Unternehmer Brennar Macfadden herausgab, hatten Polizeiphotos und Reproduktionen von Fingerabdruckkarten um 1924 die bis dahin üblichen gestellten Photo-Abbildungen als wesentliche Illustrationen von Kriminalgeschichten fast völlig ersetzt. Diese 'dokumentarische' Wendung wiederum fiel mit dem Aufbau des Federal Bureau of Investigation und der Glorifizierung von J. Edgar Hoover's mit Maschinenpistolen bewaffneten Männern ("G-men") in der Sensationspresse zusammen. Ich möchte behaupten, daß das Auftauchen einer dominanten, dokumentarischen Ästhetik in den Vereinigten Staaten, das allgemein auf die 30er Jahre festgelegt wird, tatsächlich in der Massenkultur bereits ein Jahrzehnt früher in den mit Photos illustrierten Krimi-Heften und von Lesern verfaßten 'Bekenntnis'-Heften stattfindet, die Macfadden publizierte, in *True Detective* und *True Confessions*. Ende der 30er Jahre hatte der Fetisch des Archiv-Dokuments außergewöhnliche Ausmaße erreicht. Im Foliantenformat und in limitierter Auflage wurde eine teure Reihe von Kriminalromanen publiziert, die auf den Anspruch einer Erzählung fast völlig verzichteten und statt dessen auf die überzeugende Simulation von Polizeidossiers abzielten, einschließlich beigelegter Cellophan-Tüten mit menschlichem Haar sowie 20 x 25 cm großen Hochglanzabzügen von Tatortphotos. Dieser betonte 'Archivismus' suchte jedoch ein anderes Publikum als jenes, das die billigen Halbtonphotos der Groschenhefte erreichte. Letzteres lebte sehr viel näher an der Wahl zwischen einer Verbrecher- oder einer Polizeilaufbahn.

Während die Surrealisten in Frankreich - wie sowohl in *La Révolution Surréaliste* wie auch in *Minotaure* deutlich wird - ganz offensichtlich von den Handbüchern für Polizeieinsätze und der Arbeit der Spurensichernden Kriminologen fasziniert waren, lernten die amerikanischen Künstler die Ikonographie der Polizeiarbeit - wenn überhaupt - wahrscheinnlich ausschließlich durch Groschenhefte und Boulevardzeitungen kennen.

Wenn also Archiv und Polizeiphoto den frühen modernen Kunstphotographen als zweckmäßige 'schlechte Ziele' dienten, die einen brutalen Realismus konstituierten, über den die 'Kunst' hinausgehen mußte, so übten beide doch auch einen verführerischen Reiz aus. Dieser verführerische Reiz war dem ähnlich, der die fiktiven Kriminalgeschichten mit Leben erfüllte, der Faszination, die von der Möglichkeit ausging, das Spurendetail an einem Subjekt festzumachen, es für eine den sozialen Beziehungen im Kapitalismus zugrundeliegende realistische Poesie des kriminellen Demiurgen zu gewinnen.

4

Die extremste und raffinierteste, in ihrer Mischung aus Anti-Positivismus und Anti-Romantizismus und damit in ihrer Ablehnung jeglicher Physiognomik zerstörerischste Antwort auf diese mehrdeutige Situation innerhalb des Stieglitz-Kreises ist - nicht überraschend - in der Arbeit von Marcel Duchamp zu finden, in seinem lässigen 'Gesucht'-Plakat als 'Selbstportrait' von 1924. Abgesehen von Duchamps kalkuliertem Aufgeben der physiognomischen Identität stammt die komplexeste und intellektuell anspruchsvollste Antwort auf das Modell des Polizeiarchivs von Walker Evans. Evans Antwort beginnt 1931 mit einer in Lincoln Kirsteins *Hound and Horn* veröffentlichten Sammelbesprechung mehrerer Bücher. Der junge Photograph rezensierte eine Reihe gerade erschienener Photobände, darunter August Sanders *Antlitz der Zeit*, Carl Sandburgs *Steichen the Photographer*, die französische Ausgabe von *Atget*, Albert Renger-Patzschs *Die Welt ist schön* und *foto-auge* von Franz Roh und Jan Tschichold.

Evans beginnt mit einer Klage über die "Unehrlichkeit der Sicht" der immer noch um sich greifenden Bildermacher-Ästhetik der Photoclub-Photographen und verbindet diese, ohne Namen zu nennen, mit einem brutal knappen Katalog von Photographien von Edward Steichen und Clarence White, die in frühen Nummern von *Camera Work* publiziert worden waren: "Bilder von diesigen Oktober-Feldwegen, Winterlandschaften, reflets dans l'eau, junge Mädchen mit Kristallkugeln." Aus den Reihen der bildermachenden Photoclub-Mitglieder "erhebt sich der laute und verdächtige Protest dagegen, daß Photographie eine Kunst sei. Sie finden daher, '*da Sie ja nette Dinge mögen*', in einer der hier besprochenen Anthologien das Photo einer Leiche in einer Blutlache. Plötzlich gibt es einen Unterschied zwischen einer idyllischen Beschwörung der Vergangenheit und einem offenen Fenster, durch das der Blick geradewegs durch einen Stapel von Jahrzehnten hindurch nach unten fällt."

Die unvermittelte Beschreibung des Polizeiphotos fungiert als dadaistisches Schockmittel, das das Ziel von Evans Angriff grundlegend verschiebt. Die literarische Strategie ist die der Schnellfeuer-Wort-Montage, der Parodie auf Werbetexte. Die brutale Beschreibung kollidiert nicht nur mit dem antiquarischen Ästhetizismus der Bildermacher, sondern implizit auch mit dem "Hochglanz"-, "Parvenu"- und "Banknoten"-Charakter von Steichens jüngeren Werbephotos von Betten und Feuerzeuge, die in der opulenten, von ihm selbst finanzierten Monographie *Steichen the Photographer* reproduziert waren. Da Evans bis dahin noch nicht dazu gekommen war, seine Klagen über dieses spätere Stadium in Steichens Karriere zu artikulieren, ist dies ein Schritt von telegrammstilartiger Antizipation, eine Strategie, die er in den Photosequenzen in seinem Buch *American Photographs* von 1938 wiederholen sollte. In diesen wenigen Sätzen demonstriert Evans in der Tat einen Weg, mit einem Mal durch den "Stapel von Jahrzehnten" hindurchzuschneiden.[5]

Das Polizeiphoto, das Evans hier kurz beschreibt, war auf einer der letzten Seiten von *foto-auge* reproduziert. Es stammte aus dem Archiv der Stuttgarter Polizei und trug die Bildunterschrift "Mord im Frieden". Ihm gegenüber war ein Photo aus dem Archiv der deutschen Regierung abgebildet, das drei lebende Soldaten und ein totes Pferd auf einer zerstörten Brücke zeigte mit der Unterschrift "Mord im Krieg". (Das Polizeiphoto verwendete später John Heartfield in einer seiner antifaschistischen Collagen.)[6]

So brutal und tendenziös diese Gegenüberstellung in *foto-auge* auch war, so war sie doch nur eine blasse Spiegelung der obsessiven Archiv-Dokumentation, die der Anarchist und militante Pazifist Ernst Friedrich unmittelbar nach dem Ersten Weltkrieg betrieb. Friedrich publizierte mehrere Auflagen eines Buches mit dem Titel *Krieg dem Kriege*, von denen die erste 1924 erschien. Das Buch mit einem Text in Deutsch, Französisch, Englisch und Holländisch war illustriert mit Photos der grauenhaftesten menschlichen Blutbäder und mit medizinischen 'Portraits' von überlebenden Männern, deren Gesichter von Kugeln und Schrapnellen zerstört worden waren. Von Friedrich kann man sagen, daß er zutiefst besessen war von der brutal umformenden Physiognomik moderner Kriegstechnik. Frei von jeglicher Vorstellung vom Todesinstinkt glaubte er - wie auch die Weimarer Polizei, die seine Arbeit hartnäckig zensierte -, daß derartige Bilder die positive pädagogische Basisarbeit für den Pazifismus leisten könnten. Friedrichs zentraler Slogan, "Krieg ist Pestilenz - und Soldaten sind die Bazillen"[7], war praktisch eine Umkehrung des futuristischen Kriegshygiene-Kults.

Wenn in Deutschland das Polizeiphoto in den Kampf gegen Krieg und Faschismus umgeleitet wurde, so richtete es Evans in den Vereinigten Staaten gegen Kunstphotographie und Kommerz. Diese Stoßrichtung war der von Duchamp in seinem 'Gesucht'-Plakat von 1924 nicht unähnlich. In beiden Fällen ist das Bild des Verbrechens Mittel zu einem anderen Zweck.

Evans bewahrte sich sein entschiedenes Interesse an der Polizeiphotographie bis in die Mitte der 30er Jahre und darüber hinaus. Möglicherweise vor allem durch das inspiriert, was er in seiner Buchrezension als den "klinischen Prozeß" in August Sanders "photographischer Aufbereitung der Gesellschaft" beschrieben hatte, stellte Evans eine knappe Sachliste von Sujets für eine photographische Studie der "New Yorker Gesellschaft der 30er Jahre" zusammen. Die Liste enthält eine zentrale, telegrammstilartige, unterstrichene Zeile: "*Projekt kriegt Polizeiakte.*" [8]

1938 und dann noch einmal 1941 ließ Evans sich auf die Zusammenstellung eines Archiv heimlicher U-Bahn-Portraits ein, die er mit einer unter seinem Mantel versteckten Kamera aufnahm. Das war seine stärkste Annäherung an die Methoden der Kriminalpolizei und des FBI. Als organisiertes Ensemble von Bildern wurde diese Arbeit jedoch erst sehr viel später, mit seinem 1966 erschienenen Buch *Many Are Called* vollendet. Was Evans in diesem Projekt tatsächlich sowohl entdeckt als auch darstellt ist die Sartresche Logik serialisierter, sozialer Beziehungen. Sartre definierte Serialität als die "Pluralität von Isolationen" in der modernen Stadt, deren charakteristischste Manifestation er in der Schlange an der Bushaltestelle sah.[9] Evans' Kamera folgt der U-Bahn, indem sie eine Gruppierung von Menschen schafft, die weniger in gegenseitigen Beziehungen existieren, als vielmehr in Beziehungen beiderseitiger Andersartigkeit. Die Gruppe existiert als solche nur kraft der Tatsache, daß sie von der U-Bahn-Maschine und der Kamera-Maschine organisiert wird. In seinen Notizen und Entwürfen zu diesem Projekt, die er zwischen 1942 und 1966 niederschrieb, fühlte sich Evans von der eigenartigen Abstraktheit, der Ungewißheit und der zufälligen Auswahl dieses fließenden Ensembles angezogen. Sein "unerfülltes Ziel" war, "in der Lage zu sein, schlicht zu konstatieren, daß innerhalb eines bestimmten Zeitraums zweiundsechzig Menschen unbewußt in die Reichweite eines unpersönlichen, feststehenden Aufzeichnungsgeräts kamen,

und daß all diese Individuen, die in den Sucher kamen, photographiert wurden, und zwar ohne irgendeine Auswahl durch einen Menschen während des Belichtungsmoments." Eine andere Notiz faßt es so: "Diese Menschen sind Jedermann. Ihre Bilder wurden natürlich ausgewählt und in eine bestimmte Reihenfolge gebracht, aber das Gesamtergebnis der Aufstellung hat Anspruch darauf, ein gewisser Zufallsdurchschnitt zu sein."[10]

Wenn Evans' Strategie auf Duchamp zurückgeführt (und weiter bis zu Cage fortgeführt) werden kann, so berührt sie auch die dem Kriminalroman zugrundeliegende Thematik, den Gedanken vom ökonomischen Leben als Spiel, als Wurf eines Würfels, als etwas, das nur flüchtig und teilweise, nur irrational zu begreifen und zu kontrollieren ist.

Optik und Statistik kollidieren wieder einmal, aber dieses Mal ist das Aufeinandertreffen an der Figur eines wachsamen aber vorsätzlich nahezu machtlosen Künstlers, des Dandys-Spielers-Voyeurs, des Meisters des "Dokumentarstils" estzumachen. Obwohl Walter Benjamin vorgeschlagen hatte, daß "ganz gleich, welchem Weg der Flaneur folgen mag, jeder ihn zu einem Verbrechen führen wird", vermied Evans dieses letzte Rendezvous und betonte den wesentlichen Unterschied zwischen seinem "Dokumentarstil" und dem "buchstäblichen Dokument" wie zum Beispiel "einem Polizeiphoto des Tatorts eines Mordes".[11]

Einmal berührt ist der Flecken, den der Tatort eines Verbrechens hinterläßt, jedoch schwer zu entfernen. Das U-Bahn-Projekt war Evans' große Anstrengung, optische Ermittlungsarbeit mit dem Gesetz des Zufalls zu konfrontieren und so in der Kunst das philosophische und praktische Problem zu rekapitulieren, das sechzig Jahre zuvor Bertillon in Angriff genommen hatte, der über den Gedanken einer 'Kunst' der Photographie ebenfalls verärgert war. Evans jedoch in seiner gedachten, flachen, mechanischen Passivität - wie Sartres Voyeur, der durch ein Schlüsselloch sieht und merkt, daß er von der anderen Seite her selbst beobachtet wird - schafft es, das Kraftfeld umzukehren: "Während es passiert, erkennt man unter ihnen nicht das Gesicht eines Richters oder Senators oder eines Bankdirektors. Was man sieht ist gleichzeitig ernüchternd, überraschend und offensichtlich: Dies sind die Damen und Herren Geschworenen." Dennoch, wie Evans hier für die Leser von Harper's Bazaar schrieb, verdankt dieser letzte ernüchternde Gedanke mehr LeBon als Sartre oder selbst Jefferson. Die U-Bahn ist die Rache des "l'homme moyen" an denen, die "nette Dinge mögen."[12]

Los Angeles Mai 1992

Walker Evans en de Politie

Allan Sekula

Als rationalisme dé universele methode is om kennis
te vergaren over het gehele bestaan (...) wordt de noodzakelijke
correlatie met het principe van het irrationalisme cruciaal:
het holt het hele systeem uit en lost het op.

Georg Lukács, 1923

1

Hoe kunnen we een patroon van spanningen, kruispunten en
verschillen in kaart brengen tussen de afstammelingen van
'kunst'-fotografie en 'toegepaste' fotografie, tussen de vaak
heikele, soms pathetische, wisselend succesvolle aspiratie naar
een autonome kunst van de fotografie en de bestaande grote
hoeveelheid aan praktische realismen?

Die vraag blijft hangen, ondanks de recente inspanningen
van John Szarkowski om de negentiende-eeuwse industriële
fotografie uit de Krupp-archieven te beschouwen als een
onontwikkeld modernisme avant la lettre. Szarkowski's
Photography until Now wordt gekenmerkt door een
triomfalistische maar ook een treurige crypto-Hegeliaanse
teleologie: het project van de zelfontwikkeling van de
fotografie, de 'Bildungsroman' van deze 150-jarige adolescent,
leidt tot een vlucht uit het rijk van de noodzakelijkheid
(toegepaste fotografie) naar het rijk van vrijheid (kunstfotografie). Het rijk van vrijheid (net als de Pruisische staat)
staat 'nu' heel dicht voor de deur en loopt vrijwel samen met
Szarkowski's benoeming als directeur van de fotografie-
afdeling bij het Museum of Modern Art in New York.
De picturale geest die onschuldig sluimerde in de slaafse
mimetische foto's waarop negentiende-eeuwse machines en
fabrieken staan afgebeeld zou binnen het vroeg-modernisme
ontwaken als een Schone Slaapster en 'nu', in een periode van
laat-modernisme, anti-utopisch en elegisch en zelfs een beetje
apocalyptisch zijn. In het proces gaat een zekere 'gespierdheid'
verloren. Het is de prijs van zelfbewustzijn en het resultaat
van vrijheid. De Prins trekt zich terug.[1]

En zo zet het discours over de fotografie zijn blinde
schommelingen voort tussen wat Georg Lukács, als hij het
heeft over de beperkingen van de moderne rationalistische
filosofie, de "tegenstrijdigheden van de bourgeois-gedachte"
noemt. Rationalisme geeft voorrang aan irrationalisme en doet
zichzelf slechts weer gelden als een daad van puur idealistisch
geloof. Menselijke werktuigen kunnen de totaliteit "indenken",
maar ze kunnen het niet praktisch aanpakken ondanks de
enorme en toenemende technische macht over de "details"
in het maatschappelijke bestaan.[2]

1 Siehe Szarkowski, John, *Photography until Now*, Museum of Modern Art,
New York, 1989.
2 Lukács, Georg, *Geschichte und Klassenbewußtsein*, Neuwied und Berlin,
1970, S. 214ff.
3 Eine vollständigere Fassung der hier gerafften Argumentation findet sich in:
Sekula, Allan, "The Body and the Archive", *October,* no. 39, winter 1986, S. 3-64.
4 Sheeler, Charles, "The Recent Photographs of Alfred Stieglitz",
The Arts, May 1923, S. 345.
5 Evans, Walker, "The Reappearance of Photography", *Hound and Horn, no.* 5,
October-December 1931, S. 126-127.
6 Roh, Franz, Jan Tschichold (Hrsg.), *foto-auge*, Stuttgart, 1929, Abb. 73-74.
7 Friedrich,Ernst, *Krieg dem Kriege*, Berlin, 1926.
8 Abgebildet in: Thompson, Jerry (ed.), *Walker Evans at Work*, New York 1982, S. 107.
9 Sartre, Jean-Paul, *Kritik der dialektischen Vernunft*, Reinbek, 1967.
10 Evans, Walker "Unposed Photographic Record of People", in: Sarah Greenough,
Walker Evans: Subways and Streets, Washington D. C., 1991, S. 126. Evans, Walker,
undatierter handschriftlicher Entwurf, Department of Photographs, J. Paul Getty Museum,
Santa Monica, California.
11 Benjamin, Walter,*Charles Baudelaire. Ein Lyriker im Zeitalter des
Hochkapitalismus*, Frankfurt 1974. Katz, Leslie, "Interview with Walker Evans",
Art in America no.2, March-April 1971, S. 87.
12 Evans, Walker "The Unposed Portrait", *Harper's Bazaar*, no. 95, March 1962, S. 120.

In de kleine wereld van de fotografie, de kunst van de "details" (als zodanig bespottelijk gemaakt door Lukács om zowel anti-modernistische alsook anti-naturalistische redenen), worden in één adem objectivistische en subjectivistische aanspraken gemaakt. Wetenschappelijk instrumentalisme en estheticisme gooien het op een akkoordje. De oude mythe van de fotografische waarheid en de recentere mythe van de foto-fische onwaarheid maken zich op voor een topontmoeting. Neo-'Neue Sachlichkeit' en neo-'Subjektive Photographie' in een grote pot? Waarom niet? Op de een of andere manier kan de behoefte aan zekerheid, aan helderheid en exacte omschrijvende beperkingen, vreedzaam samenleven met de behoefte aan semantische meervoudigheid, dubbelzinnigheid en niet te herleiden en niet te stoppen uitspattingen. Iedereen wil van twee walletjes eten.

2

Een goede begin om orde te brengen in deze warboel is de poging om een bijzonder figuur van irrationaliteit en uitspatting te duiden: de criminele figuur. De crimineel is symbolisch gezien het vleesgeworden principe van het burgerlijke zelfbelang. Verder subjectiveert de crimineel het alledaagse egoïsme en het onberekenbare opportunisme van economische activiteit in een kapitalistische maatschappij. Criminelen geven aan de 'onverbiddelijke wetten' van het kapitalisme een vergankelijk en verwrongen menselijk gezicht. (Dat maakt de morele verontwaardiging over plundering zo'n interessant fenomeen).

In beeldtaal botst het probleem van de crimineel met het probleem van het portret, het piсturale genre dat in de negentiende eeuw trachtte de optimistische veelheid van de bourgeoisie zelf vast te leggen. Vererende en onderdrukkende karakteristieken vormden vanaf de jaren '60 van de vorige eeuw de functionele uitersten in de dagelijkse praktijk van portretvervaardiging. Op de eerste plaats was het fotografische portret bedoeld om een geïdealiseerd, bezittend subject te individualiseren. Ten tweede individualiseerde het portret het subject van medisch-gerechtelijke regulering en bewaking. De fysionomie, die gedurende de hele negentiende eeuw een krachtig hermeneutisch paradigma vormde, diende om deze twee manieren van visuele constructie van het Zelf samen te brengen. Volgens het werk van Georges Canguilhem en Michel Foucault over het ontstaan en de logica van de bio-sociale wetenschappen, kunnen we bestrijden dat het 'normale' en 'respectabele' Zelf slechts voortkomt op basis van een gelijktijdige constructie: die van de 'pathologische' en de 'afwijkende' Ander. Hoewel de wijdverspreide fysionomie en de fotografische portretkunst de maatschappelijke verschillen dreigden op te lossen in een ongedifferentiëerde en permanent bewegende massa, konden beide worden gebruikt op een proto-technocratische wijze om in de staat de orde en de hiërarchie te herstellen. De sleutel naar deze laatstgenoemde belofte ligt in de exacte fixatie van het beeld van de crimineel, zowel individu als type. Maar de jacht op het

criminele lichaam liep spaak op het probleem van de categorisatie en het onderzoek. Hoe kon er redelijkheid en orde gebracht worden in een nog nooit eerder voorgekomen aantal beelden?

Tussen pakweg 1885 en 1900 werd een institutioneel model voor fotografische middelen uitgevonden: het archief. Dit model was het antwoord op de behoefte om een enorme, functionele collectie van foto's samen te brengen en te ordenen. Nergens anders werd het archiveren zo noodzakelijk en zo rigoreus toegepast dan in een aantal nieuwe, aan elkaar verwante en verbonden 'wetenschappen' ten behoeve van de sociale regulering en controle: criminologie, het praktische politiewerk (criminalistiek) en de eugenetica.

Deze oorspronkelijke archivering van fotografie werd echter gesystematiseerd op basis van onmiddellijke herkenning van de onvolwaardigen en van de beperkingen van de gewone procedures om criminelen visueel te identificeren en te typeren. Dit in tegenstelling tot de alledaagse opvatting over de 'mug shot' (portret van de verdachte) als het schandelijke voorbeeld van een machtig, beschrijvend visueel empirisme. De anarchie van vruchtbare produktie van de camera moest worden getemd door de archiefkast. Het betekende een afname van het door de kenleer geschraagde prestige van de gezichtsleer en een daarmee samenhangende toename van het prestige van de statistiek. Denkbeelden uit de Verlichting over de fysionomische inzichten over het menselijke karakter verloren aan waarde.

Hoe kon dit gebeuren? In de jaren '80 van de vorige eeuw ontstonden twee nieuwe beschrijvingssystemen voor de criminele figuur. Beide waren gebaseerd op de poging om de waarde van het fysionomische bewijs te redden door toevlucht te nemen tot meer abstracte statistische methodes. Met als gevolg dat de mogelijkheden van de optica ondergeschikt werden gemaakt aan regelmaat van de statistiek. Beide systemen borduurden voort op de centrale conceptuele categorie van maatschappelijke statistiek: het mathematische begrip van de gemiddelde mens ("l'homme moyen") dat in de jaren '30 van de vorige eeuw was voorgesteld door de Belgische astronoom en wiskundige Adolphe Quetelet. De Parijse politiefunctionaris Alphonse Bertillon vond het eerste moderne systeem van identificatie van criminelen uit door gestandaardiseerde foto's en face/en profile te combineren met een numerieke antropometrische serie van negen lichamelijke afmetingen op een enkele fiche. Daarna werden deze kaarten in een archiefsysteem ondergebracht op basis van hun relatieve positie binnen een statische verspreiding. De Engelse psycholoog en grondlegger van de eugenetica, Francis Galton, vond een methode uit van compositie-beelden ("beeld statistieken") in een poging om actuele fotografische indrukken van abstracte, statistisch gedefinieerde bio-sociale types te produceren. Hij was in het bijzonder geïnteresseerd in de isolatie van een bepaald crimineel type op basis van erfelijkheid.

Bertillons praktische nominalisme en Galtons theoretische essentialisme waren de twee methodologische polen van positivistische pogingen om maatschappelijke afwijking te definiëren en te reguleren. Hun begrip van de juiste relatie tussen beeld en archief stonden weliswaar diametraal tegenover elkaar, maar vulden elkaar ook aan binnen een intellectuele arbeid die de criminologie onderscheidde van gewoon politie onderzoek. Bertillon wilde het beeld zo efficiënt en foutloos mogelijk laten passen in het archief. Galton wilde het archief vastleggen binnen een enkel generisch beeld. Hoewel hun beider projecten specialistisch en sterk persoonlijk waren, gaven ze algemene kennis-theoretische parameters voor de bureaucratische afwerking van visuele documenten. Tussen 1895 en 1910 werd dit bredere, meer encyclopedische project gevolgd door een aantal internationale congressen over de rationalisatie van bibliotheekwetenschap en de verfijning van methodes voor fotografische documentatie.[3]

3

Als we Szarkowski's metafysische teleologie van het beeld afwijzen, welke verbindingen kunnen dan wel worden gevonden tussen het archiefgebruik van fotografie en de opkomst van het fotografisch modernisme? Tot op welke hoogte richtte de zelfbewuste modernistische praktijk zich naar het model van het archief? Tot op welke hoogte boden modernisten, bewust of onbewust, weerstand of ondermijnen ze het archiefmodel, dat er toe neigde de individuele fotograaf de status van precisiewerker te geven die een apparaat dat voorbij ging aan zijn of haar controle, voorzag van fragmentarische beelden? Een paar provisorische onderzoekslijnen kunnen in kaart worden gebracht.

Het proto-modernisme van de Photo Secession en zijn gelieerde bewegingen die tot ruwweg 1916 bestonden, kan worden gezien als een poging weerstand te bieden aan de archiefmethode door een strategie van ontwijking en ontkenning gebaseerd op ambachtelijke produktie. De elegante minderheid stond tegenover de gemechaniseerde meerderheid, dat gold voor zowel beelden als auteurs. Deze strategie vereiste een ostentatief vertoon van "eervolle herkenning van handenarbeid", een zinsnede van de Amerikaanse socioloog Thorstein Veblen uit 1899. De tweede verzetsrichting tegen het archiefmodel kwam voort uit de poging om de picturale fotografie binnen een anti-positivistische filosofisch discours te plaatsen, daarbij afwisselend leunend op het intuïtionalisme van Bergson, en het symbolisme en mysticisme van Swedenborg. Na 1916 echter, stapten esthetisch ambitieuze fotografen af van de technieken uit de schilderkunst en hingen een picturale retoriek aan, die nauwkeuriger was dan die reeds gebruikt werd binnen de instrumenteel realistische en archivistische paradigma's. Het is verleidelijk om te bestrijden dat de triomf van de statistiek over de optica als resultaat had dat het optische beeld 'bevrijd' was en gebruikt kon worden voor 'doelloze' esthetische doeleinden.
De filosofische veranderingen waren echter minder duidelijk en direct.

Ik keer terug naar de kwestie van het portret en de mogelijkheid dat de gezichtsleer overging in een schemergebied binnen het modernisme, uitgeblust noch overgoten door en met hetzelfde gloeiende optimisme uit de Verlichting waarmee ook het realisme van Balzac en Nadar werd gevoed. Natuurlijk kunnen we een formele en semantische crisis van het portret ontdekken, die voortkomt uit het cubisme, maar we kunnen ook een nieuwe monumentalisatie en herwaardering herkennen van het zwijgzaam expressieve gezicht van de close-up in de film. We moeten ook niet vergeten dat fysionomie een nieuwe staat van officiële moorddadigheid had verworven binnen het 'reactionair modernistische' programma van het Nationaal-Socialisme. Op dit moment echter ben ik geïnteresseerd in de situatie zoals die zich voordoet in de Verenigde Staten, waar politiek, in het bijzonder rassen- en klassepolitiek, doorgaans neerkomt op een discours over misdaad.

De kritische taal die werd gebruikt binnen de kring van Stieglitz over de portretten van na 1915 van Paul Strand, en van Stieglitz zelf, wordt gekenmerkt door verwijzingen naar de pathologie, afwijkingen, criminele overtredingen en opsporingen, alsof hier*f*in aangespoord door de geest van Zola. Zo is er de verwijzing in 1917 in *Camera Work* waar gesproken wordt over de "wreedheid" van Strands clandestiene Newyorkse straatportretten, en Charles Sheelers recensie van Stieglitz' tentoonstelling in de Anderson Gallery in 1923 met portretten "die zo dicht bij het rijk van de pathologie hangen, dat slechts een lichte storing als de trilling van een voorbij rijdende vrachtwagen hen daar kan doen belanden."[4]

Dit Amerikaanse modernistische 'neo-naturalisme' viel samen met een brede algemene erkenning van gerationaliseerde politiemethodes gericht op de gedocumenteerde bewijsvoering zoals die werd aangeboden door politiefoto's. Deze werden gereproduceerd of nagemaakt in een detective-tijdschrift dat vanaf begin jaren '20 verscheen. In *True Detective*, een pulpblad dat werd uitgegeven door de ondernemer in lichaamscultuur Brennar Macfadden, hadden rond 1924 politiefoto's en reproducties van vingerafdruk-fiches de geënsceneerde fotografische tableaux als illustraties bij misdaadverhalen zo goed als vervangen. Deze omwentelingen in 'documentatie' vielen op hun beurt samen met de oprichting van het Federal Bureau of Investigation en de verheerlijking in de roddelpers van J. Edgar Hoovers', met machinepistolen spelende 'G-men'. Ik zou willen zeggen dat de opkomst van een overheersende documentatie-esthetiek binnen de massa-cultuur van de Verenigde Staten, die gewoonlijk wordt teruggevoerd naar de jaren '30, eigenlijk al tien jaar eerder plaatsvond met de geïllustreerde pulptijdschriften over misdaad en de magazines van Macfadden waarin lezers bekentenissen deden, zoals *True Detective* en *True Confessions*. Eind jaren '30 had de fetisj van het archiefdocument al uitzonderlijke proporties aangenomen. Een serie van dure detective-romans werden uitgegeven in beperkte oplage die het konden stellen zonder de aanspraak op het narratieve en in plaats daarvan gericht waren op een overtuigende simulatie van politiedossiers, compleet met doorzichtige afsluitbare zakjes met mensenharen, en met 20 bij 25 cm foto's van de plaats van de misdaad. Dit ostentatieve 'archivalisme' wilde echter een ander publiek dienen dan dat van de goedkope in halftonen gedrukte pulpbladen. De laatsgenoemden stonden veel dichter bij de keus tussen misdadiger of politieman worden.

Terwijl in Frankrijk de surrealisten duidelijk gefascineerd waren door de politie-handboeken en het werk van de gerechtelijke criminologen, zoals aangetoond in *La Révolution surréaliste* en in *Minotaure*, valt aan te nemen dat Amerikaanse kunstenaars slechts in aanraking kwamen met de iconografie van het politiewerk, als dat al gebeurde, via de pulpbladen en de schandaalpers.

Als het archief en de politiefoto voor de vroeg-modernistische kunstfotografen als een handig 'slecht object' diende, gekenmerkt door een wreed realisme dat 'kunst' diende te overtreffen, dan hadden beide ook een verleidelijke aantrekkingskracht. De aantrekkingskracht hield nauw verband met de levendigheid van de detective fictie, een fascinatie voor de subjectivering van het gerechtelijke detail, en zet het om in een realistische verskunst waarin de criminele schepper schuilgaat onder de kapitalistische maatschappelijke betrekkingen.

4
De meest extreme en sluwe respons op deze dubbelzinnige situatie binnen de Stieglitz-kring, zeer sarcastisch met zijn amalgaam van anti-positivisme en anti-romantiek en dus in zijn afwijzing van iedere fysionomie, kan, nogal voor de hand liggend, worden teruggevonden in het 'zelfportret' van Marcel Duchamp uit 1924 in de vorm van een opsporingsbiljet.

De meest gecompliceerde en intellectualistische weerklank op het model van het politie-archief, zonder Duchamps berekende afwijzing van de fysionomische identiteit, is die van Walker Evans. Evans' respons begint in 1931 met een boekrecensie in Lincoln Kirstein's *Hound and Horn*. De jonge fotograaf recenseerde een aantal pas verschenen fotoboeken, waaronder August Sanders' *Antlitz der Zeit*, Carl Sandburg's *Steichen the Photographer*, de Franse editie van *Atget*, Albert Renger-Patzsch's *Die Welt ist schön* en *foto-auge* van Franz Roh en Jan Tschichold.

Evans begint zich te beklagen over de "oneerlijkheid van het zien" van de nog steeds aanwezige beeldesthetiek van de foto-club fotografen en verbond dit zonder namen te noemen met een zeer beknopte catalogus met foto's van Edward Steichen en Clarence White die waren gepubliceerd in vroege uitgaven van *Camera Work*: "beelden van lanen in de oktober mist, wintertaferelen, spiegelingen in het water, jonge meisjes met kristallen bollen." Van de picturalistische foto-clubleden "komt

het luide en verdachte protest tegen de fotografie als kunst. Vandaar dat in een van de anthologieën die besproken werden een foto van een lichaam in een bloedplas werd afgebeeld '*omdat je van leuke dingen houdt*'. En plotseling is er een verschil tussen een vreemde bezwering van het verleden en een open raam dat uitkijkt op een hoopje vergane jaren."

De onverhoedse beschrijving van de politiefoto's werkt als een dadaïstisch schokmiddel dat het doel van Evans' aanval diepgaand verlegt. De literaire strategie is die van de spervuur-woordmontage, een parodie op reclameteksten. De wrede beschrijving botst niet alleen met het antiquarische estheticisme van de picturalisten, maar impliciet ook met de "hoogglans-", en het "parvenu-" en "bankbiljet-" karakter van Steichens latere reclamefoto's voor bedden en aanstekers die in de rijke, door hem zelf verzorgde monografie *Steichen the Photographer* gereproduceerd zijn. Omdat Evans nog niet zo ver was zijn klachten over de latere carrière van Steichen te verwoorden, is deze stap een anticipatie in telegramstijl, een strategie die hij later zou herhalen in de foto-sequenties in zijn boek *American Photographs* uit 1938. In die paar zinnen demonstreert Evans eigenlijk een manier om met één beweging door het "hoopje vergane jaren" heen te snijden.[5]

De politiefoto, die Evans kort beschrijft, was gereproduceerd op een van de laatste pagina's van *foto-auge*. Het kwam uit de archieven van de politie in Stuttgart en droeg als bijschrift "moord in vredestijd". De foto stond naast een afbeelding uit het archief van de Duitse overheid met daarop drie levende soldaten en een dood paard op een kapotgeschoten brug dat als bijschrift droeg "moord in oorlogstijd". (De politiefoto gebruikte John Heartfield later in een van zijn anti-fascistische collages.)[6]

Hoe wreed en tendentieus deze tegenoverstelling in *foto-auge* ook was, vergeleken met de obsessieve archief-documentatie die de anarchist en militante pacifist Ernst Friedrich kort na de Eerste Wereldoorlog bedreef, was zij slechts een zwakke afspiegeling. Friedrich publiceerde vanaf 1924 meerdere edities van het boek *Krieg dem Kriege* (Oorlog aan de oorlog). Het boek, met teksten in het Duits, Frans, Engels en Nederlands, was geïllustreerd met foto's van de meest gruwelijke menselijke bloedbaden en met medische 'portretten' van overlevende mannen, wiens gezichten waren vernietigd door kogels en schrapnel. Van Friedrich kan gezegd worden dat hij zeer geobsedeerd was door de wrede transformerende fysionomie van de moderne krijgskunst. Vrij van welke voorstelling van doodsinstinct ook, geloofde hij - net zoals de Weimarer politie die zijn werk hardnekkig bleef censureren - dat dergelijke beelden een positieve pedagogische basis legden voor het pacifisme. Friedrichs slogan, "Oorlog is de pest - en soldaten zijn de bacillen" was praktisch een omkering van de futuristische cult van de hygiënische oorlog.[7]

Terwijl in Duitsland de politiefoto werd gebruikt in de strijd tegen oorlog en fascisme, richtte Evans deze in de Verenigde

Staten tegen de kunstfotografie en de commercie. Deze richting was niet totaal vreemd aan Duchamps 'opsporingsbiljet' uit 1924. In beide gevallen is het beeld van de misdaad een middel voor een ander doel.

Evans behield zijn uitdrukkelijke belangstelling voor politiefotografie tot halverwege de jaren '30 en verder. Mogelijk geïnspireerd door wat hij in zijn boekrecensie als het "klinische proces" van August Sanders' "fotografische redactie van de maatschappij" beschreven had, stelde Evans een kleine lijst samen met onderwerpen voor een fotografische studie van de "Newyorkse samenleving in de jaren '30". Deze lijst bevat een centrale, telegramstijlachtige, onderstreepte zin: *"Voor dit project, kijk in politiedossiers."* [8]

Later, in 1938 en nog een keer in 1941, begon Evans met de samenstelling van een archief van stiekem, met de camera onder zijn jas verstopt, in de metro genomen portretten. Hiermee kwam hij het dichtst bij de methodes die de recherche en de FBI hanteerden. Dit werk werd echter pas vele jaren later als georganiseerd ensemble voltooid met het boek *Many Are Called* uit 1966. Wat Evans werkelijk met dit project heeft ontdekt en heeft laten zien is de Sartreaanse logica van geserialiseerde sociale betrekkingen. Sartre definiëerde serialiteit als "de veelvuldigheid van isolaties" in de moderne stad die zich karakteristiek manifesteerde in de rijen bij bushaltes.[9] De camera van Evans volgt de metro en produceert groepjes mensen. Maar in plaats van hun saamhorigheid te benadrukken, accepteert Evans hun onderlinge verschillen. Een groep bestaat slechts bij de gratie van het feit dat ze onderworpen is aan de organisatie van de ondergrondse-treinmachine en de camera-machine. Uit zijn notities en ontwerpen voor dit project, die hij tussen 1942 en 1966 bijhield, blijkt dat Evans zich aangetrokken voelde tot de eigenaardige abstractie, de ongewisheid en de toevallige keuze van dit vloeiende ensemble. Zijn "onvervulde doel" was " het simpelweg constateren dat binnen een bepaalde tijdspanne tweeënzestig mensen onbewust binnen het bereik kwamen van een onpersoonlijk, gefixeerd registratie-apparaat en dat al deze individuen, die in de zoeker kwamen, gefotografeerd werden zonder een menselijk ingegeven keuze tijdens het moment van belichting." In een andere notitie staat het zo: "Deze mensen zijn iedereen. Hun beelden werden natuurlijk geselecteerd en in een bepaalde volgorde gelegd, maar het totale resultaat van de opstelling doet een beroep op een soort toevalsgemiddelde."[10]

Als Evans' strategie kan worden teruggevoerd naar Duchamp (en verder naar Cage), dan raakt zij ook de uit de detective-roman stammende thematiek, het idee van het economische leven als een gokspel en de worp van de dobbelsteen, als iets dat slechts vluchtig en gedeeltelijk, slechts irrationeel te begrijpen en te controleren is.

Optica en statistiek botsen wederom, maar dit keer is de botsing te koppelen aan de figuur van een waakzame maar opzettelijk bijna machteloze kunstenaar, de dandy-gokker-voyeur, de meester van de "documentaire stijl". Hoewel Walter Benjamin heeft voorgesteld dat "welk spoor de flaneur ook volgt, het brengt hem bij een misdaad", ontweek Evans dit laatste rendez-vous en benadrukte het wezenlijke verschil tussen zijn "documentaire stijl" en het "letterlijke document" zoals de "politiefoto van de plaats waar de moord is gepleegd."[11]

Eenmaal aangeraakt is de achtergelaten vlek op de plaats van de misdaad moeilijk uit te wissen. Het metro-project was Evans' grootste inspanning om optisch speurwerk te confronteren met de wet van het gemiddelde en op die manier in de kunst het probleem van het filosofische en het praktische te recapituleren; het probleem dat zestig jaar eerder door Bertillon, die zich ook geërgerd had aan een 'kunst' der fotografie, al werd aangepakt. Maar Evans, in zijn geïmagineerd vlakke, mechanische passiviteit - zoals Sartre's voyeur door het sleutelgat kijkt en merkt dat hij van de andere kant zelf wordt bespied - slaagt er in het krachtenveld om te keren: "Men herkent onder hen niet het gezicht van een rechter of een senator of een bankdirecteur. Wat men ziet is tegelijkertijd ontnuchterend, verrassend en voor de hand liggend: dit zijn de dames en heren juryleden." Hoe dan ook, zoals Evans hier schreef voor de lezers van *Harper's Bazaar*, is deze 'ontnuchterende' laatste gedachte meer eigen aan LeBon dan aan Sartre of zelfs Jefferson. De metro is de wraak van de "l'homme moyen" op hen die " van leuke dingen houden".[12]

Los Angeles mei 1992

1 Zie Szarkowski, John, *Photography until Now*, Museum of Modern Art, New York, 1989.
2 Lukács, Georg, *History and Class Consciousness: Studies in Marxist Dialectics*, trans. Rodney Livingston, Cambridge, Mass., 1971, pp. 110-148.
3 Zie voor een meer complete versie van de hier samengevatte argumentatie: Sekula, Allan, "The Body and the Archive", *October*, no. 39, winter 1986, pp. 3-64.
4 Sheeler, Charles, "The Recent Photographs of Alfred Stieglitz", *The Arts*, May 1923, p. 345.
5 Evans, Walker, "The Reappearance of Photography", *Hound and Horn*, no. 5, October-December 1931, p. 126-127.
6 Roh, Franz, Jan Tschichold (Hrsg.), *foto-auge*, Stuttgart, 1929, p. 73-74.
7.Friedrich, Ernst, *Krieg dem Kriege*, Berlin, 1926.
8 Gereproduceerd in: Thompson, Jerry (ed.), *Walker Evans at Work*, New York, 1982, p. 107.
9 Sartre, Jean-Paul, *Critique de la raison dialectique*, Paris, 1960, p. 308 ev.
10 Zie: Evans, Walker, "Unposed Photographic Record of People", in: Sarah Greenough, *Walker Evans: Subways and Streets*, Washington D.C., 1991, p. 126. Evans, Walker, ongedateerd handgeschreven ontwerp, Department of Photographs, J. Paul Getty Museum, Santa Monica, California.
11 Benjamin, Walter, *Baudelaire: Een dichter in het tijdperk van het hoog-kapitalisme*, vert. Wim Notenboom, Amsterdam, 1979, p. 35. Katz, Leslie, "Interview with Walker Evans", *Art in America* no. 2, March-April 1971, p. 87.
12 Evans, Walker, "The Unposed Portrait", *Harper's Bazaar*, no. 95, March 1962, p. 120.

Moments of History in the Work of Dan Graham (1977)

Benjamin H.D. Buchloh

Asked about the essential feature of his work Graham answered by calling it 'photojournalism',[1] an ironical quotation of a term Marcel Duchamp had once used to describe his own activities. Thus Graham voluntarily followed a misunderstanding and misnomer that his work had stirred since his earliest publication in 1965. Still in 1970, the critic Lucy Lippard could ask during a discussion with Carl Andre, Jan Dibbets and Douglas Huebler: "Dan, you've been called a poet and a critic and a photographer. Are you an artist now?"[2]

But even his own contemporaries, artists-friends of the Minimal phase whose work had found in Dan Graham's analytical criticism since 1965 a rarely qualified protagonist, refused - by misinterpreting his own visual art production - the recognition of changing basic concepts within the visual arts since 1965. Dan Flavin, for example, even though having been among the first to have been seriously interested in Graham's work and the first who published one of his photographs, wrote on Graham's "Homes for America" (1966): "Your fine photographic approach seems to recall the consistently clear and plain deviceless reportage of Henri Cartier-Bresson, which you apply not to people, as he did, but to their 'feats' of banal vernacular architecture and landscape."[3] This false classification is of particularly revealing historical irony as it shows that from a minimalist's perspective photographical information/ documentation obviously could not even be conceived as possibly being 'art' (unless 'photographical' art). Moreover the misapprehension reveals an unconscious attempt to eliminate radically innovative implications of post minimalist art activity by relating Graham's photographs to a particularly restaurative ideology of photography, namely Cartier-Bresson's idea of the 'Decisive Moment'. Whereas these photographers tend to celebrate their passive-receptive activity as a medium of the one historical moment, which they try to conserve in its photographical transubstantiation, it is Graham's intention quite to the contrary, to construct functional models of recognition of actual history by his (photographical) media.

"Homes for America" (1966) which we consider along with Graham's "Schema" (1966) to be the most complex and relevant of his early works, shall serve as an example. This piece of 'photojournalism' which he referred to as "the transition from earlier 'conceptual' pages in magazines and the 1967-1969 articles" takes off from the by then growing recognition that information about the artworks is disseminated primarily by reproduction in the (art) media, as for example Carl Andre had described it in 1968:

"The photograph is a lie. I'm afraid we get a great deal of our exposure to art through magazines and through slides, and I think this is dreadful, this is anti-art because art is a direct experience with something in the world and photography is just a rumour, a kind of pornography of art."[4] It is precisely at this anti-art point of 'pornography' that Graham starts his inquiry and it is significant for his post-minimalist attitude that he almost literally inverts Andre's disgust with the media and turns it into a basis for his own artistic strategies and works.

Graham has commented on this key work in a description which in itself repeats the intertwinement of the various formal and (art) historical relations and dialectical inversions of the work: "First it is important that the photos are not alone, but part of a magazine layout. They are illustrations of the text or (inversely), the text functions in relation to/modifying the meaning of the photos and the text are separate parts of a schematic (two-dimensional grid) perspective system. The photos correlate (to) the lists and columns of serial information and both 'represent' the serial logic of the housing developments whose subject matter the article is about. Despite the fact that the idea of using the 'real' outdoor environment as a 'site' on which to construct 'conceptual' or 'earth works' (remember the article was written some years before Smithson's and Oppenheim's works), I think the fact that "Homes for America" was, in the end, only a magazine article, and made no claims for itself as 'Art', is its most important aspect."[5]

Thus the informational frame of an art magazine's coverage becomes the 'found' formal structure. This is however juxtaposed with the subject matter of a found 'reality' structure - the miserability of everyday industrial housing. At the same time its formal stylistic qualities - the serial order of the cubic house forms, their permutational principles of single but repetitive elements (whose sum constitutes the 'wholeness' of a given formation) - reflect in an obviously ironic and ambiguous manner the formal and stylistical principles of minimal sculpture. The dialectical combination of reality structure and formal structure, this capacity of reading 'buildings and grammars' - i.e. reality systems and formal systems - which is most typical and significant for all of Graham's early writings and conceptual works, ranges them into a category of structure as simulacrum of the object of history, as Barthes has defined it, "...a pointed, international simulacrum, because the imitated object reveals something which remained invisible or even more incomprehensible with the mere object ... This simulacrum is intellect added to the object; and this addition has anthropological value as it is the human being itself, its history, its situation, its freedom and the resistance which nature opposes to his mind."[6]

The general understanding and delayed recognition of Graham's work may have had one reason in the work's specifically 'non-aesthetical' from of appearance, which are not only a result of Graham's functionalizing of formal concerns, but which are probably also the result of an entirely different approach to those historical sources of constructivism that had become a point of reference in american art since Stella and which had finally received a 'formalist' reading by the generation of the minimal artists, if only reluctantly acknowledged, like in a sentence by Donald Judd in 1974: "With and since Malevich the several aspects of the best art have been single, like unblended Scotch. Free."[7]

Dan Graham and the Minimal Heritage
"The split between art and real problems emerged in the Sixties in an essentially apolitical and asocial art - to the extent that, for most artists, political engagement meant moving to an extra art activity...The neutrality which this art assumes excludes the possibility of a critical relation to a capitalist form of life." [8]
Formalism in aesthetical practice and the correlating equivalent, and entrepreneurs' morality have not been the original position of the Minimal generation. They had not only oriented their formal and material strategies according to constructivist axioms, but also attempted to reactivate their socio-political implications. This meant demanding an objective functionalism of materials which had to originate from technological products and processes, an unlimited capacity of technical reproduction as well as its dialectical counterpart, namely the idea of the unique and specific work which could only find its actual function and realization in a particular segment of the time/space continuum, and finally the abolition of the artwork's commodity status and the attempt to replace its exchange and exhibition value with a new concept of functional use value.

Even though Flavin may not have understood or appreciated Graham's work, this is not true for the opposite: Graham has frequently pointed out how important his knowledge and understanding of Flavin's work has been to his own development as an artist. And it remains an open question whether the work of the elder artist offered in fact the complexity of aspects that Graham discerned in it, or whether he read those aspects into the work that should become the key issues in his own artistic production, thus anticipating his own future development by projecting it onto the historical screen of the predecessor's work. Especially the transformation of 'formalist' terms into a more 'functionalist' context could be called to be one of the essential qualities Graham's work has introduced into the visual arts around 1965. For example Flavin's (and equally Andre's and LeWitt's) notion of 'place' - the fact that the work referred to the gallery space as the spatial container - and the notion of 'presence' which had meant in Flavin's work that an installation was contingent on its present time situation, furthermore being specifically conceived for one particular architectural situation, became key issues in Graham's early conceptual work as well as in his critical analytical writings which preceded his development of performance, film and video works.

This transformation from plastic-material modes of analyzing perceptual (aesthetical) processes to literal-verbal analyses and conceptualization takes obviously place in Graham's descriptions of the work of Andre, Flavin, Judd, Nauman, Serra and LeWitt, which Graham wrote and published starting in 1965. Therefore it seems adequate to read these texts more as artistic arguments indicating the development of new forms of aesthetic work rather than as art criticism. On a first level of reading, these critical texts open up a historical perspective through their minute descriptive precision, in as much as they show basic principles of Minimalism to be derivatives of constructivist fundamentals. All of these for example appear as though catalogued in Graham's analysis of Carl Andre's sculpture "*Crib, Compound, Coin*" (1965) as well as in a description of Flavin's work, both published in 1967: "Fluorescent light objects in place are re-placeable in various contingently determined interdependent relations with specific environmental relations and are also replaceable from their fixture and in having a limited existence. The components of a particular exhibition upon its termination are re-placed in another situation - perhaps put to a non-art use as a part of a different whole in a different future."

Or even more systematically and explicitly on Andre:
"The component units possessed no intrinsic significance beyond their immediate contextual placement being 'replaceable'. Works are impossessible by the viewer in the monetary sense, the sense of an artist being possessed of a vision or of a satisfying personal inner needs of the viewer. Unweighted with symbolic transcendental or redeeming monetary values, Andre's sculpture does not form some platonically substantial body, but is recoverable; for which no one may be poetically transported from view when the exhibition is terminated (the parts having been recovered and perhaps put to an entirely non-related use as part of a whole in a different future)."[10]

A second reading would be the historicity of the writings themselves, from a present point of view, their acuity in the way they denote almost systematically all the elementary principles of visual thinking as they had been developed by minimal art practice. At the same time these texts connote by the very precision of their verbal apprehension of the visual facticity, the change of the artistic procedure into concepts of verbalized materiality and materialized language. This has been quite accurately observed by Robert Smithson, who as early as 1967 seems to have seen, more clearly than Flavin, the historical and aesthetic implications of Graham's writings and photographical works as being those of a new definition of art axioms (updating modes of aesthetic production to the general standards of means of recognition) and thus further approaching them to their use value potential: "Like some of the other artists Graham can 'read' the language of buildings ("*Homes for America*", 1966), ... The reading of both buildings and grammars, enables the artist to avoid out of date appeals to 'function' or 'utilitarianism'."[11]

In most of his writings Dan Graham has reflected on the double nature of those processes, in as much as they could be formalized and integrated into the context of his work by referring to them with the term 'in-formation', thus indicating that to him formal procedures as well as their material content are invisible units. The materiality of the formal processes in Graham's works could therefore be called 'specific' in the sense originally coined by Donald Judd for painterly-sculptural works of the minimal phase: "Materials vary greatly and are simply materials - formica, aluminum, cold-rolled steel, plexiglass, red and common brass and so forth. They are specific. Also they are usually aggressive."[12]

Graham's critical analysis of the formal and material heritage of minimal aesthetics not only seems to have led him to the discovery that these artists' ideas about materiality were in fact rather traditional and positivist (oriented at a constructivist craft ethos), but moreover he seems to have acknowledged that their original radicality in questioning the role of the artwork in its social context had been given up and that minimal work had been restored easily into the commodity status acquiring exchange value in as much as they gave up their context-bound idea of use value. Therefore, the materials of reality are with Graham no longer simply 'found objects' or the 'ready-made elements' of technological everyday reality as they are in Flavin's fluorescent lights or even Andre's metallurgical elements (these being much more technologically 'cultivated' than their elementary 'natural' look might at first reveal), but rather the found structures beyond visible reality and its seeming concreteness, thus determining reality, however, with a more subtle and effective impact: equally the psycho-physiological motivations of subjective behavior of the socio-economical conditions of objective political practice, or even more precisely, the omnipresent mechanisms of interdependence of those systems in the acutely observed situations of their joined effects.

Graham's authentically 'conceptual' early magazine publications, which were written before the critical articles on fellow artists, had the conventional standard magazine page as a formal ground and common denominator, they were in a sense about 'themselves'. These works like "*Figurative*" (1965), "*Schema*" (1966) or "*Detumescence*" (1966) which were among the first artworks - if not the very first at all - to be published in magazine-advertisement form, sum up the reflection of Minimal presuppositions by translating them into an entirely different formal language. The historical distance and degrees of differentiation that have been actually achieved by Graham's theoretical thought as well as by his aesthetical production can be easily understood by comparing Judd's position regarding materials of art objects and Graham's attitude towards the materiality of art in his "*Other Observations*" (1969), a text written as a later comment on his "*Schema*" (1966), which reads in parts almost as a word for word comparative study and critique of minimalist formal thought and its transformation: "A page of "*Schema*" exists as a matter of fact materiality and simultaneously semiotic signifier of this

material (present): as a sign it unites, therefore, signifier and signified.(...) In the internal logic, there is the paradox that the concept of 'materiality' referred to by the language is to the language itself as some 'immaterial' material (a kind of mediumistic ether) and simultaneously is to it as the extensive space. There is a 'shell' placed between the external 'empty' material of place and the interior 'empty' material of 'language', (systems of) information (in-formation) exist halfway between material and concept, without being either one."[13]

The consequent radicality of Graham's formal procedure to reduce "*Schema*" to a mere formula of self-referential reflectivity, finds its dialectical material equivalent in his decision to publish this work in the context of a (art) magazine advertisement, as Graham has pointed out in later notes on "*Schema*": "But, unlike a Stella painting, for example, the variants of "*Schema*" are not simply self-referential. This is because of the use of the magazine system support. Magazines determine a place or a frame of reference both outside and inside what is defined as 'Art'. Magazines are boundaries (mediating) between the two areas...between gallery 'Art' and communications about 'Art'."[14]

Thus Graham is clearly attempting to include the analytical reflection on those determining elements which had been ignored before, the different aspects of the socio-economical framework as well as the individual's psychological framework which conditions the production as well as the reception of the artwork, and by inverting his perspective from formalist concerns to functionalist strategies makes them the very subject matter of his art. Again Graham's own retrospect comment is most illuminating in regard to the transformational changes that his work initiated in comparison to the given (art) historical conditions:

"It was interesting then, that aesthetically (but not functionally, that is, in material, economic terms) some of the Minimal Art seemed to refer to the gallery interior space as the ultimate frame or structural support/context and that some Pop Art referred to the surrounding media-world of cultural information as framework. But the frame (specific media-form or gallery/museum as economic entity concerned with value) was never made structurally apparent. "*Schema*"'s strategy was to reduce these two frameworks, to coalesce them into one frame so that they were made more apparent and the 'art product' would be radically de-valued. I wanted to make a 'Pop' Art which was more literally disposable (an idea which was alluded to in Warhol's idea of replacing 'quality' for 'quantity' - the logic of a consumer society), I wanted to make an art-form which could not be reproduced or exhibited in a gallery/museum. And I wanted to make a further reduction of the Minimal object to a not necessarily aesthetic two - dimensional form (which was not painting or drawing): printed matter which is mass reproduced and mass disposable information. Putting it in magazine pages meant that is also could be 'read' in juxtaposition to the usual second-hand art criticism, reviews, reproductions in the rest of the magazine and would form a critique of the functioning of the magazine (in relation to the gallery structure)."[15]

Therefore Graham's "*Schema*" (1966) and the later comments like "*Other Observations*" (1969) or his "*Magazine/Advertisements*" (1969), starting with the sentence "Art is a social sign", have to be read along with Daniel Buren's "Limites critiques" (1969) (published in English as "Critical Limits" in 1973) [16] as one of the first and most relevant attempts of that period to make art's most extraneous, repressed and camouflaged conditions obvious and invert them to become art's subject matter. Ahead of Hans Haacke's somewhat comparable reflections twenty years ago (published under the title of *Framing and being framed:7 Works 1970-75*, Halifax/New York, 1975) Graham's framework analysis differs considerably from both Buren's and Haacke's work. Different from Buren who reflects on the historical and museological determinations of the artwork, and other than Haacke who takes as well the social conditioning of art reception into consideration as well as art's historical transformation by becoming an object of capital investment, Graham analyzes in particular the general social conditions of production and reproduction of (art) information, and their formal and material consequences (see also later his "*Income/Outflow*", 1969)

Graham's processes -in comparison to Judd's "*Specific Objects*"- are specific in a threefold manner: first in regard to their proper epistemological and historical context (i.e. the visual arts) as they dialectically reflect and transcend the given conditions of minimal aesthetics; second in their relation to objective methodology, which consciously and clearly inserts them into a context of more general principles of (recognition) production, like for example their explicit dependence on semiology. And finally Graham's works could be called specific because of their very concrete reference to a particular segment of reality. It is not at last for this reason that Graham's works, his 'specific processes', seem to lack any surface of visual-aesthetic attractivity, which would more easily allow them to be read in a cultural context of art history. On the other hand their lack of surface aesthetics, rooted in their potential function, their insistence on the idea to reinvest the artwork with a potential use value, makes them more similar to certain works of productivist art than superficial comparison might recognize. It is precisely this lack of aesthetic attraction which denounces all forms of reconciliation that more craft oriented artworks bring into the world as cultural commodities. Their service to the dominating principles are among others the attempt to restore art into its traditional role, namely that of functioning as the mere decorum of the ruling order.

Graham's 'Subject Matter' and Post Minimalism

Dan Graham's complication of critical paraphrases, which was first published in 1969 in his privately edited "End Moments" under the title "*Subject Matter*", indicated in its subtitle the paradigmatical change which was going on in the visual arts around 1965: "1. the subject (rather than the object), 2. matter

(as process not as object)." This collection of 'art-critical' writings which includes one of Graham's earliest pieces on Donald Judd (1964) as well as his in the time latest analysis of his viewing experience of a performance work by Bruce Nauman (1969), goes further than the pieces discussed in its attempt to overcome the Minimalist presuppositions. "*Subject Matter*" in part has even to be considered as a reviewing and critical reflection of Graham's own work of the "*Schema*" period that he felt still somehow to be part of the "non-anthropomorphic ideology of late 60's New York Minimal Art". Parallel to these writings Graham initiates his own first activities, within which he transformed the notions of visual and spatial concretions into the less 'aesthetical' but yet more concise and immediate perceptual modes of experience, 'acted out' by actual performers. Graham's concern for the immediacy of the perceptual experience shows that he consequently pursued the reductivist approach to art that had been induced by Stella and had been at issue all through Minimalism and that he quite necessarily arrived at a concern for the 'behavior' of people themselves, their actual practice of perception (the subject) instead of a concern for their behavior in relation to a perceived sculptural object. As Graham has been most lucidly describing and analyzing the gradual shift from the Minimalist object into the post minimal processual attitudes, he seems to have undergone in his own work a similar change, however, quite as specific and consistent in his attitude, as his works of the "*Schema*" period had been. Again the starting point of reflection goes back to Graham's perception of Flavin's work as he has been describing it in retrospect: "I liked that as a side effect of Flavin's fluorescents the gallery walls became a 'canvas'. The lights dramatized the people (like 'spotlights') in a gallery - throwing the content of the exhibition onto the people in the process of perceiving: the gallery interior cube itself became the real framework..."[17]

In Graham's essay on Sol LeWitt this reading of a sculptural work and its apprehension in a manner which is announcing the future development that Graham's own art was going to take, is even more explicit: "As the viewer moves from point to point about the art object the physical continuity of the walk is translated into illusive self-representing depth: the visual complication of representations 'develops' a discrete, non-progressive space and time. There is no distinction between subject and object. Object is the viewer - the art and subject is the viewer, the art. Object and subject are not dialectical oppositions but one self-contained identity: reversible interior and exterior termini. All frames of reference read simultaneously: object/subject." [18]
This reveals at the same time the absolutely consequent logic of the extension of 'formalist' concerns into the more 'functional' reality of Graham's later performance activities as it elucidates the strictly non-literary and non-theatrical quality of Graham's understanding of performance activities. 'Acting' in the context of visual arts is relevant only in as much as it performs the elementary procedure of perceiving the network of relationships between performer and perceiver, both being

simultaneously subject and object, as Graham had observed in detail when confronted with the works of Bruce Nauman and his performance practices whose description in "*Subject Matter*" clearly show the process of assimilation and transformation of Nauman's impact on Graham's future work. In a comment on "*Subject Matter*", in particular its parts concerning the musical and performance influences on Graham's thought, he has clearly described the importance of these phenomena for his own development:
"I had the idea of the reciprocal inter-dependence of perceiver (spectator) and the perceived art-object/or the artist as performer (who might in the case of Nauman present himself as or in place of this 'object'). In this new subject-object relation the spectator's perceptual processes were correlated to the compositional process (which was also inherent in the material...thus a different idea of 'material' and the relation of this materiality to nature(-al) processes was also developed). This change in compositional process came from the developments in music and dance...where the performer or performance was the center of the work, executed and perceived in a durational time continuum.
This was the opposite of Minimal Art's durationless 'presence'... a series of discontinuous instances, related by a generating self-contained compositional idea (which was a priorio to the performance
or execution of the piece). From music also came the idea of the physiological presence ... a work about the perceptual proces itself, taking place simultaneously as an external phenomenon and inside the brain as part of the brain's interior process (...) "*Subject Matter*" was written at the same time as my first films and performances. I wanted to explain these new types of works I was relating to." [19]

The outline of Graham's interests and strategies of his formal enterprises appear in the writings and in the works as what one could call a microscopical analysis of segments of the processes of history itself, their given structures as well as the modes of perceiving them, as well as the perceptives of analyzing and transforming them. And it is to the degree that the analysis succeeds in mediating the patterns of a given reality structure (individual behavior, modes of interaction like for example the subtle processual revealing of stereotyped male-female role behavior in his video-performance "*Two Consciousness Projections*" (1972), the gradual increase of awareness of group-behavior versus individual behavior in performances like "*Intention/Intentionality Sequence*" (1972) or "*Performer/Audience Sequence*" (1974) and the open structure inducing and elucidating the mechanisms of group identification in his "*Public Space/Two Audiences*" (1974) - their processual mechanics as well as their reified dynamics) that the works open up an instrumental perspective of further historical proceedings (thus endowing the viewer with what he experiences as their artwork quality, their aesthetical value).

Epilogue on the Idea of Use Value

"A spindle maintains itself as use value only by being used for spinning. Otherwise, by the specific form which has been given to the wood or metal, both the work which produced the form and the material which was shaped by the form, would be spoiled for use. Only by being applied as a medium of active work, as an objective moment in its very being, are the use value of wood and metal as well as the form, maintained."
(Karl Marx, *Notizen zur Grundrisse der Kritik der Politischen Ökonomie*, Moskau, 1938)

Use value in art-aesthetic's most heteronomous counterpart - defining the artistic activity as organon of history, as instrument of materialist recognition and transformation, determines itself primarily and finally by its historical context: as it can only result from the most advanced state of aesthetic reflection it must function at the same time within the specific conditions of a given particular historical situation.
For example the artist as engineer in revolutionary Russia was in fact a functional and aesthetic necessity, whereas the constructivist engineering aesthetics forty years later in the era of monopoly necessesarily functions merely as art.. Those restorations however on the formal surfaces of social reality effect the contrary of their original intentions as can be clearly seen in the development of architecture since Constructivism and the Bauhaus. On the other hand, if artistic production gives up altogether the idea of use value, it abolishes its own inherent potential to cause dialectics within the reality of cultural history, thus producing mere artistic facticity incapable of initiating further processes of development. This seems to be true of much current post-conceptual work, either the so called 'new' painting and sculpture and even more so the photographic stories and the new theatricality of performances, - all of which show the features of a decadence in art which is deprived of its inherent and innate demand to cause effects in reality, to exist otherwise than just aesthetically, to have a functional potential of historical recognition (thus much present-day art is either infantile or demonic pretension, either decorative or dramatic, as it has nothing 'to do' but being 'art' and somewhat new). These works' false vivacity which seems to denounce the rigorous abstraction of the best conceptual art and reacts against the tautological cul de sac of conceptual academicism at its worst, does not seem aware of the fact that art, once having been transformed onto the level of language, had achieved a state of most advanced (potential) communicatability and thus endowed the artwork with its highest form of abstract use value potential.
One could hypothetically argue then, that if present-day aesthetic language does not maintain either notion in its acute and necessary tendency and claim for a new body of material reality, as well as the general level of abstraction achieved by language and its counterpart the concretion of a specific use value potential (as it does most efficiently in the recent works of Dan Graham or equally in those of Michael Asher, Daniel Buren and Lawrence Weiner) then art gives ignorantly in to the general conditions of production and therefore,

on the level of superstructure reflects and shares their dilemma: "Boredom, resulting from the experience of destroyed use value, until now a problem of the privileged, has now also become a problem of the masses. The avoidance of proletarian revolution enables the capitalist development to take a final step in completing its basic apory: namely to produce wealth by destroying use value. What will be left over in the end is the unresisted and unquestioned production of simple trash."[20]

1 See Battock, Gregory (ed.), "Photographs by Dan Graham", *Minimal Art*, New York, 1968, p. 175.

2 Lippard, Lucy, *Six Years, the Dematerialization of the Art Object*, New York, 1973, p. 155.

3 Flavin, Dan, "Some other Remarks", *Artforum*, December 1967, p. 27. Sol LeWitt at the same time seems to have had quite a different understanding of Graham's photographical work which is proven by the fact that he included one of Graham's photographs as illustration for his ."Paragraphs on Conceptual Art", *Artforum*, Summer 1967.

4 Sharp, Willoughby, "Interview with Carl Andre", *Avalanche*, 1970.

5 Dan Graham in a letter to the author.

6 Barthes, Roland, "L'activité structuraliste", *Essais Critiques*, Paris 1964, p. 216.

7 Judd, Donald, "Malevich", *Complete Writings*, Halifax/New York 1975, p. 212.

8 Beveridge, Karl, Ian Burn, "Donald Judd", *The Fox*, no.2, 1975, p. 129 ff.

9 Graham, Dan, *Dan Flavin*, cat. Museum of Contemporary Art, Chicago 1967, reprinted partly in: Graham, Dan, *End Moments*, New York 1969, p. 15.

10 Graham, Dan, "Carl Andre", *Arts Magazine*, no.3, New York, 1967, p. 34.

11 Smithson, Robert, "A Museum of Language in the Vicinity of Art", *Art International* no.3, 1968, p. 22.

12 Judd, Donald, "Specific Objects", Contemporary Sculpture (1965), *Arts Yearbook* VII, p. 74-83. Reprinted in: *Complete Writings*, loc.cit. p. 181.

13 Graham, Dan, "Other Observations", *For Publication*, Otis Art Institute of Los Angeles County, Los Angeles 1975, n.p.

14 Dan Graham in a letter to the author.

15 ibid.

16 On his relationship to the work of Daniel Buren, Graham commented as follows: "I found out about Buren's theory and works many years later. I think of them as a clear advancement on Flavin's, Judd's, LeWitt's positions. It now seems to me that some of the ideas in "*Schema*" foreshadow aspects of Buren's theory/practice (I don't think he knew about the piece until 1970...although it is possible that he did, as it was published in *Art & Language* in 1968)." (in a letter to the author)..

17 ibid.

18 Graham, Dan, "Sol LeWitt - Two Structures", *End Moments*, loc. cit. p. 65.

19 In a letter to the author.

20 Pohrt, Wolfgang, *Theorie des Gebrauchswertes*, Frankfurt, 1976.

Moments d'histoire dans l'oeuvre de Dan Graham (1977)

Benjamin H.D. Buchloh

Pour caractériser son oeuvre, Dan Graham employa un jour le mot de 'photojournalisme'[1], ironisant sur le terme employé par Marcel Duchamp pour décrire ses propres activités. C'était une manière d'accréditer une fausse définition et un malentendu suscités par son travail dès 1965 . Lucy Lippard, au cours d'une discussion avec Carl Andre, Jan Dibbets et Douglas Huebler en 1970, posait la question suivante: "Dan, on t'a considéré comme un poète, un critique, et un photographe. Es-tu un artiste, maintenant?"[2]

Les contemporains de Dan Graham, et ses amis artistes de la période minimaliste même, dont les recherches avaient trouvé dans son travail de critique analytique depuis 1965 une référence extrêmement élaborée, refusaient de reconnaître - faute d'avoir compris son travail visuel - que certains concepts fondamentaux en matière d'arts visuels avaient évolué, précisément depuis 1965 . Dan Flavin, par exemple, même s'il fut parmi les premiers à s' intéresser à son travail, et le premier à publier une de ses photographies, écrivait à propos de "*Homes for America*" (1966): "Ton utilisation remarquable de la photographie peut faire penser à la clarté logique, directe et sans stratagème de la méthode de reportage de Cartier-Bresson, que tu appliquerais non à des personnes comme il le fait mais à leurs "miracles" en matière de paysage et d'architecture vernaculaires."[3] Cette comparaison erronée est très révélatrice de l'ironie de l'histoire: elle montre que du point de vue des minimalistes, une information ou une documentation photographiques ne pouvaient absolument pas être considérées comme de l'art (sinon de l'art 'photographique'). Le malentendu révèle, plus encore, un désir inconscient de nier radicalement la portée novatrice de l'activité post-minimaliste, en établissant une relation entre les photographies de Dan Graham et cette idéologie particulièrement réactionnaire que représente le "moment décisif" de Cartier-Bresson. De tels photographes tentent de faire de leur activité réceptive et passive le medium d'enregistrement de l'instant historique qu'ils voudraient transférer, intact, dans sa transsubstantiation photographique - tandis que le propos de Graham est au contraire d'élaborer, au moyen de la photographie, des modèles fonctionnels d'identification de l'histoire réelle.

"*Homes for America* "(1966), l'une de ses premières oeuvres (avec "*Schema*", qui date également de 1966) les plus complexes et les plus pertinentes, servira d'exemple. Ce travail de 'photojournalisme', dont il a parlé comme d'une pièce de "transition entre les premières pages 'conceptuelles' de magazine et les articles de 1967 -1969" est parti de cette idée, courante à l'époque, que l'information concernant les oeuvres d'art circule avant tout grâce à leur reproduction dans les medias (artistiques). Ce que décrivait Carl Andre, par exemple, en 1968: "La photographie ment. Je crains que nous n'ayions accès à l'art, en général, qu'au travers de reproductions et de magazines, et je considère cela dramatique et contraire à l'art, puisque l'art est de l'ordre d'une expérience directe avec quelque chose, dans le monde, tandis que la photographie n'est qu'une rumeur, une espèce de pornographie de l'art."[4] Or c'est précisément à partir de cette notion d'anti-art, de "pornographie", que commence à travailler Dan Graham; cette manière de prendre à rebours le mépris de Carl Andre pour les medias, en en faisant la base même de sa stratégie et de son oeuvre est caractéristique de son attitude post-minimaliste.

Graham a commenté cette oeuvre clé dans une description qui reprend le principe du tressage des relations entre forme et histoire (de l'art), ainsi que les renversements dialectiques de l'oeuvre: " Il est important, a-t-il précisé, que les photographies ne soient pas regardées seules, mais comme faisant partie intégrante de la mise en page de l'article. Ce sont des illustrations du texte et, à l'inverse, le texte fonctionne en relation étroite avec les photographies, dont elles modifient le sens. Les photographies et le texte ne sont que les éléments doubles d'une même grille de lecture. Les photographies sont liées aux listes en série et aux colonnes de la documentation écrite; les unes comme les autres 'représentent' la logique sérielle du développement suburbain dont traite l'article. L'idée de départ était de se servir de l'environnement extérieur réel comme d'un 'site' sur lequel construire des oeuvres conceptuelles ou de land art. Mais, (il ne faut pas oublier que j'ai écrit cet article bien avant les travaux de Smithson ou d'Oppenheim) ce qui me semble le plus important, finalement, c'est que "*Homes for America*" n'ait été précisément qu'un article de revue, sans prétendre d'aucune manière au statut d' "oeuvre d'art ."[5]

Le support informatif de la page de magazine devient ainsi la structure formelle 'trouvée'. A ceci s'ajoute la structure d'une 'réalité trouvée', en l'occurrence la misère des logements des zones industrielles. De plus les caractéristiques stylistiques et formelles de ces logements, - l'ordonnancement des maisons cubiques, le principe de l'interchangeabilité des éléments séparés mais répétitifs, dont l'ensemble constitue l'intégrité d'un dispositif donné - rappellent d'une manière évidemment ironique et ambigüe les principes formels et stylistiques de la sculpture minimaliste. La confrontation dialectique de la structure du réel et de la structure de la forme, le désir d'associer 'architecture et grammaire' - systèmes du réel et systèmes formels - caractérisent les premiers textes et les premiers travaux de Dan Graham, et les classent dans la catégorie du simulacre de l'objet d'histoire défini par Barthes: "...un simulacre dirigé, intéressé, puisque l'objet imité fait apparaître quelque chose qui restait invisible, ou si l'on préfère, inintelligible dans l'objet naturel ... le simulacre, c'est l'intellect ajouté à l'objet, et cette addition a une valeur anthropologique, en ceci qu'elle est l'homme même, son histoire, sa situation, sa liberté et la résistance même que la nature oppose à son esprit."[6]

On peut peut-être expliquer le malentendu général sur l'oeuvre de Dan Graham, et sa reconnaissance tardive, par la forme spécifiquement 'non-esthétique' qu'il lui a donnée: ce qui n'est pas seulement, de sa part, une manière de rendre plus efficaces ses parti pris formels, mais la conséquence d'une approche radicalement différente des origines historiques du constructivisme, devenu la référence de l'art américain depuis Stella, et que les artistes minimalistes avaient fini par réduire à une interprétation "formaliste". Ce qu'ils n'ont reconnu qu'à demi-mot, comme dans cette phrase de Don Judd (1974): "Avec et depuis Malevitch, tout ce qui s'est fait de mieux dans l'art est d'une parfaite simplicité. Comme du whisky pur. Libre."[7]

Dan Graham et l'héritage minimaliste
"Le divorce entre l'art et la réalité est apparu à travers l'art fondamentalement apolitique et asocial des années 1960. A cette époque s'engager sur un plan politique signifiait pour la plupart des artistes, changer d'activité...La neutralité affichée par cet art excluait toute possibilité d'une critique du mode de vie capitaliste."[8] Ni le formalisme, sur le plan de la pratique esthétique, ni son corollaire, la valeur éthique de l'entreprise, n'ont été inventés par les minimalistes. Ils n'ont pas seulement aligné leurs stratégies matérielles et formelles sur les principes constructivistes, ils ont également voulu actualiser leur portée socio-politique. Cela supposait d'exiger des matériaux un fonctionnalisme objectif; d'appliquer le modèle des produits et des procédés technologiques; d'avoir un potentiel illimité de reproduction technique ainsi que sa contre-partie dialectique: l'idée d'une oeuvre singulière et spécifique, qui ne trouverait sa fonction et sa réalisation effectives que dans un segment bien précis du continuum spatio-temporel; cela supposait enfin d'abolir le statut de l'oeuvre d'art comme commodité, et de remplacer sa valeur d'échange et d'exposition par une conception nouvelle, la valeur d'usage fonctionnel.

Bien que Flavin semble n'avoir ni compris ni apprécié l'oeuvre de Graham, celui-ci a souvent évoqué, en revanche, l'importance qu'avaient eue pour l'évolution de son propre travail la pratique et l'étude de l'oeuvre de Flavin. Et aujourd'hui encore on peut se demander si cette oeuvre est aussi complexe que voulait bien le prétendre Dan Graham, ou s'il lui prêtait à l'époque certains aspects de cette complexité qui allaient fonder sa propre production artistique, projetant ainsi sa future évolution sur l'écran historique de l'oeuvre de son prédécesseur. Pour être plus précis, on peut considérer l'évolution du sens de certains termes 'formalistes' à l'intérieur d'un contexte devenu plus 'fonctionnaliste', comme une des caractéristiques essentielles apportées par l'oeuvre de Graham aux arts visuels autour de 1965: la notion de 'lieu', par exemple, - le fait que l'oeuvre se réfère à la galerie comme contenant d'espace - ou celle de 'présence', qui avait

signifié dans l'oeuvre de Flavin la contingence d'une installation par rapport à sa situation actuelle, a fortiori quand l'installation était spécifiquement conçue pour un contexte architectural précis . Ces notions devinrent des données fondamentales des premières oeuvres conceptuelles de Dan Graham, comme de ses textes critiques et analytiques, juste avant l'époque des performances, films et travaux en vidéo.

Cette évolution des modes d'analyse des phénomènes de perception (esthétique) en termes plastiques et matériels vers une conceptualisation et un style d'analyse littérale et verbale apparaît clairement dans les textes sur les travaux d'Andre, Flavin, Judd, Nauman, Serra et LeWitt, écrits et publiés par Graham à partir de 1965. Il faut donc lire ces textes plus comme des débats artistiques signalant l'apparition de nouvelles formes de recherches esthétiques, que comme des textes de critique d'art proprement dits. A un premier niveau de lecture, ces textes critiques, d'une minutieuse précision, ouvrent une perspective historique en montrant en quoi les principes du minimalisme sont des dérivés des notions fondamentales du constructivisme. Toutes ces notions apparaissent répertoriées, par exemple, dans son analyse de la sculpture de Carl Andre "*Crib, Compound, Coin*" (1965), ou dans cette description d'une oeuvre de Flavin (les deux textes ont été publiés en 1967): "Les objets de lumière fluorescente placés dans la galerie peuvent être dé-placés selon de nouvelles relations d'interdépendance - déterminées par diverses contingences -, dans des environnements spécifiques; leur place à l'intérieur de l'installation peut également être modifiée; et ils ont un temps d'existence limité. Les éléments qui constituent une exposition, pendant toute sa durée, sont ensuite déplacés dans une situation différente jusqu'à perdre leur fonction artistique en devenant partie d'un tout différent projeté dans un futur différent."[9]

Ou de manière plus systématique et plus explicite à propos de Carl Andre: "Les unités de la composition n'avaient de signification intrinsèque qu'à condition d'être dé-plaçables de leur contexte immédiat. Le spectateur ne peut pas s'approprier une oeuvre au sens monétaire du terme; cela supposerait que l'artiste ait pu s'approprier le regard et les aspirations personnelles du spectateur. Privée de valeurs symboliques et transcendentales, ou monétaires et rédemptrices, la sculpture d'Andre ne forme pas une sorte de corps platoniquement substantiel, elle est "récupérable"; et on ne peut métaphoriquement jamais la soustraire à la vue de personne, une fois l'exposition terminée, puisque ses éléments seront récupérés et sans doute destinés à un usage sans rapport avec le précédent, intégrés dans un ensemble différent et projetés dans un futur différent."[10]

A un deuxième niveau de lecture apparaît l'historicité des écrits eux-mêmes, quand on les lit aujourd'hui, et la pertinence avec laquelle ils indiquent presque systématiquement tous les principes de pensée visuelle appliqués ensuite par les artistes minimalistes. Ces textes évoquent aussi, par une approche verbale très précise du fait visuel, l'évolution de la procédure artistique vers des concepts de verbalisation du matériau et de matérialisation du langage. Robert Smithson l'avait bien compris, au point de reconnaître, dès 1967 et avec plus de clarté que Flavin, que la portée historique et esthétique des écrits et des travaux photographiques de Dan Graham allait jusqu'à redéfinir les axiomes de l'art (rapportant les modes de production esthétique à leurs cadres de réception courants) et à les rapprocher ainsi de leur potentielle valeur d'usage: "Graham, comme quelques autres artistes, sait 'déchiffrer' le langage de l'architecture ("*Homes for America*" 1966)... L'analyse conjointe de l'architecture et de la grammaire permet à l'artiste d'éviter un recours périmé à la 'fonction' ou à l''utilitarisme'." [11]

Dan Graham s'est penché, dans la plupart de ses textes, sur ce double phénomène, dans la mesure où il pouvait le formaliser et l'intégrer dans le contexte de son travail en y faisant référence sous le terme d''in-formation'; ce qui était une manière d'indiquer que selon lui, les procédures formelles et leur contenu matériel étaient indissociables. La matérialité des procédés formels des travaux de Dan Graham peut donc être qualifiée de 'spécifique', selon le mot employé par Donald Judd pour désigner les travaux de sculpture-peinture de l'époque minimaliste: "Les matériaux varient énormément, et sont simplement des matériaux: formica, aluminium, acier laminé à froid, plexiglas, cuivre rouge ou ordinaire, etc . Ils sont spécifiques.... En outre, ils sont habituellement agressifs." [12]

L' analyse critique par Dan Graham de l'héritage formel et matériel de l'esthétique minimaliste semble non seulement lui avoir révélé le caractère traditionnel et positiviste des idées de ces artistes sur le matériau (inspirées de la morale constructiviste du 'métier'), mais également lui avoir fait prendre conscience que les interrogations radicales des débuts, sur le rôle de l'oeuvre d'art dans son contexte social, avaient disparu; et que les oeuvres minimalistes avaient tranquillement acquis une valeur d'échange et donc le statut de 'commodité', dès l'instant où elles avaient renoncé à l'idée de la valeur d'usage liée au contexte. Dès lors ces matériaux prélevés dans la réalité cessèrent d'être, selon Graham, des 'objets trouvés' ou des 'éléments ready-made' de la réalité technologique quotidienne, comme c'est le cas des lumières fluorescentes de Flavin ou même des éléments métallurgiques de Carl Andre (ces derniers étant beaucoup plus sophistiqués, sur un plan technologique, que ne le laisse penser de prime abord leur aspect 'naturel' élémentaire); ils devinrent les structures trouvées sous la réalité visible et sous son apparence tangible, qui déterminent en fait cette réalité en produisant sur elle un effet plus subtil, et plus efficace: il s'agit des ressorts psychophysiologiques du comportement subjectif, des conditions socioéconomiques de la pratique politique objective, ou même plus précisément, des mécanismes omniprésents d'interdépendance de ces systèmes, au point précis et repérable où leurs effets se conjuguent.

Les premières publications strictement conceptuelles de Dan Graham, parues avant ses articles critiques sur ses amis artistes, avaient comme dénominateur commun et comme support formel la page de magazine standard, conventionnelle, et se prenaient donc en quelque sorte elles-mêmes pour objet. "*Figurative*" (1965), "*Schema* "(1966), ou "*Détumescence*" (1966), qui sont parmi les premiers travaux artistiques - si ce n'est les tout premiers - à paraître sous forme de publicité de magazine, reprennent les principes minimalistes en les transposant dans un langage formel entièrement différent. On comprend facilement la distance historique et les nuances produites par la pensée théorique et la production artistique de Graham si on compare le point de vue de Judd sur le matériau d'objet d'art et celui de Graham sur la matérialité de l'art en général, qu'il expose dans un texte de 1969, intitulé "*Other Observations*". Ce texte fut écrit sous la forme d'un commentaire rétrospectif de "*Schema*"(1966), et il doit se lire pour ainsi dire comme une étude critique et comparative, terme à terme, de la pensée minimaliste et de son évolution: "Une page de "*Schema*" existe à la fois sous la forme d'un fait matériel et concret, et sous celle du signifiant sémiotique de ce fait (actuel): en tant que signe il associe donc signifiant et signifié... A l'intérieur de cette logique, il reste ce paradoxe que ce concept de 'matérialité' auquel on se réfère par le langage, fonctionne vis à vis du langage lui-même à la fois comme une sorte de matériel 'immatériel' (quelque chose comme un ether 'mediumnique') et comme l'espace dans son extension. Il y a un 'creux' entre le matériau extérieur vide que constitue le lieu et le matériau intérieur, également vide, que constitue le langage; des systèmes d'information (in-formation) existent, à mi-chemin entre matériau et concept, sans participer entièrement ni de l'un ni de l'autre ." [13]

Le radicalisme de Graham, dans sa démarche formelle, quand il réduit "*Schema*" à une pure formule de reflectivité auto-référentielle, trouve un écho dialectique et matériel dans sa décision de publier ce travail sous la forme d'une publicité de magazine (d'art), comme il l'a lui-même précisé dans ses notes postérieures à cette publication: "Mais, contrairement à ce qui se produit pour un tableau de Stella, par exemple, les variantes de "*Schema*" ne sont pas simplement auto-référentielles. Et ceci parce que j'utilise le système du magazine comme support. Les magazines définissent un lieu ou un cadre de référence à la fois extérieur et intérieur à ce qu'on appelle l''Art'. Les magazines sont à l'interférence de deux domaines....celui des galeries d' 'Art', et celui de la communication sur l''Art'..." [14]

Il s'agit donc clairement pour Graham d'entreprendre une réflexion analytique sur ces éléments déterminants, et jusqu'alors négligés que sont les différents aspects du contexte socio-économique et de la psychologie individuelle, - qui conditionnent la production et la réception de l'oeuvre d'art - et de faire de ces stratégies fonctionnalistes, qui ont remplacé ses préoccupations formelles, le sujet même de son oeuvre. Ce même commentaire de "*Schema*" éclaire parfaitement les modifications apportées, par son travail, au contexte historique (artistique) de ces années-là: "Ce qu'il y avait d'intéressant à l'époque, c'est que, sur un plan 'esthétique' (et non fonctionnel, c'est à dire en termes matériels et économiques), certains artistes minimalistes semblaient se référer à l'espace intérieur de la galerie comme au cadre ou au contexte (ou support) structurel absolu, et que certains artistes du Pop Art prenaient, eux, comme référence absolue, le monde médiatique environnant de l'information culturelle. Mais le cadre lui-même (la structure des medias ou de la galerie/musée proprement dite, comme entité économique affectée d'une valeur) n'apparaissait jamais. La stratégie de "*Schema*" consistait à réduire ces deux contextes, à les fondre en un seul de manière à les rendre plus apparents, et à ce que le 'produit artistique' soit définitivement dé-valué. Je voulais faire du Pop Art qui soit littéralement accessible (ce qui figurait déjà dans l'idée de Warhol de remplacer la qualité par la quantité, selon la logique de la société de consommation). Je voulais trouver une forme artistique qui ne pourrait être ni reproduite ni exposée dans une galerie ou dans un musée, et je voulais réduire l'objet 'minimaliste' à une forme bi-dimensionnelle (ni peinture ni dessin) qui ne soit pas nécessairement d'ordre esthétique: d'où l'idée des imprimés, qui représentent de l'information reproduite à grande échelle et accessible à tout le monde. Publier ces travaux dans des pages de magazine signifiait aussi qu'ils seraient 'lus' au milieu des chroniques d'art, des articles et des reproductions, et qu'ils fonctionneraient par la même occasion comme une critique du magazine (et de la structure de la galerie simultanément)."[15]

Il faut donc considérer "*Schema*" (1966) - ainsi que ses commentaires postérieurs, comme "*Other Observations*" (1969) ou "*Magazine/Advertisement*" (1969) qui commence par la phrase "L'art est un signe social" -, avec le texte de Daniel Buren, *Limites Critiques* (1969)[16], comme les tentatives les plus pertinentes, à l'époque, de mettre en évidence les aspects de l'art les plus ignorés, les plus réprimés et camouflés, et d'en faire, à l'inverse, le sujet même du travail. Le cadre d'analyse de Graham se distingue sensiblement de celui de Buren et Haacke, avant même que Haacke ne tienne des propos semblables (publiés sous le titre *Framed and Being Framed: 7 Works 1970-75*, Halifax/New York, 1975) . La réflexion de Buren porte sur les déterminations historiques et muséologiques de l'oeuvre d'art; Haacke prend en considération le contexte social de réception de l'art ainsi que son évolution historique au moment où il devient un objet d'investissement capitaliste. Graham, lui, analyse de près les conditions sociales générales de la production et de la reproduction de l'information (artistique), ainsi que leurs conséquences sur le plan formel et matériel (voir aussi plus tard son article "*Income/Outflow*", qui date de 1969).

Les procédés de Graham - si on les compare aux "*Specific Objects*" de Judd - sont spécifiques à trois égards: tout d'abord si on considère leur contexte épistémologique et historique propre (c'est à dire les arts visuels), puisqu'ils transcendent et

reflètent dialectiquement les principes établis de l'esthétique minimaliste. Ensuite dans leur relation à une méthodologie objective, qui les place délibérément et clairement dans le contexte des principes généraux de la production, par leur dépendance explicite à l'égard de la sémiologie, par exemple. Ils sont spécifiques, enfin, par leur référence concrète à un aspect précis de la réalité. Cette spécificité n'est pour rien dans le fait que ces travaux, ces 'procédés spécifiques', semblent privés de la surface d'attrait visuel qui les rendrait plus acceptables et plus accessibles dans le contexte culturel de l'histoire de l'art. Mais cette absence de qualité esthétique, - que justifie leur fonction virtuelle -, et l'insistance sur l'idée que l'oeuvre d'art doit être réinvestie d'une potentielle valeur d'usage, apparente les travaux de Dan Graham à certaines oeuvres d'art productivistes mieux que ne saurait le faire une comparaison superficielle. Et c'est précisément cette absence d'attrait esthétique, enfin, qui dénonce tous ces faux consensus formés autour des oeuvres qui relèvent du 'métier', et qui abreuvent le monde en commodités culturelles. Placées au service des idées dominantes, ces productions contribuent à restaurer l'art dans son rôle traditionnel d'un pur décorum de l'ordre au pouvoir.

Le "Subject Matter" de Dan Graham et le post-minimalisme
Une élaboration des paraphrases critiques apparaissait pour la première fois dans "*End Moments*", publié par Dan Graham à compte d'auteur, sous le titre de "*Subject Matter*". L'évolution paradigmatique en cours dans les arts visuels autour de 1965 était évoquée par le sous-titre: 1) Le sujet (plutôt que l'objet). 2) Le matériau (comme processus et non comme objet). Ce recueil de textes de 'critique d'art', qui inclut l'un des premiers essais de Graham sur Donald Judd (1964) ainsi qu'une de ses premières analyses d'une performance de Bruce Nauman (1969), pousse encore plus loin sa remise en question des principes minimalistes. "*Subject Matter*" doit même être considéré comme une révision et une auto-critique de son travail de l'époque de "*Schema*", qu'il considère encore faire partie de "l'idéologie non-anthropomorphique de l'art minimaliste de la fin des années 1960 à New-York". Parallèlement à ces textes, Graham entreprend ses premières activités propres, au cours desquelles sa conception d'une réalisation visuelle et spatiale se transforme en un mode d'expérience moins 'esthétique', mais plus concis et plus direct, 'joué' par de vrais performers. Cet intérêt de Graham pour l'immédiateté de l'expérience de perception montre donc d'une part qu'il avait mis en question l'approche réductiviste de l'art à l'origine de laquelle se trouvait Stella, et à laquelle le minimalisme était resté fidèle; et d'autre part qu'il en était arrivé à s'intéresser au 'comportement' des gens eux-mêmes, à leur pratique réelle de la perception (au sujet), plutôt qu'à leur comportement en fonction de la perception d'un objet plastique. Au fur et à mesure qu'il observait, avec une parfaite lucidité, le passage de l'objet minimaliste aux attitudes processuelles du post-minimalisme, son propre travail semblait subir la même évolution, sans se départir pour autant de la singularité et de la cohérence caractéristiques de ses travaux

de l'époque de "*Schema*". Pour comprendre il faut revenir une fois de plus à la manière dont Graham a perçu l'oeuvre de Flavin, et à ce qu'il en a dit rétrospectivement: "J'aimais bien l'effet secondaire produit par les fluorescents de Flavin: les murs de la galerie devenaient comme des "toiles". Les lumières mettaient en scène les spectateurs (comme l'auraient fait des projecteurs) dans la galerie, projetant sur eux le contenu de l'exposition, au moment même où ils la percevaient; l'intérieur de la galerie, le cube lui-même, devenaient le cadre de l'oeuvre...." [17]

Cette appréhension de la sculpture, qui annonce les développements de son propre travail, est encore plus clairement exprimée dans son essai sur Sol LeWitt: "Tandis que le spectateur se déplace de point en point autour de l'objet d'art, la progression physique de la marche provoque un effet d'illusion de profondeur: la complexité visuelle de ces représentations 'produit' un espace-temps discontinu, sans progression. Il n'y a plus de distinction entre le sujet et l'objet. L'objet est le spectateur - l'art, et le sujet est le spectateur - l'art. L'objet et le sujet ne sont plus dialectiquement opposés, ils forment une seule identité qui s'auto-définit: un intérieur réversible et un extérieur terminal. On peut tout interpréter en fonction de cette double référence: objet/sujet." [18]

Tout ceci permet de comprendre selon quelle logique absolument cohérente les préoccupations "formalistes" de Graham ont évolué vers le réalisme plus "fonctionnel" de ses activités de performance; en même temps que cela rend plus clair sa conception strictement non-littéraire et non-théâtrale de la performance. "Le jeu" dans le domaine des arts visuels ne prend de sens qu'à condition de représenter le fonctionnement élémentaire de perception du réseau de relations entre le performer et le spectateur, chacun étant simultanément sujet et objet: ce qu'il avait parfaitement observé dans les travaux et dans les performances de Bruce Nauman, dont la description dans "*Subject Matter*" montre clairement la manière dont il a assimilé et transformé l'influence sur son propre travail. Parlant de "*Subject Matter*", et plus particulièrement des influences subies en matière de musique et de performance, Dan Graham a décrit clairement l'importance de tous ces phénomènes pour son évolution: "Je croyais à l'inter-dépendance entre celui qui perçoit (le spectateur) et l'objet d'art perçu, ou l'artiste comme performer (qui peut, dans le cas de Nauman, se présenter comme, ou à la place de, cet 'objet'). Dans cette nouvelle relation sujet-objet, le processus de perception du spectateur était lié au processus de composition (lequel était également inhérent au matériau.... Il s'ensuivait une nouvelle conception du matériau et de la relation de cette matérialité avec des processus naturels). Cette évolution des processus de composition venait de changements survenus dans la musique et la danse...où le performer, ou la performance, devenait le centre de l'oeuvre, exécutée et perçue dans un continuum temporel. C'était le contraire de la 'présence'

atemporelle de l'art minimal... une série d'instances discontinues, reliées par un principe de composition générateur, auto-défini (principe qui existe d'ailleurs en a priori d'une performance ou de l'éxécution d'une pièce). L'idée de la présence physiologique venait également de la musique....un travail sur le processus de perception lui-même, se produisant à la fois comme un phénomène extérieur, et à l'intérieur du cerveau, comme partie du fonctionnement interne du cerveau...(...) J'ai écrit "*Subject Matter*" en même temps que mes premiers films et mes premières performances. Je voulais expliquer quels nouveaux types de travaux j'abordais." [19]

Les axes de la pensée de Dan Graham et les stratégies de ses recherches formelles apparaissent dans les écrits et dans les oeuvres, sous la forme de ce qu'on pourrait appeler une analyse microscopique des segments des processus de l'histoire elle-même, de leurs structures de base, de leurs modes de perception, et de la perspective de leurs analyses et de leurs transformations. Cette analyse peut même servir de médiateur pour mettre à jour des schémas de structure d'une réalité donnée (le comportement individuel; les relations d'interférence, les comportements homme-femme types, par exemple, qu'il met subtilement à jour dans sa vidéo-performance "*Two Consciousness Projections*"; l'apparition d'une prise de conscience progressive dans les comportements de groupe, opposés aux comportements individuels [dans des performances comme "*Intention/Intentionality Sequence*", de 1972, ou "*Performance/Audience Sequence*", de 1974]; les mécanismes d'identification de groupe, présentés et résolus par la mise en place d'un dispositif précis [dans "*Public Spaces/Two Audiences*", 1974], leurs mécaniques processuelles aussi bien que leurs dynamiques de réification). Ces oeuvres ouvrent ainsi sur une perspective instrumentale de mise en acte de l'histoire, et confirment le spectateur dans l'expérience qu'il fait de leur qualité artistique, de leur valeur esthétique.

Epilogue sur l'idée de la valeur d'usage
"Un fuseau ne conserve sa valeur d'usage que s'il est utilisé pour filer. Faute de quoi, étant donné la forme spécifique donnée au bois et au métal, le travail qui a produit cette forme et le matériau qui a été mis en forme deviennent inutilisables. Le bois et le métal, ainsi que la forme qui leur a été donnée, ne conservent leur valeur d'usage que dans la mesure où ils sont mis en pratique comme moyen de travail effectif, comme un moment objectif dans sa plénitude."(Karl Marx, *Notizen zur Grundisse der Kritik des Politischen Okonomie*, Moscou, 1938).

La valeur d'usage - si on considère son équivalent dans l'histoire de l'art - qui définit l'activité artistique comme organe de l'histoire, comme instrument de transformation et d'identification matérialiste, se détermine au point de départ et à la fin par son contexte historique: puisqu'elle ne peut résulter que d'un stade très élaboré de réflexion artistique, elle doit fonctionner en même temps à l'intérieur des conditions

spécifiques d'une situation historique particulière donnée.
Par exemple l'artiste constructiviste et ingénieur, dans
la Russie révolutionnaire, correspondait en fait à une nécessité
fonctionnelle et esthétique, tandis que l'esthétique
constructiviste de l'ingénierie, quarante ans plus tard,
à l'époque du monopole, fonctionne nécessairement et
strictement comme art. Ces retours à l'ordre, même s'ils
affectent la surface apparente de la réalité sociale, obtiennent
le résultat inverse à leurs intentions de départ, comme on
le voit très bien dans l'évolution générale ou dans l'architecture
depuis le Constructivisme et le Bauhaus. D'autre part,
si la production artistique abandonne tout à fait l'idée de la
valeur d'usage, elle compromet son propre pouvoir de créer
de la dialectique à l'intérieur de la réalité de l'histoire culturelle,
et elle se contente de produire de purs faits artistiques,
incapables de générer des développements ultérieurs. Ceci
semble vrai d'une grande partie des recherches post-
conceptuelles contemporaines, qu'il s'agisse de la soi-disant
'nouvelle' peinture, des fictions photographiques ou de la
théâtralité apparue dans la performance. Ces recherches
portent les stigmates d'un art dont la décadence se manifeste
dès qu'il est privé de sa vocation à produire de la réalité,
à exister autrement que sur un plan strictement esthétique,
à exercer un pouvoir fonctionnel d'identification historique
(ce qui explique que l'art, aujourd'hui, soit dans sa majeure
partie infantile ou d'une prétention démente, décoratif ou
spectaculaire, puisqu'il n'a rien à 'faire' sauf à être de l'art et
produire quelques vagues nouveautés). Ces travaux faussement vitaux ont la prétention de remettre en question à la fois
l'abstraction rigoureuse de l'art conceptuel le plus sophistiqué,
et la stérilité tautologique de l'art conceptuel le plus académique. Ces artistes semblent ignorer le fait que l'art, depuis
qu'il a eu accès à ce statut de langage, a atteint le seuil le plus
avancé de sa communicabilité (potentielle), et qu'il a donc doté
l'oeuvre d'art de sa forme la plus élevée de valeur abstraite
potentielle d'usage. Si le langage esthétique contemporain ne
poursuit pas cet effort et cette revendication acharnés et
nécessaires d'un nouveau corpus de réalité matérielle; s'il
n'entretient pas le niveau général d'abstraction atteint par le
langage et sa contrepartie dans la mise en oeuvre d'une valeur
d'usage spécifique potentielle (comme on le voit le mieux dans
les travaux récents de Dan Graham, mais aussi dans ceux de
Michael Asher, Daniel Buren et Lawrence Weiner); alors cela
signifie que l'art se plie en toute innocence aux conditions
générales de production et donc, sur le plan des
superstructures, qu'il fait écho à l'impasse dans laquelle elles
se sont engagées:"L'ennui, qui est la conséquence de
l'expérience de la destruction de la valeur d'usage, et qui fut
jusqu'à maintenant le fait des privilégiés, est devenu aussi le
fait des masses. L'évitement de la révolution prolétarienne
permet à l'évolution capitaliste de franchir un dernier pas et
d'accomplir son aporie fondamentale: produire de la richesse
en détruisant de la valeur d'usage. Pour en arriver à la fin à ne
plus produire, sans résistance ni questionnement, qu'un tas
d'ordures." [20]

1 Voir Gregory Battock (ed.), "Photographs by Dan Graham", *Minimal Art*,
New York, 1968, p. 175.

2 Lucy Lippard, *Six Years, The Dematerialization of the Art Object*,
New York,1973, p.155.

3 Dan Flavin, "Some other Remarks", *Artforum*, décembre 1967, p.27. Sol LeWitt
semble avoir eu, à la même époque, une approche très différente du travail photographique
de Dan Graham, puisqu'il a illustré d'une de ses photographies son article
"Paragraphs on Conceptual Art", *Artforum*, summer 1967.

4 Willoughby Sharp," Interview with Carl Andre", *Avalanche*, 1970.

5 Dan Graham, dans une lettre à l'auteur. Le texte français reprend ici la traduction
de Claude Gintz, parue dans le cat. de l'exposition *L'art conceptuel, une perspective*,
Musée d'Art Moderne de la Ville de Paris, ARC, Paris 1989-1990, p.155.

6 Roland Barthes, "L'activité surréaliste", *Essais Critiques*, Paris 1964.

7 Donald Judd, "Malevich", *Complete Writings*, Halifax/New York 1975, p.212.

8 Karl Beveridge, Ian Burn, "Donald Judd", *The Fox* no.2, New York 1975, p.129 et sq.

9 Dan Graham, *Dan Flavin*, cat. Museum of Contemporary Art, Chicago 1967,
repris partiellement in: Dan Graham, (ed.), *End Moments*, New York 1969, p.15.

10 Dan Graham, "Carl Andre", *Arts Magazine*, no.3, New York 1967, p.34.

11 Robert Smithson, "A Museum of Language in the Vicinity of Art",
Art International no. 3, 1968, p.22.

12 Donald Judd, "Specific Objects", Contemporary Sculpture (1965),
Arts Yearbook VIII, p.74-83. Traduit en français par Claude Gintz in
Regards sur l'art Américain des années soixante, Paris, 1979, p.65.

13 Dan Graham, "Other Observations", *For Publication*,
cat. Otis Art Institute of Los Angeles County, Los Angeles 1975, n.p.

14 Dan Graham, dans une lettre à l'auteur.

15 ibid.

16 Dan Graham parle en ces termes de sa relation au travail de Buren:
"Je n'ai découvert la théorie et les travaux de Buren que très tard. Je pense qu'ils étaient
en avance sur ceux de Flavin, Judd ou LeWitt. J'ai le sentiment aujourd'hui que certaines
des idées de "Schema" annonçaient la théorie et la pratique de Buren (je ne crois pas qu'il
ait connu la pièce avant 1970, mais ce n'est pas exclu puisqu'elle avait été publiée dans
"Art & Language" en 1968). Dans une lettre à l'auteur.

17 ibid.

18 Dan Graham, Dan, "Sol LeWitt-Two Structures", *End Moments* (cf note 9).

19 Dans une lettre à l'auteur.

20 Wolfgang Pohrt, *Theorie des Gebrauchswertes*, Frankfurt, 1976.

Augenblicke der Geschichte in der Arbeit von Dan Graham (1977)

Benjamin H.D. Buchloh

"Metaphysik ist überhaupt nicht ein Bereich von Invarianz, dessen man habhaft würde, wenn man durch die vergitterten Fenster des Geschichtlichen hinausblickt; sie ist der sei es auch ohnmächtige Schein des Lichts, der ins Gefängnis selber fällt, umso mächtiger, je tiefer ihre Ideen in Geschichte sich einsenken, umso ideologischer, je abstrakter sie ihr gegenübertritt."

Adorno, T.W., "Klangfiguren", *Musikalische Schriften 1*, S.43Frankfurt 1959

Dan Graham hat einmal, befragt nach dem wesentlichen Aspekt seiner Arbeiten, eine ironische Selbstbeschreibung Duchamp's zitierend, geantwortet, es handele sich um "Photo-Journalismus". In ironischer Untertreibung folgte er so einem Vor-und Fehlurteil, das den Arbeiten Graham's seit ihrer ersten Veröffentlichung um 1965 folgt und eine wirklich angemessene Einschätzung der Bedeutung seiner Arbeiten verhindert hat. Noch 1970 konnte in einer Diskussion mit Carl Andre, Jan Dibbets und Douglas Huebler die Kritikerin Lucy Lippard die Frage stellen:
"Dan, du wurdest für einen Poeten gehalten, für einen Kritiker und einen Photographen. Bist du jetzt ein Künstler?"[1]
Selbst mit Graham befreundete Künstler und Zeitgenossen der Minimal Art, deren eigene ästhetische Produktion in Graham einen selten qualifizierten Analytiker und Exegeten (und Kritiker) gefunden hatte, verwahrten sich durch ihre Fehleinschätzung vor der Erkenntnis der veränderten Bedingungen der Kunstproduktion, wie sie in Graham's frühen photographischen Werken erkennbar wurden. So schrieb zum Beispiel Dan Flavin an Graham, dessen Photographien kommentierend:
"...deine guten photographischen Ansätze scheinen die durchgängig klare und offensichtlich unverstellte Reportage eines Henri Cartier-Bresson wiederaufzunehmen, nur daß du diese nicht auf Menschen anwendest, wie er es getan hat, sondern auf ihre 'Leistungen' einer banalen umgangsprachlichen Architektur und Landschaft."[2]
Von besonderer Beredheit ist dieses Mißverständnis, weil ein Künstler des Minimal gleich in einem Satz versucht, sowohl die sich anbahnende Möglichkeit einer photograpischen Dokumentation als eines legitimen und vollwertigen ästhetischen Mittels zu bestreiten, wie er zugleich deren neue inhaltlich-politische Implikationen auszuschalten sucht, indem er die photographischen Arbeiten Graham's in gerade jene Tradition der Photographie zu stellen unternimmt, die im Begriff des 'Decisive Moment' ihre Ideologie formulierte: der Photograph als Medium des einen geschichtlichen Augenblicks, den es in der photographischen Transsubstantation zu erhalten gilt, steht der Haltung Graham's zu seiner Kunst wie deren funktionalem Medium Photographie konträr gegenüber, da es ihm gerade um die akute Konstruktion eines Modells zur Erkenntnis von Geschichte zu tun ist. Eine wesentlich angemessenere Einschätzung der photographischen Arbeiten Dan Graham's, die neben den frühen konzeptuellen Stücken und den kritisch theoretischen Texten die erste Phase seiner Produktion bestimmt, zeigte jedoch schon Sol LeWitt's Entscheidung, seine "*Paragraphs on Conceptual Art*" (1967) mit einer Abbildung einer dieser Photographien einzuleiten.

Mißverständnis und Fehleinschätzung mögen ihre allgemeine Erklärung im Konflikt zweier aufeinanderfolgender Künstlergenerationen finden. Eine weitere Ursache dürfte überdies jedoch in einer den Arbeiten Graham's spezifischen ästhetischen Unkenntlichkeit liegen, die nicht zuletzt jenen anderen historischen Voraussetzungen sich verdankt, auf die sich Graham's Arbeiten berufen: die Erkenntnisse der konstruktivistischen Materialästhetik und die Ideen des Produktivismus.

Minimal Art und ihre Überwindung im Werk Dan Graham's

"Der Bruch zwischen der Kunst und den Problemen des Wirklichen zeigte sich in den 60er Jahren in einer wesentlich apolitischen und ungesellschaftlichen Kunst - in einem Ausmaß das für die meisten Künstler politisches Engagement in dieser Zeit bedeutete, sich außerhalb der Kunst zu betätigen. (...) Die Neutralität, welche diese Kunst angenommen hatte, verhindert jede Möglichkeit einer kritischen Beziehung zu den kapitalistischen Organisationsformen des Lebens."
(Beveridge, Karl, Ian Burn, "Donald Judd", *The Fox* no.2, 1975 s.129 ff)

Formalismus is nicht seit je die Haltung der Künstler des Minimal gewesen wie man fälschlich aus heutiger Perspektive schließen könnte. Insofern ist auch die Kritik von den ehemaligen Art & Language Künstlern Beveridge und Burn eine historische Rückphantasie, die sich in dieser Form allenfalls auf die späten Werke des Minimal anwenden ließe, welche monumentale Größe annehmen und neue Herrschaftsformen vermitteln. Das ursprüngliche Selbstverständnis dieser Künstler hatte sich nicht nur an den formalmateriellen Axiomen der konstruktivistischen Kunstauffassung orientiert, vielmehr auch deren gesellschaftspolitische Implikationen für die gegenwärtige Situation zu aktualisieren versucht: objektive Funktionalität des Materials, das seinen Ursprung in allgemein gegebenen technologischen Produktionsprozessen zu nehmen hatte, technische Reproduzierbarkeit und deren dialektische Entsprechung in der Vorstellung vom einmaligen, ja spezifischen Werk, das nur in diesem einen besonderen Ausschnitt aus Raum und Zeit seine gegenwärtige Funktion finden konnte, die Aufhebung des Warencharakters und der

Versuch, an die Stelle des ästhetischen Tauschwertes und des Ausstellungswertes den ästhetischen Gebrauchswert zu setzen, hatten zu Beginn der Entwicklung der Minimal Art im Zentrum der Überlegungen der Künstler gestanden. So zitiert Dan Graham in seinem Aufsatz "*Subject Matter*"[3] eine Aussage Flavin's die diese am Konstruktivismus orientierte Haltung und eine Reihe der Kriterien des produktivistischen Denkens belegt: "Leuchtstoff-Röhren-Objekte an einem bestimmten räumlichen Punkt sind repläzierbar in verschiedenen, zufällig zu bestimmenden, untereinander abhängigen Beziehungen zu spezifischen Situationen innerhalb des umgebenden Raumes und sind ebenso wieder aus ihren Befestigungen zu lösen und haben als solche nur eine begrenzte Dauer ihrer Existenz als Kunstwerke. Die Komponenten einer jeweiligen Ausstellung können nach Ihrem Abschluß in einem völlig anderen Zusammenhang replaziert werden, vielleicht für einen Gebrauch außerhalb der Kunst in einem anderen Gesamtkontext in einer anderen Zukunft."[4]
Oder wie Dan Graham selbst - offentlich von Flavin's Denken beeindruckt - an den Skulpturen von Carl Andre, "*Compound Coin, Crib*" (1965) beobachtete.

"Die konstituierenden Elemente besaßen über ihre unmittelbare kontextuelle Plazierung hinaus keinerlei innerste Bedeutung, sie waren 'replazierbar'. Diese Werke können vom Betrachter nicht in einem monetären Sinne erworben oder besessen werden, ebenso wenig wie es einen Künstler gibt, der von einer Vision besessen wäre oder dem Wunsch, die inneren Bedürfnisse des Betrachters zu befriedigen. Indem diese Werke unbefrachtet sind mit irgendeinem symbolischen transzendentalen oder sontstwie vielversprechenden pekuniärem Wert, bildet die Skulptur von Andre nicht etwa einen platonischen substantiellen Körper, sondern sie ist wiederhelstellbar; damit niemand poetisch entrückt werde, werden die konstituierenden Teile wortwörtlich gerückt aus dem Blickfeld des Betrachters, wenn die Ausstellung erst einmal beendet ist, (die Teile sind wieder einzelne Teile geworden und können in einem zukünftigen Zusammenhang wieder einem völlig verschiedenen Verwendungszweck zugefürt werden).[5]

Zum einen wird hier deutlich, in welchem Maße die Kunst des Minimal für die frühen photographischen und sprachlichen Arbeiten von Dan Graham von Bedeutung war, - man könnte geradezu von einer unmittelbaren Umwandlung formaler Prinzipien einer immer noch perzeptuell definierten Kunst in die konzeptuelle sprachliche Kunst Dan Graham's ablesen, wenn man diese Texte Graham's als eigenständige und zugleich noch abhängige Werke zu sehen bereit ist und sie nicht ausschließlich auf die Ebene der Kunstkritik reduziert. Zum anderen verdeutlicht die Lektüre der frühen Aufsätze Dan Graham's und seine prägnante formale Deskription und Analyse der Werke von Andre, Flavin, LeWitt, Nauman, Serra e.a., in welchem Maße deren eigene Definitionen der künstlerischen Arbeit unbewußt oder explizit auf die historischen Grundlagen des Konstruktivismus rekurrierten:

das plastische Werk, das nicht nur die Grenzen der eigenen traditionellen Kategorien Malerei, Skulptur und Architektur aufhebt, sondern zugleich auf die unmittelbare Funktionalität des ästhetischen Prozesses selbst zielt als Teil einer allgemeinen historischen und gesellschaftlich-politischen Transformation. Als Kritiker hat Graham jene theoretischen Implikationen der Minimal Art und ihre formalen Praktiken erkannt und beschrieben zu einem Zeitpunkt, als die offiziöse Kunstkritik diese Werke noch heftigst befehdete. Die problematischen Aspekte dieser Kunst jedoch, eben jene verdinglichte Übernahme historischer Voraussetzungen, die sich als für den gegenwärtigen Stand der Entwicklung der (ästhetischen) Produktionsmittel als unangemessen erwies, reflektierte und veränderte er in seiner eigenen künstlerischen Produktion spätestens seit 1966. Dies erkannte Robert Smithson 1967 sehr genau, als er über Graham's erste größere Arbeit in Form einer Zeitschriftenveröffentlichung, "*Homes for America*" (1966) schrieb: "Wie auch einige der anderen Künstler kann Graham die Sprache der Architektur ("*Homes for America*") lesen ... Die Lektüre jedoch von Architektur und von ihrer Grammatik erlaubt es dem Künstler, obsolete Bezüge und Ansprüche auf 'Funktion' und 'Utilitarismus' zu vermeiden."[6]

Doch Graham's kritische Auseinandersetzung mit den formalen und materiellen Praktiken der Minimal Art war nicht nur in der Erkenntnis ihrer relativ traditionellen Materialauffassung und eines technologisch aufgearbeiteten Konstruktions-Ethos begründet. In seinen Arbeiten wie "*Schema*" (1966), "*Side Effect*", "*Common Drug*" (1966) oder "*Homes for America*" (1966) werden jene für die Minimal Künstler spezifischen formalen Prozesse wie Elementarisierung und Systematisierung, Objektivation und Autonomie der ganzheitlichen Gestalt gleichsam aus der Sphäre der plastisch-materiellen Objekte in die der sprachlichen Konzeption und des Informations-Diagramms transformiert. Wenn Merleau-Ponty in seiner "Phänomenologie der Wahrnehmung", die ein theoretisches Kernstück der Minimal-Theorie gewesen war, gesagt hatte: "Ich kann einen Würfel niemals so sehen, wie er mir von seiner geometrischen Definition präsentiert wird. Ich kann ihn nur denken", und dies von Künstlern wie Judd und Morris in konkrete Gestalt umgesetzt worden war, so wendete Graham dieses Theorem wieder auf jene Ebene des Begriffs zurück und entließ die Kunst aus der Rolle, Illustration der Theorie geworden zu sein. Für Graham's Auffassung, einer den Ideen des Produktivismus verpflichteten Kunst, war es unabdingbar geworden, daß sich diese einer instrumentalen Form der Erkenntnis, die außerhalb der ästhetischen Praxis entwickelt worden war aber notwendig auf diese einwirken mußte, zu bedienen hatte (im Falle Graham's etwa Teilaspekte von Linguistik und Semiologie, Medientheorie und Psychologie). Überdies hatte sich zu diesem Zeitpunkt bereits gezeigt, daß die ursprüngliche Radikalität der Reflektion des Kunstbegriffs, ihre Auseinandersetzung mit den die ästethische Produktion determinierenden Mechanismen des Marktes und der kulturellen Institutionen in einer Serie von Kompromissen wieder aufgelöst wurden und in einer fraglosen Einschätzung des Kunstwerks als einer neuerlich konvertierbaren Ware endeten. Was als analytische Konstruktion der Modalitäten sinnlicher Erkenntnis instrumental entwickelt worden war, hatte sich bereits wieder in handelbares kulturelles Produkt verwandelt. Am besonderen Beispiel einer Arbeit von Robert Morris hat Dan Graham diese Veränderungen der Motivation der Minimal Künstler analysiert und ihnen die eigenen Alternativen entgegegesetzt:

"Anstatt die Beziehung der Kunst - als einem ökonomischen Phänomen - zu ihren Inhalten zu untersuchen (oder zu unterwandern) und die Welt der Kunst als einen Teil der realen ökonomischen und gesellschaftlichen Welt zu sehen, hat Morris' Stück dieses Thema abgeblockt und die weitere Verfolgung dieses Problems durch andere Künstler - entweder individuell oder als Kollektiv - unmöglich gemacht. Der hauptsächliche 'Wert' von Morris 'Unternehmung' war eben 'Kunst'. Es handelte sich um eine abgesicherte Struktur - mit einem garantierten Resultat in dem Sinne, daß das Feedback eine Bestätigung des bestehenden Status bedeuten würde und der Idee der Kunst als einem geschlossenen elitären System. So werden Morris und die Kunst zugleich aufgewertet. Ich würde hingegen wünschen, daß ich mich selbst und meine Kunst weniger psychologischen Selbsttäuschungen öffnete und dem gesamten sozio-ökonomischen System, von dem man die Kunst immer hat ausnehmen wollen, wie man auch das 'Selbst' des Künstlers als einen Sektor außerhalb dieser Bedingungen betrachtet hatte. Ein Ziel meiner Arbeit war es, 'Motivationen' von Gesichtspunkten außerhalb der Kunst zu sammeln, die ihrerseits andere Kategorien der Selbst-Definition in sich geschlossen regulierten. Dieser Ansatz führt zu einer Situation, in der eine gesellschaftlich definierte Idee des 'Selbst' oder des 'Individuums' gegen das eigene Selbst eingesetzt wird, um dieses unter gesellschaftliche Kontrolle zu bringen, und es darin zu halten. Das 'Selbst' ist keine unteilbare Entität sondern ist im Netz der Zwischenbeziehungen und der Strukturen des Environments gegeben. Als einen Versuch, sich dagegen zu verteidigen, versuchen Individuen oder Gruppen von Individuen immer wieder (wie in Morris' Gebrauch der Kunstgeschichte), sich selbst zu definieren oder aber das Netz ihrer Beziehungen zu verschiedenen anderen Parametern neu zu definieren." [7]

Diese Aussagen Dan Graham's haben programmatischen Charakter sowohl rückwirkend betrachtet für seine Arbeit seit 1966 wie sie auch die Themen und 'Motive' seiner späteren Arbeiten definieren. Das 'Selbst' des Künstlers (stellvertretend für das geschichtliche Subjekt allgemein), seine Tätigkeit wie deren Produkte werden in einer, der ästhetischen Reflektion bislang - wenn man von den Theorien Buren's seit 1969 absieht - unbekannten Rigorosität als abhängige Teile umfassenderer gesellschaftlicher, historischer, politischer und psychologischer Wirkungszusammenhänge gesehen, die sich gegenseitig bedingen und definieren als der eigentliche 'Raum' und die eigentliche 'Materie' der ästhetischen Praxis als einer bewußten Erfahrung des historisch Gewordenen und aus ihr

sich bildenden intentionalen Initiation der Veränderung gegebener Realität. Person und Arbeit des Künstlers, 'Art and Artist's Self', subjektive Prozesse und objektive Resultate werden als analoge Phänomene verstanden, ganz im Gegensatz zum in der Minimal Art unbefragt gebliebenen Autonomie-Begriff des Künstlers und seiner 'craft': gerade weil beide gleichermaßen der Realität und ihren Determinanten unterworfen sind, können sie zum Subjekt der ästhetischen Praxis werden ... Die Arbeit Dan Graham's ließe sich somit als eine mikroskopische Analyse von Segmenten der geschichtlichen Prozesse selbst verstehen, und eben in dem Maße, wie es dieser Analyse gelingt, die stereotype Systematik des Gewordenen, dessen prozessuale Mechanik, wie auch seine verdinglichte Dynamik wieder in einer dialektischen Bewegung zu vermitteln, eröffnet die Kunst Graham's instrumentale Erkenntnis fernerer Geschichte. Materialien der geschichtlichen Realität sind nun nicht mehr 'objets trouvés' oder 'Ready-made Elements' technologischer Produktionprozesse wie noch in Flavin's "*Fluorescent Light Objects*" oder selbst noch in Andre's metallurgischen Element Gruppen, sondern bedingt durch den Wechsel der Erkenntnisperspektive in Graham's Werk werden nun die vorgefundenen Strukturen der jenseits sichtbar-materieller Realität und ihrer konkreten Dinghaftigkeit liegenden - diese darum umso mehr determinierenden - Gesetzmäßigkeiten menschlicher Produktion und deren Motivationen. Mehr jedoch als andere zeitgenössiche Arbeiten reflektiert die Kunst Graham's auf die Prozesse der (Kunst) Information selbst. Allerdings findet die formale Darstellung der Bewegungsgesetze geschichtlicher Abläufe - seien sie nun subjektiv-individualpsychologischer Natur oder seien sie objektiv sozio-ökonomischen Charakters, seien sie zumeist eben das System des Zusammenwirkens aller dieser Aspekte in einem konkreten geschichtlichen Modell - in den Arbeiten Graham's immer auch ihre je spezifische Konkretion, die "*Subject Matter*", finden die Modelle der Bewegungsgesetze ihre exemplarische Inhaltlichkeit, ihren realen materiellen Körper, der Erkenntnis konkret vermittelt und nicht nur formalisiert. Dies begründet die reale Dialektik der Arbeiten Graham's und unterscheidet sie von anderen proto-konzeptuellen akademischen Kunstreflektionen oder aber dem tautologischen Idealismus der reinen konzeptuellen Kunst. Graham selbst hat in seinen theoretischen Ausführungen den Aspekt der formalen Prozesse in bildnerischer Produktion immer wieder mit dem Begriff der In-Formation zu fassen gesucht, und er deutete durch diese Schreibweise bereits den doppelten Standpunkt seiner Beobachtungen an: das sie sich richten auf die formalen Abläufe des Geschichtlichen wie auf dessen konkrete Inhaltlichkeit als einem unauflösbaren Moment von einheitlicher Bewegung plastischer Gebilde (wie etwa auf der Ebene des subjektiven Erfahrungsmodells "Symptom" eine vergleichbare Einheit von formalem Prozeß und historischem Inhalt gegeben ist). Die Materialität dieser von Graham dargestellten Prozesse ist ebenso spezifisch - allerdings transportiert auf jene Ebene der Erkenntnis, derer Graham sich als Künstler des Post-Minimal zu bedienen hatte - wie Donald Judd dies für die Materialität der Minimal Skulptur in überzeugend genauer Weise zu formulieren gewußt hatte: "Die Materialien sind sehr verschieden, und sie sind einfach Materialien - Formica, Aluminium, kalt gewalzter Stahl, Plexiglas, Kupfer und Messing und so weiter. Sie sind spezifisch. Wenn sie unmittelbar angewendet werden, sind sie noch spezifischer. Auch sind sie im allgemeinen aggresiv." [8] Spezifisch sind die Arbeiten Graham's in ihrer Materialität also in einem dreifachen Sinne: zum einen hinsichtlich ihres ureigensten historischen Kontextes der bildenden Kunst, den sie reflektierend vortreiben, indem sie eben jene besonderen Voraussetzungen der Minimal Art analysiert und verändert haben. Zum anderen hinsichtlich ihrer objektiven Methodik, sich in Abhängigkeit von allgemein verbindlichen Prinzipien der Erkenntnis (der Produktion) in anderen Diziplinen zu entwickeln und zu definieren. Und zuletzt sind sie spezifisch in einem je konkreten Bezug auf ein besonderes Segment gegebener Realität, das ihre Materialität ausmacht, die sie mit der formal-ästhetischen Praxis auf den Stand des Modells bringen. Somit entledigen sich die Arbeiten Graham's gerade im Maße ihrer spezifischen Funktion jedes ästhetischen Scheins, jeder vordergründig sinnlich-plastischen Attraktion, die sie in einem kulturellen Kontext leicht lesbar und subsumierbar werden ließe. Im Maße ihrer Funktionalität insistieren sie auf ihrem eigensten Potential an ästhetischem Gebrauchswert. Jene instrumentale Unmittelbarkeit und deren unbedingter Anspruch auf die Realisierung und Einlösung von historischer Erkenntnis als prozessualer historischer Wahrheit verleiht den Arbeiten Graham's eben jene ästhetische Unkenntlichkeit, die schon den Werken der Produktivisten zu eigen war. Gerade sie denunziert alles Versöhnliche, das die mittlere Kunst in die Welt bringt und was sie als kulturelle Dienstleistung - das nämlich ist ihre Realität, die sie gegen das Tabu des ästhetischen Gebrauchswertes aufzubieten hätte - sowohl an den interessierten Mann zu bringen weiß, wie dieser sich ihrer für seine Zwecke zu bedienen versteht.

Konzeptuell ist das Werk Graham's im besten Sinne deshalb, weil in seiner Arbeit die objektive Verdinglichung des Kunstwerks auf den Begriff gebracht worden ist, der Begriff jedoch nicht zum neuen Kunstobjekt verkommt. Dieser Begriff jedoch, die konzeptuelle Durchdringung des geschichtlich Gewordenen, des Verdinglichten im Kunstwerk wie in der Realität, setzt eine Genauigkeit der Betrachtung voraus, die nur der materialistische Historiker zu leisten vermag, wie sie zugleich die antizipierende Praxis des produktivistischen Künstlers verlangt, um als Organon fernerer Geschichte zu fungieren. Diese funktionale Auffassung der konzeptuellen Kunst, die zugleich symbolische (sprachliche) wie auch reale (systematische) Prozesse der Veränderung auslöst, erscheint mit Graham's Arbeiten erstmals in der Kunst des Post Minimal mit solcher formalen Präzision und inhaltlichen Komplexität, mit ihr ist jene Gefahr einer neuen Materialästhetik und klassizistischer Funktionslosigkeit, wie sie sich in den späteren Werken der Minimal Künstler

abzeichneten, aufgehoben, eine Gefahr wie sie schon fünfzig Jahre zuvor für den Konstruktivismus von Boris Arvatov gesehen und formuliert worden war:

"Entsprechend den Regeln der bourgeoisen Kunst erzogen, ist der Ingenieur-Künstler fast so sehr ein Fetischist wie sein Blutsbruder, der Architekt. So verfällt das Ingenieurswesen der süßen Umarmung des Ästhetizismus und verdammt sich somit freiwillig entweder zu einer Verengung der Probleme oder aber zu einer Haltung gesellschaftlichen Konservatismus." [9]

1 Lippard, Lucy, *Six Years: The Dematerilization of the Art Object*, New York, 1973, S.155.

5 Flavin, Dan, "Some Other Remarks", *Artforum*, December 1967, S.27.

3 Graham, Dan, *End Moments* (Collected Essays and Early Work), New York, 1969. S. 15.

4 Das in dem Aufsatz "*Subject Matter*" wiedergegebene Zitat von Dan Flavin stammt aus dem Ausstellung-Katalog *Dan Flavin*, Chicago Museum of Contemporary Art, Chicago, 1967.

5 Graham, Dan, "Carl Andre", *Arts Magazine*, no.3, 1967, S.34ff.

6 Smithson, Robert, "A Museum of Language in the Vicinity of Art", *Art International*, no.3, 1968, S.22.

7 Graham, Dan, "Notes in Income (Outflow) Piece" - From a Talk to Students at the University of the State of New York at Oswego, New York, 1973, *Interfunktionen* No.11, 1974, S.115.

8 Judd, Donald, "Specific Objects", Contemporary Sculpture (1965), *Arts Yearbook* VIII, p.74-82; Judd, Donald, *Complete Writings*, Halifax, New York 1975, S.181

9 Arvatov, Boris, "Materialized Utopia", *Lef* Nr.1, Moscow 1923, zitiert nach: Bann, Stephan, "The Tradition of Constructivism", *The Documents of the 20th Century Art*, London, 1974, S.85 ff.

Momenten van Geschiedenis in het werk van Dan Graham (1977)

Benjamin H.D. Buchloh

Toen Dan Graham eens gevraagd werd naar het wezen van zijn werk, antwoordde hij: "fotojournalistiek"[1], een ironisch citaat van de term die Marcel Duchamp ooit gebruikte als omschrijving van zijn eigen bezigheden. Graham hield daarmee een foutieve opvatting en een foutieve interpretatie van zijn werk in stand, waartoe het trouwens al vanaf de vroegste publikatie (1965) aanleiding had gegeven. Nog in 1970 stelde de critica Lucy Lippard hem, tijdens een discussie met Carl Andre, Jan Dibbets en Douglas Huebler, de vraag: "Dan, je bent als dichter, als criticus en als fotograaf beschouwd. Ben je nu een beeldend kunstenaar?"[2]

Zelfs zijn tijdgenoten, bevriende kunstenaars uit de minimale kunst-periode, wier werk sinds 1965 in Dan Graham en zijn analyserende kritiek een zeldzame en bekwame protagonist had gevonden, weigerden - door zijn werk verkeerd te benoemen - te erkennen dat de fundamentele opvattingen binnen de beeldende kunst sedert 1965 aan het veranderen waren. Zo schreef Dan Flavin, één van de eersten die een serieuze belangstelling toonde in Graham's werk, en als eerste een van zijn foto's publiceerde, over Graham: "Je zuivere fotografische benadering roept de heldere en eenvoudige, ongekunstelde reportage-methode van Henri Cartier-Bresson op, die je niet, zoals hij, toepast op mensen, maar op hun 'verrichtingen', de banale, alledaagse architectuur en het landschap."[3] Deze foute rubricering getuigt van een onthullende historische ironie, want er blijkt zonneklaar uit, dat vanuit het standpunt van de minimalist, gefotografeerde informatie/documentatie nooit als 'kunst' beschouwd kan worden (behalve 'fotografische' kunst). Bovendien onthult deze misvatting een onbewuste poging om impliciete vernieuwingen in de post-minimale kunst radicaal te ontkennen, Graham's foto's worden immers in verband gebracht met de, juist zo behoudende, ideologie van de fotografie als Cartier-Bresson's concept van het 'enig juiste moment'. Terwijl Cartier-Bresson en de zijnen hun grootste voldoening vinden in een passief-ontvangende bezigheid, als medium voor dat ene historische ogenblik dat zij trachten te conserveren in zijn fotografische transsubstantiatie, staat Graham's bedoeling daar lijnrecht tegenover: hij construeert namelijk werkmodellen voor het herkennen van de actuele geschiedenis door middel van de (fotografische) media.

"*Homes for America*" (1966), dat samen met "*Schema*" (1966) beschouwd kan worden als de meest complexe en relevante exponent van zijn werk, dient als voorbeeld. Dit 'fotojourna-listieke' werk , dat hij kenschetste als "overgangswerk van de vroegere 'conceptuele' tijdschriftpagina's naar de artikelen van 1967-1969", vindt zijn oorsprong in het, in die periode, groeiende besef, dat informatie omtrent kunst in de eerste plaats verspreid wordt door reprodukties in de (kunst)media. Zoals bijvoorbeeld Carl Andre in 1968 beschrijft: "Een foto is een leugen. Ik vrees dat een groot deel van wat we van kunst zien via tijdschriften en dia's tot ons komt, en dat vind ik vreselijk; dat is anti-kunst, want kunst is een directe ervaring van iets dat echt bestaat, en foto's zijn niet meer dan een gerucht, een soort pornografie van kunst."[4] En juist vanuit de anti-kunst van 'pornografie' begint Graham zijn onderzoek, waarbij het tekenend is voor zijn post-minimalistische houding, dat hij Andre's afschuw van de media bijna letterlijk omkeert tot de basis van zijn eigen methoden en werk.

Graham geeft een commentaar op "*Homes for America*" in een beschrijving waarin de verstrengeling van de verschillende (kunst)historische en formele relaties en de dialectische omkeringen van zijn werk herhaald worden: "Ten eerste is het belangrijk dat de foto's niet op zichzelf staan, maar deel uitmaken van de lay-out van het tijdschrift. Ze zijn illustraties bij de tekst of, omgekeerd, de tekst functioneert in relatie tot/als modificatie van de betekenis van de foto's. De foto's en de tekst zijn afzonderlijke delen van een schematisch (twee-dimensionaal) perspectiefsysteem. De foto's correleren (aan)de lijsten en kolommen van de in rijen geordende informatie, en beide representeren ze de rijtjeslogica van de woningprojecten waarover het in de tekst gaat. Ondanks het idee om het 'echte' landschap te gebruiken als 'lokatie' waarop 'conceptuele' kunst of 'land art' tot stand komt (n.b.: het werk is ontstaan enkele jaren vóór het werk van Smithson en Oppenheim), geloof ik dat het belangrijkste aspect toch was, dat "*Homes for America*" uiteindelijk niet meer was dan een tijdschriftartikel en als zodanig geen aanspraak maakte op het predikaat 'Kunst'".[5]

Zo wordt het informatie verstrekkende kader van een kunsttijdschrift de 'gevonden' formele structuur. Daarnaast is er de inhoud, de eveneens gestructureerde 'gevonden' werkelijkheid - de alledaagsheid van een industriële woonwijk. Gelijktijdig weerspiegelt de stilistische vormentaal - reeksen vierkante huizen en hun permutatie door middel van enkelvoudige, zich steeds herhalende elementen (die samen het 'geheel' van een gegeven formatie vormen) - op ironische en dubbelzinnige wijze, de formele en stilistische principes van de minimale beeldhouwkunst. De dialectische combinatie van de structuur van de werkelijkheid en die van de vormentaal, de capaciteit om 'gebouwen en taal' te lezen - i.e. systemen van de werkelijkheid en van de vorm - die het meest typerend en het meest herkenbaar is in al Graham's vroege teksten en conceptueel werk, plaatst ze in de categorie van het simulacrum van het geschiedenisobject, zoals Barthes het definieert: "...een toegespitst, opzettelijk simulacrum, omdat het nagebootste object iets onthult dat voordien onzichtbaar en onbegrijpelijk was, zelfs bij het object zonder meer... Het simulacrum is intellect, toegevoegd aan het object, en deze toevoeging heeft een antropologische waarde, want het is de mens zelf, zijn omstandigheden, zijn vrijheid, en de tegenstand van de natuur die zich tegen zijn geest keert."[6]

Eén reden voor het algemene misverstand omtrent, en de late erkenning van, Graham's werk is misschien de zo kenmerkende 'niet-esthetische' verschijningsvorm ervan. Deze is niet alleen het resultaat van Graham's behoefte tot het functioneel maken van de vormentaal, maar waarschijnlijk ook het gevolg van zijn geheel eigenzinnige benadering van historische bronnen als het constructivisme. Sinds Stella waren dit al bakens in de Amerikaanse kunst en ze kregen een diepgaande 'formele' betekenis voor de generatie van minimale kunstenaars, zoals schoorvoetend erkend werd in een uitspraak van Donald Judd in 1974: "Door en sedert Malevitsj zijn de afzonderlijke aspecten van de beste kunst onversneden, zoals malt whisky. Vrij."[7]

Dan Graham en de erfenis van het minimalisme

"De kloof tussen kunst en de problemen van de werkelijkheid werd in de jaren zestig zichtbaar in de kunst, die in wezen a-politiek en on-maatschappelijk was. Zozeer zelfs, dat dit voor de meeste kunstenaars uit die tijd - als ze zich al politiek geëngageerd voelden - iets was dat zich buiten de kunst afspeelde (...) De neutraliteit die inherent is aan deze kunst, sluit iedere mogelijkheid tot een kritische houding ten opzichte van een kapitalistisch geordende maatschappij uit."[8] Formalisme bij het maken van kunst en de daarmee samenhangende equivalenten, én ondernemersmentaliteit, waren niet de uitgangspunten van de minimale kunstenaars. Niet alleen richtten zij hun formele en materiële opvattingen op het constructivisme, ze poogden ook de sociaal-politieke gevolgen daarvan nieuw leven in te blazen. Dit betekende in de eerste plaats, dat zij van hun materiaal de objectieve functionaliteit eisten van technische produkten en werkmethoden. Ten tweede, het werk diende oneindig reproduceerbaar te zijn, maar ook de dialectische tegenpool daarvan, nl. uniek en specifiek, zodat het zijn eigenlijke functie en verwerkelijking slechts kon vinden in een bepaald segment van een tijd/ruimte continuüm. Tenslotte was er de afschaffing van de marktwaarde van het kunstwerk en een poging om de geld- en expositiewaarde te vervangen door een nieuw concept van functionele gebruikswaarde.

Flavin mag dan Graham's werk niet begrepen hebben, of onjuist beoordeeld als visuele kunstuiting (zoals zijn bestempeling als fotografie duidelijk maakt), andersom was dat niet het geval: Graham heeft meer dan eens duidelijk gemaakt hoe belangrijk zijn kennis en begrip van Flavin's werk geweest is voor zijn eigen ontwikkeling als kunstenaar. Het blijft een open vraag of het werk van de oudere kunstenaar in feite wel die rijkdom en facetten bezat, die Graham er aan toekent, of dat hij er zelf achteraf aspecten in leest, die later sleutelgegevens in zijn eigen werk werden, daarmee vooruitlopend op zijn eigen ontwikkeling, en deze projecterend op het historische werk van zijn voorloper. In het bijzonder de omzetting van 'formalistische' termen in een meer 'functionalistische' context

kan men één van de essentiële eigenschappen noemen, die Graham's werk heeft geïntroduceerd in de beeldende kunst van omstreeks 1965. Zo werden bijvoorbeeld Flavin's (en ook Andre en LeWitt's) idee van 'plaats' (het feit dat een kunstwerk verwijst naar de tentoonstellingsruimte als de ruimtelijke container) en het idee van 'aanwezigheid' (dat in Flavin's werk betekent, dat een installatie afhankelijk is van zijn situatie op dat moment, en bovendien geschapen is voor één bepaalde architectonische situatie) sleutelgegevens, zowel in Graham's vroege conceptuele werk, als in zijn kritisch-analytische teksten, die aan de ontwikkeling van zijn performance-, film- en videowerk voorafgingen.

De transformatie van een plastisch materiële manier om esthetische waarnemingsprocessen te analyseren, via een literair-verbale analyse en conceptuele methode, vindt merkbaar plaats in Graham's beschrijvingen van het werk van Andre, Flavin, Judd, Nauman, Serra en LeWitt, die ontstonden en verschenen vanaf 1965. Het lijkt daarom juister om deze teksten te beschouwen als een betoog over kunst, waarin de ontwikkeling van nieuwe vormen van esthetisch werk worden aangeduid, dan als louter kunstkritiek. In eerste instantie bevatten deze kritische teksten een historisch perspectief door hun beschrijvende precisie, voor zover een aantal principes van de minimale kunst afgeleiden zijn van constructivistische ideeën. Deze verschijnen als het ware gecatalogiseerd in Graham's analyses van Carl Andre's beeldhouwwerk "*Crib, Compound, Coin*" (1965) en ook in een beschrijving van Flavin's werk, beide verschenen in 1967: "Objecten van tl-buizen die ergens staan opgesteld zijn willekeurig verplaatsbaar al naar gelang de ruimtelijke situatie, en ze zijn ook verplaatsbaar in de zin dat ze uit de fittingen genomen kunnen worden, en een bepaalde levensduur hebben. De afzonderlijke delen van een bepaalde tentoonstelling worden na afloop verplaatst naar een andere omgeving - misschien ook in gebruik genomen als niet-kunst, als onderdeel van een ander geheel, in een andere toekomst."[9]

Of nog systematischer en duidelijker over Andre: "De samenstellende delen bezitten geen intrinsieke betekenis buiten hun directe, context gebonden plaatsing, die opnieuw 'verplaatsbaar' is. Het werk kan door de toeschouwer niet in bezit genomen worden in de monetaire betekenis van het woord, in de zin van een kunstenaar die bezeten is van een idee, of van het bevredigen van een persoonlijke, innerlijke behoefte van de toeschouwer. Onbelast met symbolische, transcendentale of inwisselbare geldelijke waarde, vormt Andre's beeldhouwwerk geen substantieel lichaam in Platonische zin, maar is het herbruikbaar; zodat niemand poëtisch vervoerd raakt van het beeld na afloop van de tentoonstelling (de onderdelen zijn weer losse delen geworden en kunnen in een andere toekomst voor een ander doel gebruikt worden)."[10]

Een andere benadering zou, vanuit het gezichtspunt van vandaag, de historiciteit van de teksten zelf betreffen, om de precisie waarmee ze als het ware systematisch alle elementaire beginselen van het visuele denken, zoals dat door de praktijk van minimale kunst was ontwikkeld, aantonen. Gelijktijdig beschrijven deze teksten door het precise woordgebruik dat de zichtbare werkelijkheid analyseert, de omzetting van het maakproces van de kunst in concepten van verwoorde materialiteit en gematerialiseerde taal. Robert Smithson heeft dat zeer juist opgemerkt, want al in 1967 schijnt hij, duidelijker nog dan Flavin, de historische en esthetische implicaties van Graham's geschreven en fotografisch werk te beschouwen als een nieuwe definitie van kunstaxioma's (het herwaarderen van het esthetisch produkt zodat het komt te vallen onder de algemene maatstaf van kijk- en herkenningswerktuig). Hiermee brengt hij ze nog dichter bij hun mogelijke potentieel van gebruikswaarde: "Net als sommige andere kunstenaars, kan Graham de taal van gebouwen 'lezen'. Het lezen van zowel gebouwen, als geschreven taal, maakt het de kunstenaar mogelijk ouderwetse verwijzingen naar 'functie of 'nut' te vermijden."[11]

In zijn meeste teksten gaat Dan Graham in op het dubbele karakter van deze processen, voorzover ze in de context van zijn werk geformaliseerd en geïntegreerd kunnen worden, door ze de naam 'in-formatie' te geven. Daarmee geeft hij aan dat voor hem zowel formele processen als hun materiële inhoud ondeelbare eenheden zijn. De stoffelijkheid van de formele processen in Graham's werk kunnen daarom 'specifiek' genoemd worden, in de zin waarin Donald Judd die term voor het eerst gebruikte voor de picturale beeldhouwkunst uit de minimale periode: "Materialen variëren aanmerkelijk en zijn niet meer dan materialen - formica, aluminium, staal, plexiglas, rood en geel koper, enz. Zij zijn specifiek. Meestal zijn ze ook agressief."[12]
Graham's kritische analyse van de formele en materiële erfenis van de minimale esthetiek, schijnt hem niet alleen tot de ontdekking gebracht te hebben dat de ideeën van deze kunstenaars omtrent materialiteit in feite tamelijk traditioneel en positivistisch waren (gericht op een constructivistische nijverheidsethiek), maar bovendien schijnt hij te hebben ingezien dat ze hun oorspronkelijke radicale houding, als gevolg waarvan ze de rol van het kunstwerk in zijn maatschappelijke context ter discussie stelden, opgegeven hadden. Daarmee was het minimale werk moeiteloos teruggegleden naar de status van consumptie-artikel, waarvan de handelswaarde steeg naarmate het context-gebonden concept van gebruikswaarde werd opgegeven. Daarom zijn bij Graham de materialen van de werkelijkheid niet langer eenvoudigweg 'objets trouvés' of 'ready-made' elementen van de technologisch alledaagse werkelijkheid, zoals bij Flavin's tl-buizen of Andre's metallurgische elementen (die overigens technisch veel gecultiveerder zijn dan hun elementaire 'natuurlijke' uiterlijk op het eerste gezicht doet vermoeden), maar gebruikt hij structuren die te vinden zijn achter de zichtbare en tastbare werkelijkheid. Daardoor wordt bij Graham de werkelijkheid gedefinieerd op een veel subtielere en doeltreffender manier. Hetzelfde doet Graham met de psycho-

fysiologische motiveringen van subjectief gedrag, met sociaal-economische condities voor objectieve politieke handelingen, of, nog scherper, met de alomtegenwoordige mechanismen van onderlinge afhankelijkheid van deze systemen (in de nauwkeurig geobserveerde situaties van hun gecombineerde uitwerking).

Graham's authentiek 'conceptuele', vroege publicaties in tijdschriften, die hij schreef vóór de kritieken op zijn mede-kunstenaars, kenden als formele en gemeenschappelijke noemer de standaard tijdschriftpagina, en in zekere zin gingen ze ook over 'zichzelf'. "*Figurative*" (1965), "*Schema*" (1966) of "*Detumescence*" (1966), die tot de eerste werken behoren - als ze al niet de allereerste zijn - die in tijdschrift-advertentievorm uitkwamen, geven een totaalbeeld van de vooronderstellingen van de minimale kunst door hun vertaling in een volstrekt andere vormentaal. De historische afstand en het gamma van verschillen, die bereikt worden door Graham's theorieën en zijn werk, kan men beter begrijpen als men Judd's standpunt over het materiaal waarvan een kunstwerk gemaakt moet zijn, vergelijkt met Graham's houding vis à vis de stoffelijkheid van kunst in "*Other Observations*" (1969). "*Other Observations*" is een tekst die hij schreef als commentaar op "*Schema*" (1966) en die op sommige plaatsen bijna klinkt als een vergelijkende studie van, en een kritiek op, de minimalistische formele ideeën en hun transformatie: "Een pagina van "*Schema*" bestaat als een feitelijke werkelijkheid en tegelijkertijd als een semiotische duiding van het aanwezige materiaal; als signaal bergt het in zich zowel de betekenis als de betekenisgever (...). In deze interne logica ontstaat de paradox, dat het concept van 'stoffelijkheid' waar de taal naar verwijst, zich tot de taal zelf verhoudt als 'onstoffelijk' materiaal (een soort mediamieke ether) en tegelijkertijd de allesomvattende ruimte ervoor is. Er ligt een 'scheidingswand' tussen het uiterlijke 'lege' materiaal van de plaats en het innerlijke 'lege' materiaal van de 'taal', (het systeem van) de informatie (in-formatie) is te vinden halverwege materiaal en concept, zonder zelf het één of het ander te zijn."[13]
De consequente radicaliteit van Graham's formele methode om "*Schema*" te reduceren tot niet meer dan een formule van een naar zichzelf verwijzend systeem, vindt zijn dialectisch-materiële equivalent in zijn besluit, het werk te publiceren in de context van een advertentie in een (kunst)tijdschrift, zoals hijzelf in een later commentaar op "*Schema*" opmerkt: "Maar, in tegenstelling tot een schilderij van Stella bijvoorbeeld, verwijzen de varianten van "*Schema*" niet eenvoudigweg naar zichzelf. Dit komt, omdat het tijdschrift-systeem als vehikel wordt gebruikt. Tijdschriften leggen een plaats of een referentiekader vast, zowel buiten als binnen datgene wat men als 'kunst' definieert. Tijdschriften zijn grensgebieden (die de verbinding leggen) tussen twee terreinen....tussen de 'kunst' uit de galerie en de communicatie over 'kunst'."[14]

Graham probeert dus klaarblijkelijk de analyse van bepalende elementen die voorheen verwaarloosd waren gebleven, mee te laten spelen, als ook de verschillende aspecten van het sociaal-economische stelsel, alsook de psychologische achtergrond van het individu, die bepalend zijn voor zowel de produktie als voor de ontvangst van een kunstwerk. Door de optiek te veranderen, nl. de omzetting van de drijfveren van de formalist in de strategie van de functionalist, maakt hij deze juist tot het onderwerp van zijn kunst. Weer is Graham's eigen terugblik het meest verhelderende commentaar op de radicale veranderingen van de heersende (kunst)historische condities, waarvan zijn werk het beginpunt is geweest, : "Het was interessant, vanuit esthetisch oogpunt gezien (niet functiona-listisch, d.w.z. in materiële, economische zin), dat een gedeelte van het minimale werk leek te refereren aan de tentoonstellingsruimte als ware die in laatste instantie het kader of de structurele 'drager'/referentiekader, en dat enkele werken van de Pop Art zich op dezelfde manier verhielden tot de culturele informatiemedia, maar dat het kader (een bepaalde media-vorm of de tentoonstellingsruimte/ museumzaal als economisch geheel, die zich bezighouden met (geld)waarde) nooit structureel zichtbaar werd gemaakt. De werkwijze, gebruikt bij "Schema", bestond er uit, om deze twee soorten kaders samen te voegen tot één kader, zodat deze duidelijk zichtbaar werden, waardoor het 'kunstprodukt' radicaal in waarde daalde. Ik wilde Pop Art maken, die letterlijk wegwerpbaar zou zijn (een idee waar al in Warhol's concept van de vervanging van 'kwaliteit' door 'kwantiteit' op gezinspeeld werd - de logica van de consumptiemaatschappij), ik wilde een kunstvorm maken, die niet gereproduceerd of tentoongesteld kon worden in een galerie/museum, en ik wilde het minimale kunstwerk nog sterker reduceren, tot een niet noodzakelijk esthetische, twee-dimensionale vorm (die schilderij noch tekening was): drukwerk, dat massa-geproduceerde informatie is en massa-wegwerpartikel. Het plaatsen ervan op de bladzijden van een tijdschrift, betekent dat het 'gelezen' kan worden naast de gewone kunstkritieken, besprekingen en reprodukties in de rest van het tijdschrift, zodat het werk functioneert als kritiek op de werking van het tijdschrift (in relatie tot de galerie-structuur)."[15]

Daarom moeten Graham's "Schema" (1966), en zijn latere commentaren als "Other Observations" (1969), of zijn "Magazine/Advertisements" (1969), dat begint met de zin: "Kunst is een sociaal signaal", gelezen worden naast Daniel Buren's "Limites critiques" (1969).[16] Zij behoren tot de eerste en meest relevante pogingen uit die periode om de kunst die zich aan de periferie bevindt, die onderdrukt of gecamoufleerd is, zichtbaar te maken en tot onderwerp te maken van zichzelf. Lang vóór Hans Haacke's enigszins vergelijkbare commentaren van ruim twintig jaar geleden, (in het engels verschenen onder de titel *Framing and Being Framed: 7 Works 1970 - 75*, Halifax/New York, 1975), geeft Graham een analyse van het kader, die aanzienlijk van zowel Buren als Haacke verschilt. De analyse verschilt van Buren, omdat deze commentaren geeft op de historische en museologische determinatie van een kunstwerk, en van Haacke, omdat deze ook de sociale receptie van een kunstwerk in beschouwing neemt, evenals de historische transformatie van kunst, veroorzaakt doordat

een object tot kapitaalinvestering wordt. Graham analyseert speciaal de algemene maatschappelijke condities voor produktie en reproduktie van (kunst)informatie, en de formele en materiële gevolgen daarvan (zie ook zijn latere "*Income/Outflow*"(1969)).

Graham's processen zijn - in tegenstelling tot Judd's "*Specific Objects*" - in drie opzichten specifiek. In de eerste plaats ten opzichte van hun epistemologische en historische context (nl. de beeldende kunst), want ze becommentariëren en transcenderen op dialectische wijze de bestaande condities van de minimale esthetiek. Ten tweede, specifiek in hun relatie tot de objectieve methodologie, die ze zeer bewust en duidelijk indeelt in een context van meer algemene principes van herkenning (produktie), zoals bv. hun expliciete afhankelijkheid van de semiologie. Ten derde kan men Graham's werken specifiek noemen om de zeer concrete verwijzingen naar een specifieke segmenten van de werkelijkheid. Het is niet in de laatste plaats om deze reden dat Graham's werk, zijn 'specifieke processen', elke uiterlijke visueel-esthetische aantrekkelijkheid lijkt te missen, waardoor zijn werk makkelijker te plaatsen zou zijn in de context van de kunstgeschiedenis. Aan de andere kant maakt juist dit gebrek aan uiterlijke schoonheid, dat wortelt in een potentiële functionaliteit, binnen het idee dat het kunstwerk weer een potentiële gebruikswaarde moet krijgen, dat de werken meer overeenkomsten hebben met bepaalde voorbeelden van produktivistische kunst, dan men op het eerste gezicht zou zeggen. Het is juist dat gebrek aan esthetische aantrekkelijkheid, waardoor elke vorm van valse inschikkelijkheid aan de kaak wordt gesteld, dat door meer op kunstnijverheid gerichte kunst wordt gebruikt als culturele pasmunt. De dienst die deze kunst verleent aan de heersende principes, ligt onder meer gevat in de poging om aan de kunst zijn meest traditionele rol terug te geven, nl. die van een louter decorum voor de heersende orde.

Graham's "Subject Matter" en het post-minimalisme
Graham's bundel kritische parafrases, die voor het eerst werden gepubliceerd in het door hemzelf geredigeerde "End Moments", onder de titel "*Subject Matter*", draagt een ondertitel waaruit duidelijk blijkt welke belangrijke verandering zich aan het afspelen was in de beeldende kunst rond 1965: "1. het subject (in plaats van het object) en 2. materie (als proces, niet als object)." Deze verzameling van kunst-kritische teksten, waartoe een van Graham's eerste stukken over Donald Judd (1964) en zijn (destijds) laatste analyse van de ervaringen van de toeschouwer bij een performance van Bruce Nauman (1969) behoren, gaat verder dan de eerder besproken stukken want Graham poogt de vooronderstellingen van de minimale kunst van zich af te schudden. "*Subject Matter*" moet men zelfs gedeeltelijk beschouwen als een herziening op en een kritische overdenking van Graham's eigen werk uit de "*Schema*"-periode, waarvan hij voelde, dat het nog steeds deel uitmaakte van de "non-anthropomor-fische ideologie van de Newyorkse Minimal Art uit de late zestiger jaren". Tegelijk met deze teksten begint Graham met

zijn eerste eigen activiteiten, waarbinnen hij bestaande ideeën van visuele en ruimtelijke eenheden verandert in minder 'esthetische', directe perceptuele methodes, gespeeld door beroepsacteurs. Graham's belangstelling voor de directheid van de kijkervaring, toont aan dat hij consequent toewerkte naar een reductivistische benadering van de kunst, waarmee Stella een begin gemaakt had, en die van belang was gedurende de gehele minimale periode; en dat hij bijna noodzakelijkerwijs kwam tot een belangstelling voor het 'gedrag' van mensen zelf en hun perceptie (het 'subject'), in plaats van een bekommernis voor hun gedrag tijdens het kijken naar een kunstobject. Graham, die een zeer heldere analyse heeft gemaakt van de geleidelijke verandering van de belangstelling voor het minimalistische object, naar post-minimale kijkprocédés, lijkt in zijn eigen werk dezelfde verandering te hebben ondergaan, maar hij blijft daarbij even specifiek en consequent als in zijn werk uit de "*Schema*" periode. Weer gaat hij terug naar zijn oordeel over Flavin's werk, zoals hij dat terugblikkend beschrijft: "Wat mij beviel, was dat als gevolg van Flavin's tl-buizen, de wanden van de galerie tot 'doek' werden. De lichten werkten als spots op het publiek in de galerie - zodat de inhoud van de tentoonstelling geprojecteerd werd op het publiek, dat zich op dat moment bezig hield met kijken; de binnenruimte van de galerie zelf werd het echte kader..."[17]

In Graham's essay over Sol LeWitt wordt de lezing van een sculptuur en de manier waarop het werk dient te worden opgevat, zo beschreven, dat de ontwikkeling van Graham's eigen werk expliciet eruit op te maken valt: "Terwijl de toeschouwer zich beweegt van punt naar punt rondom het kunstobject, wordt de fysieke continuïteit van zijn bewegingen vertaald in een illusionistische-zelf-representatieve diepte: de visuele complicatie van het voorgestelde 'ontwikkelt' zich in een duidelijke, niet-progressieve ruimte en tijd. Er bestaat geen verschil meer tussen subject en object. Het object is de toeschouwer - de kunst en het subject zijn de toeschouwer, de kunst. Object en subject zijn geen dialectische tegengestelden meer, maar één geheel, een in zichzelf besloten identiteit: omkeerbare uiterlijke en innerlijke eindstations. Alle referentiekaders geven gelijktijdig te lezen: object/subject."[18] Dit onthult ook de consequente logica van de uitbreiding van de 'formalistische' bedoelingen van Graham naar de 'functionele' realiteit van zijn latere performances, terwijl eveneens een licht wordt geworpen op de strikt a-literaire en on-toneelmatige kwaliteit van Graham's opvatting van performances. 'Acteren' is in de context van de beeldende kunst slechts relevant voor zover de elementaire procedure wordt getoond van het zichtbaar maken van het netwerk van verhoudingen tussen uitvoerder en kijker, die beide tegelijk subject en object zijn: zoals Graham al in detail opmerkte, toen hij geconfronteerd werd met de performances van Bruce Nauman. De beschrijving ervan in "*Subject Matter*" toont duidelijk het proces van assimilatie en transformatie van Nauman's invloed op het toekomstige werk van Graham. In een commentaar op "*Subject Matter*", speciaal in het gedeelte waar hij de invloed van muziek en performances op zijn ideeën behandelt, wordt het belang van deze fenomenen voor zijn eigen ontwikkeling duidelijk: "Ik had het idee van een wederzijdse, onderlinge afhankelijkheid van de kijker (toeschouwer) en het bekeken object of de kunstenaar als acteur (die in Nauman's geval zichzelf voorstelt als, of in de plaats van, 'object'). In deze nieuwe subject/object relatie komen de kijkprocessen van de toeschouwer in verband te staan met het proces van de compositie (hetgeen ook inherent is aan het materiaal ... en zo ontwikkelt zich ook een ander idee van het 'materiaal' en de verhouding van deze 'materialiteit' tot de natuur(lijke) processen). Deze mutatie in het compositie-proces komt voort uit de ontwikkelingen in muziek en dans ... waar de (uitvoerende) kunstenaar of de performance het centrale punt is, uitgevoerd en bekeken in een eindig tijdscontinuüm. Dit is het tegenovergestelde van de tijdsduurloze 'presentie' van de minimale kunst ... een serie van niet-aaneengesloten momenten, bijeengehouden door een ter plaatse ontstaan, in zichzelf besloten gearrangeerd concept (dat vóór de voorstelling of performance al is vastgelegd). Uit de muziek kwam ook het idee van de fysiologische presentie (...) een werk dat gaat over het kijkproces zelf, dat plaatsvindt tegelijkertijd als uiterlijk fenomeen, en binnen de hersenen als deel van innerlijke processen...(...) "*Subject Matter*" werd geschreven in dezelfde periode, waarin ook mijn eerste films en performances zijn ontstaan. Ik heb deze nieuwe werken, waarmee ik een binding voelde, willen uitleggen."[19]

De contouren van Graham's belangstelling, en het ontstaan van zijn formele ideeën tekenen zich af in zijn teksten en zijn werken, als een microscopische analyse van segmenten van historische processen: hun gegeven structuren en de verschillende manieren waarop men die kan bekijken en ook de manier waarop ze geanalyseerd en getransformeerd worden. Het is in dezelfde mate waarin de analyse erin slaagt om de patronen van een gegeven werkelijksheidstructuur over te brengen (individueel gedrag, manieren van interactie, zoals bijvoorbeeld de subtiele, stapsgewijze ontleding van het stereotype man-vrouw rolpatroon in de video-performance "*Two Conscious Projections*" (1977), het langzame bewust-wordingsproces van groepsgedrag versus individueel gedrag in performances als "*Intention/Intentionality Sequence*" (1972) of "*Performer/Audience Sequence*" (1974) - het mechanisme ervan zowel als de tastbaar gemaakte dynamiek) dat zijn werk een perspectief opent dat bruikbaar is bij historische gebeurtenissen (waarmee de kijker datgene wordt toebedeeld, wat hij ervaart als de kunstwerk-kwaliteit van het werk, zijn esthetische waarde).

Epiloog over het concept van gebruikswaarde
"Een spindel handhaaft zichzelf in zijn gebruikswaarde, alleen door gebruikt te worden bij het spinnen. Als dat niet zo was, zou juist doordat men een specifieke vorm geeft aan hout of metaal, zowel het werk dat nodig was om deze vorm te maken, als het materiaal waaruit de vorm werd gemaakt, nutteloos zijn geworden. Alleen door zijn toepassing als medium voor actief

gebruik, als objectief moment in zijn eigen bestaan, wordt zowel de gebruikswaarde van hout en metaal, als de vorm, gehandhaafd".
(Karl Marx, *Notizen zur Grundisse der Kritik der politischen Ökonomie*, Moskau, 1938).

Gebruikswaarde in de kunst, de meest door regels bepaalde tegenhanger van de esthetiek - als men het maken van kunst definieert als het werktuig der geschiedenis, als instrument voor materialistische herkenning en transformatie - wordt in de eerste en laatste plaats bepaald door de historische context. Omdat gebruikswaarde alleen kan ontstaan als gevolg van het meest geavanceerde stadium van esthetisch besef, moet het tegelijkertijd functioneren binnen de specifieke omstandigheden van een bepaalde historische situatie. Zo was bijvoorbeeld de kunstenaar als constructivist/ingenieur in revolutionair Rusland een voorbeeld van functionele en esthetische noodzakelijkheid, terwijl de constructivistische ingenieurs-esthetiek van veertig jaar later, uit het monopolie-tijdperk, noodzakelijkerwijs alleen als kunst functioneert. Dergelijke restauraties aan de formele buitenkant van de maatschappelijke werkelijkheid, bereiken echter het tegenovergestelde van wat ze bedoelen, zoals dat duidelijk te zien is in de ontwikkeling van de architectuur sinds het constructivisme en het Bauhaus. Als anderzijds, bij het maken van kunst, de gebruikswaarde helemaal opgegeven wordt, worden daarmee aan de kunst de mogelijkheden ontnomen een dialectiek op gang te brengen binnen de culturele geschiedenis, zodat er iets ontstaat dat de naam draagt van kunst, maar dat niet in staat is een verdere ontwikkeling op gang te brengen. Dit lijkt zeer van toepassing op een groot deel van het tegenwoordige post-conceptuele werk, de z.g. nieuwe schilderkunst en beeldhouwkunst en in nog grotere mate bij de fotoverhalen en de nieuwe dramatiek van de performancebeweging. Alle tonen zij decadente trekken waarbij de kunst niet meer haar inherente en ingeboren taak vervult: een effect in de werkelijkheid teweegbrengen, inwerken op andere gebieden dan alleen maar het esthetisch veld, een functioneel arsenaal van historische aanknopingspunten offreren. (Veel hedendaagse kunst is dan ook óf infantiel, óf vol demonische pretenties, decoratief of dramatisch, omdat ze niets anders 'te doen' heeft dan 'kunst' zijn, en min of meer nieuw). De valse levendigheid van zulk werk, die een flagrante ontkenning is van de rigoureuze abstractie van het beste conceptuele werk, en die een reactie is op de tautologische cul-de-sac van een conceptueel academisme op z'n starst, schijnt er zich niet van bewust, dat de kunst, zo gauw die zich transformeert tot het niveau van taal, haar hoogste graad van communicatie (mogelijkheid) heeft bereikt en zo het kunstwerk voorziet van zijn maximale abstracte gebruikswaarde. Men kan dan ook stellen dat, als de esthetische taal van vandaag, deze indringende en noodzakelijke begrippen en eisen voor een nieuwe materiële realiteit niet blijft steunen, en tegelijk het niveau van abstractie verwaarloost zoals dat bereikt wordt door de taal en haar tegenhanger, met name de belichaming van het potentieel aan specifieke gebruikswaarde (zoals dit zeer

efficiënt gebeurt in de recente werken van Dan Graham, en ook van Michael Asher, Daniel Buren en Lawrence Weiner), dat dan de kunst in alle onwetendheid toegeeft aan de algemeen geldende condities voor produktie en bovendien in dezelfde dilemma's dient te delen als: "Verveling, voortkomend uit de aan den lijve ondervonden vernietiging van gebruikswaarde (tot nu toe een probleem van de welgestelden) wordt een probleem voor de massa. Het vermijden van een proletarische revolutie maakt het voor het kapitalisme mogelijk, om de laatste stap te nemen en zijn fundamenteel onoplosbare tweeledigheid tot het einde door te voeren: het vervaardigen van overvloed door de vernietiging van gebruikswaarde. Wat uiteindelijk overblijft is de gedwee toegelaten en de vanzelfsprekende produktie van rommel."[20]

1 Zie Battock, Gregory (ed.), "Photographs by Dan Graham", *Minimal Art*, New York, 1968, p. 175.
2 Lippard, Lucy, *Six Years, the Dematerialization of the Art Object*, New York, 1973, p. 155.
3 Flavin, Dan, "Some other Remarks", *Artforum*, December 1967, p. 27. Sol LeWitt had in diezelfde periode een geheel ander idee van Graham's fotografische werk, hetgeen bewezen wordt door het feit dat hij een van Graham's foto's gebruikte als illustratie voor zijn "Paragraphs on Conceptual Art", *Artforum*, Summer 1967.
4 Sharp, Willoughby, "Interview with Carl Andre", *Avalanche*, 1970.
5 Dan Graham in een brief aan de schrijver.
6 Barthes, Roland, "L'activité structuraliste", *Essais Critiques*, Paris 1964, p. 216.
7 Judd, Donald, "Malevich", *Complete Writings*, Halifax/New York 1975, p. 212.
8 Beveridge, Karl, Ian Burn, "Donald Judd", *The Fox* no.2, 1975, p. 129 e.v.
9 Graham, Dan, *Dan Flavin*, cat. Museum of Contemporary Art, Chicago, Chicago 1967, gedeeltelijk herdrukt in: Graham, Dan, *End Moments*, New York 1969, p. 15.
10 Graham, Dan, "Carl Andre", *Arts Magazine*, no.3, New York, 1967, p. 34.
11 Smithson, Robert, "A Museum of Language in the Vicinity of Art", *Art International* no.3, 1968, p. 22.
12 Judd, Donald, "Specific Objects", Contemporary Sculpture (1965), *Arts Yearbook* VII, p. 74-83. Reprinted in: *Complete Writings*, loc.cit. p. 181
13 Graham, Dan, "Other Observations", *For Publication*, Otis Art Institute of Los Angeles County, Los Angeles 1975, n.p.
14 Dan Graham in een brief aan de schrijver..
15 ibid.
16 Over zijn verhouding tot het werk van Daniel Buren schrijft Graham het volgende in een brief aan de schrijver: "Ik hoorde van Buren's theorie en werk pas vele jaren later. Volgens mij zijn ze de standpunten van Judd, Flavin en LeWitt vooruit. Het lijkt me, dat een aantal ideeën uit "*Schema*" voorlopers zijn van aspecten van Buren's theorie/praktijk (ik geloof dat hij het stuk pas zag in 1970 ... hoewel hij het mogelijk eerder had kunnen zien omdat het in 1968 in *Art & Language* was verschenen)."
17 ibid
18 Graham, Dan, "Sol LeWitt - Two Structures", *End Moments*, loc. cit. p. 65.
19 Dan Graham in een brief aan de schrijver.
20 Pohrt, Wolfgang, *Theorie des Gebrauchswertes*, Frankfurt, 1976.

Jean-François Chevrier

teaches contemporary art history at the Ecole Nationale Supérieure des Beaux Arts de Paris. From 1983 to 1985 Chevrier was editor of the magazine *Photographies*. In 1988 Chevrier curated, with James Lingwood, the photography exhibition Matter of Facts, (Musée des Beaux Arts, Nantes et al.); and in 1989, with James Lingwood, Une Autre Objectivité/Another Objectivity, (Centre National des Arts Plastiques, Paris et al.); and organized, the exhibition and the book *Photo Kunst*, on behalf of the Graphische Sammlung of the Staatsgalerie Stuttgart and Edition Cantz. In 1991 Chevrier curated, with Ann Goldstein, the exhibition A Dialogue about Recent American and European Photography, (The Museum of Contemporary Art, Los Angeles), followed by Lieux communs, figures singulières, (ARC,Musée d'Art Moderne de la Ville de Paris), and the exhibition of Craigie Horsfield, with James Lingwood (ICA, London et al.). Chevrier is the author of *Portrait de Jurgis Baltrusaitis* (Paris, 1989) and a contributing editor to *Galeries Magazine*.

Jean-François Chevrier

Enseigne l'histoire de l'art contemporain à l'Ecole Nationale Supérieure des Beaux-Arts de Paris. De 1983 à 1985, Chevrier est rédacteur en chef du magazine *Photographies*. En 1987, il est commissaire, avec James Lingwood, de l'exposition de photographie Matter of Facts (Musée des Beaux Arts, Nantes et al.). En 1989, il réalise, également avec James Lingwood l'exposition Une Autre Objectivité/Another Objectivity (Centre National des Arts Plastiques, Paris et al.), et supervise, pour la Graphische Sammlung de la Staatsgalerie Stuttgart et les éditions Cantz, l'exposition et l'ouvrage *Photo Kunst*. En 1991, Chevrier est commissaire, avec Ann Goldstein, de l'exposition A Dialogue about Recent American and European Photography (The Museum of Contemporary Art, Los Angeles), suivie par Lieux communs, figures singulières (ARC, Musée d'art Moderne de la Ville de Paris) et, avec James Lingwood, de l'exposition Craigie Horsfield (ICA, Londres et al.).Par ailleurs Chevrier est l'auteur de l'ouvrage *Portrait de Jurgis Baltrusaitis* (Paris, 1989) et collabore régulièrement à *Galeries Magazine*.

Jean-François Chevrier

unterrichtet zeitgenössische Kunstgeschichte an der Ecole Nationale Supérieure des Beaux Arts de Paris. Von 1983 bis 1985 war er Herausgeber der Zeitschrift *Photographies*. 1988 zeichnete er zusammen mit James Lingwood verantwortlich für die Photo-Ausstellung und den Katalog Matter of Facts, (Musée des Beaux Arts, Nantes, und andere Orte) und 1989, wieder zusammen mit James Lingwood, für Une Autre Objectivité/Another Objectivity, (Centre National des Arts Plastiques, Paris, und andere Orte), sowie für die Ausstellung und das Buch *Photo Kunst* für die Graphische Sammlung der Staatsgalerie Stuttgart und die Edition Cantz. 1991 organisierte Chevrier zusammen mit Ann Goldstein die Ausstellung A Dialogue about Recent American and European Photography, (The Museum of Contemporary Art, Los Angeles) und anschließend Lieux communs, figures singulières, (ARC,Musée d'art aoderne de la ville de Paris) sowie, zusammen mit James Lingwood, die Ausstellung von Craigie Horsfield (ICA, London, und andere Orte). Chevrier ist der Autor von *Portrait de Jurgis Baltrusaitis* (Paris 1989) und schreibt für das *Galeries Magazine*.

Jean-François Chevrier

doceert hedendaagse-kunstgeschiedenis aan de Ecole Nationale Supérieure des Beaux Arts de Paris. Van 1983 tot 1985 was Chevrier hoofdredacteur van het magazine *Photographies*. In 1988 stelde Chevrier, samen met James Lingwood, de fotografietentoonstelling Matter of Facts, (Musée des Beaux Arts, Nantes et al.) samen; en in 1989, samen met James Lingwood, Une Autre Objectivité/Another Objectivity, (Centre National des Arts Plastiques, Paris et al.). Voor de Graphische Sammlung van de Staatsgalerie Stuttgart en Edition Cantz stelde hij de expositie en het boek *Photo Kunst* samen. In 1991 organiseerde hij samen met Ann Goldstein de tentoonstelling A Dialogue about Recent American and European Photography, (The Museum of Contemporary Art, Los Angeles), gevolgd door Lieux communs, figures singulières (ARC, Musée d'Art Moderne de la Ville de Paris) en samen met James Lingwood de tentoonstelling van Craigie Horsfield, (ICA, London et al.). Chevrier is de auteur van *Portrait de Jurgis Baltrusaitis* (Paris, 1989) en medewerker van *Galeries Magazine*.

Allan Sekula

is a photographer and critic. He is the author of, amongst others, "Photography between Labour and Capital" in *Mining Photographs and Other Pictures: A Selection from the Negative Archives of Shedden Studio, Glace Bay, Cape Breton, 1948-1968*, Halifax, Nova Scotia, 1983; *Photography Against the Grain: Essays and Photo Works 1973-1983*, Benjamin H.D. Buchloh (ed.), Halifax, Nova Scotia, 1984; "The Body and the Archive" in *October* no. 39, Winter 1986; "Some American Notes", *Art in America*, February 1990. He has shown his work in, amongst others, the Folkwang Museum, Essen (1984); the Institute of Contemporary Art, Boston (1986); P.S. 1, Long Island City, New York (1987); Washington Projects for the Arts, Washington D.C. (1988); Vancouver Art Gallery, Vancouver (1991) and the Museum of Contemporary Art, Los Angeles (1991).

Allan Sekula

Photographe et critique. Il est l'auteur, entre autres de "Photography between Labour and Capital", in *Mining Photographs and Other Pictures: A Selection from the Negative Archives of Shedden Studio, Glace Bay, Cape Breton, 1948-1968*, Halifax, Nova Scotia, 1983; *Photography Against the Grain: Essays and Photo Works 1973-1983*, Benjamin Buchloh (et al.), Halifax, Nova Scotia, 1984; "The Body and Archive", *October* no. 39, Winter 1986; "Some American Notes", *Art in America*,

February 1990. Son oeuvre a, entre autres, été exposée, au Folkwang Museum, Essen (1984), à l'Institute of Contemporary Art, Boston (1986), à P.S.1, Long Island City, New York (1987), au Washington Projects for the Arts, Washington D.C. (1988), à la Vancouver Art Gallery, Vancouver (1991) et au Museum of Contemporary Art, Los Angeles (1991).

Allan Sekula

ist Photograph und Kritiker. Einige seiner Aufsätze sind: "Photography between Labour and Capital", in *Mining Photography and Other Pictures: A Selection from the Negative Archives of Shedden Studio, Glace Bay, Cape Breton, 1948-1968*, Halifax, Nova Scotia, 1983; *Photography Against the Grain: Essays and Photo Works 1973-1983*, Benjamin H. D. Buchloh (Hrsg.), Halifax, Nova Scotia, 1984; "The Body and the Archive", in *October* 39, Winter 1986; "Some American Notes", in *Art in America*, February 1990. Seine Arbeiten hat er unter anderem im Folkwang Museum, Essen (1984), im Institute of Contemporary Art, Boston (1986), im P. S. 1 auf Long Island City, New York (1987), im Washington Projects for the Arts, Washington D.C. (1988), in der Vancouver Art Gallery, Vancouver (1991) und im Museum of Contemporary Art, Los Angeles (1991) gezeigt.

Allan Sekula

is fotograaf en criticus. Hij is auteur van onder andere "Photography between Labour and Capital" in *Mining Photographs and Other Pictures: A Selection from the Negative Archives of Shedden Studio, Glace Bay, Cape Breton, 1948-1968*, Halifax, Nova Scotia, 1983; *Photography Against the Grain: Essays and Photo Works 1973-1983*, Benjamin H.D. Buchloh (ed.), Halifax, Nova Scotia, 1984; "The Body and the Archive" in *October*, no. 39 Winter 1986; "Some American Notes" in *Art in America*, February 1990. Zijn werk werd onder meer tentoongesteld in het Folkwang Museum, Essen (1984); the Institute of Contemporary Art, Boston (1986); P.S. 1, Long Island City, New York (1987); Washington Projects for the Arts, Washington D.C. (1988); Vancouver Art Gallery, Vancouver (1991) en het Museum of Contemporary Art, Los Angeles (1991).

Benjamin H.D. Buchloh

is associate professor of art history at the School of Architecture of the Massachusetts Institute of Technology in Cambridge, Massachusetts, is director of critical studies at the Independent Study Program of the Whitney Museum of American Art in New York and an editor for *October* magazine. Buchloh has published, amongst others, important essays on Michael Asher, Joseph Beuys, Dara Birnbaum, Marcel Broodthaers, Daniel Buren, Jacques de la Villeglé, Dan Graham, John Knight, Gerhard Richter, Allan Sekula, Thomas Struth, Andy Warhol and Lawrence Weiner. The first two volumes of his collected essays have recently been published in French translation, *Essais historiques I, art moderne* and *Essais historiques II, art contemporain*, Lyon, art édition, 1992.

Benjamin H.D. Buchloh

Professeur d'histoire de l'art à The School of Architecture of the Massachusetts Institute of Technology à Cambridge, Massachusetts. Directeur des études critiques de l'Independent Study Program du Whitney Museum of American Art à New York et membre du comité de rédaction du magazine October. Buchloh a publié entre autres, d'importants essais concernant Michael Asher, Joseph Beuys, Dara Birnbaum, Marcel Broodthaers, Daniel Buren, Jacques de la Villeglé, Dan Graham, John Knight, Gerhard Richter, Allan Sekula, Thomas Struth, Andy Warhol et Lawrence Weiner. Une traduction française des deux premiers volumes de ses écrits a récemment été publiée, *Essais historiques I, art moderne* et *Essais historiques II, art contemporain*, Lyon art édition, 1992.

Benjamin H. D. Buchloh

ist außerordentlicher Professor für Kunstgeschichte an der School of Architecture des Massachusetts Institute of Technology in Cambridge, Massachusetts sowie Direktor für Kritische Studien des Independent Study Program des Whitney Museum of American Art in New York. Buchloh hat unter anderem wichtige Aufsätze über Michael Asher, Joseph Beuys, Dara Birnbaum, Marcel Broodthaers, Daniel Buren, Jacques de la Villeglé, Dan Graham, John Knight, Gerhard Richter, Allan Sekula, Thomas Struth, Andy Warhol und Lawrence Weiner veröffentlicht. Außerdem ist er einer der Herausgeber der Zeitschrift *October*. Kürzlich sind die ersten beiden Bände seiner gesammelten Aufsätze in französischer Übersetzung erschienen: *Essais historiques I, art moderne* und *Essais historiques II, art contemporain*, Lyon, art édition, 1992.

Benjamin H.D. Buchloh

is buitengewoon hoogleraar in de kunstgeschiedenis aan de School of Architecture of the Massachusetts Institute of Technology in Cambridge, Massachusetts, is directeur kritische studies bij het Independent Study Program van het Whitney Museum of American Art in New York en is redacteur van het tijdschrift *October*. Buchloh publiceerde onder andere belangrijke essays over Michael Asher, Joseph Beuys, Dara Birnbaum, Marcel Broodthaers, Daniel Buren, Dan Graham, John Knight, Gerhard Richter, Allan Sekula, Thomas Struth, Andy Warhol en Lawrence Weiner. De eerste twee delen van zijn verzamelde essays zijn onlangs verschenen in een Franse vertaling, *Essais hisoriques I, art moderne* en *Essais historiques II, art contemporain*, Lyon, art édition, 1992.

Colophon/Colophone/Impressum/Colofon

Exhibitionconcept/Conceptiondel'exposition
Ausstellungskonzept/Tentoonstellingsconcept:
Jean-François Chevrier

General coordination/Commissariat général/
Allgemeine Austellungsleitung/Algemene coördinatie:
Chris Dercon

Research/Recherches/Recherchen/Onderzoek:
Sandra Alvarez de Toledo, Jean-François Chevrier, Chris Dercon and the staff of/et
l'équipe de/und die Mitarbeiter von/en de staf van Witte de With

Organisation of the exhibition/Organisation de l'exposition/Organisation der
Ausstellung/Organisatie van de tentoonstelling:
Witte de With, center for contemporary art, Rotterdam:
Chris Dercon, Paul van Gennip
Museum Boymans-van Beuningen, Rotterdam:
Karel Schampers, hoofdconservator
Musée Cantini, Marseille:
Bernard Blistène, Directeur des Musées de Marseille, Philippe Vergne, Direction des
Musées de Marseille
Westfälisches Landesmuseum für Kunst und Kulturgeschichte, Münster:
Prof. Dr. Klaus Bußmann
Whitney Museum of American Art, New York:
David A. Ross

Catalogue/Catalogue/Katalog/Catalogus:
Jean-François Chevrier, Chris Dercon, Mat Verberkt

Editor/Redaction/Redaktion/Redactie:
Mat Verberkt

Editorial assistants/Assistants d'édition/Redaktions-Assistenten/Redactie-assistenten:
Barbera van Kooij, Robin Resch

Design/Graphiste/Gestaltung/Ontwerp:
Ton Homburg (Opera)

Translations/Traductions/Übersetzungen/Vertalingen:
Sandra Alvarez de Toledo, Jacob Groot, Barbara Flynn, Brian Holmes, Françoise
Joly, Brigitte Kalthoff, Regina Sasse, L. Schwarz, Robin Resch, Mat Verberkt

Photography/Photographie/Photographie/Fotografie:
Bob Goedewaagen, Sylvain Pelly, Adam Rzepka

Printing/Impression/Druck/Druk:
Snoeck-Ducaju & Zoon, Gent, België

Lithography/Photogravure/Lithographie/Lithografie:
Twin Type, Breda

Edition/Tirage/Auflage/Oplage:
3500

A co-production of/Une co-production de/
Eine Koproduktion von/Een co-produktie van:
Witte de With, center for contemporary art, Rotterdam
La Direction des Musées de Marseille
Westfälisches Landesmuseum für Kunst und Kulturgeschichte, Münster
Whitney Museum of American Art, New York

Witte de With, center for contemporary art, Rotterdam
Witte de Withstraat 50
3012 BR Rotterdam
Nederland
Tel. 31 (0)10 4110144
Fax. 31 (0)10 4117924
Witte de With is een activiteit van de Rotterdamse Kunststichting en wordt
ondersteund door het Ministerie van WVC.
Staf: Gé Beckman; Chris Dercon; Paul van Gennip; Roland Groenenboom;
Chris de Jong; Barbera van Kooij; Gosse Oosterhof; Miranda Spek;
Gabrielle Terlaak; Mat Verberkt

La Direction des Musées de Marseille
Centre de la Vieille Charité
2, rue de la Charité
13002 Marseille
France
Tel. 33 91 562838
Fax. 33 91 906307

Remerciements: Christian Poitevin, Adjoint au Maire Délégué à la Culture,
Nicolas Cendo, Conservateur du Musée Cantini, Marseille; Véronique Legrand,
Conservateur, responsable du Département Editions; Ginette Bouchet,
Administrateur des Musées; Alain Franzini et l'Equipe Technique des Musées de
Marseille et pour cette exposition: Robert Dubois-Chabert, Sauveur Frutto,
Erasme Galli, Edmond Médioni, Jean-Claude Rosa, Antoine Toscano, Paul Toscano;
Robert Filippi, Régie des espaces; Maggie Gilchrist, Conservateur,
Chargée des Relations Internationales des Musées de Marseille; Florence Ballongue,
Véronique Traquandi, Michel Blancsubé, Presse Communication

Westfälisches Landesmuseum für Kunst und Kulturgeschichte
Domplatz 10
4400 Münster
Bundesrepublik Deutschland
Tel. 49 251 590701
Fax. 49 251 5907210
Prof. Dr. K. Bußmann

Whitney Museum of American Art
945 Madison Avenue
New York, New York 10021
USA
Tel. 1 212 570-3600
Fax. 1 212 570-1807
David A. Ross
Director

We would like to thank the lenders/Nous tenons à remercier les prêteurs/
Wir danken den Leihgebern/Wij danken de bruikleengevers:
Walker Evans:
The Art Institute of Chicago, Chicago; Collection particulière, Paris;
The Metropolitan Museum of Art, New York; The Minneapolis Institute of Arts,
Minneapolis; The Museum of Modern Art, New York; Sander Gallery, New York
Dan Graham:
Mac Adams, New York; Benjamin H.D. Buchloh, New York;
The Carnegie Museum of Art, Pittsburgh; Le Case d'Arte, Milano; Collection Daled,
Bruxelles; Collection particulière, Bruxelles; Collection particulière, Paris;
Collezione Pasquale Leccese; Dannheiser Foundation, New York;
Galerie Durand-Dessert, Paris; Marian Goodman Gallery, New York; Dan Graham,
New York; Dr. Susanna Hegewisch-Becker, Hamburg; Galerie Johnen & Schöttle,
Köln; Kasper König, Frankfurt am Main; Lisson Gallery, London; Galerie Roger
Pailhas, Marseille/Paris; Privatbesitz, Köln; Galerie Micheline Szwajcer, Antwerpen

Documents/Documents/Dokumenten/Documenten:
De Appel, Amsterdam; Argos Films, Paris; Artforum International, New York;
Galerie Art & Project, Slootdorp/Rotterdam; Jane Ryan Beck and Craig H.
Winkelman, New York; BRTN Dienst Kunstzaken en Stefaan Decostere;
Collection Daled, Bruxelles; Collection particulière, Paris; DAAD, Berlin;
Sylviane De Decker Heftler, Paris; DIA Center for the Arts, New York; Fondation pour
l'Architecture, Bruxelles; Haags Gemeentemuseum, Den Haag; Marian Goodman
Gallery, New York; Dan Graham, New York; Friedrich Wolfram Heubach, Köln;
Ton Homburg, Breda; Audio-visuele dienst van de Katholieke Universiteit Leuven;
Walther König, Köln; Ernst Mitzka, Hamburg; Particuliere verzameling, Rotterdam;
Privé collectie, Schiedam; René Pulfer, Basel; Real Life Magazine, New York;
Bob Rogers, Nova Scotia College of Art and Design, Halifax, Nova Scotia; Harry
Ruhé, Amsterdam; Sonic Youth, New York; Stedelijk Van Abbemuseum, Eindhoven;
Hans Sonneveld, Brussel

Photography credits/Crédits photographiques/Photonachweis/Herkomst foto's:
Walker Evans:
p. 93, 97, 102, 117 © 1992, The Art Institute of Chicago, Chicago. All Rights Reserved;
p. 73, 76-83, 86-88, 90, 91, 104, 110, 111, 121 Collection particulière, Paris;
p. 74, 89, 98, 99, 106, 107, 112-115, 118-120 The Museum of Modern Art, New York;
p. 100, 101, 103, 109 The Minneapolis Institute of Arts, Minneapolis;
p. 92, 105 The Metropolitan Museum of Art, New York
Dan Graham:
p. 170 The Carnegie Museum of Art, Pittsburgh;
p. 132 Collection Daled, Bruxelles;
p. 178 Galerie Jürgen Becker, Hamburg;
p. 149, 150, 157 Galerie Durand-Dessert, Paris;
p. 137 Privatbesitz, Köln;
p. 182 Galerie Micheline Szwajcer, Antwerpen

CIP-GEGEVENS KONINKLIJKE BIBLIOTHEEK, DEN HAAG
Walker

Walker Evans & Dan Graham / [Jean-François Chevrier ... et al. ; ed.: Mat
Verberkt ; transl.: Sandra Alvarez de Toledo ... et. al.; photography: Bob
Goedewaagen ... et al.]. - Rotterdam : Witte de With. - Foto's
Catalogus van de gelijknamige tentoonstelling in museum Boymans-van
Beuningen, in Witte de With, centrum voor hedendaagse kunst, Rotterdam,
Musée Cantini, Marseille, in Westfälisches Landesmuseum für Kunst und
Kulturgeschichte, Münster, in Whitney Museum of American Art, New York. -
Tekst in het Engels, Frans, Duits en Nederlands.
ISBN
90-73362-20-2
NUGI 921
Trefw.: Evans, Walker ; tentoonstellingscatalogi / Graham, Dan ;
tentoonstellingscatalogi / fotografie ; geschiedenis ; 20e eeuw